Sidney Lumet

Sidney Lumet

Film and Literary Vision

FRANK R. CUNNINGHAM

THE UNIVERSITY PRESS OF KENTUCKY

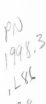

Library of Congress Cataloging-in-Publication Data

Cunningham, Frank R., date
    Sidney Lumet : film and literary vision / Frank R. Cunningham.
        p.   cm.
    Includes bibliographical references and index.
    ISBN 0-8131-1745-3 (alk. paper)
    1. Lumet, Sidney, 1924-   —Criticism and interpretation.
    I. Title.
    PN1998.3.L86C8   1991
    791.43'0233'092—dc20   91-10230

For MĀRA

In a dark time, the eye begins to see. . . .
            The edge is what I have. . . .
A man goes far to find out what he is—
Death of the self in a long, tearless night,
All natural shapes blazing unnatural light.

                    —Theodore Roethke

Contents

The Films of Sidney Lumet

12 Angry Men (1957)*
Stage Struck (1958)
That Kind of Woman (1959)*
The Fugitive Kind (1960)*
A View from the Bridge (1962)*
Long Day's Journey into Night (1962)*
Fail Safe (1964)*
The Pawnbroker (1965)*
The Hill (1965)*
The Group (1966)*
The Deadly Affair (1967)*
Bye, Bye Braverman (1968)*
The Sea Gull (1968)*
The Appointment (1969)
King: A Filmed Record . . . Montgomery to Memphis (1969)
Last of the Mobile Hot-Shots (1970)
The Anderson Tapes (1971)
Child's Play (1972)
The Offence (1973)*
Serpico (1974)*
Lovin' Molly (1974)*
Murder on the Orient Express (1974)
Dog Day Afternoon (1975)*
Network (1976)*
Equus (1977)*
The Wiz (1978)
Just Tell Me What You Want (1980)
Prince of the City (1981)*
Deathtrap (1982)
The Verdict (1982)
Daniel (1983)*
Garbo Talks (1984)
Power (1986)*
The Morning After (1986)
Running on Empty (1988)
Family Business (1989)
Q & A (1990)*

Films marked with an asterisk receive emphasis in this book.
Dates refer to release in the United States.
All are narrative, fictional films except King, a documentary.

Acknowledgments

The fifty-nine degrees below zero wind-chill factor outside my study window as I wrote an earlier draft of the introduction was a cogent reminder that serious study of literature-and-film is challenging in the rural northern Midwest and that I am significantly indebted to many institutions and individuals in the research and writing of this book. I thank especially Mr. Sidney Lumet for several informative interviews that enriched my knowledge of his work and also of film; throughout the book, uncited comments are quotations from Mr. Lumet's interviews with me. Stephen E. Bowles's *Sidney Lumet: a guide to references and resources* (G.K. Hall, 1979), the sole previous book-length study of the director's work, provided invaluable bibliographical assistance; it contains as well helpful cast lists and production information on all Lumet's films from *12 Angry Men* (1957) through *Equus* (1977). Among other items listed in my bibliography and chapter notes, the writings of Stephen Farber, Graham Petrie, and Maurice Yacowar have been especially illuminating. I am very grateful to the following research institutions and libraries: the Library of Congress, Motion Picture Division, where I was able to study Lumet's films; the Pacific Film Archive, Berkeley, California; the New York Public Library, Lincoln Center; the Museum of Modern Art, Film Division; the Museum of Broadcasting, New York; and the graduate schools of Princeton University, Yale University, the University of California, Berkeley, Stanford University, the University of Nebraska–Lincoln, and the University of Minnesota, which permitted use of their library facilities. I thank the Office of Research of the University of South Dakota for support that aided some of the research for this book. For permission to reprint a small portion of the section on *The Pawnbroker* and the section on *12 Angry Men*, which first appeared in *Literature/Film Quarterly*, I thank the editors at Salisbury State University, Maryland. I appreciate the opportunity to have read a shorter version of the section on *Long Day's Journey into Night* a few years ago before members of the English Department at the University of Nebraska–Lincoln; during the discussion period I learned from the helpful comments of professors June Levine, Robert E. Knoll, Frederick M. Link, and R.D. Stock. Discussions with A. Walton Litz, Princeton University; Warren G. French, Swansea, Wales;

Robin W. Winks, Yale University; and Haskell F. Norman, M.D., San Francisco Psychoanalytic Institute, deepened and enriched my knowledge of literature, of film, and of collateral concerns reflected in this book. While their lessening of my ignorance does not implicate them in the book's limitations, I am grateful for their friendship.

I have no words adequate to express my love for and gratitude to my wife, Māra Lemanis, for her superb intellectual and spiritual collegiality and for her encouragement and sustenance at all stages in the preparation of this book. Without her inestimable professional and personal qualities, and her love, both work and life would be greatly diminished.

Introduction

For more than a generation, Sidney Lumet has pushed the edges of American film in multiple ways, extending society's awareness of social and moral issues in a rather dark time for our culture when, particularly in the last fifteen years or so, it has seemed more interested in space age or consumer fantasies than in probing examinations from its artists into its most serious personal and institutional problems. At the same time, Lumet has also extended his personal boundaries into filmic areas well beyond the intense urban tragedies and literary adaptations for which he is most noted. Musing upon his directorial career since *12 Angry Men* (1957), Lumet commented in an interview concerning his most recent film, *Q & A* (1990): "I've never been aware of it as wanting to do movies about the criminal justice system, and then I look back and there are seven, eight, nine of them involved with it. . . . I guess when you're a Depression baby, someone with a typical Lower East Side poor Jewish upbringing, you automatically get involved in social issues. And as soon as you're involved in social issues you're involved in the justice system."[1] "When I get angry, I'm angry for life," he said in that interview, and Lumet's career-long commitment to the notion that meaningful action is necessary and (sometimes barely) possible reflects the demanding optimism that, combined with a steadily meditative cinematic eye, induced the American Civil Liberties Union of Southern California in 1985 to honor the director "for his personal commitment to justice so brilliantly portrayed through his craft."[2]

The most prolific American film director of his generation, Lumet created four of the culture's most distinguished films: *12 Angry Men*, *Long Day's Journey into Night* (1962), *Fail Safe* (1964), and *The Pawnbroker* (1965). He has also directed at least another dozen films of major artistic stature, from the early *A View from the Bridge* (1962) to *Daniel* (1983); these include many films based upon literary works, such as the thoughtful comedies, *The Sea Gull* (1968) and *Bye, Bye Braverman* (1968), and the incisive examinations of women, *The Group* (1966) and *Lovin' Molly* (1974), as well as important films that are not adaptations from literature, such as *Dog Day Afternoon* (1975), *The Offence* (1973), and *Prince of the City* (1981). Throughout his films, whether or not they are adapted from literature, Lumet manifests a respect for intelligence and for the written word that is rare in contemporary American film: even such relatively minor, if competent, films like *Family Business* (1989) and *Just Tell Me What You Want* (1980) are populated by articulate, intelligent characters. Lumet's cowritten screenplay for *Prince of the City* was nominated for an Academy Award, and at age sixty-five, Lumet wrote his first independent screenplay for *Q & A*. Usually choosing to work apart from minimalist fashion and independent of the Hollywood bureaucracy (most often in New York City, sometimes in Europe), Lumet, in the Modernist spirit, frequently subverts convention and varies his approach, revealing deep, diverse human experience through various genres and styles, offering his audience new visions of established literary works as well as films from less canonical literary sources and nonliterary origins. Yet like other serious creative people in a society preoccupied with faddish deconstructions and other trivial intellectual pursuits, Lumet, while respected as a filmmaker—especially by other directors, cinematographers, and actors—has not gained the widespread critical esteem his work deserves. Sensing the director's continual cinematic growth during the 1970s, Bernard Dick in 1978 wrote that Lumet deserved a reevaluation, pointing out that, for example, William Wyler had also been seriously underrated in Andrew Sarris's important but overly generalized categories in *The American Cinema* ten years before.[3]

Sidney Lumet: Film and Literary Vision represents an attempt to reevaluate Lumet's considerable body of important work, particularly that adapted from substantial works of literature, and to establish his justifiable standing as a major artistic American director, analyzing in depth what I consider to be his most significant films, works of enduring quality, including eight films from less-recognized literary sources or original screenplays. Proceeding from André Bazin's theoretical position that the creative film director, while remaining respectful to the literary source, can capture its spirit in an independent work of cinematic art, I examine fourteen literary films in considerable detail in chapters 2-5, analyzing Lumet's thematic and cinematic visions of the works and attempting to reveal his filmic artistry in character, symbol, structure, and setting, his combining of visual and verbal language into a unified cinematic whole. In a period during which impressionistic commentary—generalized theorizing, frequently without supporting evidence or detail—threatens to erode our critical practice as well as our respect for the imaginative and formal properties of significant art, I seek to counter such impressionism through a narrative analysis of the films' visual, literary, and adaptational aspects. Insofar as possible,

I attempt to recreate the unique cognitive and emotional power of Lumet's major films by a close description of the narrative flow, the composition of shots, and the camera placements and movements, interweaving Lumet's particular stylistic vision of the original literary work. By helping readers see these sometimes unfamiliar—and frequently heretofore impressionistically criticized—films more clearly, I hope that they can better understand and appreciate Lumet's considerable craft, at its best rising to distinguished art.

Chapter 1 considers elements in Lumet's television background and other formative artistic influences that have affected his cinema of social and individual conscience and commitment, drawing, as elsewhere, upon published and personal interviews that reflect the conception and execution of Lumet's films. Employing critical approaches that are predominantly formalist, psychoanalytic, and social, I also attempt to introduce some central Lumetian thematic concerns through a brief examination of two recent films not adapted from celebrated literary sources, *Q & A* and *Power* (1986). Chapter 2 discusses a central theme in all Lumet's work, common to his psychological, sociopolitical, and moral concerns; examining five films from different periods of the director's career, the chapter demonstrates how Lumet's adaptational skills improve the three dramas and two novels considered. Chapter 3 focuses on such concerns in regard to notable films dealing specifically with women. Chapter 4 examines with substantial detail, justified, I believe, by the remarkable artistic quality of the films, what may be considered Lumet's supreme cinematic/humanistic accomplishments, four films that—perhaps with the later *Daniel* and *Prince of the City* and the middle-period *The Sea Gull* and *Dog Day Afternoon*—mark his most significant contribution to American and world cinema. While the thematic organization of chapters 1, 2, 3 and 5 is appropriate for a director so interested in ideas as Lumet, chapter 4 (like chapter 6) is organized chronologically, in order to show the development of the director's style, in his most distinguished films from literature and his major films from nonliterary sources. Chapter 5 examines Lumet's central comic achievements, *The Sea Gull* and *Bye, Bye Braverman*. Chapter 6 studies major films not adapted from canonical literary sources, attempting to reveal how the director's creativity functions beyond the adaptational mode and to disclose thematic and technical similarities to the most important literary films. The final chapter advances Lumet's case for major artistic stature from another direction: with the detailed analysis of twenty-two films as background, I discuss Pauline Kael's and Andrew Sarris's criticisms of Lumet and the frequently illogical and impressionistic nature of their commentaries, using, as appropriate, examples from other of Lumet's films—"minor" only for this director—such as *Garbo Talks* (1984), *Family Business*, and *Running on Empty* (1988), to establish Lumet's thematic and stylistic qualities.

Even a book-length study cannot treat in depth all thirty-six narrative fictional films of such a versatile director as Lumet; I made choices on the basis of my judgment of the aesthetic qualities of the finished films in deciding whether to accord a film detailed examination or to employ it briefly in illustration of Lumet's stylistic or thematic concerns. Some solid, competent films are relegated to "minor" status, films that might loom more prominently in the career of a lesser director. Some interesting films, such as *The Verdict* (1982) and *Running on Empty*, are not treated extensively because they are somewhat static visually. Others that feature splendid individual performances, like James Mason's in *Child's Play* (1972) and Alan King's in *Just Tell Me What You Want*, are de-emphasized because of their lack of textural richness and dimension in other critical respects. While the author of *Murder on the Orient Express* is a veritable cultural commodity compared with the authors of *Fail-Safe* and *That Kind of Woman* (1959, based on "Layover in El Paso"), the latter two films represent a deeper, more emotionally and intellectually challenging achievement than *Murder on the Orient Express* (1974) in my view and thus are given extended analysis. Designation as a major, significant film need not imply that a film has previously been considered "major" (for example, *Fail Safe, Lovin' Molly,* or *The Deadly Affair*) but rather that the film deserves to be judged significant because of hitherto ignored cinematic/artistic qualities. An achieved filmic result that, from a variety of critical perspectives, attains thematic and symbolic complexity and density, a fully dimensional human applicability, entitles it to the designation of a major film in the Lumet oeuvre. If, in my opinion, an interesting film has been accorded sufficient discussion elsewhere—such as Stephen Farber's treatment of *The Appointment* (1969) or Maurice Yacowar's work on *Last of the Mobile Hot-Shots* (1970)—then I have directed my critical attention elsewhere.[4] Sufficient notice of the fourteen "minor" films (for example, the role of *Murder on the Orient Express* in helping Lumet achieve a more sprightly *Network*) is given to demonstrate their thematic and stylistic relevance to the totality of Lumet's artistic career.

Chapter One

A Cinema of Conscience

Commenting in a 1982 interview on the nature of his artistic approach, American director Sidney Lumet spoke out in a voice that at once reflected a social commitment to "the flag of protest—which is what a lot of us start with," his legendary energy, and his affection for a more authentic New York rather than a superficial Hollywood as a place to make films:

Your "vision" comes in your selection of material; your frame is only there to serve the material. So, for me, the frames are always going to be different. In the so-called "New York School," there's an emphasis on literal humanity. . . . We're not sugar-coating much in New York. . . . I'm more interested in the motives that aren't so easy. . . . There's a life force that makes one person turn out a hell of a painting and somebody else stab his cousin. But I'll tell you the real difference between New York and Los Angeles. [Lumet leans forward, grins wickedly:] In *Dog Day Afternoon*, when the bank is robbed, it looks like night. I've never seen a shot in Los Angeles that looks like night. The city is incapable of looking like night![1]

In 1967, ten years after his landmark first feature film, *12 Angry Men*, and about a decade and a half before *Prince of the City* and *Daniel*, relatively recent major films that equally affirm the significance of the morally engaged life, Lumet wrote that film is "the last and only medium in which it is possible to tell a story of conscience, outside the printed word."[2] When in 1982 another interviewer reminded him that sixteen years before he had written, "While the goal of all movies is to entertain, the kind of film in which I believe . . . compels the spectator to examine one facet or another of his own conscience," Lumet replied, "the pictures I've done that I'm proudest of have something to say about the human condition. I don't think *The Anderson Tapes*, which is a first-rate caper movie, can matter as much as *Long Day's Journey Into Night*."[3] Lumet's prolific, versatile, and frequently distinguished record of thirty-six narrative fictional films from *12 Angry Men* (1957) through *Q & A* (1990), at least twenty of which are either fine adaptations from literature or are, independently, themselves serious cinematic literature, amply fulfills his goal to be remembered for "getting something truthful done."[4] Rarely making a film in Hollywood and usually risking unfashionable or unconventional subjects and themes, Lumet has skillfully managed to secure commercial viability in a marketplace directed increasingly during his career toward the artistically reductive and culturally trivial, while maintaining a consistently high artistic level in his major films and frequently creating emotionally arresting and thoughtful themes and values in his minor, more commercial work. Lumet is one of a diminishing group of filmmakers who remembers Snowden's secret, "The spirit gone, man is garbage,"[5] in a cultural environment so vapidly materialistic and conformist that *American Film* was prompted in 1986 to sponsor a major symposium, "What's Wrong with Today's Films?"[6] Lumet has "been able to get my kind of movie made—pictures like *12 Angry Men, The Pawnbroker, Fail Safe, Long Day's Journey Into Night*. They were pictures out of which I got a lot of . . . personal, inner satisfaction—but they were only made because creative people were given opportunities by companies willing to take real risks."[7]

In these four films—which because of their thematic depth and aesthetic brilliance deserve a place among America's finest cinematic achievements—and in more accessible works such as *Serpico, Dog Day Afternoon,* and *Q & A,* the director addresses moral as well as social malaise, challenging his audiences toward mature thought and feeling instead of prompting easy minimalist, facile responses. He says of *Serpico* what has often been latently thematic in his work, that "the acceptance of corruption [is] a way of life [in] the American system. It's this . . . attitude we have of 'What can *we* do? *We* can't fight city hall' that's at the root of our problems."[8] Lumet succeeds in his best films in integrating social and political themes with complex psychological motivations, characterizations, and visual correlatives expressive of meaning. Convinced, like Robert Alter, of realism's importance to contemporary humankind, Lumet posits abiding moral values in his films that are not simply the culturally conditioned artifacts of fashionably ideological and relativistic times.[9] Sharing André Bazin's adaptational respect for the literary text, Lumet seems to employ film to restore our integration with reason and the natural world and thus to construct a base for a more just human society. Yet the director's celebrated realism is balanced with an unheralded and subtle lyricism as well; his meditative eye observes through leisurely camera movements the poetic in human experience, for example, in the opening sequences of *The Sea Gull* and *The Pawnbroker* and during intervals of otherwise harried lives in *Bye, Bye Braverman, Lovin' Molly, That Kind of Woman, The Appointment,* and *Long Day's Journey into Night.*

Honored by other film directors—the Directors Guild of America has nominated Lumet seven times for outstanding direction for *12 Angry Men, Long Day's Journey into Night, The Pawnbroker, Serpico, Murder on the Orient Express, Dog Day Afternoon,* and *Network*—Lumet throughout his career has insisted on the collaborative nature of film direction, even ridiculing the auteur theory, so fashionable during recent decades, of the dominance of the "personal" director, scorning it as merely symptomatic of the era's preoccupation with celebrity and sensationalism. Firmly in control of all artistic and pragmatic elements of the film at hand, Lumet is renowned among both actors and cinematographers for his flexibility in the sharing of creative ideas with the writer, actor, and other artists. He has no equal in the distinguished direction of superior actors, frequently from the theater, including Ralph Richardson, Marlon Brando, Richard Burton, Harry Andrews, Katharine Hepburn, James Mason, Geraldine Fitzgerald, Blythe Danner, Rod Steiger, Vanessa Redgrave, Paul Newman, Sean Connery, Henry Fonda, Dustin Hoffman, Albert Finney, Simone Signoret, and Anne Bancroft. Lumet often casts such luminaries in roles that stretch both their imagination and his own. He has also drawn remarkable performances from previously less fully dimensional actors such as Tab Hunter, Sophia Loren, Nick Nolte, Anthony Perkins, Barbara Nichols, Raf Vallone, Dean Stockwell, Larry Hagman, Omar Sharif, Alan King, Ali MacGraw, Beau Bridges, Armand Assante, Jane Fonda, Faye Dunaway, and Timothy Hutton. If the material requires it, Lumet may choose an untrained actor, but "over ninety per cent of the time I want the best tools I can get: actors, writers, lighting men, cameramen, propmen. . . . I don't see why knowledge hurts, why craft hurts. Something doesn't have to be lifeless simply because it's accomplished."[10]

These and other fine, if less celebrated, performers (Jack Warden, Maureen Stapleton, Edward Binns, Joseph Wiseman, Judd Hirsch, Kathleen Widdoes, Ian Bannen, Christine Lahti) have shared Lumet's keen interest in themes of psychological and moral entrapment, the unrealization of human potentiality, the eternal tension between our attractions toward security and opportunity, the struggle toward self-definition, dilemmas unique to women's self-development (a subject of interest to Lumet long before its dispersion into popular culture), the ambiguities of betrayal and of self-delusion, and the significance of the acceptance of risk and of an individual, personal responsibility. Such concerns, so dominant in Lumet's great films, are present even in works not adapted from major literary sources, such as his recent films *Family Business, Power, Running on Empty,* and *Q & A.* These films can serve well as a brief introduction to some of Lumet's characteristic ideas and techniques, reflecting a literary seriousness and depth that attract the director in his good or competent films even as in his most serious, multidimensional work. *Family Business* transcends its caper genre to study relations among generations, as the character portrayed by Dustin Hoffman must gain the crucial understanding of his past that is required of so many of Lumet's loners before he can gain reconciliation with the future, his beloved son. Similarly, the characters in *Running on Empty* must come to terms with past concepts of self before they can become free of their present moral containments and attempt to establish a claim upon an ambiguous and frightening future. Both generations must reach for such personal responsibility, as the young musician (River Phoenix), told by his grieving revolutionary father to "go and make a difference" while the older rebels attempt to pursue their private revolution apart from him, must watch his parents with pride and sorrow as Lumet reveals the truck making one extra circle around the boy, his parents centering him visually in their love and dreams. Especially in *Q & A* and *Power,* among his recent films, Lumet focuses upon what has been an almost archetypal concern throughout his long career—the single character isolated in a vast system, succored perhaps only by deeply held principles or, after a long aridity of the spirit, embracing a principle apart from mere self-interest or behaviorist impulse. The frequent presence in his films of such characters and situations forges an important part of Lumet's persistent and most demanding optimism, the sense throughout his films—even in the remarkably stark worlds of *Power* and especially of *Q & A*—that the human experience is ultimately meaningful and potentially purposive, but that it can be made so only by the diligent exercise of human inventiveness, resourcefulness, and unstinting rationality and courage.

Q & A: Heart of Darkness

Lumet's most recent film joins many of its fine predecessors in positing that the causes for humankind's most deeply rooted evils and sadnesses lie sequestered and usually unrecognized within the individual human heart. As in earlier films concerning the criminal justice system, such as *12 Angry Men, Serpico, Dog Day Afternoon,* and *Prince of the City,* individual self-delusion and class inequities figure prominently in the political and moral inferno of *Q & A* (1990), but the depths of the cauldron are racial bigotry and prejudice. A key role in the film is played by Jenny Lumet, one of the two daughters of the director and his former wife, Gail Jones, the daughter of singer Lena Horne. Sidney

Lumet commented that it "was largely the observations of racism that my children brought home that made it all the more urgent to me. . . . Their awareness became my awareness."[11] Jenny Lumet, in the role of Nancy, becomes a catalyst amid a web of political intrigue and murder that nearly strangles her former lover, the young assistant district attorney played by Timothy Hutton, in his nascent moral regeneration at the film's conclusion. On the Caribbean beach, with a lone black man almost invisible in deep rear left frame, the Hutton character finally realizes that his own unrealized racial attitudes have subtly blended with, reinforced, and been used by the ignorant and hate-filled white power structure that has turned a once honorable tough cop (Nick Nolte) and his administrative superior (Patrick O'Neal) into moral monsters.

Hutton gives a restrained, nuanced performance reminiscent of his fine portrayal in *Daniel*, as he embodies the director's long preoccupation with the perennial tension between self-delusion and the struggle toward self-definition. His look of rejection toward Nancy and her father at his sudden discovery that the light-skinned young woman is black, though not visually shown by the director in the film, becomes, as Peter Travers has observed, "the film's grieving heart."[12] For it grows with the progression of the film's seamy horrors (from precinct houses to transvestite clubs) into a metaphor of a racism, subliminally present before in Lumet's films of the ignorant and the fearful (*12 Angry Men, The Pawnbroker*), which permeates the worlds of *Q & A*, from that of the basically decent nonwhite policemen (Charles Dutton and Luis Guzman) and their white colleagues and superiors to that of the mafia lords (Dominick Chianese) they grill in the Q&A, and even to the world of the racially oppressed themselves, whether Puerto Rican gangster (Armand Assante) or drug victim (Paul Calderon). In Gary Giddens's view, the film, "though flawed, is one of [Lumet's] strongest films, and, in some respects, a culmination of his most serious work. . . . All the coercive people in this film—mobsters and pols—are defined by the specificity and strength of their hatreds." And David Ansen, previously a perceptive critic of *Prince of the City*, praises *Q & A* as "an uncommonly ambitious thriller . . . full of fury and despair at an ingrown old-boy network that has institutionalized prejudice as a form of self-protection."[13]

While *Q & A*'s artistic weaknesses—including a blatant musical score (by Rubén Blades) unusual in Lumet's work, some plot coincidences (though the intricate, even convoluted plot is generally well designed by Lumet from Edwin Torres's novel), and a rather histrionic performance by the young Jenny Lumet—keep it below the level of achievement some of Lumet's films not adapted from major literature, the films' themes are mordantly sustained by the brutally funny dialogue, by Lumet's superior direction of Hutton's tough-innocent Irish lawyer and Nolte's horrifyingly dead-eyed, violent Irish police lieutenant, and by what Vincent Canby has carefully observed as the film's probing, "by extension, [of] the ethics of an increasingly complex, pluralistic society."[14] As the old mafia don (Leonard Cimino), his business interests perhaps endangered by the developing blood-feud against Assante by Nolte and O'Neal, rails about how business has changed since the old days and decides on a new operation—"Clean out the pipes, you see what happens when you go outside your own? . . . anybody know any Chinks?"—his casual, unconscious stereotyping reminds us of Faulkner's warning of the rot at our social center, the heart of our darkness.

Lumet said in 1982, "Now I want to find a way of telling real stories in abstract terms that make it even *more* real," as he recognized that *Dog Day Afternoon* was as far as he could go with realism and that *Network* and *Prince of the City* had been moves toward greater stylization. Gavin Smith noted the elliptical quality of the apparently realistic *Prince*, and Lumet was pleased when Akira Kurosawa visited him to discuss the stylization of the film. Lumet observed, "I want [stylization] to be done with such subtlety that you can't see it happening. . . . The only one . . . who really spotted [*Prince*'s stylization] and could talk to me about it in great detail was Akira Kurosawa. . . . I think he's the greatest living director in movies and maybe that has ever lived, and he liked my work."[15] Stylistically, *Q & A* continues the direction of *Prince of the City*, from its opening hellish shot of the vomitous greenish streets just before Nolte's vicious, premeditated murder of the Puerto Rican drug dealer to the series of shots of Hutton's approaches to O'Neal's office, each causing Hutton to seem more lost in the darkness of the narrow corridor through which he must walk. The somewhat sympathetic Assante, trapped aboard the boat, has just before his death a scent of what will come, and Lumet memorably captures his arching head and the strange light in his eyes as he seems to intuit his doom with a sense as nonrational as the bigotry that has oppressed him since the barrio of his youth. Especially Nolte, the law's assumed protector, is enshrined in an ironic white light periodically throughout the film that renders his high-pitched, repressed hiss ethereal, incongruent with his massive physical stature; this lighting is particularly evident during his final, self-justifying speech to Hutton and during his grilling of the prostitutes early in the film. As he stands over the sniveling Calderon before he murders the informant, Nolte is lighted eerily from behind through the curtained boat window, yet visually oppressed like his victims through Lumet's additionally lighting him from the bright ceiling lights above. Also visible in a mirror at the left of the frame, this feared killer seems almost insubstantial, from a visual perspective, as Lumet suggests the ephemerality and banality, along with the moral idiocy, of the unconscious malice that alone animates him.

Power: Packaging the System

More concrete and tangible than the abstractions that dominate the people and institutions of *Q & A*, the media technology in the service of a frequently irrational contemporary electoral system is to Lumet no less destructive to our social and moral heritage. Lamenting "the mechanization of our lives, the loss of contact," the director spoke of Gavin Smith's interpretation of *Power* (1986) as a film about a "terminally compromised" political process: "Well, there's a whole new ballgame now. . . .That is what's happened since television began, because television really has taken over our lives, from the mid-Seventies on, when we first had a generation that had never lived without television. Which is what *Network's* about. And that does frighten me. . . . Because the nature of human experience is shifting rapidly, rapidly."[16]

Few Lumet films have been as misunderstood as *Power*. The *Variety* reviewer wrote, "Not so much about power as about p.r., this facile treatment of big-time politics and media, featuring Richard Gere as an amoral imagemaker, revolves around the unstartling premise that modern politicians and their campaigns are calculatedly packaged for tv."[17] Even the perceptive Jack Kroll, in a review entitled "The Selling of the Candidates" saw Gere's continual jazz drumming on his rubber drum pad, as his private jet whisks him from one image-consulting job to another, simply as a symbol of his "emotional and ideological detachment from his job," construing Gere's character "as all slickness and no substance. Ironically, *Power* becomes as slick as the world it tries to expose."[18] Perhaps the presence of the iconic Gere, almost archetypally the Hollywood macho male star, in a Lumet film caused a hastily considered dismissal of *Power*. Critics might have reflected, however, upon the presence in the film's cast of such brilliant actors as Gene Hackman, as a more ethical media manager of an earlier era; E.G. Marshall, who lent such distinction to *12 Angry Men,* as a liberal senator whose wife's dubious judgment has caused his surreptitious withdrawal from an election campaign; and Beatrice Straight, so memorable in *Network,* another Lumet study of abused electronic technology, as

Marshall's errant wife. The cast also includes such excellent performers as Julie Christie, as a journalist who is also Gere's estranged wife; Denzel Washington, as a political manipulator who is at least a match for Gere; and Fritz Weaver, whom Lumet introduced in *Fail Safe*, as a bumbling rich man hoping that Gere's media expertise will capture for him the governorship of New Mexico. Commenting in a 1986 interview that everyone "is obsessed with image instead of substance," Lumet said that Gere had not been his first choice for the smooth, jet-setting Pete St. John, that he had been unimpressed with most of Gere's recent acting. "But he came in; we talked two long days. He was so intelligent, with such a strong sense of self, and he showed such a real desire to act again—to get back to real acting." [19]

Lumet's fabled ability to draw the most from his actors again proved fruitful: Gere's performance in *Power* is glitzy, but it also embodies the essence of sleaze as well as intelligence. Lumet coaxes Gere far beyond the mumbling Method performance of the actor's fine *American Gigolo*, and Gere is truly witty and articulate in his scenes with his client who hopes, despite her recent divorce, to retain her Washington state governorship (Michael Learned). Lumet also astutely turns Gere's superstar image against him, as he is finally bested by the (black) villain of the film, Washington, whose Machiavellian brilliance and psychological subtlety outrun even Gere's and who teaches Gere that his own neutral behaviorism is inferior to Washington's commitment to his Arab employers' antisolar policies and schemes, that mere pursuit of technical expertise for its own sake is an arid enterprise, indeed.

Especially interesting in *Power* is Lumet's continual use of Gere's jazz drumming. The liberation and creativity inherent in jazz have been attractive to the director throughout his career; his association with the jazz arranger and composer Quincy Jones, in such films as *The Pawnbroker*, *Last of the Mobile Hot-Shots*, and *The Anderson Tapes*, has particularly enriched those films, and Blades's jazz-influenced score for *Q & A* is, when tempered in volume, effective in enhancing the film's themes. The image-master's simulated accompaniment to Gene Krupa's noted solo in Benny Goodman's "Sing, Sing, Sing" is usually a resort to escape some further betrayal or other moral compromise: Gere's playing is the film's initial visual image, and similar images are repeated after Gere has manipulated his Latin American politico's reality, after the drunken Hackman has accused him at the airport of degrading their mutual craft through his cynicism, and after Gere has employed electronic chicanery to refashion Weaver's fall from his horse into a pictorial illusion of John Wayne–like mythic invincibility. In one of the film's most stylized scenes, following Gere's honest praise of his friend Marshall's sincere political values, Lumet reveals the media man in a motel room, drumming away the ugly reality of Marshall's withdrawal from politics; here the camera discloses Gere's reality, slipping downward right in a mirrored reflection as if to suggest visually his attempt to come to grips with his own political values. Significantly, following his humiliation by Washington and his nascent reevaluation of the meaning of Marshall's career and his own while he sits in Marshall's old office chair, Gere is seen, not playing, but holding the drumsticks to his face, deep in reflection. While before the music functions unconsciously as an avenue of emotional wholeness, during Gere's self-assessment and eventual change the music's liberating, healing aspects become integrated with a more conscious self.

Lumet stylizes the illusory ambience of Gere's world somewhat as he does in *Network*: cinematographer Andrzej Bartkowiak's harsh whites and grays provide a shimmering equivalent to the moral squalor achieved through darker shadings in *Q & A* and *Prince of the City*, with the camera sometimes positioned at an Ozu-like floor level to suggest the moral level of Gere's political policies. Possible sentimentality accruing from Gere's finally supporting an honest candidate for idealistic reasons and from his reconciliation with Christie is avoided by the director's relentless parade of electronic technology, at the end of the film as well as earlier. Even as the idealistic young candidate speaks sincerely, abetted both by Gere and Hackman, his second-place finish is visually accompanied by the television camera relentlessly approaching us, making its demands upon us as well as the candidate. Lumet's concern at the future derationalization of our political discourse through the careless or malicious use of such seductive instruments is underscored by his ironic use of a penultimate "Stars and Stripes Forever," before the screen goes black to Goodman's final "Sing, Sing, Sing." As the young district attorney discovers in *Q & A*, in Lumet's vision politics begins within.

Lumet's words during the filming of *The Verdict* (1982) reveal that such themes are undergirded by autobiographical elements: "For me . . . that personal struggle toward self-knowledge in a world that doesn't help you to it is there all the time." Lumet observed in an interview that he was greatly influenced by his early viewing of Carl Dreyer's *Day of Wrath* and *The Passion of Joan of Arc*, which provided his "first inkling . . . about the potential of movies . . . an enormous emotional experience."[20] Perhaps his early admiration of the paintings of Chagall and of late nineteenth-century and modern American writers (he especially mentions Whitman and Sandburg) also informs to some degree

Lumet's fondness for urban settings and for themes of struggle and enlightenment. "This great Romanticism about cities, about the energy of them . . . that's something I always felt very close to because I find cities romantic . . . the sense of vitality. It's exactly on the potential for your life changing moment by moment, the closeness to destruction and the infinite potential for growth." Certainly his early experiences in the theater in New York were formative. Lumet commented in an interview that his early connections with the theater, including his child membership in the Group Theatre, first as a child actor and later as a director, exerted a substantial influence upon his themes and styles as a film director: "I think almost automatically what did get into the work was a real Depression baby. I was a kid actor with the Group Theatre, and that was probably the single greatest taste-setter for me. The social or realistic playwrights, Odets, Kingsley, and plays I saw in the Federal Theatre, I think all of these are woven into the work."

Son of the Warsaw-trained actor-director Baruch Lumet, Sidney at age four in 1928 made his acting debut through his father's association with the Maurice Schwartz acting group at New York City's Yiddish Art Theatre, two years after Baruch moved the family from Philadelphia, Sidney's birthplace. At age eight he was reading Karl Marx, and during the late 1920s and early 1930s Lumet continued to act in his father's series of radio dramas for a small Brooklyn station. Lumet was pleased that the station's call letters contained the initials of socialist Eugene V. Debs.[21] Reflecting on these formative years in an interview Lumet said, "Acting was an economic necessity in our family during the Depression, and for two years—1931 and 1932—I was on a weekly WEVD radio show, in Yiddish, called 'The Rabbi from Brownsville.' My father wrote and directed the show and acted the leading man and the grandfather. My mother was the leading lady, and I played the son. All together, our weekly salary came to $35."[22]

Lumet treasures his childhood memories. "I was exposed to Maxwell Anderson, to Kurt Weill . . . taken by somebody [I respected] to see Chagall—first the paintings and then the *man*. . . . Philip Loeb did [this] for me when we worked together in *My Heart's in the Highlands*." This mixture of the realistic and the lyrical was a feature of Lumet's first Broadway appearance at the Belasco Theater in 1935, in Sidney Kingsley's social drama, *Dead End*. "I was 11 at the time and had already been in eight Jewish plays. But since I was always small for my age, I couldn't play one of the Dead End Kids. So Sidney, who adored me, wrote a special bit into the play for me. We've remained friends all these years. In fact, the loft we used for the party scene in *Serpico* was Sidney's loft on Sixteenth Street. He was so excited the day we shot there."[23]

Growing up in a working-class neighborhood, Lumet was exposed to the leftist ideas that flourished during the 1930s. In an interview with Don Shewey, he termed himself a "street Jew." As an adolescent he was politically active in groups like the Young Communist League.[24] Many years later, Lumet reflected that during the early preparations for *Daniel*, he played Paul Robeson recordings for the cast: "That's the music I was brought up with."[25] During the filming of *The Group*, Lumet mused about the period: "To me the sub-text of the Thirties was commitment, passionate, idealistic commitment to the best of all possible worlds. . . . I remember the times vividly. I felt it surging all around me—that emotion . . . Even in the Depression. And I remember Roosevelt and the Group Theatre and the Spanish Civil War. Everything contained the excitement of commitment."[26]

Asked by Gavin Smith in 1988 if the 1930s of his childhood seemed to him a golden era, Lumet replied, "Not at all. Painful. But rich. Only those of us who lived through it and survived it came out with something that provided us with something very positive over the rest of our lives." During the late 1930s Lumet's acting roles included his initial exposure to the film profession; he played with Sylvia Sidney in the filmed play *One Third of a Nation*, a social drama of tenement life that had been a Federal Theatre project of 1938. (The production was filmed at the old Astoria Studio, which Lumet was to help resuscitate in the late 1970s and 1980s.) Twice during this period Lumet portrayed the young Jesus, in the 1937 production of Franz Werfel's *The Eternal Road* (in which he worked alongside Lotte Lenya and Kurt Weill) and in Maxwell Anderson's *Journey to Jerusalem*, directed by Elmer Rice, in 1940. Lumet reminisced to Smith, "Many of the young kids [in *The Eternal Road*] were going off to Spain to fight with the Lincoln Brigade." To these socio-artistic experiences were added Lumet's appearance as Stanley in Francis Faragoh's *Sunup to Sundown* (1938), directed by Joseph Losey, as the young hood Willie Berg in John Bright and Asa Bordages's *Brooklyn, USA* (1941), and most memorably as Johnny in Saroyan's *My Heart's in the Highlands* (1939), which earned acting accolades from Brooks Atkinson: "Young Sidney Lumet playing the part of a boy with winning charm and manly technique."[27]

Educated at New York's Professional Children's School, Lumet was for a semester a student of dramatic literature in Columbia University's extension division before his enlistment and five years' service in the Army Signal Corps upon the entry of the United States into World War II. His service included a radar instructorship at Camp Murphy, Florida— "I got everything I know about sound there" —and more challenging experiences as well: "In 1943, Lumet volunteered for a 'blind' overseas assignment. He and five other men were shipped to India, to be air-dropped into China to teach signal communications to the Chinese army. Japanese troops overran the proposed landing site and, Lumet recalls, 'there was no place for us to move out to. I spent two years in the jungle in northern India, where the mountains prevented the radar from working. . . . But at least I didn't fight the war in the Russian Tea Room, which is the way most of my good left-wing friends did.' "[28] Lumet said, "I was in big trouble when I got out of the army in 1946: five foot seven, no great beauty, not a leading man. That was before ethnic was beautiful. It was a terrific reading time . . . drifting in the Village."[29] Lumet's main acting experiences during this period of gradual transition from acting to directing were as a replacement for Marlon Brando as David in Ben Hecht's *A Flag is Born* in 1946, a production directed by Luther Adler that raised funds for a free Palestine, and as Tonya in Arthur Goodman's utopian political play *Seeds in the Wind* in 1948, a performance that also earned Atkinson's praise for acting of "exceptional force and clarity."[30] Of this postwar readjustment period, Lumet reminisced: "I knew at that time that if I stayed in acting, the best I could hope for was getting the part of the little Jewish kid from Brooklyn who got shot down by the mean Japs or Nazis, and then Clark Gable would pick me up and then with tears in his eyes would rush forward and single-handedly wipe out their machine gun nest. That was an area of drama that didn't particularly interest me."[31]

Lumet studied with Sanford Meisner at the Neighborhood Playhouse while forming his own theater group in the late 1940s, and Smith writes that "Meisner's very practical and specifics-oriented technique is one of Lumet's formative influences."[32] The future director's usual independence of spirit was revealed in 1947 when he was thrown out of the newly formed Actor's Studio after a few months because of his disagreement with the studio over its "constant reinvestigation of realistic acting. . . . My God, we're the best in the world at it, how long can you investigate one style? It's only one style, nothing could have been more boring." With about a dozen other rebel actors from the Studio, Lumet formed one of the first off-Broadway acting groups, the Actor's Workshop at University Place. This group, expanded to include about thirty others, explored Lumet's three-year course, studying in reverse chronological order from modern realism the development of styles in world dramatic literature, back through Shaw and the high comedy writers to Shakespeare's comedies and tragedies and finally to the Greeks, thus embarking "on what I thought was a much more sensible approach to acting." Supporting himself by odd acting jobs and by teaching at the High School of Performing Arts for forty-nine dollars a week, Lumet like the others kept the workshop going on a contribution "of five bucks a week. . . . We could make it run on about two hundred bucks a week. Anthony Tudor would give us the body movement that each period required, and Marian Rich would be working on voice problems for each style . . . but there was nobody to direct, and that's how I began directing." During the late 1940s, Lumet directed his first of five plays in New York, Molière's *The Bourgeois Gentleman*, which would be followed by other plays whose social themes perhaps stimulated his future cinematic social concerns, such as Shaw's *The Doctor's Dilemma* in 1955, Arch Oboler's nuclear war science fantasy, *Night of the Auk*, starring Claude Rains and Christopher Plummer, in 1956, and Camus's *Caligula* in 1960.

The transition to television direction that would launch him to prominence and into his film directing career, Lumet says, came about most fortuitously. "I fell into directing by accident. It was luck—a gathering of knowledge and circumstance. Being at the right age when TV came along was an incredible piece of luck."[33] In 1950, Lumet gained an assistant director's post at CBS through the help of an old friend, Yul Brynner: "Yul was directing at CBS at the time. We'd had some rough days together, were good buddies; he called up and said, 'listen, come on in, nobody knows what the hell they're doing, it's a ball,' and so I went in as Yul's A.D. and then when Yul left to do *The King and I*, I took over *Danger* from him, so I really sort of backed into it." The weekly *Danger* murder mystery series launched a decade of approximately five hundred Lumet productions following his rise to staff director in 1951, including shows in such series as *Mama* and *You Are There*, and the direction after 1953 of many plays in such drama series as *Play of the Week*, *Best of Broadway*, *Goodyear Playhouse*, *Playhouse 90*, and *Studio One*. Television directing taught Lumet many skills that would benefit his future film directing career. Since the pace of live television direction was exacting, he learned concentration, the ability to work on different projects simultaneously and quickly, and the discipline of working within cramped budgets and schedules. At the same time, he was afforded the opportunity to do creative work with thousands of fine New York theater actors in an environment that encouraged projects of high literary quality. Further, the improvisatory nature of early live television encouraged, indeed demanded, such directorial qualities as experimentation and versatility in theme and technique: Lumet learned expertise in camera placement and technique as well as in working with diverse actors, in lighting and shot selection as well as in set design. Always the atmosphere was experimental, for "there were no rules about what could or could not be done."[34]

Lumet's entry into television during its prime creative period led directly to his opportunity to become a feature film director. Although he had not seen Franklin Schaffner's television production of Reginald Rose's *Twelve Angry Men*, he had worked with Rose often; still he stressed his good fortune in an interview. Producers Rose and Henry Fonda needed a director for the film, and "Fonda—bless him—had seen something I had directed off-Broadway two or three years before when he was in New York with *Mister Roberts*, and he had no problems trying me out as director. It was as easy as that."[35] Such social forces as the rise of independent production and the gradual decline of the Hollywood studio system in the fifteen years after World War II (which prompted Gerald Mast's judgment that this period may have been "the least innovative, most tentative years in the *art* of the American film")[36] allowed artists from television to contribute to the commercial film scene what Gene Moskowitz termed a "new hold on reality, with its comment on important issues of the day, and, in consequence, a firmer stand on morality. The cinema, meanwhile, seemed to be straying in the opposite direction, in an increased emphasis on spectacle, sensation, and a return to comedy which tried to treat of current affairs without having a firm basis in today's needs."[37] With other directors with television experience who brought to film this increased sense of social reality, such as Delbert Mann (*Marty*, 1955), Martin Ritt (*Edge of the City*, 1957), Robert Aldrich (*Kiss Me Deadly*, 1955), John Frankenheimer (*The Manchurian Candidate*, 1962), and Arthur Penn (*The Left-Handed Gun*, 1958), Lumet in his first film began to dispel the Hollywood doldrums represented by Douglas Sirk's sentimental melodramas, low-budget horror movies, and inflated, self-important spectaculars. Its strong social themes, gritty urban implications, and splendid characterization all are outgrowths of Lumet's superior television experiments of the early and middle 1950s.

In 1952 *Cue Magazine*'s television editor termed Lumet's first series, *Danger*, "the finest half-hour dramatic series in television." In a guest column for the editor, the then twenty-eight-year-old Lumet talked about his and producer Charles Russell's efforts to create a program of high quality within a melodramatic framework that would satisfy the sponsor and the advertisers in early television's glut of programs devoted to "dog acts [and] idiotic give-away shows." The series, said Lumet, "was the direct responsibility of the people doing the work. . . . With the realization that there was no point in waiting for taste and content to come down from above . . . some of us decided to try to do what we believed in."[38] He continued,

I think it's interesting to note that *Danger,* basically a melodrama in which someone has to be involved in some sort of perilous situation, has succeeded in being human, honest, and occasionally illustrative of some major point about living. . . . For example, I remember a wonderful moment coming out of the line, 'Stay away from that girl—she goes for you.' The line immediately suggests every cliché in the books. However, instead of its being said as a threat, we had the actor deliver it in terms of a sincere plea from a physically unattractive man to one who was more appealing. The fact that the first man was the gangster and the other man the hero of the story no longer mattered.[39]

Lumet estimated that "one out of every five shows we do is totally satisfying in form and content" and that another 40 percent "are interesting and somewhat rewarding." He said, "At the rate of 52 shows a year, we figure that we've been hitting a very satisfying average. . . . We've set our sights pretty high, but that's the only way we'd care to work. . . . Most flattering is the fact that when there's a night ball game on . . . at the same time we don't lose any of our audience."[40]

Lumet has said that among the television productions he remains most proud of after more than three decades are the CBS News-aided *You Are There* segments "The First Salem Witch Trial" and "The Death of Socrates," and the plays *Tragedy in a Temporary Town* (*Alcoa Hour*) and *No Deadly Medicine* (*Studio One*), along with, of course, his monumental production of O'Neill's *The Iceman Cometh*.[41] "We always took pride in 'Salem Witch Trial' because we did it the same week that Ed Murrow did his McCarthy show, so we like to think we were slight contributors to the general attack on him." In this thirty-minute dramatic re-creation of a great historical moment, Lumet reveals what will become a consistent thematic concern: loners or outsiders who suffer at the hands of a static community for their ideals or special visions. Joseph Anthony gives a fine performance as Rev. Willard, defending the strong, unconventional tavern owner, Bridget Bishop (played by Janet Ward, in a sensitive performance foreshadowing her splendid small role as Mrs. Grady in *Fail Safe*), from the irrational charges of the denouncing women whose perceptions have been distorted by the privations constantly confronting the settlers. Lumet alternates rhythms well, with frenetic cuts for the accusers balanced with slow pans and tilts and medium close shots to reveal both the dignity and resolve of the accused and the solidity of the courageous youth who tries to present a deposition favorable to her. The final scene in which the witch who is not supposed to be capable of tears weakens to the extent of letting a tear fall is strong evidence of Lumet's superior skill with actors and of his frequent assertion that he regards as the most significant landscape the variegated moods of the human face.

In "The Death of Socrates," Lumet again prefigures his future interest in characters, from Kay in *That Kind of Woman* to the fugitive family in *Running on Empty,* who are prepared to make substantial sacrifices for their deeply held principles. Before we see Socrates in his cell, Lumet holds Aristophanes (E.G. Marshall) in close-up showing profound admiration of the thinker though the playwright has satirized him in *The Clouds*. The theme of the necessity of rationality is apparent here, as it will be in such Lumet films as *12 Angry Men* and *Fail Safe,* suggested by the stark vertical columns that frame Marshall (columns will likewise frame the opening action in Lumet's first feature film) while he identifies the actual self-protective motives of Socrates' enemies. An energetic Plato (Paul Newman) also argues rationally with Socrates' main accuser. We first see Socrates (Barry Jones) symbolically descending stairs, although his spirit soars as he jokes that the women will not need to wash his body since he has just bathed and he continues to discourse on the soul's immortality. Socrates gently insists to the crying Phaedo (John Baragrey) that his enemies only offer him death, because they do not realize that he only lives through his sincere beliefs. In close-ups, Lumet reveals that the philosopher's real choice is life, achieved through continual doubt and questioning. After Socrates drinks the hemlock, Lumet reveals his hand reaching toward the bars and the sunset beyond them, emblematic of his hoped-for kingdom of reason, as Kenyon Hopkins's cool flute score anticipates Val's passion for truth and its musical signature in *The Fugitive Kind*.

Although not emphasized by Lumet as among his own memorable television works, another *You Are There* program, "The Death of Stonewall Jackson," also anticipates the director's future cinematic work, particularly Lumet's concern with social issues and his oft-implied disapproval of those, like the jurors the Fonda character must oppose in *12 Angry Men* and the static members of *The Group,* who hide in self-delusion and ignorance rather than assume the human responsibilities of risk and an active engagement with the world. Lumet satirizes some Confederate and Union soldiers, with the gentle pressure reminiscent of the director's treatment in *The Sea Gull, Garbo Talks,* and *Bye, Bye Braverman,* in this historical reconstruction of events that hastened the demise of the South in the Civil War. As Jackson (Andrew Duggan) lies dying after the South's victory at Chancellorsville, a boosterist Virginia civilian bigwig proclaims that "our army is invincible," though it becomes known that Jackson has been shot accidentally by his own soldiers. Significantly reduced in visual scope at the rear of the frame, a Southern major (Kendall Clark) realistically reminds the civilian nonetheless that Washington will probably fall in ten days: "If we lose General Jackson, sir, how much do you think we have won?" As he oratorically accuses the major of being defeatist, the civilian's head is seen carefully backgrounded by many grids within a window, symbolically suggesting the emotional narrowness and insecurity that represses the great cost of the South's victories.

As he will do especially in the major films, Lumet here expands Howard Rodman's fine screenplay through cinematic commentary; he does this also in succeeding scenes involving the contesting soldiers, suggesting the fragility of their positions by the toy boat on which they trade corn whiskey for coffee with the opposing side. The gritty world of the combatants is reminiscent both of the worlds of *Fail Safe* and of the contemporary urban strife in such films as *Serpico* and *Prince of the City*. (Indeed, two of the soldiers are portrayed by Frank Overton and Edward Binns, who are prominently featured in Lumet's film of contemporary apocalypse.) As Overton suggests inviting Union soldiers over the river for some singing during a lull in the fighting and sends the invitation via the frail boat, Lumet's camera follows it part way into the dirty stream, until its little sail begins to luff, dashing the possibility of the communal plan. Lumet then cuts to Binns, a prisoner in Lee's camp, satirizing his own superpatriotism: "I'm the sort o' man that has got to do something foolish every time he hears a band play." Laughing at his former illusory notions of glory while he munches on grass, Binns seems less concerned about the war's outcome than about the increasing pollution from the North's great industrial might, now hazing the cities for which the soldiers daily risk their lives. As Binns speaks, Lumet's camera reveals a Union lieutenant, yet as hungry for glory as his counterpart from Virginia, framed carefully against a background grid of thin, tall trees suggesting his emotional rigidity. In contrast with his excessive zeal is the reasoned dignity of General Lee (Tom Chalmers), who insists upon a grieving tone for the lieutenant's reading of the names of their dead, that their deaths not be deprived of moral significance. But like many Lumet central characters, Lee is also ironically aware of his own weaknesses, as, resolutely facing the camera, he criticizes himself for what may approach sentimental philosophizing. The short dramatization concludes with Jackson's death and a fine shot of the major that anticipates Lumet's future visions of various emotional and spiritual vacancies. Jackson's realistic subaltern is visually cornered from a sharp low angle by two edges of the room's ceiling, reminding us that social order and justice are ever vulnerable to the forces of irrationality.

Equally illustrative of the development of Lumet's directorial viewpoint in his future career as a film director are his television productions of Arthur Hailey's *No Deadly Medicine* and Reginald Rose's *Tragedy in a Temporary Town*. In both works, Lumet reveals his consistent interest in men in crisis situations who grope, however tentatively, toward moral capability and maturity. In *No Deadly Medicine*, Lee J. Cobb brilliantly portrays an aging medical administrator, anticipating his incandescent performance in Lumet's first film, *12 Angry Men*. While Lumet's assured direction cannot entirely save Hailey's "General Hospital" plot in which a baby's life is lost as a result of a botched lab test supervised by the tired Cobb, Lumet shows his ability to animate even a near soap opera, foreshadowing his skill in bringing to life such seemingly unpromising film material as that of *Lovin' Molly* and *That Kind of Woman*. In the process Lumet draws a competent performance even from the usually wooden William Shatner as the young doctor who lacks compassion for the more harried senior physicians. The conclusion is one of early television's gems, as Cobb, forced to resign as a result of a mistake in medical judgment and in personal loyalty to a perhaps incompetent long-time technician-friend, prepares to leave a world he has loved for more than a quarter of a century. As he packs his things, Shatner comes in, barely knowing how to approach a distinguished senior he has long treated coolly. In a long, compassionate speech, during which Lumet's careful close-ups catch every nuance of Cobb's pain, the old doctor warns his successor not to get lost in vast administrative detail and as a result fall behind in medical knowledge and, worse, become tired. Gently holding Shatner's lapels, Cobb warns him to keep reading and listening and above all not to "allow yourself to get tired."

At Shatner's departure, Lumet ends the drama with a wordless two-minute sequence that looks forward to some of the director's finest film sequences that depend on nonverbal resources, such as the mannequin episode in *That Kind of Woman*, the scene in Miss Birchfield's living room in *The Pawnbroker*, and the lyrical opening of *The Sea Gull*. As the younger man starts out the door behind Cobb, the old doctor reaches back with his right hand without turning, laying the hand on Shatner's elbow, at once conferring forgiveness and awareness of the irrevocable, and ushering the younger man toward his new life. Then barely suppressing tears in an action utterly without sentimentality, Cobb lights a cigar but watches as the match will not go out, though he shakes it twice. He then must blow at it with the part of his lips not holding the cigar, his stubborn life force perhaps stifled but refusing to go gentle, before a final look around his office precedes his departure.

Reginald Rose's *Tragedy in a Temporary Town* focuses on a transient camp for workers at a dam. Amid talk of economic layoffs, an angry, frustrated Jack Warden (who, with fellow worker Edward Binns, will also distinguish Lumet's *12 Angry Men*) whips up other workers to beat savagely a Puerto Rican youth for supposedly making a slight sexual advance to a young white girl. Losing all respect for rational behavior, Warden incites a McCarthy-like hysteria that threatens to erode society's cherished traditions of liberal humanism. Lumet demonstrates his ability to draw significant performances from marginal actors, as Lloyd Bridges stands alone against the vigilante mentality, admitting his own fear in shielding his son (the actual offender), while defending humanity's best potentialities against the encroachment of a beast similar to the one that a more professional healer must attempt to exorcise in Lumet's *Equus*. Frequently attracted to themes of the pernicious social effects of unthinking conformity and obedience to authority, Lumet shows that even the moderately heroic Bridges cannot understand Warden's warped motivations and gives way to fear concerning his son's minor culpability. Even the father of the unharmed girl (played by Robert Emhardt, who memorably portrays Polly's father in *The Group*) readily sacrifices the unfairly accused youth to placate the group's conformist behavior. Lumet's conclusion makes skillful use of set decoration and lighting as Bridges drags the brutally beaten boy down the long central path separating the houses of the shantytown off into darkness. Visible only is a broken-branched, leafless tree in right foreground and the camp water pump, the visual center of the action, dripping very slowly, its symbolic life force barely sustained against humankind's apparently limitless potential for irrational, unconsidered violence.

Chapter Two

The Loner and the Struggle for Moral Capability

Throughout his career as a film director, Lumet has evidenced a major thematic concern with humankind's ceaseless struggle for self-definition and self-understanding. Even in such minor works as *The Wiz*, *The Verdict*, and *Family Business*, the director has investigated the reasons behind self-delusion and emotional self-estrangement, the contribution of evasion and denial to the eventual betrayal of others and to self-betrayal, and the necessity of the reasoned imagination for the avoidance of emotional fragmentation. In five films—the most recent of which, *Daniel* (1983), approaches the aesthetic and thematic standard of Lumet's four most distinguished works, discussed in chapter 4—Lumet's career-long interest in psychological themes and in the outsider's struggle toward some measure of self-realization are significantly evident. In *Equus* (1977), *The Deadly Affair* (1967), *The Fugitive Kind* (1960), *A View from the Bridge* (1962), and *Daniel*, Lumet's adaptational skill improves upon the originals, two works of fiction and three of dramatic literature, in important areas while involving significant themes that conjoin the director's recurrent moral and sociopolitical interests. Three of these films emphasize personal ignorance, denial, and self-enclosure, while in *The Deadly Affair* and *Daniel* Lumet explores the connections between personal vacancy and political evil. In all five films, major protagonists must struggle against personal dependencies that, if unrecognized, will inevitably lead to deepening levels of inferiority and insecurity. A sense of psychological and moral renewal is possible only when the characters reach toward a more intellectually conscious and rigorous, and sometimes less sentimental, confrontation with frequently harsh realities.

Equus: Martin Dysart and the Death of the Gods

During a more than thirty-year career as a director of feature films, Lumet has often revealed a preoccupation with psychoanalytic themes, particularly in his many adaptations of literary works. In such films as

A View from the Bridge and *The Last of the Mobile Hot-Shots*, Lumet treats themes of fragmented identity; in *The Group* and *Lovin' Molly*, he explores aspects of insecurity and compensation; and in *Long Day's Journey into Night, Prince of the City*, and perhaps most memorably, *The Pawnbroker*, he deals with guilt and psychological regeneration. In his 1977 adaptation of Peter Shaffer's popular play, *Equus*, however, Lumet demonstrates his most marked interest in the processes of analytic healing. It is in his adaptation of Shaffer's flawed drama that Lumet's strongest images of the psychoanalytic process become evident.

Shaffer's *Equus* concerns the rebellion against the "God of Normal" by Alan Strang, a disturbed adolescent boy whose religious fantasies and repressed sexuality cause him to blind six horses with a metal spike in a Hampshire stable. Assigned by the court to explore the causes of this savage act is Martin Dysart, a child psychiatrist renowned for his exceptional analytic skill and sensitivity in diagnosing and healing the pain in youths that so frequently causes greater suffering for others and for themselves. Beginning therapy with a youth so estranged from reality that he can only mumble inane jingles from television commercials, Dysart, with the support offered by his friend from magistrate court, Hesther Salomon, manages to induce abreaction of Alan's crucial boyhood experiences concerning horses with the eternally all-seeing power of the "jealous God" that Alan—and his mother—so fear. Dysart also begins the long process of exorcising these besetting Nature Gods from Alan; but during the therapeutic process he becomes progressively more troubled at the thought that he may be "taking away his worship" and substituting for Alan's "passion" mere adjustment to the God of Normal, those mechanical and institutionalized values against which the boy may partially have been rebelling. Feeling that an illusion may undergird his psychoanalytic career, Dysart at one point proclaims to Hesther, "I feel the job is unworthy to fill me," and ends his experience with Alan convinced that, because psychoanalysis does not understand all the mysteries of the etiology of neurosis, his "profession is based upon a total mystery!" and that he, no less than Alan, lives in the dark, striking at heads with sharp weapons.

It is not surprising that Shaffer's play was so popular throughout the 1970s, a period during which even many among the intellectual sectors of society enshrined instinct while conferring diminished status upon rationality, intellectual dedication, and competence. More probing viewers, however, were asked by Shaffer to accept sentimental visions of reality: horse lovers were obliged to welcome Alan's madly destructive act because of the supposed sincerity and "individuality" of the religious passion underlying it; audiences were supposed to accept that the moral content of the psychotic's and the psychoanalyst's actions were identical. As Molly Haskell complained, this sentimentalization of "the antisocial impulse" assumed that "neurosis is equated with passion and passion—the visible excess, the self-display of emotion—is mistaken for emotion itself."[1] Andrew Sarris acidly remarked, "The psychiatrist . . . assures the audience that the demented stableboy has performed a valid ritual from some obscure do-it-yourself religion. . . . Sanity is thus equated with mediocrity as in the most dubious dicta of R.D. Laing."[2] Reflective audiences found it difficult to accept that Dysart, in attempting to heal Alan, was merely processing his eventual adjustment to a plastic, freeway-saturated industrial complex, rather than, as a passionate scholar of ancient Greek myths, more probably opening the disturbed boy to a life in which he could be freer to make more authentic choices toward less instinctual, though equally impassioned, visions of the divine. Stanley Kauffmann noted that the film at least would have the advantage of making more apparent "the dubiousness of the material" and accused Shaffer of loading the dice with his flimsy plot: "The contrivance of choosing just this one doctor . . . the whole jerry-built pseudo-Lawrentian comment on the lack of ecstasy in modern life utterly collapses."[3] Shaffer's simplistic Manichaean conceptions assume that because, as Dysart admits, his profession "doesn't stock replacements" for the devils it attempts to exorcise, society can easily dispense with what psychotherapy can do well: helping, by the enlightened and imaginative use of reason, to free the confused psyche enough so that it can begin the arduous process of finding for itself more humane replacements for destructiveness.

Lumet's long-standing interest in psychoanalytic situations and themes does not, unfortunately, allow him to escape unscathed from Shaffer's confusions. Richard Burton's controlled performance as Dr. Dysart includes all the play's major set-speeches indicting rational inquiry (Shaffer served as the film's screenwriter). Since Lumet always exercises final control of what appears on the screen, he must share with the playwright the aesthetic burden of the lines uttered by the guilt-ridden psychiatrist.[4] But through the pictorial images Lumet employs to establish a context for Shaffer's words, the director manages to ameliorate somewhat the drama's conceptual weaknesses, to demystify Shaffer's mystical pseudoprofundities through a visual style that, typically for Lumet, is based more in pictorial realism than in stylization. Gordon Gow has praised Lumet's versatile style of "heightened naturalism";[5] the director's images sometimes suggest, in contrast with the literary source, the deeply rooted psychosexual issues that—rather than any ceremonial Nature God worship—truly underlie Alan Strang's antisocial behavior toward his community, as well as his own psychic agony.

Among the film's most memorable images is the pre-credits sequence, as Lumet holds in midshot a knife with a white bone handle shaped like a horse's head. As the hilt begins a slow clockwise turn, Lumet's camera very slowly tracks into an extreme close-up of the horse's head, skeletonlike, then even closer in to the horse's hollowed-out eyes and clenched teeth, suggesting the death of equine beauty that time and madness will surely bring about. This image merges into a real horse's head, then to a shot of a horse standing next to a naked boy in a thin shaft of light in a darkened field as Burton begins to speak the opening lines. Lumet's use of real horses instead of Shaffer's expressionistic stage masks underscores the fact that real horror stems from such misplaced "worship" as Alan's and that the Nature Gods are masters, not slaves as the boy conceives them.

After Dysart's first self-deprecatory speech, decrying that his "educated average head" lacks the "horse power, if you like" to understand the alleged complexities of the animal's nature, Lumet represents scenes of Dysart's therapeutic work as background to the film's credits, scenes that counter the analyst's self-doubts. Working with different groups of disturbed children and adolescents, Dysart is seen functioning healingly in the real world of his provincial hospital: He halts a fight, listens to a youth lying on a couch who dreams of getting through a gate so "then I could see everything," works in a group therapy circle with eight children, and, most poignantly, holds a large punching bag as it is pummeled silently by a youth, making the boy assume, finally, the responsibilities of both striking and shouting for himself.

Lumet's first shot of Alan (Peter Firth) shows the boy shuffling along a corridor, a door closing on his path from the side. He is alone, his Godlike fantasies having crumbled into his near-institutionalization at Dysart's hospital. As if to indicate Alan's self-entrapment, Lumet reveals him at the entrance to Dysart's office framed by two opaque windows, a vertical window frame at each side of his head and a horizontal one exactly dividing his head at midlevel. As Alan responds to Dysart's initial queries by ritualistically repeated television jingles, the camera pans diagonally across him from left to right (he is in left side view toward the camera in the previous shot), to suggest the fragmented nature of his mind.[6]

One of Lumet's most effective visual sequences follows this interview, as Dysart, seated at his desk, speaks into the camera about his recurrent dream in which, as a chief priest in Homeric Greece, he functions as the ritual knife-slayer of hundreds of young children, at once praising his own "unique talent for carving" and expressing his fear both at the emotional discomfort his profession causes him and at the threat posed by the other gods once they sense his self-doubt. During his speech, Lumet reveals Dysart in original domestic scenes that accentuate the psychological problems that are in the main responsible for his self-accusations, rather than Shaffer's mystical causalities. During the opening lines, we observe Dysart at home, shaving, through a steamy translucent mirror, his face framed tightly by four diagonal mirror edges. As he describes the horrifying masks worn by him and his assistant priests, Lumet shows him entering his bedroom from a slightly low angle, standing over the bed in which his wife (Kate Reid) lies, her body turned away from him, toward camera, her eyes sharply open. As Dysart relates his execution of the children, Lumet shows him in long shot, from a slight low angle, at the far end of his kitchen, again confined within white, vertical window frames, walls and ceiling. As he loses confidence in his ceremonial role, Lumet again frames him tightly in the garage doorway, before showing the analyst driving away in his car past a dead tree. (Later, as Dysart tells Hesther of the sterility of his marriage, Lumet reveals the couple raking and carrying piles of dead leaves.) These shots of his bleak home life are interspersed with six cuts to Dysart behind his desk, the close-ups drawing ever nearer, as if to suggest the psychological reasons behind his malaise countering the mystical concerns overtly expressed in the lines he speaks.

As Alan readies himself to tell Dysart about his childhood experiences on the beach and his discovery of horses at age six, he first bows his head, horselike, and then momentarily plunges his head into a drawer in the doctor's filing cabinet (another episode not in the play), to suggest to Dysart and to us that he is subliminally preparing to accept the sightlessness of the horses he has maimed. While Shaffer's lines convey the connection between Alan's passion for horses and the pictures in the bedroom of his childhood of a hideously suffering Christ and the horse-replacement substituted by his neurotic father, Lumet manages to emphasize through congruent visual images the psychological etiology of the boy's psychosis, although the director's cut from a bit in the horse's mouth to the image of Christ's shackled hands is too overt and forced. In the next scene, as the boy complains to Dysart about the vulnerability of horses and reveals unconsciously his disgust for his social-climbing equestrian mother and his sexually repressed father, Lumet shoots him in shadows, cornered by the vertical and horizontal planes at the end of his small room in the hospital. Alan is later seen compressed by similar boundaries when he first sees Jill astride a horse before she obtains for him a post at the stables.

Lumet again films with almost abrasive realism the sequence of Dysart's visit to the boy's parents: as Alan's father must watch his son flay himself before the domineering picture of his God Equus in his own bedroom, the camera catches the masochism of son and father; yet father is divided from son by a stair railing, a fine visual correlative of the self-entrapment of both the son and the father, who could not allow himself openly to discuss sexuality with his son. Lumet's film emphasizes more strongly than the play the emotional distance between them that is a major factor in the human, rather than mystical, forces that victimize Alan. And Lumet underscores the father's own unrealized need for fathering at the scene's conclusion as Dysart binds up an accidental wound in the father's hand.

Lumet's initial presentation of Alan in the stables visually recreates the probable circumstances of his mother's indoctrination of him into the constraining externals of institutionalized religion, which has led him to confuse Jesus with Equus. He stands fascinated with all the equestrian memorabilia, the medals, the equipment. As Jill seductively begins to instruct him in the art of currying, Alan smells the curry brush, then the horse; then he rubs his face on the horse's flesh. As he gazes transfixed at the other horses, Lumet's camera walls him in by the barriers of the pen in the foreground. As he enters the empty rear pen, he is now enclosed by two sets of constraining walls. He then runs his hands over the bars of the windows in the stall, entranced by the masochism of his attachment, eroticized by the distorted fusion of his mother's religious zealotry and its equine symbol. Wetting his hands in the horse's trough, Alan stands for several seconds bowing his head in a horse's posture, joined to the animals in ways so destructively unconscious that he lashes out blindly at them when he feels he has betrayed their Godliness because of Jill's later arousal of his sexual desire.

As Alan is led to reexperience the circumstances of his night ride on the horse-God, Lumet's images again stress the psychological rather than the ritualistic elements of the literary source. Although the director does reveal the magic the experience holds for the boy, he also underscores the emotional sickness at its base, unremittingly reminding us that Alan's psychosexual disorientation eventually destroys what Alan says he so loves, because of his rational incomprehension of his myth. In an interview with Tom Burke, Lumet said of this sequence:

"I knew that in the movie, if the boy's wild horse ride was to have its full impact, the horror of the blinding must be graphic. It is, and the ride's incredible! Orgasmic, and real! Four-and-a half minutes at full gallop, one uninterrupted shot, got it in one take!"[7] As Alan and the horse walk together in the bluish moonlight, Lumet frames them between even rows of low plants, confining them unawares within the boy's compulsion. During the wild ride, Lumet's camera focuses on an extreme close-up of Alan's fingers pressed on the horse's flank as though in attempted sexual stimulation. As Alan recites half-educated religious gibberish to the animal in mounting frenzy, Lumet interprets his release as clearly sexual rather than religious: instead of the "AMEN!" that closes act 1 of the play, Lumet holds the sound of Alan's high-pitched orgiastic scream for several seconds after the screen goes black following the sight of the boy's silhouette, with head thrown back, held by the camera in freeze-frame.

Although Shaffer's play does give Hesther some opportunity to counter Dysart's doubts, Lumet's film adaptation gives her rejoinders greater prominence.[8] In the scene in her kitchen, for example, she gently implies that, if Alan's implied accusation that Dysart himself might "gallop" more has merit, then this can be done without the sacrifice of other life. Hesther sensibly defends normality as not having to be hypocritical or excessively conventional, and Lumet frames the pair at one point approaching the dining room through a very narrow hallway, suggesting visually Hesther's sense of Dysart's guilty self-abasement regarding his attempted healing of Alan and her intuition that Alan, unlike the great Romantic heroes of legend and history, does not freely choose his life, his "extremity." Lumet heightens for us Hesther's awareness that Dysart's unique gift can bring to Alan the precious gifts of freedom, of choice.

And, indeed, Alan is nearly ready to begin to choose Dysart's rational methodology in preference to his own pain. Perhaps the most powerful visual sequence in the film is Lumet's handling of the blinding scene, as Dysart convinces the boy, with some sadness, that old gods do, indeed must, die, and through another of his "tricks" induces a reexperiencing of the crucial episode that Alan has understandably repressed more deeply than any other previous experience. Dispensing with Shaffer's stylized presentation, which softens the enormity of Alan's destructiveness, Lumet typically spares us no ugliness in revealing the ordained end of madness such as Alan's. Of this scene, Ralph Applebaum commented: "On stage, the blinding scene was rather tame, since it was done in mime. . . . But when it occurs on screen it is a paroxysm of fury."[9] In red light, Alan flails upon the straw in the stable, flaying himself; then, to Dysart's voice-over, "The Lord thy God is a jealous God, he sees you, Alan, forever and forever he sees you," Alan leaps down upon the horses, a sickle in his hand. Lumet cuts to an extreme close-up of the horse's head dagger hilt used in the film's first sequence, showing the point of Alan's instrument chopping into it; then to a shot of blood on Alan's body; then to the horrible shot of the point of the sickle in the eye of what is seemingly an actual horse.[10] After fourteen fast cuts of this carnage, Lumet's camera slows to an extreme high-angle shot of Alan, jets of blood pouring down upon him in the terrible wash of holy wrath he needs, before his final scream and wish for annihilation precedes Dysart's merciful bringing of exhausted sleep.

Lumet's realistic adaptation of the Shaffer drama reveals that Dysart's guilt-ridden closing lines confuse his unsatisfying marriage with the erroneous assumption that skill and the life of the intellect are somehow more destructive than the psychoses they sometimes can dispel. Dysart forgets that, if to some degree his profession is based upon mystery, then to some degree the same is true of all of life and he picks at heads not as a destroyer but as a saver of life. Lumet's handling of Shaffer's sometimes sentimental material, intensifying through camera work and shot selection the psychotic rather than the allegedly incantatory origins of Alan's behavior, lends greater credence to Hesther's view that some aspects of normality are preferable to mania and that by beginning to heal him, the analyst allows Alan's potential for future pursuit of other visions that may create new gods. Lumet's film gives credence to Lionel Trilling's idea in "Art and Neurosis" that creativity is far more than psychic distortion and reminds us that Dysart forgets that passion can be enhanced, if not created, by his passion for rational investigation that can make humans more loving and more free. Finally, Lumet's vision of *Equus* reminds us of Trilling's words at the conclusion of his important essay "Freud and Literature": "One is always aware in reading Freud how little cynicism there is in his thought. His desire for man is only that he should be human, and to this end his science is devoted. . . . the poetic qualities of Freud's own principles . . . suggest that this is a view which does not narrow and simplify the human world for the artist but on the contrary opens and complicates it."[11]

The Deadly Affair: Varieties of Betrayal

Lumet's work in mystery and crime film can be compared with the entertainments of Graham Greene in fiction, works that, while maintaining thematic seriousness, are either sometimes somewhat lighter in tone or are designed to appeal to a wider audience because of their roots in these more popular types. In chapter 6, I will examine some films of this kind, such as *Dog Day Afternoon* and *Serpico*, which Lumet directed from original screenplays or nonliterary sources. Elsewhere I will briefly refer to minor films of the type adapted from popular novels such as *The Anderson Tapes, Murder on the Orient Express,* and *The Verdict*. Perhaps the best of Lumet's films in the mystery genre is *The Deadly Affair* (1967), adapted from John Le Carré's competent first novel, *Call for the Dead* (1961). Here Lumet remains faithful to the central political action concerning the increasing mechanization of the contemporary bureaucratic individual, while further darkening the novel through an investigation of his frequent thematic preoccupations with the victimizing power of self-delusion and the moral gaps that cause betrayal in human relationships.

Few popular novelists have so well depicted both the corruption inherent in much modern bureaucratic organization and the resulting isolation and brutalization of the individual within such structures as has Le Carré. In a series of taut, well-known novels, from *The Spy Who Came In from the Cold* in the early 1960s to the recent *The Russia House*, Le Carré has written of the social hardening and consequent spiritual loss that has accompanied the progressive routinization of the British Secret Service, once a highly personal and individualistic organization but since World War II an increasingly impersonal and self-aggrandizing bureaucracy, hardened into attitudes of self-protectiveness, time-serving, and, ultimately, moral squalor. After the onset of the Cold War, as John Kirk has written, the exoticism and romance of espionage seem remote; in a period when our survival depends upon our instant knowledge of our adversaries' capabilities, espionage on an expanded scale has become a regrettable but necessary fact of international life. Ian Fleming's stories of the glamor of espionage tend less and less to be taken seriously by the mature reader, and yet, as Kirk notes, "Espionage, realistically treated, is still a tremendously exciting theme for fiction. And now, added to the old stand-by ingredients of mystery and suspense are the comparatively recent elements of immediacy and significance. In the hands of contemporary masters such as Eric Ambler, Graham Greene . . . tales of espionage become considerably more than escapist entertainments. They show us, in human terms, something frightening and true about the world we live in."[12] Le Carré's most frequent protagonist is George Smiley, an overweight, mild, scholarly spy, atypical in that he manifests none of the James Bond derring-do; indeed, amid the sabotage and murder usual in

international espionage, Smiley attempts to preserve the prewar sense
of honor and decency. Gentle, insightful, psychologically astute,
Smiley is fond of musing upon Hesse in *Call for the Dead* as he puzzles
out the personal motivations and sufferings of his prey: "Strange to
wander in the mist, each is alone. No tree knows his neighbor. Each is
alone" (48). He suffers when he finds that he must betray his moral
values and principles. Implicit beneath Le Carré's tortuous plots and
tense pacings lies the key question: "Can a man be a decent spy? What
happens to his character if he tries?" [13]

The central action in *Call for the Dead* concerns the agent's efforts to
understand the labyrinthine reasons behind the death of Samuel Fennan, a respected Foreign Service official who briefly skirted Communist party membership in the 1930s. Assigned by the Adviser to
investigate an anonymous letter sent to the Foreign Office identifying
Fennan as a Communist sympathizer and thus a possible security risk,
Smiley interviews Fennan and determines that the official should be
given a complete clearance. Later Smiley discovers that Fennan has
been found shot, apparently by his own hand. Although the Adviser is
content to close the case quickly as an undoubted suicide, Smiley,
believing that considerable circumstantial evidence supports the idea
that Fennan may have been murdered, resigns from the Service and
presses his investigations privately. Several murders later, Smiley has
experienced the bureaucratic corruption of the Adviser, who wishes to
suppress evidence in the case to preserve the reputation of the Service
and to avoid any threat to their sister bureaucracy, the police. Smiley
must also face betrayal by Fennan's wife, Elsa, who presents a nearly
convincing charade for sympathy as a former victim of a Nazi concentration camp, casting a haze of misleading evidence to implicate her
dead husband as a spy, when in truth she is a secret agent under the
control of the East German intelligence service. Le Carré's depiction of
institutional and personal betrayals also includes Smiley's early abandonment by his wife, Ann; the deceptions of Adam Scarr, a Battersea
garage owner unknowingly used by the East Germans and later murdered by them; and Smiley's own moral defection at the end of the
novel when his present nemesis and former World War II espionage
colleague, Dieter Frey, sacrifices himself rather than harm his former
mentor. Smiley must face the fact that he has unnecessarily killed his
closest friend.

With screenwriter Paul Dehn, Lumet makes some alterations in the
novel's plot while employing imaginative camera work and an unusual
color scheme to heighten the personal and moral aspects of the various
characters and to focus upon the emotional insufficiencies that inevita-

bly lead to the many betrayals of trust and intimacy.[14] He is particularly effective in his choice of actors, typically making unusual selections that lend original shadings to the novel's themes: James Mason matches his fine performances in Lumet's *The Sea Gull* and *Child's Play* with a memorably cold, conflicted depiction of the agent, who in the film is deglamorized and renamed, more simply, Charles Dobbs. Simone Signoret fully realizes the ambivalent motivations of Elsa Fennan in a performance that equals her excellent portrayal of Arkadina in *The Sea Gull*. Harry Andrews's portrayal of Mendel, the retired police inspector, well balances Dobbs's theoretical brilliance with a passion for fact in a role reminiscent of performances in Lumet's *The Hill* and *Equus*. Roy Kinnear's boozer is one of Lumet's finest depictions of working-class people's self-victimization, adding stature to the actor's work in *The Hill*. And Harriet Andersson is splendid in the amplified role of Dobbs's wife, Ann, from whom the agent learns deeper meanings of the nature of self-estrangement, betrayal, and potential self-renewal.[15]

Indeed, betrayal and self-betrayal are almost ubiquitously present in Lumet's stark vision of Le Carré's pessimistic novel. Perhaps the most visually impressive sequence in *The Deadly Affair* occurs as Dobbs visits Elsa Fennan's house for the first time to question her about her husband's possible reasons for taking his life. This episode achieves greater significance than in the novel, because Lumet presents it just after a scene, original to the film, in which Dobbs and Ann are shown through their mutual insecurities to have further estranged themselves from one another; Elsa's lies to Dobbs point up the agent's own consistent betrayal of his wife and of himself. As Dobbs enters the house, a steady rain can be heard that continues, soft but unrelenting, throughout the scene. He stands for a moment, again isolated, against a bare blue-gray wall, before Lumet's camera pulls back, leaving Dobbs in the hallway. From his perspective the camera follows Elsa as she slowly goes back through a door to the kitchen and closes it, to reemerge at the far end of the living room at a table where she begins to pour tea. As she does this, Lumet pans right, showing Elsa in rear center frame, separated from Dobbs by the entire length of the room. Dobbs now steps into the living room, and Lumet holds him there, standing alone, his back to the camera, for a seemingly interminable forty-five seconds as Elsa stolidly pours the tea and stirs in the sugar. At the edge of the frame but clearly visible is a blanket, stained with blood, that covers the place on the floor where Samuel Fennan's body was found. In one of Lumet's most remarkable cinematic evocations of theme, each character is visually isolated, Elsa framed between a window and a door frame on the rear living room wall, and Dobbs enclosed within the door frame he has just passed through, still standing, hat in hand. Lumet then cuts to the blanket, and Elsa's slowly moving feet, clad in old white socks, gradually enter the frame, as we hear her otherwise disembodied voice say quietly, "Who can one ask to clean such things?"

At the words the camera tilts upward to Dobbs in deep background, cornered now between the living room door he has just passed through and the main living room window facing the street, through which can be observed the falling rain and a tall, leafless tree. The moral aridity of the two characters is heightened by Lumet's visual ironies through camera placement: as Lumet reins in Le Carré's verbosity in the interchanges (29-31), the director separates the two characters in two-shots. Frequently Elsa, attempting to manipulate Dobbs's sympathy for her wartime past and her recent loss as well as to conceal the truth about Fennan's death, is shot from above, as if to minimize her, while her speeches, accusing Dobbs's bureaucracy, seem to enhance her credibility. Dobbs, however, is usually shot from below, which seems to confer moral superiority upon him through visually dominant positioning, while his apologetic words all but admit the guilt he harbors over his investigatory work. One low-angle shot pins him in a corner of the room as he says lamely, "We had to check." The sequence closes with a fine shot as Dobbs accidentally receives the wake-up call Fennan had placed before the murder without his wife's knowledge: as Dobbs begins to realize that the dead man must have arranged the call and that this fact makes more questionable the bureaucratic judgment of suicide, Lumet shows him sitting down very close to the camera as the camera also tracks slowly toward the agent until he is in extreme close-up, before his hurried departure from the house.

Other sequences involving Elsa also sustain Lumet's concern with the individual corruption that enmeshes most of the film's characters. When Dobbs returns to Elsa's house to break her story, following the murders of Scarr and the East German agent Harek, telling her, "They get their strength from day-dreamers like you," he is framed by Lumet from low angle within the window with the barren trees behind him. Dobbs's position again suggests his own moral complicity with Elsa's personal, if not political, acts of betrayal. During their interchange the ticking of a clock can be heard, metaphorically referring to earlier scenes showing the agent's awareness that he may soon lose Ann to the attractive, younger Dieter Frey (Maximilian Schell). While Signoret is brilliant in Lumet's closely adapted confessional scene (122-33), again pleading for sympathy as she continues to withhold vital information about her allegiance to Frey, Lumet depicts Dobbs as hypocritically sympathizing with her to learn the identity of her control.

He discovers only at the theater performance of Marlowe's *Edward II* that Dieter is indeed Elsa's control and is also using Ann for his political purposes. Earlier in the film, Lumet employs *Macbeth* more extensively than in the novel (99ff.) for reasons of exposition that afford Lynn Redgrave a fine comic cameo as an understudy; at this point he uses Marlowe's history play in a more detailed manner than does Le Carré to enhance Dieter's ultimate betrayal of Elsa. As Lightborn prepares to murder Edward, Lumet creates suspense while Dobbs and his associates await the arrival of Elsa's control, not yet knowing that it is Frey. A side door opens, casting some light upon Elsa's expectant face, and Lumet reveals Frey sliding into the empty space beside her, smiling as he plans her murder. Direct quotes from the play, performed by the Royal Shakespeare Company directed by Peter Hall, parallel Frey's actions.[16] "To pierce the windpipe with a needle's point" approximates Frey's manner of killing Harek, and his presently suspected pawn senses with Edward, "Something tells me if I sleep I'll never wake," just before Frey soundlessly compresses her windpipe. Typically, Lumet indulges in little of the gory details so frequently found in crime films over the past two decades: the scene of Edward's horrible murder by Lightborn and his associates is distanced, and Frey's betrayal of his agent is achieved with subtle, even gentle, gestures to accompany the intelligently employed Marlovian allusions. With ostensible kindness, Frey reaches to adjust Elsa's coat around her for warmth as he quietly applies pressure to her neck before her head is seen from the rear to droop slightly.

Lumet's depictions of Mendel and Scarr are altered from the novel to emphasize Lumet's concern with the personal absences that can lead to or lie at the roots of political betrayals. Lumet adds to the novel's material on Scarr (67-79) both to deepen the moral ugliness of the petty criminal who provides Harek with a car for his meetings with Elsa and to make the social unfortunate more sympathetic. As Dobbs and Mendel visit Scarr's neighborhood in Battersea to question him, Lumet's bleached color again is employed effectively as a sharply low-angle shot includes the building that houses both the garage and the pub Scarr habitually uses to lessen any ambitions he might have to escape the seaminess of his life. The horror of his environment is revealed as Mendel sees Scarr's little daughter leaning out of the window toward him; when the policeman asks where her mother is, the child replies, "Which one?" indicating that her father is in the pub. Lumet further individualizes the grossness of the social background when, following Harek's near-killing of Dobbs at his discovery of the loaned car, the camera in an extreme low-angle shot discovers a bedraggled hobo, asleep on papers and rags, whose aroused cries scare off Dobbs's attacker after Harek has stumbled over him. The usually serene and rational Mendel, realizing that Scarr's earlier lie to him has nearly killed his friend, takes the garageman from the pub and pummels him half the length of the dusky street, as the camera tracks along, heightening the dissolute environs with imaginatively employed bluish lighting.

As Mendel leaves the bleeding Scarr in front of his garage, Lumet adds an original, brief scene, cutting to Scarr's little girl, alone in the street except for the doll she holds, staring at her father and Mendel in wonderment. After Mendel walks away, not looking at the child, Lumet shows Scarr staggering to her, gentling her by asking, "Did you eat the egg I boiled for you?" She answers affirmatively, flatly and without self-pity saying that she gave some of the dinner to the doll, who is dying. Dimly sensing her self-reference, her father says that he will have to buy her another doll, as both walk slowly toward the pub where two women come toward them and enfold them in their arms. Then all stand in the street in deep center frame. The tenderness of this scene is heightened when Scarr starts to pick up his child, but does not. Lumet generally brooks no sentimentality, especially here: Scarr has formerly stooped to blackmailing a homosexual and is similarly morally lax in much of his professional and domestic life. But this small episode is reminiscent of sketches in later Lumet films, such as *Serpico* and *Dog Day Afternoon*, in which both the harshness and the potential for sympathy among disadvantaged or working-class people is made evident. As can be seen in these films and in Lumet's stark *The Offence*, few characters wear black or white hats in his cinematic world.

Also distinguished from Dobbs's privileged class background is Mendel, the retired policeman who assists the agent in solving the espionage mystery. Unlike the literate Dobbs, Mendel has little time for the theoretical aspects of investigative work; he is supremely intelligent and lives by the values of reason and fact. In the novel he is thin and "weasel-faced" (35), but in the film he is more developed and even more energetic, characteristics emphasized further by Lumet's omitting the character of Dobbs's clever ally, Peter Guillam. When interviewing Scarr in the pub, Mendel is all reasoned politeness, even placing his gloves atop his hat. Lumet emphasizes his factual orientation even more than Le Carré does: visiting Dobbs in the hospital after his beating by Harek, Mendel falls asleep when the agent speculates on the nature of the possible espionage plot; following Elsa, the animal lover must quickly excuse himself from conversation with a collie owner as his quarry strolls by. In the film, Mendel leaves the theater to follow the escaping Frey before Dobbs can warn him of the crucial fact that Elsa has been murdered, a situation that leads to the inspector's death in Lumet's vision of the novel. Here as in other films, Lumet is alert to the necessity of continual vigilance if the reasoned man is to survive in a world of appearances and self-delusion that can betray and destroy even the momentarily unwary.

Lumet's most marked and original departure from the literary source is his treatment of the tangled relationship between Dobbs and his wife, Ann. In the novel, Ann is a distant figure, a memory in Smiley's down-at-heel emotional self-estimate (47, 54-55), who, the omniscient narrator recalls, thought her husband "breathtakingly ordinary" (7). Even after the ending clash (melodramatic in both book and film) between Smiley-Dobbs and Ann's latest lover, Dieter Frey, Le Carré presents the British agent's final flight to Zurich as similarly resigned, "fatalistic" (192). But Lumet's Dobbs, while often pathetic in his self-estrangement and abdication of sexual desire for and responsibility to the woman he deeply loves, is a man struggling toward feeling and present-tense self-definition, and his final flight to see Ann is not done completely from weakness. In his deepening of Dobbs's emotional life Lumet makes his most notable contribution to creating *The Deadly Affair* as an independent work of art.

Dobbs is presented as a man in considerable emotional turmoil from his initial appearance on the screen. Over the film's credits, backgrounded by cinematographer Freddie Young's blanched color technique developed especially for the film in response to Lumet's request for a subdued coloration process to achieve his thematic purpose, we first see purplish silhouettes of Ann and her husband, arguing soundlessly, Ann characteristically near the bed, Dobbs framed vaguely along a wall.[17] Just as Lumet employs unusual color schemes to achieve comic effects in such films as *Network* and *Garbo Talks*, he does so in this sequence to suggest the emotional costs of isolation and broken communication in intimate relationships. Over the jazz score by Quincy Jones, Dobbs looms over Ann in bluish green shadows, her back in close-up, before the couple is shown embracing on the bed and finally estranged again in a hellish red-black composition. In the initial post-titles sequence, Lumet reveals the meeting between Dobbs and Samuel Fennan (Robert Flemyng), recounted from Dobbs's memory in the novel (85-88), a scene that emphasizes Fennan's decency and truthfulness (as well as his foolhardiness, improbable enough in both book and film, in meeting Dobbs openly in a public park, where Lumet shows Dieter watching the conversation).

That Dobbs is convinced Fennan is not engaged in espionage is made clear in the next sequence, which includes one of the most evocative yet simple camera movements in the director's career. Following his meeting with Fennan, Dobbs is seen being awakened with the telephoned information of Fennan's probable suicide. Dobbs protests his astonishment, since he believed Fennan's story and was going to give Fennan a full security clearance. As the phone conversation ends, Lumet frames Dobbs in the corner of the bed, then pulls the camera back fairly quickly from his crumpled figure with a slight movement right to left, centering Dobbs in the frame but showing his head in the corner of the room. He has just admitted to the agency that he does not have the car because Ann is not at home, and the camera movement isolates and entraps him emotionally in reference to both his relationship and his professional work. His confidence thus shaken, Dobbs walks in his pajamas, shot from behind as the camera pulls back from him, to Ann's bedroom in bluish darkness. Faintly calling his wife's name, he steps to her door, framed between it and the opening to the hallway and stairs. Though isolated visually, Dobbs gently turns down her bedcovers in anticipation. Lumet next reveals him emerging toward her returning car, and they speak with her door open, cut off further from each other through separate shots and separated from us by the car's mass. Quietly he asks, "Did you have a good evening?" and she replies, "Yes, I'm afraid so." He blunders, "Who was it, this time?" but with real affection she asks if he needs the car, before he cuts her off with, "Go back to bed, darling." He tries to recover his loss by calling after her with affection, but she has run from him.

Their future scenes together establish that her affairs result mainly from his self-estimate; his gallant attempts to tolerate her liaisons only alienate her further from him, as she seeks a deeper intimacy with him that he seems unable to provide. Her affair with Dieter, Dobbs's old friend as well as former espionage protégé, is motivated mainly by an attempt to bring Dobbs closer to her, to have him reveal more of himself to her. Mason well balances coldness and desire as he portrays Dobbs alternately seeking Ann's love and pushing it away. Obviously jealous when Dieter first visits the house, Dobbs says, "It's the nice ones I'm terrified of," in fear that Ann will love someone else and leave their relationship. As Ann and Dobbs argue after Dieter's visit, Lumet separates them into distant spatial planes; Ann says from deep rear frame, "If I could love one man it would be you, Charles," but the subtle, decisive agent cannot grasp the ambiguity of interpretation that would favor his candidacy. Not understanding her need for at least his anger, he stammers, "I always thought being aggressive was the way to keep my job and being gentle was the way to keep you." Although Dobbs visually looms over Ann at this point, again Lumet shows that the agent is in an inferior emotional and moral position to the woman he loves because of his need for spiritual isolation, his unwillingness to achieve self-understanding and thus emotional intimacy. Dobbs once confesses to an associate that he and Ann are "addicted" to one another, and Lumet indicates this by the too-frequent use of the Astrud Gilberto recording of a love song listened to by Ann and sometimes by other characters. As so often occurs in Lumet's films, such unreasoned addictions cause much human misery.

A weakness in the film is that until the final sequences Lumet does not sufficiently connect masochistic attitudes in Dobbs's personal life with his participation in stifling political bureaucracies, except perhaps to imply that the agent's commitment to ethically suspect political practices, even after his resignation from the Service, betokens other unconsidered spaces in him. That Lumet is more interested in Dobbs as a man than an agent is possibly contributed to by Le Carré's improbable *scène à faire*, the confrontation between Dobbs and the cornered Dieter (172-73). It is doubtful that the killer floridly described by Smiley (169) would sacrifice himself for his mentor as Dieter does. Lumet adapts this scene accurately but heightens Dobbs's sense of guilt for his more considered killing of his old friend following (in the film) Dieter's admission that he consciously used Ann to reach Dobbs. After Dobbs has kicked Dieter's hands to ensure his being ground to death between the boats and the pier, Lumet emphasizes his guilt and uses it and Dieter's admission to motivate Dobbs's final visit to Ann in Zurich. As Dobbs cries out in shame at his loss of principle through his action, Lumet ends the film's penultimate sequence with a long shot of the agent clearly realizing his guilt, his head compressed by the bank at bottom frame and a building ledge above him. In the final sequence, after he scorns the agency's offer to reemploy him, Dobbs flies to Zurich perhaps to attempt to redirect the energy he will no longer give in the service of professional betrayal finally to open himself to Ann's needs. What seems most important at the end of the film is not a conventional happy ending but Dobbs's partial spiritual renewal. At the airport, Ann runs down a long stairway to meet her husband, happy that he is slightly drunk; but he immediately speaks the film's last line of dialogue, "I have to tell you," as they walk away from the camera, his arm around her. As the film ends she abruptly stops in middle distance and stands a little apart from him, engaged by his attempt at greater emotional authenticity but also confronted by his betrayals of his friend, of his honor, and of her in needlessly killing a man she has cared for. His courageous disclosure by no means ensures that Dobbs and Ann can regain a relational integrity that years of layered betrayals and flights from responsibility have assaulted, perhaps, in Lumet's uncompromising vision, beyond all remedy.

The Fugitive Kind: Orpheus Ascending

Old Jabe Torrance, cadaverous and weak from his terminal illness, manages to "scramble down" the steps in Tennessee Williams's verbose fantasy, *Orpheus Descending*, send two slugs through his wife, Lady, then rush out into the street shouting with sufficient gusto to attract the attention of the town rednecks.[18] They soon enter the store and dispatch Williams's ostensibly mythic stud hero, Valentine Xavier, with a blowtorch. Here the thoughtful reader of Williams's play and viewer of Lumet's film version, *The Fugitive Kind* (1960), may pause to recall that a consistent feature of Lumet's career has been an ability to create significant cinematic art either by deepening fairly successful literary material (*The Deadly Affair, The Group, 12 Angry Men*) or significantly improving weak literary sources (as in *Equus, Lovin' Molly, A View from the Bridge*). Perhaps Lumet's most remarkable salvaging of a deeply flawed literary work is his adaptation of Williams's long-hatched drama that so sentimentalizes sexuality that audiences could enjoy feeling safe with it. In the drama a religious zealot presses the hand of the hero to "her great heaving bosom" (92) and actually engages in an exchange—sometimes in capital letters:

VEE: Yes, yes, light. YOU know, you know we live in light and shadow, that's, that's what we *live* in, a world of—*light* and—*shadow*. . . .
VAL: Yes. In light and shadow. [He nods with complete understanding and agreement. They are now like two children who have found life's meaning, simply and quietly, along a country road.]
VEE: A world of light and shadow is what we live in, and—it's confusing. (92)

Lumet, skilled in defusing Arthur Miller's pomposities in *A View from the Bridge* a few years later, manages, in collaboration with screenwriters Williams and Meade Roberts, to reduce the elements of sensationalism and sentimentality in the film adaptation of *Orpheus Descending*. Lumet also clarifies somewhat the symbolic and mythic confusions in the play to create a work that, while not among his outstanding films, is more tough-minded and compressed than the original source.[19] One reason for Vee's perplexities is that, as Signi Falk has explained, Williams indistinguishably runs together in *Orpheus Descending* actions concerning Orpheus's descent to the nether world, his being torn asunder by frenzied women, and his functioning as poet.[20] Val-Orpheus further functions as a comic-book figure who can hold his breath for three minutes at a time and whose sexual temperature always hovers a bit beyond that of other mortals, as Jesus Christ, as Nietzschean life force, and as a snakeskin-clad, guitar-playing, pre-hippie road warrior. Exercising more discipline upon the play's excesses, Lumet, Williams, and Roberts concentrate the many archetypal evocations, allowing the loveliness of Williams's best poetry in the play to emerge at its most lyrical. The basic idea—the playwright's great theme of the eternal war between life's animalistic, conscienceless oppressors and those they dominate—surfaces with something approaching the moral power and significance of such Williams works as *A Streetcar Named Desire* and *The Glass Menagerie*.[21]

Lumet's opening sequence shows immediately that the director intends to omit much of the play's early expository material and instead to focus upon Val's background as one of life's fugitive kind who, like the freest birds, try ever to keep flying, not to touch earth until they die. Gone are the prologue's surrealistic stage directions concerning the store and its confectionary and the background information provided by the two gossipy middle-aged women of the southern town on hate-filled marriages, on the town's common knowledge that Jabe led the gang that killed Lady's Italian immigrant father by burning his wine garden. Lady would surely now possess this information, making dramatically preposterous her ever having married Jabe, even after being abandoned by the town's richest scion, David Cutrere. Lumet instead begins the film with one of its most memorable sequences.

Before the credits, a guard comes to lead Val to a courtroom just before 7:00 A.M. Val (Marlon Brando) is first viewed inside a wire cage of a jail cell barely large enough to hold him and three derelicts, cleaning his ear with his finger, his snakeskin jacket thrown over his left shoulder. Next, Val stands before a judge we never see, and he is visually made further vulnerable by being framed within a jury box behind him. Val realizes that the ever-aloft birds of this world are ignored by conventional men, as he must redeclare his name to the bailiff and must listen to the judge label him "Snakeskin." As Val starts to give details of the party fight that resulted in his arrest, he reveals himself as a man who lives by his feelings and by principles. Lumet slowly pans left to right to a close-up of the left front view of Val's face as he says he had a "real bad feeling" at seeing his guitar—"You know, this is my life's companion"—on display in a pawnshop window before the party. His face is lighted as he tries to explain to the unheeding judge the importance of the guitar: "I can't explain it to you but everybody's got something that's very important to them and with me it's my guitar. It was a gift from a very great man, Leadbelly." But the judge prods him to hold his head up so that he can hear him better, caring nothing about the great blues singer's relationship to the man in the dock. Brando's famous "Method mumble" is perfectly audible here, as throughout Lumet elicits an incandescent performance from the great actor. Straining to be cooperative, ashamed of the fight, Val steps closer to the judge's desk, placing his hand on its edge, his face now in extreme close-up. The shot intensifies his vulnerability by visually cutting off his body at neck level, his snakeskin jacket now barely visible. Kenyon Hopkins's soft reed music is just audible as Val moodily explains that his anger at his rootless life caused him to start the disturbance, and he raises his hand in pledge to the judge that he will get his guitar and leave New Orleans. As the credits appear, the scene dissolves into a view of a long, deserted country road at dawn with a row of telegraph poles stretching into the distance, to the sound of Hopkins's score for guitar and flute and of birds awakening.

Lumet's next major sequence further demystifies Val and reveals Vee Talbott (Maureen Stapleton) as a much richer and more dimensional character than the visionary religious zealot of the drama, a woman who first introduces the wandering Val to the oppressiveness of the small Mississippi town outside which his car has broken down in the rain. Lumet's camera lingers on the useless car, its left headlight still dominating frame left as Val runs through the downpour to the first lighted house, as if guided by the lights from both his headlight and Vee's home. As Vee admits him, their faces are joined in a small shaft of light, sustaining through imagery the essential goodness of the two characters as distinguished from what both will soon experience from Vee's husband, Sheriff Talbott. As Val enters the house, Lumet frames him in the shadows of jail cell bars on the wall behind him. Though Val doesn't ask for a bed, "just a little dry place," Vee offers him the bed in the lockup, explaining that a prisoner has just escaped and her husband is out tracking him down. Val approaches the cell cautiously, the camera viewing him from the cell, showing him again dominated by the shadows of the bars along the wall. As Vee talks of Eddie's escape, saying, "I'm rarely disappointed when I put trust in people," she comes toward the cell door, in up angle close-up, and is visually oppressed by the ceiling of the cell and the heavy iron door in left frame. The two characters continue to be joined in light, however, as Lumet reveals light falling upon Vee's frightened eyes as she declares, "He said excuse me!" of the escaped boy, as if to console herself. As her husband's dogs yelp and the sounds of three shots are heard, the two realize that the boy has been caught.

Lumet's next composition eloquently reveals Williams's frequent theme of the inexorable entrapment of the sensitive by the powerful and unethical: as Vee walks between the cell and the stairs, the camera behind her, into visual enclosure, Val comes into the camera backed by a grid of bars, and he holds his guitar so that it seems compressed in the foreground of the same frame into which she, in the rear, is entrapped. The guitar's neck further seems oppressively upon her back, and Lumet holds the two vulnerable, sensitive people for several seconds in this position before Vee, sobbing at the realization that Eddie is dead, starts to ascend the stairs to make coffee and to show Val her religious paintings. As she describes to a kindred soul how her painting makes her feel "elevated!"—"I paint a thing how I feel it" —this disclosure means far more than her casual similar announcement to the gossipy ladies in the play (17), for Vee and Val are joined by a common creativity, compassion for suffering, an honest awareness of their loneliness in the universe. Their intimacy is reinforced by Val's revelation to Vee, earlier in the play, that he has decided to stop his nightlife, that "you're not young at 30 if you've been on a party since you were 15." Trusting his change she tells him of the clerking job at Lady's. Appreciating each other's warmth they smile as they share the coffee. As the sheriff (R.G. Armstrong) and his men reenter the house with their grisly news, Lumet's camera returns inside the cell to view the men in a fast pan as they move through the room, visually echoing Vee and Val's victimization in the men's spiritually imposed oppression. Just after the sheriff is momentarily shown against a bare wall, Lumet holds Vee's face in light from high angle as she looks at her husband climbing the stairs and reminds him that the boy excused himself before he broke jail. As she speaks, the great sun-eye of her painting of the church is visible over her shoulder. At his condescending laugh, "They'll give him a crown in heaven," Lumet cuts to Vee, holding her in close-up for several seconds, faced away from the men's brutality and trying to adjust emotionally to it by looking steadily at the religious art she has created. Attempting to draw strength from it, to gain salvation as Val attempts to do through his art, Vee responds to her husband's parting request to know Val's last name.

Before Jabe's return from the hospital to the welcomes of the sheriff and his fawning neighbors, director of photography Boris Kaufman reveals his mastery of the rural as well as the urban scene in Lumet's films. We see the town's daily life, its drab grayness and peeling wood frame storefronts. Now that Lumet has explored some major members of the fugitive kind, as well as their potential legal oppressor, he faithfully adapts most of the material of the play's first act, including the first appearance of David Cutrere's bohemian sister, Carol (Joanne Woodward), outlawed from the county by her conventional family for her wild ways, and Uncle Pleasant, the strange Negro "conjure man" who has a spiritual affinity with Carol. While we are spared the conjure man's "Choctaw cry," Lumet adds material that confirms his humanistic alliance with the slender forces of good in the town. The conjure man helps Carol after she slips on the steps to the store, and the two are visually dominated by Jabe's large store sign as they stand together, shot from low angle. The shabbily dressed, nearly toothless old man strikes fear into the hearts of the town's bourgeois gossipy ladies, who are terrified by his talismans and other evidences of naturalness. Lumet comments wittily on their conventionality as, while they shriek at the old man's bird-bone charm, we observe in deep frame a far more frightening vision of lifelessness in the white clothes dummy. Lumet has Carol stare at the gossips as she asks the old man to make sure "every sign of corruption is burned and washed away" from the bone by the sun.

As the moral corruption of Jabe (Victor Jory) enters the store, Lumet's treatment of Lady (Anna Magnani) establishes at once her membership among the emotionally victimized. As the neighbors pander to the wealthy merchant, Lumet cuts to Lady standing apart in a full shot against the drab street. She enters the store last and again stands apart as her husband is surrounded by the sycophants who hope to benefit materially at his death. During his verbal abuse of Lady concerning her attempt to change some displays during his absence for the store's commercial advantage, Lumet shoots over her shoulder at Jabe, who leers hatefully into the camera at her. Using his cane to stomp up the stairs until he is visually lost behind the grid of the railing, as Lady stares after him, Jabe is barely in his room before he knocks with his cane for her to come to aid him, and she mounts the stairs with weary slowness.

If Lumet's vision of Jabe as a death figure is nearly as broad as the monomaniacal presentation in the play, then his treatment of Carol, the sexual force of the film, is more complex and interesting than her role in *Orpheus Descending*. He coaxes from the fine actress, Joanne Woodward, an unusually steamy performance that is one of the notable vamp roles in serious American films of this period. Transferring Carol's attempted seduction of Val (20-28) from the store to the world outside, Lumet shows Val first moving Carol's sultry legs to the passenger's side of the gearshift (Carol is forbidden to drive in the county) before they depart for a place to begin their "jooking." She shimmies to the juke box in the most tawdry of settings, a place with broken venetian blinds as well as shattered dreams and lives. In her famed speech, Carol defines jooking's ascent from dancing to carnal pleasure (22) as she successively gives a man a playful push who requests a definition of jooking while lasciviously licking her lips at Val, starts to dance as she takes a sip from another man's paper bag, comes into camera attracting a man from his date, and pours some liquor on her brother David's head. As she utters the splendid last line of the speech, "Well, that depends on who you're jookin' with!" she takes another drink, hurls the bottle through a window, and, her body stretched full length in a chair, throws her legs into the camera with great abandon. When her socially conscious brother slaps her for her behavior, Carol slaps him harder, knocking him to the floor.

Then Carol and Val leave for the next stop on their jooking journey, their drive to Wisteria Hill, the town cemetery, during which Carol describes to Val her journey from failed town reformer to "lewd vagrant." Lumet allows us to see the cemetery (merely referred to in the play on p. 28) to reinforce Williams's frequent theme of the necessity and dignity of simply living amid the death-in-life common to so many people. The cemetery episode is one of the most imaginatively lighted in the film, as Lumet shoots it entirely in shadows, except for eerie horizontal strips of light coming from rear frame.[22] Lying against a gravestone, Carol challenges Val that the dead talk, gazing up at him with their message "Live" repeated five times. "It's all they know. It's the only advice they can give." Lumet combines the play's wordy scene (57ff.) with the cemetery scene, moving Carol's propositioning of Val and his refusal of her to a more dramatically effective site. Val compares her breaking "like a bundle of sticks" to the dead whom the hedonist Carol in some ways resembles, as he rejects her style of life for what he hopes will be a more generative future working at the store. Lumet shoots over Carol's shoulder toward Val, who walks away from her toward the car past the twisted treetrunks, then turns on the car's lights and awaits her until she rises and slowly walks to the car framed by gravestones and vines.

Lumet adapts consistently the events and the best speeches of the scenes concerning the developing relationship between Lady and Val. As Val awaits her decision about whether he is hired as the store's clerk, watching Lady call the druggist for medicine to aid her sleeplessness, Lumet catches his image in a mirror right behind her. As she continues to lament her sleeplessness, the director shoots Val's image circling her both in the mirror and in a slow pan shot from behind her. Brando is brilliant as his eyes tell her of his love for the great blues guitar players who have influenced his playing and inspired his life, his face lighted by Lumet here as it is when Val's great humanity is revealed through his words and actions. As Val tries to teach Lady her lamentable status as one of the world's people who "get bought" and the desirability of being among the birdlike creatures who try never to touch the earth until they die, Lumet reveals Lady staring up toward Jabe and shows Val's dreaming face in imagery of liberation, yet foreshadowed entrapment. His face is in shadow except its lower right quadrant just below eye level, but Lumet holds it at low angle framed by the railing of the upper landing and by two windows. When Val reaches the words "I seen one once, it died and fell to earth," Lumet holds his face at a sharper up angle, his eyes raised and now lighted, the lower face dark, but the rear window lighted.[23] Near the end of the speech, as he says that the birds, in an image of archetypal freedom, "just spread their wings out and go to sleep on the wind," Lumet cuts to his face in extreme close-up from low angle, his eyes rapt with wonder, gazing upward, and then cuts to Lady's lighted eyes, rapt with appreciation of him, before she shows him her dream of the refurbished confectionary.

After a melodramatic, overly expository scene in which Lady tells an accusing and jealous Jabe how he has always physically repelled her and the literally adapted lugubrious episode in which Lady reminds David Cutrere how beloved he was by her and how that summer "I carried your child in my body" (61), Lumet regains his disciplined approach to the material. First he adds a scene in which Val and Lady drive to a lovely wooded spot, the former site of her father's beloved wine garden; its burned-over yet gradually burgeoning aspect serves as a fine visual equivalent for the film's themes of conflicting destruction and renewal. As Lady sings the songs she and her father sang and Val gently strums his "life's companion," Lumet frames Lady within the right angle of two blackened beams. But as she relates the grim story of her father's being burned by the town rednecks, Lumet divides her from Val by a vertical beam and shoots Val from the rear; suddenly she faces into the camera and cries, "I'm full of hate!" But the director's sensitivity to the play's potential meanings is at its finest in the scene in which Val and Lady consummate their newly found love. While Val is often gentle in the play, in the crucial seduction scene he also tests Lady, making her come to the alcove "like a spellbound child" after she has barred the door with her arms and screamed her need for him (81). He then walks to the bedroom alcove and, crooning a song, waits for her to enter it, making her, in effect, come to him. Lumet's vision of this important scene does not reduce the strength required of Lady, but does make Val even more tender toward her and honors their avowal by making it more mutual as well as less melodramatic. In the film, after mutual accusations and Val's preparation to leave the store permanently, Lady runs toward him, and Lumet coaxes a firm but not histrionic interpretation of the memorable lines from Magnani as she says with soft urgency, "I need you . . . to live . . . to go on living." Val pulls the curtain of the alcove aside, lighting her face. Then looking at and believing her, he kisses her softly, and they enter the alcove together. For several seconds Lumet's camera remains on the peacock-design curtain and the gradually darkening shadows of Lady and Val upon it.

Lumet's conclusion also somewhat tempers the melodramatic excesses of the play's final act. He faithfully adapts such episodes as Jabe's hissing dismissal of Lady's attempt through the confectionary to re-create the beauty of her father's wine garden, Jabe's admission that he was among the gang that caused the death of her father by burning his orchard, the sheriff's warning to Val to get out of town before the next morning, and the ostensibly streetwise guitarist's eventual realization that he is, indeed, in considerable danger. (There is a fine shot of Jabe's menace even at long range as he limps along, the camera held slightly tilted, at ground level.) Like the play, the film also strains credibility when Lady's operatically announced pregnancy is sufficient to keep Val in town for the confectionary's grand opening, when even in the play the lovers admit that safety dictates their meeting later, out of the county.[24] But despite weak objective correlatives for actions that undergird the themes, Lumet's vision of the final catastrophe is stronger and more convincing than that in *Orpheus Descending*. The director adds a brief episode in which the lovers walk into the confectionary for a moment of peace; the camera is behind Val as Lady returns at one point to embrace him to the sound of the tinkling wind chimes, telling him that, like the green fig on the apparently barren tree, these events call for celebration.

After one final shot of Lady enjoying her festivities, bathed in lights and tinsel, the embracing couple looks up to see the vindictive Jabe setting fire to the easily combustible confectionary, while calling out a window that Val is looting the store. After a shot of Jabe's crazed eyes through the grid of the stair railing, Lumet risks an unusual shot that successfully indicates Lady's confused horror at what she sees: the

director tilts the camera, showing Lady completely upside down rushing out of the confectionary, then up the stairs into close-up as Jabe kills
her point-blank. Lumet then cuts to Val, like Lady's father caught in fire
while trying vainly to extinguish it. Carol screams for him to flee, but
Val pauses, seeing Lady upon the stairs. They silently say each other's
names as he watches her die, her face visually pinned between the
railings.[25] Then in a symbolic gesture more evocative than a blowtorch
of the townsmen's repressed sexual jealousy and hostility toward Val,
the mob forces him back into the burning confectionary with their
powerful fire hoses, the force of the water exceeding even his strength
to resist. Carol presses Val's snakeskin jacket to her face while speaking
the memorable lines about the wild things' skins as "tokens passed
from one to another so that the fugitive kind can follow their kind."
Lumet's final shot shows Carol, driving now, heading out of the town,
viewed from a tree in which a lone bird is visible. Lumet's vital and
original imagery in support of Williams's themes, together with a more
disciplined approach to potentially melodramatic and sentimental material renders *The Fugitive Kind* a more mature artistic work than its
florid original.

A View from the Bridge: The Consequences of Denial

Arthur Miller's revised two-act version of *A View from the Bridge* (1957)
provided Lumet with the literary source for his 1962 film of the same
name. The harsh trumpet background to the opening credits, together
with the information that Norman Rosten's screenplay is "based upon"
Miller's drama, indicate that Lumet's interpretation of the play will
have a different focus from Miller's sometimes didactic and sentimental
stance toward his Brooklyn dockworker, Eddie Carbone. Lumet cuts
many portentous lines throughout the play of Miller's choral figure,
Alfieri the attorney, most notably the lawyer's inaccurate but supposedly consoling bromide at the end, as "the dull prayers of the
people and the keening of the women continue" after Eddie's death.[26]
"And even as I know how wrong he was, and his death useless, I
tremble, for I confess that something perversely pure calls to me from
his memory—not purely good, but himself purely, for he allowed
himself to be wholly known."[27] Lumet's approach—typically honest,
even unsparing in this instance—to the material he chooses for adaptation results in a tragedy that is more probable than Miller's, one far less
grandiose in its attempt to connect Eddie with the ancient Greek tradition. Lumet's thematic thrust in this realistic, gritty film is precisely
that Eddie's fall results not from some mystical connection to the past,

on some "cliff at Syracuse" as Alfieri reminds us (379), but from his failure to identify and to struggle against the source of his developing hatred for his desired niece's lover, the illegal immigrant Rodolpho. Eddie resorts instead to denial, to the failure—consistently terminal in Lumet—to recognize reality and to act upon that recognition with responsibility.

Lumet's passion-blinded Eddie Carbone is more consistently motivated than the amorphous figure Miller speaks of in "Introduction to the Collected Plays": "However one might dislike this man, who does all sorts of frightful things, he possesses or exemplifies the wondrous and humane fact that he too can be driven to what in the last analysis is a sacrifice of himself for his conception, however misguided, of right, dignity, and justice" (51). Lumet's vision faces more directly that Eddie's ignorance—and Catherine's emotional immaturity and inexperience—doom Eddie and the illegal immigrants he betrays, that Eddie does not at all "allow himself to be wholly known," that this sacrifice is one to an unacknowledged and ill-understood passion rather than to any conception of "dignity and justice." Thus Lumet's Red Hook longshoreman, less reduced by sentimentality than his literary original, emerges as arguably a more fully realized tragic figure.[28]

Lumet's opening is better dramatically, more ominously revealing, than Miller's stagy, Expressionistic beginning, as the director cuts Alfieri's leaden foreshadowings and comparisons between himself and an ancient Calabrian lawyer who perhaps "sat there as powerless as I, and watched it run its bloody course" (379). Over the credits, Lumet shows at the shipyards massive loading equipment, then a large forklift with a heavy load of lumber being unloaded from a ship. From low angle, the timbers press down upon the title credits, held high above the longshoremen by seemingly disembodied hooks—an image repeated effectively in the scene of Eddie's death at the end of the film. When some timbers fall upon and hurt one of the loaders, Eddie promptly assumes command, seeming far different and more rational here than he is at home. He attempts to care for the wounded man and stresses to the foreman that whether it is a compensation case is "for a lawyer to decide," as he looks warningly at him in extreme close-up.

Much earlier in the film than in the play, Eddie meets the two "submarines," or illegal aliens, his wife's cousins from Sicily; Lumet's camera reveals him descending the long stairs deep into the ship's hull where the two men are hidden from a very high angle, as Eddie goes down into the beginning of the situation that will catalyze his doom. As he meets the men, again he seems in complete control of an arrangement that his ignorance will soon make hellish for him; he hugs the men warmly and smiles amply as Lumet shoots him from slightly low angle. It is apparent that, in his work, he is controlled, rational, able to show his emotions freely and fully, by implication in full control of the aliens and of himself. Lines of Alfieri's, original to the film, reinforce this impression, as the attorney says confidently to the foreman concerning the longshoreman's injury that "Eddie will get the facts, and they will be right," affirming Eddie's reputation among his social group as a reasonable and fair man. Eddie's apparent confidence and control are also echoed in the only lines from Alfieri's long speech (378-79) that Lumet chooses to present, as the attorney speaks less mythically about the increasingly civilized, lawful atmosphere of the neighborhood in which "we settle for half."

Yet beneath the appearance of control lurk images of the continuing presence of disorder and potential violence, for the injured loader yearns to be taken home in the ambulance, indicating the same misplaced and exaggerated concern for his public image that Eddie will exhibit so pathetically just before his street fight with Marco that results in his death. Also, the memory lingers that we have seen the two illegal aliens, Marco and Rodolpho, not just heard about their existence as in the play; their physical presence renders them more human, and their positioning in the bowels of the ship makes them more vulnerable, thus heightening Eddie's subsequent betrayal of them. Further, the faintly discordant music that has backgrounded Alfieri's lines on the law continues into Lumet's depiction of Eddie's neighborhood; as Eddie nears home, he is surrounded by yelling children in the street. Trolley wires loom over the street and his housefront and form a screened network, pressing him down toward the street's children. Though he seems happy and integrated as he passes Lipari's candy store, Lumet's camera reveals a slightly gratuitous gesture, as Eddie hits the peanut machine just a little too forcefully to get what he needs to respond to a child's request of him. As Eddie gets closer to his home, further from the rationality imposed by his social role at the shipyards, Lumet implies that more primitive emotions will rule over his social acculturation, that Eddie will be in danger because of increased proximity to and influence by the raw emotions typical of his class traditions.

Lumet closely adapts the substance and dialogue of the scene (380-90) describing Eddie's coming home to the family's evening meal and their discussion about the arrival of his wife's cousins, yet visually and gesturally heightens the scene to emphasize Eddie's excessive emotional investment in and his denial of his seventeen-year-old niece's developing attractiveness and independence. Described by Miller as "husky, slightly overweight" (379), Lumet's Eddie, as portrayed by the vibrant Raf Vallone, enters his home energetically hugging Catherine (Carol Lawrence, in her debut) with the excessive physicality revealed by Lumet just before, as the girl runs to him as soon as he enters. Whereas in the play Eddie comments more sedately and conventionally on the girl's new skirt, "Oh, if your mother was alive to see you now!" (380), Lumet draws from Eddie a more ambivalent mixture of repression and desire as he says, "Hmmm . . . your mother would be glad to see you *now*." But Lumet's most notable contribution to this sequence is in subtly revealing Catherine's unconscious encouragement of Eddie's attraction to her. While Catherine has no awareness of more than a natural need for warmth from her uncle, who adopted her following the death of her parents many years before, Lumet very early in the film stresses the truth of what Beatrice, Eddie's wife, warns Catherine of later in the play: "You're a grown woman and you're in the same house with a grown man" (405). Attuned to Eddie's every request, Catherine laughs with some abandon, with more than a young girl's playfulness, when she tells her uncle that she will get him a beer. Lumet dramatizes the play's passing reference, as next Eddie shaves, in his undershirt, as the child-woman perches near him on the edge of the bathtub, applying her perfume, having earlier asked him, concerning the day's news, "Tell me, Eddie, no secrets between us." The orphaned adolescent, naturally insecure, thus stirs in her uncle inferred levels of intimacy between them of which she remains completely unaware. Yet Catherine, aided by the circumstance of young Rodolpho's arrival, redirects her emotions, while Eddie tragically cannot admit to himself his desire for her, nor even directly confront her burgeoning sexual attractiveness. Typically, he cannot speak directly to her of this and must resort to such euphemisms as her "walkin' wavy" (381) and "I'm responsible for you."

Through suggestive use of in-depth compositions and camera placements, Lumet here establishes the different emotional planes occupied by Eddie's subliminal conceptions of Catherine and of his wife Beatrice, superbly realized by Maureen Stapleton. Beatrice becomes anxious when she hears of the imminent arrival of her cousins; her wish even to wash her walls and her continual kitchen activity establish her traditional domestic role. She has created for Eddie and Catherine a home as supportive and as sustaining as her husband's precarious longshoreman's existence and limited income can make possible. The atmosphere is warm as Eddie agrees to shelter her two relatives and is extolled by his wife for his charity, but as Bea holds his face, in deep background Lumet positions the image of Catherine's face interposed between man and wife. When Eddie sits down to dinner it is clear that he expects his wife to wait upon him. Conditioned like her husband by their origins, Bea throughout the scene is often in the kitchen, separated from Eddie and from Catherine, who at the outset sets Eddie's table. As Eddie must deal with the unwelcome possibility that Catherine is considering leaving home to work in an office, Lumet visually compresses him between two door frames in foreground and background; but his wife is back in the kitchen separated from both him and Catherine in another spatial plane and further truncated from them by the room's confining entryway. Rarely in this sequence does Lumet include Eddie and Bea in the same shot. At one point when Eddie looks intently at Catherine, he comes close into the camera, and Lumet cuts immediately to a worried Bea. Eddie serves himself first when he sits to eat his spaghetti, and, talking about his work on the docks, he is framed by a window—a rare, liberating open space—as he confidently talks of his long and subliminally satisfying hours at work. Then he passes the food, not to his wife, but to Catherine, indicating through this unconsidered gesture his reigning emotional primacy.

Throughout the episode, Lumet gives less emphasis than in the play to Miller's irony over Eddie's warning to Catherine not to alert accidentally anyone in the neighborhood to the presence of the two illegals. Lumet concentrates instead on the longshoreman's emotional vulnerability, sometimes underscored by high-angle shots; once he says, "I never counted on one thing, that you'd grow up," as his eyes roam over her. When Catherine serves him coffee, Bea comes into the room, her rising nervousness suggested by the slight jostling of the cups she carries. Lumet shows Bea going to Eddie's chair and picking up his cup, visually disclosing that her husband is no longer in the chair but that he has moved to another to be closer to his niece. When Bea is again in the kitchen as Catherine lights Eddie's cigarette, Lumet shows that Eddie is not only unconsciously neglecting his wife but also treating her like a servant. While this is in part due to Eddie's unconsidered values that a man must dominate his home, the director also reveals Eddie and Bea as mutually entrapped—Bea somewhat more consciously than Eddie—by emotional circumstances growing ever more difficult to control.

The arrival of Marco (Raymond Pellegrin) and his younger brother Rodolpho (Jean Sorel) precipitates Eddie's moral decline. Although Marco is completely cooperative and grateful, immediately telling Eddie that he and Rodolpho will leave the house as soon as they become a burden, Lumet catches Eddie in deep left frame looking at Rodolpho with a trace of discontent when the youth demonstrates his singing abilities—sometimes his sole means of coping with the abysmal economic conditions in Italy that have driven the brothers to become illegal aliens. Eddie attempts to repress his feelings by saying he's afraid the singing will be heard and the brothers discovered and deported. "We never had no singer here," he says, ironically incriminating his own future behavior. When Catherine gives Rodolpho his cake, Eddie looks menacingly at his niece for the first time; as he observes the youth put three scoops of sugar in the coffee Catherine has given him, Lumet reveals Eddie in deep background looking with intent unease at the young couple, from a viewpoint that separates the two, visually splitting them in the frame.

Unlike the play, Lumet's film shows Rodolpho's love of life on the docks, as the youth rides a great pile of logs, singing. He so entertains the other stevedores that one passes the hat around for him, and Rodolpho ends with a great, sweeping bow. As Rodolpho jokes, throwing some flour at the men, they laugh and join in the fun. Beneath the great bridge the young immigrant's genial playfulness incites the other workers momentarily to suspend the burden of their heavy work. Lumet cuts to Eddie following this action; he is separate from the group and their play for the first time, brooding alone. Then the camera pulls gradually back from him, increasing his growing emotional estrangement. The next scene in the apartment vividly conveys his isolation, as Eddie declares his dismay at Rodolpho's singing at the shipyards. Eddie's deeper jealousy of the young immigrant for his joy of life is revealed when Bea confronts him with his long sexual absence from her. In the play, Eddie's retort is almost hostile: "I got nothin' to say about it!" (399). But in the film, Eddie is more sad than angry: "I've got nothing to say about it, Bea, nothing." The slight verbal difference illuminates Eddie's increasing helplessness in not understanding the motives behind his withdrawal from Bea, from life. In a memorably composed shot, one of Lumet's finest visualizations of loneliness, Bea's head turns aside as she sits in the foreground of frame left. Seated deeper in right frame, Eddie comes forward and places his left hand on her shoulder, as Lumet shoots them from behind their left shoulders, patting each other's hands. Softly Bea says, "If you talked to me maybe I could help," but her husband turns away from her, driven from her by forces he does not even admit exist. As they speak, Lumet shows the couple's mirror image in left frame; in right frame is their picture when they were younger and more intimate. Both images are tilted at about the same angle from one another. Sharing the mirror image is another mirror on the opposite wall behind them, reflecting lined wallpaper and a doorframe that seem to fix them, to press them down.

Lumet's next sequence, like the scene of Rodolpho at the shipyards, again extends the scene of action beyond the apartment, not merely opening up the action to outside settings but with visual cogency paralleling the growing closeness of Catherine and Rodolpho, as they begin going out together, and Eddie's increasing isolation as, in secret, he watches them. At one point the young couple emerges from a bus near the house, and Eddie hovers close by but unseen in the shadows. As Catherine passes him, Eddie emotionally reenacts the scene with the children at the beginning of the film by going to the peanut machine near the candy store and staring over his left shoulder at her, merely the proximate cause of his agony and of his division from his wife. In another fine wordless scene Eddie watches from the darkness as Catherine and Rodolpho enjoy the immigrant's first experience in a Horn and Hardart automat. Taking joy in life's simplest pleasures, far from his hoped-for Broadway, Rodolpho juggles his nickels, plays a sort of roulette with the glass doors behind which strange food awaits him, runs both coffee spouts at once and slides a tray toward Catherine from many feet away, while his love enjoys him and the chutes and the noise. Eddie watches, enjoying nothing, his dark jacket pulled up to protect him as much from them as from the cold. His silence answers their laughter as he spiritlessly sips coffee, shot from low angle, pressed up against the darkness. Again Lumet shows Eddie from extreme low angle, as he walks into a frame dominated from above by a theater marquee, a look of abandonment on his face.

After watching the couple from outside a dance hall, Eddie walks into darkness, emerging again into the frame as he looks up at Alfieri's office. Lumet cuts to the stairway as Eddie's head gradually rises into the frame, cut off visually from his body, and Eddie is further fragmented and separated from the camera by the stairway railing. While the film again eliminates the lawyer's self-conscious poeticisms, Lumet's direction of Alfieri (Morris Carnovsky) illuminates the lawyer's wisdom as he tries to persuade Eddie to forget Catherine, telling him that her relationship with Rodolpho is beyond both the law— except for the alien's entry into the country—and Eddie's control. They stand by a window, with a light visible behind Eddie, while Alfieri stands almost in darkness; yet against Eddie's passionate but ignorant denunciation of Rodolpho, Alfieri's cool rebuttal possesses more justice and humanity. As Eddie is for the first time tempted to betray the illegals to the authorities, Lumet twice brings him into two sharply low-angle close-ups, his anxiety symbolized through the ceiling, oppressive above him. Vallone's splendidly intense performance is nowhere more conflicted than when he speaks of his years of difficult work in raising the girl (409-10); the camera slowly moves in upon him from low angle, the light again ironically behind his head, as Eddie screams to Alfieri, with a variation in the play's progressive present tense, "He steals from me!"

Tension in Eddie's home continues to rise in the fight scene, which Lumet adapts with only a few significant changes from the final scene of act 1 of the play. After Marco again cooperatively defuses a potential argument by ordering his brother to return home earlier from his evenings out with Catherine, the couple begins dancing, with Eddie's eyes on Catherine's swaying skirt, so close that the breeze brushes Eddie's newspaper. Suddenly Eddie's form in the background rises ominously into the frame from the dancers' hip level; he tries to deflect their joyous movement by suggesting another more violent, that they all go to the fights. Offering to teach Rodolpho to box, Eddie spars with him for a while, then suddenly strikes him so hard (more forcibly than in the play, p. 416) that he knocks him down. After Marco leads his brother away and the couple resumes dancing, Marco, more menacingly than in the play, demonstrates to Eddie a physical strength superior even to his host's. In a series of low- and high-angle shots that separate the two men into different spatial levels, Lumet's Marco slowly rises from a kneeling position, holding a chair so steadily with one hand at the bottom of one leg that it does not tip over, after Eddie has failed to manage this feat. In the film, unlike the play, Marco raises the chair slowly until it crashes into the ceiling. Lumet's final cut of this suspenseful sequence is from the topmost level of the chair, held poised by Marco over Eddie's head, sharply down into Eddie's face. But a short wordless scene original to the film underscores Marco's compassion immediately following this symbolic confrontation. Bea encounters Marco later that night in the kitchen when everyone else is asleep; he holds his hands palms up to her in weary distress, then turns again to stare wonderingly through the window's icy panes into the darkness.

The sequence of Eddie's discovery of the couple kissing, which drives him to betray the brothers, is heightened by Lumet to be both more suspenseful and more thematically thought-provoking. As Catherine talks with Rodolpho, testing his love by attempting to learn whether he would live with her in Italy as well as America, she drinks milk (only in the film), an action that further suggests her unconscious complicity in Eddie's downfall. Eddie does not see them kiss in the play (421); but Lumet shows Eddie, more tiredly than his companion carrying a Christmas tree up the dark stairway into the camera, suddenly discovering Catherine and her lover by the bedroom door. Lumet does not show Eddie's savage kiss of his niece's mouth (422); rather Eddie's repressions are displaced in his brutal Sicilian death-kiss on the mouth of Rodolpho and by his breaking of the bottle from which he has been drinking and smashing its jagged edges into the wall as he screams for Rodolpho to leave his house.[29]

"His eyes were like tunnels," Alfieri declares as Eddie seeks his advice for the second and last time in the play (423). As the attorney attempts to convince Eddie to let go of Catherine, Lumet cuts to the office door Eddie has just closed. A small pane of its translucent glass is missing: into Alfieri's legal, civilized world is entering inevitably the disorder and violence the lawyer's values are helpless to prevent. As elsewhere in the film, Lumet emphasizes more than Miller the relentless drive of Eddie's uncomprehended motive. The director photographs Eddie's crucial decision to telephone the Immigration Bureau more realistically than Miller treats the scene in the play, while retaining an Expressionistic device (original to the film) to heighten the emphasis upon Eddie's disordered mind. Lumet lengthens the distance Eddie must walk to reach the telephone booth, shooting Eddie's advance toward it from deep rear frame through the booth's glass panels, and employs asynchronous sound as an expression both of the extent to which Eddie's fixation has come to dominate him and of his approaching end. A low, metronomic ticking sound, gradually becoming louder until it is pronounced, accompanies his walk to the booth and continues even after his entrance. As Eddie makes the fateful call, Lumet's camera pans from right to left so that we can see Eddie through windows on three sides of the booth, visually reinforcing the social sweep of Miller's theme, implacably observing him as his social environment soon will, in his isolation within his fantasies and misdirected aggressions. As he identifies himself, "I'm just from the neighborhood," Lumet's visual and aural techniques accent Eddie's ironic loss of identity, both personal and social, his loss of respect and of his "name" (437).

Lumet's swift progress to Eddie's disgrace and death encompasses Miller's basic plot and reinforces Lumet's own more personal conception of Eddie's ultimate responsibility for his comprehensive losses. Just before the authorities come to arrest the illegals, Lumet draws a cooler performance from Lawrence as Catherine invites her uncle to the forthcoming wedding, revealing her quick maturing since her last terrible meeting with Eddie. The nets of his disturbance and of his denial of responsibility in not attempting to recognize the source of his anxiety tighten around Eddie as Catherine no longer unconsciously needs to gain his approval. After the brothers' arrest and Marco's spitting in Eddie's face in judgment of his betrayal, Lumet shows Eddie, more in guilt than rage, racing up the street after the departing officials' car, moving into the camera as if into society's judgmental eye. Then Eddie's isolation increases as groups of his neighbors, even the longshoremen closest to him, begin to fade silently away from him. Again walking into the camera among the denying, withholding people, Eddie tries to justify his act. But as Eddie screams that he must avenge his honor, in a shot reminiscent of Jean Renoir the people cross around him, as if in fulfillment of Alfieri's prophecy "You won't have a friend in the world."

Like the play's final street scene, Marco comes to Eddie, free on bail before his deportation, to exact an apology but not to kill. In Miller's play, the men fight, Eddie produces a knife, and Marco grabs Eddie's lunging arm and presses the knife around into Eddie, killing him. In Lumet's vision, the death is not accidental, but the director charges Eddie with greater responsibility for his end, as for his life. Eddie begins the fight, then grabs a dock spike after Marco knocks him to the ground, while a man in the crowd throws Marco a similar spike with which to defend himself. As Eddie reiterates, "I want my name!" the stronger Marco disarms Eddie of his spike. He does not stab him, but rather punches him repeatedly, driving him down on his knees to the damp street. The hovering trolley wires press him down to degradation from top frame while a fire burns in right frame. Lumet holds Vallone's taut face in extreme close-up as he registers both Eddie's frustrations and his shame. Then, rising, Eddie stands, completely alone, looking around at all he has known, before raising the spike and thrusting it down deep into his belly. Eddie accepts responsibility for his final act, finally judging his dim understanding in a manner similar to Oedipus, in wordless admission of the degradation he has brought upon his community and upon himself. In the film, Alfieri makes no moral pronouncements but just reports the facts to the police, after he visually echoes Eddie's responsibility by walking a distance to a telephone booth, a scene shown from the booth's perspective.[30] Now, judgment executed and responsibility declared and accepted, the crowd, including Alfieri, gather around Eddie's body. The camera slowly rises high above the scene, and we hear nothing but sounds of shipyard life and foghorns. Lumet's film thus ends by universalizing an individual neurosis, depicting the power of irrationality and denial to plunge humankind into self-destruction and catastrophe, as we observe from on high a moral vision of our weakness and our fall.

Daniel: The Understanding of the Past

Although political writer Andrew Kopkind has termed *Daniel* "a picture of uncommon integrity," and Stephen Farber, one of the few consistently careful critics of Lumet's films, has called *Daniel* "the most powerful film of 1983," the film engendered much harshly negative commentary.[31] Some reviewers scorned *Daniel* because they felt it did not adhere closely enough to historical facts about Julius and Ethel Rosenberg (upon whom Paul and Rochelle Isaacson are loosely based in Lumet's film, scripted by E.L. Doctorow from his 1971 novel, *The Book of Daniel*), the alleged atomic spies tried and executed—unjustly, in the minds of many—in 1953 for conspiracy to commit espionage. In this vein, Pauline Kael criticized the film as an "upsettingly personal fantasy" in which Daniel Isaacson's search for the meaning of his parents' ordeal and of his and his sister's life in relation to it is "hollow" because it does not address the specific innocence or guilt of the accused. Kael, frequently impressionistic when writing about Lumet, says that *Daniel* stimulates fears of persecution and victimization among American Jews, that it "feeds a strain of public hysteria and a fear of anti-Semitism." Considering Lumet's harrowingly realistic depiction of the Isaacsons' electrocutions, Kael can only conclude her review: "Is there any purpose in this except to make Jewish audiences quake and weep and feel helpless?" Kael is troubled by the film's fragmented time sequences (both book and film range across time from the 1930s to the 1960s); she complains that Lumet's use of Paul Robeson's spirituals at important places in the narrative is monotonous ("And boy, could this movie use something jazzy to pace it"). Kael accuses Lumet of photographing Amanda Plummer, who portrays Daniel's seriously disturbed sister, Susan, in such a way to make her appear "rodentlike. . . . I could hardly look at her."[32]

Andrew Sarris, while intelligent on the film's and the novel's Marxist analysis of capital punishment, invokes his anti-Communist Greek immigrant parents to criticize the film and, in a curious phrase for a critic who proclaims himself a social progressive, laments the "white-bread" casting for the Jewish principal roles portrayed by Timothy Hutton (Daniel) and Lindsay Crouse (Rochelle). Distressed by what he calls the "golden glow" of the scenes set in the 1930s and 1940s, Sarris then laments the film's lack of "romanticism" in Lumet's treatment of the Isaacsons.[33] Sarris's non sequitur in commenting upon

Lumet's time sequencing reveals why film writing frequently gains little credence among scholars in related humanities disciplines: "Contemporary movie theory is adamantly opposed to off-screen narration, and thus Hutton is unable to articulate the wrenching transition from present to past and back." Edward Guthmann less impressionistically faults Lumet for representing the Isaacsons simply as "symbols of martyrdom" and for crowding the film "with so many events, characters and historical reference points that we never get the time to discover any of the characters to our satisfaction."[34]

Commentators who indict Lumet for emphasizing the characters' thoughts and feelings more than their supposed historical or political accuracy forget that, even in our reductively and stridently politicized era, art is not identical with politics and history. As I will attempt to demonstrate, Lumet does not ignore social texture in *Daniel*, but he is first an imaginative artist, creating, as literary artists do, his own vision of the world's events. Certainly even (and especially) Shakespeare would fall from our creative pantheon were the sole literary criterion mere historical veracity. Lumet does imply, in the sequence involving Daniel's meeting with the *New York Times* reporter, the possible guilt of the youth's parents, faithfully adapting Doctorow at this point.[35] As he does throughout his work, however, he seeks implications behind and beyond actions and not mere social details as his thematic emphasis: in this respect he resembles Dreiser or Hemingway, not John O'Hara. The film does not rely mainly on Rosenbergian connections and memories but like all art depends upon our empathy with these characters' problems and dilemmas, reflecting the universal human dilemma. Audiences who recall the late 1940s and early 1950s may have their grief enhanced at the sufferings of the Isaacsons and their two children, but the politically uninitiated will also experience both their suffering and Daniel's potential self-renewal if they can view the film with empathy and imagination. Such observers will recognize that Daniel wishes more to understand than to justify the past. Lumet reveals Daniel struggling to understand himself, his cruelties and obsessions, and striving through an understanding of his parents' and younger sister's catastrophes to rebuild a more mature and effective selfhood.

In several interviews Lumet endeavored to set forth his deep personal commitment to the film and to explain his perception of his artistic intent. Speaking with Arthur Bell, the director commented, "This is not the story of the Rosenbergs. . . . I set out to make a movie about parents and children. To me, *Daniel* is the story of a boy who buries himself with his parents, and spends the rest of his life trying to climb out of the grave."[36] To Judy Stone, Lumet said that the film concerns Daniel and his sister, children of a convicted couple, the Isaacsons: "It's about the cost of passion. Who pays for it? What are the losses? . . . Why can't artists' children ever seem to pull their lives together? How much do my two kids . . . pay because I've done 31 movies in 25 years?"[37] Lumet and Doctorow prepared a joint statement that was presented to the press at early screenings of *Daniel*. After giving the basic narrative outline, the statement continued:

The historical event that inspired both the novel and the film is the trial and execution of Julius and Ethel Rosenberg in 1953. But except for the extremity of their legal situation, the characters in *Daniel*, as well as the setting and circumstances of their lives, are fiction. There is no attempt here to be historically accurate. The questions we ask as storytellers are not those which seek factual verification. The story is told from Daniel's point of view. He becomes a kind of detective of his own life as he investigates the annals of his family's history and relives his responses as a child and now as an adult to the extraordinary demands made on him by his parents' trial and death. Through Daniel's search for self-discovery in his own memories, as well as his contacts with people who were involved in his parents' case, we see from the inside three decades in the life of American dissent—from the Depression and World War II to the McCarthy period and the anti-war movement of the 1960s. The effects of parents on children, of ideologies on life, of history on individuals, are questions considered in the story of two generations of a family whose ruling passion is not success or money or love, but social justice.[38]

Lumet and Timothy Hutton further defended the film's conception at a press conference at the University of California, Berkeley, during which Lumet tartly observed, "This movie isn't a docudrama." Alluding to his several gritty, realistic crime films based upon the lives of real persons (*Serpico, Dog Day Afternoon, Prince of the City*), the director expressed the desire to expand beyond the limitations imposed by that kind of realism, adding that despite his interest in social themes he does not consider himself a director of "message" films: "What I like basically are character studies, and usually the most dramatic confrontations happen between characters in the context of the society they live in. . . . I can't imagine a better antagonist for the character of Treat Williams in *Prince of the City* than the government. What he had to fight was just so much more powerful than if he had had a conflict with just one individual. So I guess my taste . . . leads me to films that have political undercurrents."[39]

Lumet made the film for "the currently meager budget of $8.5 million." As with *Long Day's Journey into Night*, all major participants in the film, as well as the crew, served for amounts far below their normal salaries. Timothy Hutton worked for union scale of twenty-five thousand dollars, also passing up a million-dollar offer to star in another film so that he could do *Daniel*. At first, Lumet was not keen on casting the usually fresh-faced Hutton as the brooding Jewish intellectual, but Hutton pursued an interview with Lumet at his own expense and impressed the director with his understanding of the psychological implications of the novel. Lumet pressed upon the young star Michael Gold's fine, obscure novel, *Jews without Money*, and urged him to visit Hebrew schools and synagogues; Hutton also studied Irving Howe's *World of Our Fathers* but did no direct research on the Rosenberg case.[40] Hutton was pleased with Doctorow's reaction to the actor's transformation: "After he saw it, he said, 'You are Daniel.' That was a pretty big compliment." The young actor echoed many other fine performers who have respected Lumet's work over the years when he praised the "learning experience" he lived through during preparations for the film and said, "I won't just do it for the money. If you do . . . then you're just not being straight with yourself. . . . You've got to do something you believe in; then you'll always know you did it because you felt something from it, and because you wanted to make other people feel something from it too."[41]

In *Daniel*, Lumet creates a densely textured, multilayered film that heightens the principal characters who participate in Daniel's rediscovery of himself and his connection to the living world. As Kopkind perceptively observes, "In a deeper and richer way the film re-creates the images and ideas of the Rosenbergs' world, the dangers of an existence on the edge of idealism, 'the mythological burden,' as Doctorow wrote, 'of acts much smaller than their consequences.' " Surely the member of the Isaacson family most sundered by such acts is Daniel's younger sister, Susan: when the FBI comes to the Isaacson home and quickly sweeps away the children's toys, "family . . . culture, history, and life," Susan is condemned to sufferings even greater than those endured by her brother or her parents, ultimately descending through her own repression of rejection and guilt into catatonic psychological withdrawal.[42] Lumet and scriptwriter Doctorow begin the film with the sequence (deferred until pp. 90ff. in the book) depicting Susan's hectoring of Daniel and her foster parents, the Lewins, on the proper radical political uses of her parents' trust fund, following brief scenes of Daniel's remorseless description of the electrocution process and Lumet's subsequent cut to 1960s political demonstrations. Struggling to be rational, useful in building a better society, Susan has already begun to use political involvement as she previously employed religion, drugs, and sex, as a substitute for understanding her gnawing need to erase her consciousness. Her drivenness is revealed as she reacts with infantile gestures to Daniel's reasoned, if cynical, rejection of political responses; she foreshadows her final psychotic posture by throwing her arms up over her head while she screams invectives against her brother, as Lumet shows her cornered in the room's intersecting walls.

Following sequences that return to the Isaacsons' youth and courtship through radical activities—during one sequence in the film, unlike the novel, a pensive Communist reminds Paul that Stalinists are vicious—Daniel discovers in the car Susan's gift of an old "Free Them" poster and an open packet of razor blades in announcement of her attempted suicide. Lumet then immediately cuts to the episode after their parents' arrest, when Ascher, the attorney (Edward Asner), takes the children to a rally in support of the Isaacsons. Lumet shoots the crowd at a distance from high angle, a "distant aspect for the long historical vision."[43] Suddenly cries rise up, "Here are the children," and hands also rise to carry the bewildered and finally terrified children up to the speaker's podium. Dressed in red, the little girl screams out for her brother as the children are horizontally passed hand to hand by the mob, manipulated as political pawns while the crowd ritualistically cries, "Free them," a harbinger of Susan's future enslavement. From below, Lumet closes in on the harrowed faces of vulnerable human beings who appear helpless zombies in the crush of political fanaticism.

Also structurally reaaaranged from the novel (18-19) is Daniel's visit to see the institutionalized Susan. In the film, the visit occurs following references to Rochelle's crazed mother, periodically driven mad by the difficulty and poverty of her immigrant life. This arrangement allows a political and an emotional context for Susan's psychological disintegration. After Daniel enters the visiting area, Lumet cuts to an empty corner of the room before Susan's sudden visual appearance there. Still attempting to use her sardonic humor to counter depression, Susan mocks her beloved brother: "It's serious. . . . My whole family's here, how supportive." Then she convulses them both in laughter with her legalistic statement, "The right to do irreparable harm is a bloodright," as the camera allows a view of her heavily bandaged wrists. Rather than Daniel's thinking of the numbing of pleasure in death (18), the film gives these thoughts Susan's voice as, her humor suddenly subdued, she says, "It's just that I was overcome with it. . . . I forget what it is you're supposed to expect from being alive," as the camera reveals the windows' bars distantly behind her brother. As Susan is led away, Daniel must hear (as in the novel, p. 19) Susan's warning: with one

finger raised, she says farewell to him, "They're still fucking us . . .
Daniel. You get the picture." It is this experience that begins Daniel's
process of reexamining himself, his turning from what Kopkind describes as "passive aggression against the world and active aggression
against his surrogate family, his young wife, and their infant son."[44]

Lumet economically presents Susan's downfall to this point in the
film's flashbacks. As Paul tells the family, backgrounded by the arrival
of the first television sets at his radio store, that arrests have begun, he
catches up Susan in his arms, but the child already seems somewhat
abstracted from the scene. (Susan and Daniel as children are mar-
velously portrayed by Jena Greco and Ilan M. Mitchell-Smith.) As her
parents argue, faced with abandonment by most of their friends when
the FBI begins its visits, Susan traces the line of a shadow on the wall.
After Ascher persuades Paul's reluctant sister, Frieda (Julie Bovasso), to
take the children in, Lumet reveals a short respite in Susan's insistent
feelings of rejection as Daniel playfully lifts his little sister into the air
from a bed and she gives a momentary slight smile. When the children
are removed to a charity shelter, Lumet varies the action from the
novel, showing many children in a meal line and Susan attempting to
run to her brother from the enforced separate line for girls. When the
matron slaps her, Daniel goes wild, causing a near riot in the dining
room.

In perhaps the most moving scene in the film, Lumet heightens
the children's attempted return to their home (187-95) by showing their
lonely odyssey backgrounded by emptier landscapes. Nowhere in the
film are Paul Robeson's spirituals used more hauntingly than during
the children's journey homeward. Cinematographer Andrzej Bartkowiak's reddish browns dominate the coloring here, as, to Robeson's
rich, somber, song "This little light of mine, I'm gonna let it shine,"
Lumet traces the path of their vulnerable light through the emotionally
distant cityscapes. Sometimes separated from us by double sets of
railings, the children hold each other on traffic islands, Susan curling
into her big brother. At one point, Bartkowiak shoots them along a
wall, at a considerable distance, the curving paths and rail lines enveloping the children, diminishing them within a maze. Susan
screams as they approach their old neighborhood; Daniel runs to a
wire fence that separates him from us and stares for many seconds at
the abandoned house. After Daniel breaks into the barred-up house,
Lumet ends the sequence as Daniel comes toward the camera and then
stares at his sister, who is seen with her hands crossed over her chest.
Then she closes her eyes and places her hands over them, and Daniel
holds and kisses her. Robeson's voice is also heard over Susan's final

the adult Daniel bearing her total catatonia as she lies, arms over her head, seeing nothing. Reflecting Robeson's words, Daniel's understanding deepens while he holds her in his arms facing his picture and the "Free Them" poster, as she is finally granted her need to extinguish all feeling.

In this drama of the dissolution of parent-child relationships, Lumet's treatment of Paul and Rochelle Isaacson succeeds, as Kopkind has noted, in showing "American communism as a thoroughly American way of life, an alternative political style which was not only acceptable in its context, but in many ways rewarding and socially useful."[45] Beginning in the 1930s with the Isaacsons' courtship at City College, Lumet romantically lights the shot in which they are shown on a streetcar, slowly pulling into the barn, as Paul reads Marx aloud to his beloved. At a rally during the late 1930s, their friend and later betrayer, Selig Mindish (Joseph Leon, who also worked with Lumet in *Just Tell Me What You Want*) introduces the couple to the radical speaker, then dances with them. Early on, Paul is shown to be more abstract in his political beliefs, more credulous in his Marxism, while Rochelle never allows the system to make inroads upon her essential humanism. If somewhat fanatical, Paul (Mandy Patinkin) loves his son deeply, and in a fine scene varied from the novel (45ff.), Paul instructs the adoring Daniel on the evils of Joe DiMaggio's exploitation of himself and his audience via his picture on a cereal box. As Paul kisses his son's forehead, both are joined in laughter. Rochelle is even more solidly confirmed in the values of family; when a loyal friend comes to visit her following Paul's arrest, Rochelle echoes the novel, "To ruin a family, the lives of children" (137).

In the family's bus trip to hear Paul Robeson, an episode that occurs later in the film, heightened dramatically by its placement after the now-adult Daniel's foster father explains to him the legal and political realities behind the government's actions against his parents, Lumet shoots one of the few violent sequences in his major films as the Communists' bus is smashed by right-wing radicals, with police collusion. During the assault, Rochelle is more mature than Paul, who courageously risks serious injury but reveals his naïveté while doing so. By the time of the children's visit to their parents in prison, Paul, significantly shot from a longer range, has deteriorated to a still-loving sloganeer, while Rochelle is emotionally far stronger in considering her children's psychological needs as well as her own, attempting to sustain their strength and self-images in the face of their grievous loss and stalking from the visiting room with a proud, purposeful stride. Unlike the novel, Lumet's film reveals Paul also tending to ignore Susan, who seeks psychological support from her father, preferring to speak to Daniel in clichés, ending with a pathetic remark, "We are an ideal family." At the electrocution, Paul is even less in control than in the novel (312), falling and finally having to be dragged down a long blue hall toward the death chair. Lumet closely adapts the novel here, with Crouse giving a splendid angry performance as she stares at her oppressors until the last moment so that they cannot forget what they have done and are about to do. Yet with typical Lumetian objectivity, her watchers do not flinch, shot from the rear as they watch Paul and Rochelle's hideous deaths. Rochelle's life force is so strong that her killers must electrocute her twice in order to extinguish it.

"Ah, my pop," spoken by Daniel's adult voice, is heard over the scene of his father's burning. At last Daniel comes to terms with his past, staking some claim upon his future; the son's understanding of his parent's radical heritage merges with a softening of his previously aggressive stance toward the world, his wife, and his foster parents (37-38, 68-72). Lumet closely adapts the novel's representation of this alienation and Daniel's gradual emergence from it through his visits to Ascher's wealthy widow and to his foster parents to learn more about the history of his parents' legal ordeal and its unfairness. But the director significantly changes the novel's section describing Daniel's visit to Selig Mindish's daughter in southern California (285-309). While Doctorow sets the scene of Daniel's reunion with the now-senile old betrayer in Disneyland, laying on the rather obvious satire of middle-class capitalist consciousness through the easy symbolism of America's Ur-theme park, Lumet's approach is subtler and more humane. Lumet's depiction of Linda (Tovah Feldshuh), now a prosperous dentist, and her fiancé, a quintessential yuppie, is typically fair and balanced: while the audience's sympathy tends to lie with the bearded, searching protagonist, and Linda's office is the picture of coldness with its carefully arranged plastic flowers, Linda herself is courageous in her free admission of her own family's great emotional suffering following the trial. She graciously accedes to Daniel's desire to question Selig concerning his condemning of Paul and Rochelle, but the moving scene of their meeting takes place in a rest home, where the old man paints gestures even when no paper is in front of him. In a fine shot, Lumet shows the group from floor level approaching the door to Selig's room, headed by his strongly striding daughter, who, long before Daniel, has understood and accepted the meaning of the past. Daniel places his face in front of the staring old man, and for a moment Selig returns to life, remembering Daniel as a child and beginning to speak of Susan as a little girl; he goes toward Daniel, placing a hand upon his face, and leans forward to kiss him. Perhaps at the guilt Susan's name brings to him, Selig's face again goes blank, and Daniel rises from him, wisely speaking, in a different sense than is used by the judge in the novel (248), "There's such a thing as too much hope," before he lightly kisses Linda and leaves.

This recognition, followed by Lumet's close adaptation of the funeral scene (315ff.), in which Daniel (backgrounded by another apt Robeson spiritual) can at last weep for his past and present dead, makes possible Daniel's full return to emotional wholeness. Unlike the novel, Lumet's film ends with Daniel and his young family present among a huge crowd during an antiwar demonstration in the late 1960s. Some viewers have interpreted this conclusion as the director's endorsement of Daniel's return to politically defined commitment.[46] But Lumet's camera placements and other visual details in the final sequence suggest a more ambiguous resolution. Daniel stands somewhat apart from the crowd, as a young singer croons a less-powerful version of the Robeson spiritual heard during Daniel's childhood odyssey homeward with Susan. Lumet's camera pans over many people of many races and backgrounds, but the rock music sounds tinny against Robeson's exhortations to an earlier generation of more committed American radicalism; it seems a mere pop display, gesture without much authentic thought or feeling. Unlike Nazerman in *The Pawnbroker*, who wanders with release and awe amid those he has scorned, Daniel is pensive, reflecting on the possible value of a commitment to a sometimes more trendy radicalism than that for which his parents sacrificed their lives.

Lumet's last shot of the film is a tilt upward to a perfectly blue sky— if taken seriously, the sort of broad, sentimental sign one seldom observes in close analysis of Lumet's work. It seems more probable that as the camera pulls back to show Daniel at the edge of thousands of people at the demonstration, Lumet is commenting ironically on the sentimental and fashionable piety of the late 1960s that claimed that the revolution had spread and that thus things automatically were better than when Daniel's parents met a horrific fate at the hands of an insensitive legal system. Daniel ends the film perhaps meditating on that very question, not blindly accepting a simplistic radicalism, an easy pop Marxist communion with his generic historical past, glibly accompanied by the ever-present, self-advertising troubadour. Lumet's political and moral vision is rarely so simplistic. Doctorow spoke to Arthur Bell about his own ambiguities concerning the political levels of his novel: "When I wrote *The Book of Daniel* in the late '60s there were more interesting questions to explore than the aberrant behavior of

a pair of radicals. I was interested in the connection between the
New Left and the Old Left. What was the role of the radical in America?
Was it sacrificial? Why do the left movements always destroy them-
selves?"[47]

Timothy Hutton's comments on the ending also lend credence to
an ironic interpretation. "I don't know if it's a strong political commitment, but he's certainly free enough to try it at that point. He's a little
tentative, reluctant perhaps, but he's at least exploring the politics of
his generation. It's meant to be a healthy sign."[48] Hutton recognizes
that the major aspect of Daniel's discovery is that of a personal past, a
sense of completeness about his parents' catastrophe, an enlarged
capacity to ask hard questions and face new challenges. Lumet himself
recognized this in a comment during the filming of *Daniel*:

Sure it's a political film. . . . But I feel the best way to get at it is through the
human level. I'm not interested in agitprop or poster art. I'm an old 'thirties
leftist, and I know that politics is not about victories. It's about a constant
lifetime struggle because you feel a certain way about what the function of
government is. . . . all work is political finally. It's political by saying, 'Look,
you're a human being and these are the kinds of human beings and situations
you are up against. And this is what greed means. This is what power means.'
Now what are you—on a human level—going to do to arouse somebody
enough to make them spend their time in a sensible way. That's the best
politics.[49]

Praising Lumet's "masterful adaptation" of the novel, Andrew
Kopkind labels *Daniel* a film of "rare understatement, and terrible
power" and calls the film's seriousness and difficulty "qualities that
can hardly be expected to win mass-media critical acclaim or attract the
demographic bulge to mall cinemas." Few of the director's films more
clearly reveal his penchant for taking "grave risks with art and politics
as practiced (or avoided) in Hollywood."[50]

Chapter Three

Woman and the Progress of Self-Understanding

One of Lumet's most attractive characteristics as a director is his openness to social and psychological experience, his receptivity to ideas before they become mainstream, even fashionable, in the culture. While feminist themes had surfaced in our mass culture by the mid-1960s, Lumet's *That Kind of Woman* (1959), *The Group* (1966) and *Lovin' Molly* (1974) were among the first contemporary American films to treat in some depth the complex problems of women's psychological and social identities. Indeed, *Long Day's Journey into Night* and minor, if at times interesting, films such as *Stage Struck, The Appointment, Just Tell Me What You Want,* and *The Morning After,* among other Lumet works, reveal Lumet's continuing interest in the necessity for women, as well as for men, to plumb beneath life's surfaces into emotional risk and involvement in order to achieve secure personhood. Avoiding the didacticism, flat characterizations, and thematic sentimentality or sensationalism of more overtly "feminist" films such as *An Unmarried Woman* (1978) and *Alice Doesn't Live Here Anymore* (1975), *The Group, That Kind of Woman,* and *Lovin' Molly* dare to study women who grow beyond a dependence upon men and attempt to define themselves apart from and beyond men. These films thematically resemble the subtle *Girlfriends* (1978) in their relatively deep inquiry into the sources of the emotional thwarting underlying so much of woman's pain and into the unfashionable idea that so much of this discomfort can be self-inflicted and self-imposed. In these films, women who do not act with self-awareness and responsibility, those who choose the status of "girls" rather than women, those who prefer self-delusion to self-development, end the victims as much of their own as of men's preemption. Their spiritual and psychological isolation and failure results, as it does for Lumet's men, from failures in self-knowledge. Lumet's films that emphasize women's characters and situations strive for and usually achieve mature feminist values, values that encourage progress toward self-understanding.

The Group: Kay's Fall and the Death of Dreams

Throughout his career, Lumet has shown uncommon sensitivity to psychosexual themes and issues, as his sympathetic treatment of homosexuality in *Dog Day Afternoon* reveals. His understanding of the ambiguities involved in heterosexual relationships is evident from the compassionate representation of General and Mrs. Black in an early scene in *Fail Safe*, the heightened emphasis upon Mary's character in *Long Day's Journey into Night*, the strong if neurotic characters of the aspiring young actress in *Stage Struck* and the bohemian Carol in *The Fugitive Kind*, the sad yet assured social worker in *The Pawnbroker*, as well as the purposeful female characterizations in later films such as *Daniel*, *The Verdict*, *Garbo Talks*, and *Running on Empty*. In a 1966 adaptation of *The Group* that follows closely the plot of Mary McCarthy's witty, verbose, and sometimes didactic 1963 novel, Lumet condenses the novel's humor and closely observed social detail to concentrate upon McCarthy's depiction of the eight young women's disappointments in the seven years following their Ivy League college days.[1] Revealing more trenchantly than the novel the emptiness of lives darkened by the absence of individual responsibility, Lumet places greater emphasis upon a universal theme of loss caused by human self-delusion.[2]

The novel begins with a sometimes gauchely written opening scene describing Kay's wedding, which discloses McCarthy's fascination with recipes and with the social distinctions among members of the group. We are told of Lakey's momentary anger: " '*Fool*,' spat out the Madonna from Lake Forest, between gritted pearly teeth. . . . the fine white Renaissance nostril was dinted with a mark of pain."[3] Instead of this, Lumet begins the film with two original, nearly wordless sequences that suggest the rigid patterns dictating and controlling many of the young women's lives and the potential of many of them for early disappointment and even self-destruction. As an offscreen voice, accompanied by three quick little taps, calls a class to attention to sing the college song, we observe floor-level shots of four sets of brown and white shoes moving front to rear frame, then four others crossing in an exact perpendicular grid: unlike the stately classical opening of *12 Angry Men*, this visual image suggests the inflexible social ambience and generally unconsidered responses of the young women that will subtly influence their future lives. Offscreen the Class of '33 sings the school song while Lumet reveals typical episodes of their college lives: significantly, the first to appear is the usually dignified, highly conscious Lakey (Candice Bergen), smiling with quiet pleasure at the sight of Renaissance paintings, echoing the song's reminder of the potential inherent in life's flowing bowl for those who choose to attempt to determine their own destinies. But except for the images of the serene Polly (Shirley Knight) at work in her chemistry laboratory and the ever-pensive and rational Helena (Kathleen Widdoes) painting at her easel, the images predict by implication the future unhappiness or emotional sterility of Pokey (Mary-Robin Redd) lost in her great wealth as she casts aside her books to ride her horse, of Libby (Jessica Walter) compulsively working at her editorial desk surrounded by signs exhorting, "Be Neat" and "Get Those Subscriptions," and, most memorably, of Kay (Joanna Pettet), involved so foolishly, as the school song suggests, in her student-directing, understanding her own needs and motives much less than the roles played by the irate actresses she criticizes and who predictively abandon her.

In the credits sequence Lumet continues visually to suggest the probable arc of the future for many members of the group, using circle imagery to suggest the patterns of compulsive and unexamined repetition that will result in emotional disaster for several. As Pokey clowns with her ukulele, Lumet's camera circles the group's backs as they are seated around a table, then cuts to a painting of the group by Helena that hangs over the fireplace, her subjects scantily clad and appearing more sexual and emotionally free than most of them will be in their future lives. The next shots ironically comment on the life of the painting, as we see couples dancing stiffly on the gymnasium floor; then Lumet dissolves to another group of dancers superimposed over the first. But the camera makes a semicircular tilt over this group until they are nearly upside-down, before another dissolve reveals Kay and her ill-chosen husband, Harald (Larry Hagman), as he slips an engagement ring on her finger and she is ecstatic at his confirmation of her identity, the askew first dissolve commenting directly on the future status of their union. Lumet next cuts to graduation day, its scenes of ritualistic conventionality foreshadowing the unhappiness to come: Pokey runs to her parents, whose wealth will forever insulate her against risk and growth; Priss (Elizabeth Hartman) fingers the engagement ring for which she will all too easily abandon her New Deal principles; Dottie (Joan Hackett) is seen with her mother, in whose subtly influential values she will always be entrapped; and Libby preens for photographers, absorbed in her self-image as she will be when we last see her. Only Lakey, composed, walking alone with her private thoughts, and Polly, running with Helena to her jovial, ostensibly "mad" father (Robert Emhardt), seem to represent more flexible and informed choices that could potentially break the superficial practices that will doom the others in the group to such sterile lives. The sequence concludes with Helena's class valedictory; her face shining with hope, she reminds her classmates that they go into a time of grave economic crisis, in which only those who continue to achieve at their highest personal levels can make the greatest national contribution and thus fulfill the promise of the many advantages bestowed upon them. A female chorus, underlying her restrained passion, celebrates "our triumphant way"; this motif will occur once again in the film's somber last scene, when, less than a decade later, Kay is dead and the hopes of many of her friends lie shattered or compromised.

In keeping with his and producer/screenwriter Sidney Buchman's choice to emphasize the novel's implicit theme of disillusionment generated by individual self-delusion and failed self-development, Lumet closely adapts McCarthy's central plot. He does, however, omit or de-emphasize certain characters and events: Helena's mother, Dottie's mother, Pokey's family butler, Hatton, Harald's occasional political activity, and the reacquaintance late in the novel of Priss with Norine—whose central function in the novel is to establish a topical socio-political background. Similarly, Lumet generally follows McCarthy's organizational patterns, except that he tends to intersperse episodes involving the eight young women that, while advancing the narrative in McCarthy's directions, also illuminate via comparison or contrast the reasons for the mutual decline—or, occasionally, ascent—in the characters' fortunes. In so doing, Lumet gives further evidence of having less concern with the attentions of the viewer and critic interested mainly in films because of their immediate social or political "relevance," in favor of appealing to an audience more comfortable with closely reasoned and more universal themes.[4]

Kay's fall from her campus hotel window during her plane-spotting, presented in the novel in flashback after the occurrence, is represented as a present action in the film, underscoring Lumet's frequent concern with the palpable, concrete consequences of moral choices and actions. While Kay's fall is accidental in both book and film, Lumet's direct showing of it is a dramatic culmination of the evasions of reality that constitute emotional and moral failure for several members of the group. Lumet's depictions of the characters of Dottie, Pokey, Priss, Libby, and Kay lead inevitably to Kay's final descent and contrast sharply with Helena's intermittent life successes and the triumphs of Polly and Lakey, the two members of the group who gain greatest self-understanding and who thereby best fulfill the spirit of Helena's valedictory, having the most to offer to others as well as to themselves.

Lumet's revelation of Dottie is among the film's most poignant explorations of character. While McCarthy devotes much attention

(19-71) to Dottie's sexual initiation by Harald's friend, Dick (Richard Mulligan) and her interminable ruminations about the event, Lumet more concretely and swiftly proceeds to Dottie's ultimate disillusionment, implying rather than spelling out as in the novel (164-80) Dottie's attachment to her mother and her unconscious rejection of her mother's romantic fantasies that lead Dottie to a conventional and unsatisfying marriage with a man too old for her. Lumet's direction of Hackett is subtle and humorous as he suggests the young Bostonian's ample potential for sexual passion so appreciated by Dick without belaboring McCarthyan details. As Dottie realizes that to Dick she is merely a replacement for his unrequited lust for Lakey, yet she also yearns to mature sexually; the usually rather stern Hackett is here winsome and soft-eyed in her flirtatious responses to Dick in the restaurant. When Dick leads her to his tawdry attic room, the college song can be heard softly in the background; as he begins to remove her clothes, she assists him by thrusting her arms straight up over her head as though she were under arrest. While in the novel, following intercourse Dottie thinks of the similarities between sex and dancing (46), in the film she happily chatters to her companion, "It's like following in dancing!" McCarthy writes that Dottie "heaved and squirmed to free herself" (35) from her sleeping lover, but Lumet directs her delicately to remove his arm from across her chest as she attempts to locate the bathroom. Amusingly she creeps out of Dick's room swathed in a blanket, and as she contemplates Dick's lack of capacity for intimacy, she whistles at her image in the mirror while uttering Pokey's usual line, "Who'd a thunk it?" But after Dottie obtains her contraceptive device and waits for Dick in the park, telephoning him many times, she finally realizes that he doesn't care for her at all. Lumet shows her leaving the park in the rain, depositing on the bench her formerly precious package, whose contents Dick had urged her to buy. In the last scene of the sequence, backgrounded by the college song, Dottie boards a train for Boston, her final disillusionment begun.

Briefly interspersing her decline with the continuing stories of her seven friends, Lumet gives us only brief glimpses of Dottie for the remainder of the film: as Helena types the class newsletter, at one point Dottie is seen sitting listlessly on another train, this one moving to Arizona, where she will be engaged to the businessman she does not love. The camera pulls back slowly from an engagement ring, while Dottie's composed, listless face stares out the window, her dead spirit as folded as her hands. Near the beginning of Kay's party for Harald, celebrating his completed play, Lumet reveals Harald already drinking heavily and cuts to Dottie looking at a picture on the wall of a bohemian-looking young man. Suddenly the doorbell rings, and Dottie turns right into the camera with a look of longing, in hopes that it may be Dick. Wordlessly Lumet portrays the price exacted by her evasive, dishonest marital selection, a price confirmed late in the film by a suddenly much older-looking Dottie, fumbling with her gin bottles as she telephones her congratulations to Polly on her consciously examined marriage to a psychiatrist, Dr. Jim Ridgeley. At Helena's after a group reunion upon Lakey's return from Europe, Dottie is seen drinking excessively and in a line original to the film wistfully asks the group if the serene Polly's life is "tragic." And as the group must cope with Kay's death at Helena's, a seated Dottie is seen in a very fast, subtle shot, looking downward as she mentions that Kay's burial service will be held at the same church in which she was married—the same place where Dottie first saw Dick. Trapped in her past by her own disinclination to recognize her true emotional needs, Dottie, like some of her friends, condemns herself to a gray half-life.

Pokey and Priss also suffer, Pokey less consciously, from their tradition's very ease, circumstances that weigh against either young woman's choosing to act in ways that will allow much risk or emotional development. McCarthy and Lumet devote the least attention among the eight protagonists to the chubby, good-natured Pokey, perhaps because she possesses such enormous wealth and such comforting parents that there is almost no occasion for any conflict in her life. At Kay's reception, in the film, unlike the novel (11), it is Pokey who parrots the group's intended criterion for each of their future marriages (significantly in the film a standard attributed centrally to Priss): "Who wants to marry a broker, a banker, a cold-fish corporation lawyer?" She misses the irony that among the least happy members of the group will be those who because of their present situations and values will abandon their best hopes and potentialities and settle instead for relationships that, while financially or socially secure offer little emotional authenticity. By placing McCarthy's words in the mouth of the wealthiest, if least educated and refined, of the young women, Lumet emphasizes the moral value of relational choices ultimately made by Polly and also by the rich Lakey. Pokey's wealth is so vast that her parents have given her for graduation her own plane so that she can commute easily to Cornell for her graduate studies in agriculture (11), and the film adds a comic demurrer by Pokey, spoken in all innocent surprise: "It's just a little two-seater!" Following sequences in the film that reveal the increasing emotional vacancy of Kay's and Libby's lives, Lumet suddenly shows Pokey marrying a vapid, anorexic-looking poetry instructor, hardly a promising partner for a person whom Priss has had virtually to haul through her college career, and again the women's chorus can be heard offscreen singing of their "triumphant way." On Lakey's return from Europe with her formidable German baroness, Lumet gives Pokey a most characteristic line absent in the novel, concerning a rumor that Polly's father has either heard or concocted (373): "That dame must tote a pair of brass knuckles." "Unconscious of the passage of time" (368), as she is utterly insensitive to the possibility of human metamorphosis, Pokey as the least conscious member of the group functions almost as a symbol of the price some of them must pay for choices unconsidered and responsibilities avoided.

Priss struggles to grow beyond her wealth and security; immediately in Lumet's pre-credits sequence, the slim socialite shakes her head with satisfaction after pinning up an NRA sign. But by graduation, she has already become engaged to a pediatrician, Sloan Crockett (James Congdon), from her own monied class, whose influence will weigh strongly against her development, both politically and emotionally. By the film's third sequence, dealing with arrangements for Kay's wedding, it is clear that Kay, who is from a western state and far from the social class of the other group members, will not be extended an invitation by any of the others' parents to hold her wedding reception at their homes. Lumet concretizes this situation by specifying Pokey's and Priss's families as the proximate causes for Kay's holding her reception in a simple restaurant. These events gain added significance in the film, because Priss heads for marriage almost as fast as the insecure Kay—indeed, these two liberally inclined young women seem almost in competition to see whose marriage will be the group's first. Since Priss is the group's only Phi Beta Kappa and her mother is a Vassar trustee, she might be expected to have a more secure sense of her own future and abilities than her rush to marriage would suggest.

At the reception, Norine (Carrie Nye), a satellite of the group, criticizes Priss's sense of social responsibility, but when Harald predicts the doom of America's privileged class, Priss reacts defensively, again suggesting her deepest emotional allegiances. Shortly after the sequence on Helena's giving way to her Republican parents' wishes concerning her career, Lumet discloses the traditional atmosphere surrounding Priss's wedding, especially Sloan's markedly unprogressive manner, as the offscreen women's chorus ironically sings of freedom. After the catty Libby's reminder to the group of the experience in store for the sexually inexperienced Priss that night, Lumet adds one of his most politically revealing episodes to the plot: aboard the honeymoon train—like Dottie's trains suggestive of the incipient death of its passenger's spirit—he shoots Sloan almost upside down, leaning out of his upper berth, visually dominating the terrified Priss cowering in her lower bunk. His eyes gleam as he says, "There's so little of you, Priss, too little for both Roosevelt and me!"

Like Dottie, Priss's decline accelerates after she becomes a mother, as she becomes increasingly submissive to the wishes of her emotionally fascist pediatrician-husband, and after she loses her job following the NRA's being declared illegal. McCarthy takes far too long (224-47, 333-43) to establish Priss's fear of sex and her nursing agonies directed by the compulsive Sloan. Lumet compresses this material, adding a minor character who shows women outside the group in a far superior light than does the novel's acidulousness. Using the fine actress Hildy Parks, who also contributes the memorable cameo of Mrs. Black in *Fail Safe*, as Nurse Swenson's assistant, Lumet gently shows some of the sources of Priss's anxieties. In the novel, McCarthy describes Sloan's insistent forcing of Priss to breast-feed their infant after the section on the sexually disturbed Libby's near rape at the hands of Nils (220-23), suggesting the neurotic connections between two of the least happy women in the group. Lumet, however, more sensitively and subtly contrasts Priss's unconsciously caused sufferings with the previous sequence showing Polly's amusing, highly conscious acceptance of her sexual needs and, moreover, of her emotionally inadequate lover's preference for fantasy instead of honest attachment.

As Sloan again invokes his assumed medical as well as husbandly authority to insist on breast-feeding for a woman who has always been made sensitive and guilty about her small breasts, Priss confesses to the nurse, "I could never bear to be touched," as Lumet moves the camera in on her fear. The nurse turns in the doorway as she leaves, catering to her fear but also kindly acting in sisterly support and solidarity: "Look on the bright side; they used to say it'll develop the bust." Lumet holds Priss in a low-angle shot, smiling in appreciation at this concern. This scene is immediately followed by the domineering Sloan's insistence on rigid feeding schedules, to whose depredations the now-cowed Priss more and more easily submits. The school song is heard softly in the background as she relinquishes more and more of her dreams. When we last see Priss in the film, she is totally submerged, gossiping with Libby, who has often been unkind to her behind her back. Priss disapproves of Mr. Andrews's living with Polly and her new husband because of his past history of emotional problems, but the term she pejoratively uses, *madness*, ironically comments on the familial neurosis she has allowed Sloan to wreak upon their child. In deep rear frame, he delightedly knocks over toy soldiers, preparing to be Sloan's natural successor in the dispensation of reactionary, compulsive imperiousness.

In Libby, perhaps the least sympathetic part in the novel and film, Jessica Walter's performance and Lumet's direction of the fine actress, whose portrayal of Inez provides *Bye, Bye Braverman* with some of its most outrageous farcical moments, register the most distinguished, consistent comic aspect of the cinematic adaptation. From our first views of Libby at graduation, primping for photographers and appearing to blow a misdirected kiss at her spatially distant father, the class English major seems all frosting and no substance. At Kay's reception, she praises her classmate to her parents as a "darling," yet she is cheap with Kay's gift and points out by indirection Kay's inferior social status to the rest of the group, a fact that several of the others gently try to overlook and sometimes even to compensate for. When Kay expresses concern that her favorite, Lakey, is not present, she reacts to Libby's obviously manufactured excuse with the question "Is that true?" In lines original to the film, Libby condescendingly replies, "True? Why, Kay." Her nearly hysterical laugh accompanies a barely brushed kiss on Kay's cheek, and she wanders off looking vaguely confused, revealing that for herself even more than for her saddest cohorts, truth and authentic confrontation with reality form no part of her social or especially her psychological worldview. Profoundly emotionally repressed herself, the ironically nicknamed Libby makes sly innuendos about the speed of Kay's wedding and comments to the ever-kind Polly (whose loving father lost much of his wealth in the crash) concerning Polly's prospective life in the Village as a medical technician, "How bohemian, dear." The highly conscious Polly replies smoothly, "How cheap, dear," gently spoofing Libby's eternal lack of charity. For all her incessant attention to her appearance, Libby is antisexual at bottom, continually flirting with and teasing men to buoy up her own deep insecurity. As Dottie is first attracted to the shallow Dick, Lumet shows Libby at her mirror, praising Dick's appearance—"fascinating man, that restless, chiseled face"—ignoring Kay's good insight that Dick is "warped."

Occasionally Lumet humanizes Libby a little, as in the short scene where she visits Kay at Macy's and helpfully teases the harried sales trainee by buying a pair of gloves and tapping on the counter, "Come, come miss, let's not be all day." Yet in the next sequence, Priss's wedding, Libby is back in form, suggesting to the group, truly enough in this isolated instance, that Priss is marrying centrally for social reasons. Ever caustic and critical, continually gossiping with and at the expense of her friends to cover up the emptiness of her own social and emotional life, Libby spies the hapless Pokey in her pilot's uniform at Kay's party and cracks, "Her plane must be double parked." She also cuts her friends behind their backs especially for their alleged sexual deficiencies. Married in McCarthy's novel (360), Libby is increasingly shown as alone and isolated by Lumet. Despite her reveling in the celebrity-mongering of her job as a literary agent, Libby allows its ceaseless activity to fill her life so that she will be prevented from confronting herself, from making personally fulfilling choices. After her teasing evening with Nils (Bruno di Cosmi) ends with a physical beating and utter humiliation, Lumet adds to this episode in the novel a brief scene showing Libby on the telephone, vicariously thrilled at Polly's evening, pathetically trying to embroider her humbling experience with Nils while lying in bed, a teddy bear under her arm. During a later telephone conversation, Lumet shoots her surrounded by five stuffed animals and backgrounded by a painting of a young adolescent girl.

It is perhaps unsurprising that the least emotionally developed of the group's intelligent members is so catty about Lakey's lesbian lover; Libby's vividly red mouth gleams as she powders herself at Helena's, and, as she prepares to escort Polly on her way home, Walter is afforded her best comic moment with a finger-snapping send-up of the baroness, "Come along, dahlink, I'll drop you somewhere quiet, like the subway." And in our final experience of Libby in the film, she unsurprisingly reacts to the facts of death no better than to varieties of mature sexuality. Lumet shows Libby alone on a rear chair at Kay's funeral service, after she alienates herself even from the group by treating Kay's death as though it were suicide. Then, following Lakey's insistence that the casket be closed, she snaps, "Open or closed," to Helena's suggestion concerning sandwiches after the service, as she stares out, her scar of a mouth the quintessence of harshness. While McCarthy presents Dottie as the sole member of the group too weak to face the implications of Kay's burial (363), Lumet chooses Libby as the most frightened, the least self-aware; his final shot of Libby reveals her running off down the street in frame right as the cars prepare to depart for the cemetery. Libby's compulsive, emotionally truncated life marks her emotional and moral failure as the greatest of all the group, even deeper than Kay's, since Libby's decline lacks even the ennobling struggle of Kay's vain, deluded search for self-fulfillment. In terms of Helena's class valedictory, Libby remains unable to make any substantial contribution to the life around her because she so completely misunderstands herself and flees from self-knowledge.

As the least socially well-connected and financially secure among the group, Kay takes considerable pride in being the first to marry. But as is the case with Priss, Kay's haste and choice of partner reveal characteristics that will hasten her fall. Lumet follows closely McCarthy's plot in presenting the story of this most affecting member of the group, but he is effective visually in rendering her a haunting symbol of the absence of individual responsibility that destroys the happiness of so many of the young women. Like all her circle except Helena, Polly, and Lakey, Kay develops little identity beyond that conferred upon her by a lover, in Kay's case her intellectually lazy, womanizing husband, Harald. While in the novel the group shows no concern at Harald's keen interest in liquor stores (18), Lumet and cinematographer Boris Kaufman make use of fast cutting—an effective technique throughout for lending pace to McCarthy's often long-winded novel—in the reception sequence to show the displeasure that Harald's descriptions cause to the sensitive Helena and Polly.[5] As Kay bustles about, an efficient hostess, but one whose clacking glasses reveal her misdirected ambition, her aspiring to a casual class that is beyond her, Harald drinks too much and insults the women's class and wealth with his superficial Marxism. Lumet here shows Kay's hand only, creeping up into frame left, attempting to restrain her husband from further insulting behavior. It is a shot reminiscent of *That Kind of Woman* and *12 Angry Men*, a visual correlative of the personal fragmentation that Kay's unfortunate alliance with Harald will cause her. Lumet heightens the sense of the psychological costs to Kay in the rice-throwing scene (29), to which he adds a directional component: he photographs the group descending the subway entrance stairs into the darkness toward the camera, almost without a word, deepening our visceral awareness of the depths to which Kay and Harald are heading.

Kaufman, production designer Gene Callahan, and skilled costume designer Anna Hill Johnstone give the film an accurate 1930s atmosphere and decor, particularly in the sequence set in Kay and Harald's apartment. Kay's zealousness in accumulating the most fashionable furniture, accessories, and technological conveniences is most threatening to Harald, suggesting accurately his wife's ambition to achieve material as well as social success. At Kay's party for Harald's first completed play, Lumet's blocking of the actors is reminiscent of the rigid visual patterns that begin the film's pre-credits sequence; the movement of the actors suggests a mechanical movement of objects and correlates well with Kay's emotional mechanism as she strives continually forward, with admirable drive but with little understanding of her own motives and of the consequences for her marriage and her future. Harald's own voracious insecurities drive him to destroy the manuscript of his play by throwing it down an incinerator chute in a drunken fury at a colleague's correct insight that the play was written largely to glorify its author's personal weaknesses and will probably be an artistic failure. Lumet suggests the irrevocability of Harald's act by a significant departure from the novel; while McCarthy softens the moral significance and inevitable psychological consequences of Harald's drivenness by having Kay mention that several other copies exist (117), thus turning Harald's behavior into a self-indulgent parlor game, in the film no mention is made of other copies of the play. Thus Lumet considers Harald's destructiveness here an important harbinger of Kay's future horrors. He also indicates this by changing the playful ending of the party chapter (117-18), directing a fine performance by Pettet as she is all pretended charm coming in from the hallway, keeping up appearances at all costs to cover her near despair, walking directly into the camera composing her features to the image she has made herself believe will be socially respectable.

From this point in the film, Kay will be increasingly visually isolated as Harald becomes progressively alienated from her and from himself. In the film, Lumet does not show Harald's political activities (145); even these occasional and self-aggrandizing gestures are absent in the director's vision of a man driven totally in upon himself and upon the destruction of all his and Kay's potential happiness. While Kay is not prominently featured in the middle third of the novel, Lumet heightens her status as the symbolic center of his conception of the novel's importance by twice in midfilm juxtaposing her fragmentation with Libby's, showing Kay at one point listening to Libby's self-inflating accounts of her literary dealing and celebrity lunches, while she eats a packed cold dinner, surrounded by her bric-a-brac but without Harald, who increasingly pursues other interests. As Helena's typed class report reveals Kay's career advancement at Macy's, Lumet cuts to Harald at home, drinking, his theater career now reduced to a four-month road assignment as an assistant director. In a brief scene, following another quarrel between them, Harald takes Kay to bed, saying he will send money for her "blond Swedish showroom." Lumet hones the camera down in upon her, clearly showing Kay's great need of his desire for her, although it is now occasional and accompanied by frequent insults.

In the novel, McCarthy distances the audience from Harald's assault of Kay and her tentative threat to knife him by presenting the episode in part through Polly's serene consciousness (307-32) and spelling out laboriously, through Polly's psychiatrist husband, Jim, the motives within her paranoid insecurity. Lumet intensifies the emotional violence and the horror of the episode both by presenting it in actual, present time and linking it visually to Kay's valiant effort to assuage her loneliness by plunging into civil defense activity, suggesting both Kay's courage in trying to build a social self and her use of political activity to mask the ravening insecurities that compel her to continue in an unsatisfying relationship. As Kay talks on the phone with Polly about her fear of long-range bombers, she reveals her own uncertain sense of sexual confidence by criticizing Lakey's potential motives for asking her to join the group in college and by expressing some anxiety about visiting Lakey and her lover.

Again using quick cutting to intensify the pace, Lumet shows Harald entering after spending a long time taking Norine home, beginning to insult Kay and to break her cherished possessions, then hitting her. Kay rushes to the kitchen to flourish a knife in his direction before quickly dropping it with a sob. Harald strikes her savagely and locks her in a closet, abject and hysterical. Then she is seen against a white wall in the mental ward, framed and enclosed by the shadows of the wires on her cell windows. In one of the film's best visual sequences, Lumet shoots Kay as ultimately the prisoner of her fantasies about her husband's need for her. From low-angle shots, the camera shows her circling the room like a caged animal, exploring the walls that surround her; the corners in which she is occasionally framed are cinematic equivalents of her self-delusion in thinking that Harald, who has lied to get her committed, will be the eventual source of her release. Before Kay's accidental, yet psychologically inevitable, toppling from her campus hotel window during plane-spotting, when the women's chorus becomes louder as it accompanies the screams of her fall, Lumet alters McCarthy's section in which Harald comes to free Kay from the hospital and arranges her return to her apartment in the care of Jim and Polly.[6]

In a poignant interlude during which Kay progresses to some understanding of her shattered life, she runs through the debris of her precious apartment, picking up its broken pieces as the camera pans from room to room in pursuit of her. To the soft choral song, she dimly senses that Harald's action was inevitable, that she made a commitment to a writer with so little commitment to his work that he has left his typewriter behind. As Jim realizes her situation, however, Kay ends still comparing her status with that of others in the group she considers even less fortunate; yet Lumet also underscores Kay's courage in facing the enclosure in which she was locked for hours, shooting from within the closet as Kay enters it to retrieve her clothes before retreating to a room on the sustaining college campus of her dreams where she thought she belonged to something. But unlike Priss and Helena, Kay's problem is not lack of courage but rather the misconception that someone outside herself will cause her emotional fulfillment, will confer an identity upon her that she might better have forged through the employment of her own considerable, yet sadly unrealized, personal capacities.

Helena avoids the unwise early marriages of some of her classmates; this perhaps brightest and most variously talented of the group gains a sort of intellectual independence yet remains only partially fulfilled because of a Priss-like submission to the wishes of her politically conservative parents and her inability to make a firm, lasting professional commitment of her own. Superbly rendered by the restrained yet confident performance of Kathleen Widdoes—whom Lumet directed to a sterling Masha in *The Sea Gull*—Helena is indeed among the wisest, as well as the most wealthy, of the group. Remarkably talented (101-2), Helena is the class secretary without being an unpleasant gossip like Libby; she continually takes charge of uncomfortable arrangements for the others, from Kay's wedding to her funeral services. Ever rational and perceptive of the needs of others, she defuses trouble from the jealous Norine and others via her sly humor at several points in Lumet's film. In a fine original bit at Kay's party, when badgered by a radical about her family's money and then praised by Kay for her many talents, she coos, "You left out bird calls," and proceeds to mock her attacker with a rousing screech as she delicately slides out of the left frame. Yet Lumet well depicts the brilliant Helena's fatal choice in abandoing her dream of helping nursery school children and bowing to her business magnate father's pressure to live dependent upon his resources.

While Lumet might have strengthened the feminist component of the film by including more material from the novel describing the amusing relationship between Helena and her mother (107ff., 360ff.), he instead focuses alternately on the great strengths and unfortunate weakness of a young woman, who, with Lakey, is the most intellectually independent and assured member of the group. Norine, too, is de-emphasized in the film to show Helena in a more interesting and impressive light. After she catches Harald and Norine necking at Kay's party, Helena calls on Norine (120-43) to attempt to protect Kay's marriage. McCarthy gives Norine more good lines in the novel's interchange, while Lumet heightens Helena's contribution to reveal how costly her eventual succumbing to familial tradition will be for her. And while Norine has the last word in McCarthy, in Lumet's film Helena's rejoinder to Norine's request that Helena not repeat their discussion to anyone, "I won't . . . but you will," closes the scene with command, as does Helena's tough, cool reception of Norine's repeating Kay's cruel perception that Helena is "a neuter, like a mule," while the class song is heard in the background.

In two original, brief scenes, Lumet visually shows the professionally uncommitted Helena counterpointed with the decisive Polly, as the medical technician competently prepares to allow a weak lover to leave a relationship with her. First Helena is seen in her artist's garret, pursuing yet another temporary interest subsidized by her father, commenting on her painting of the group (which McCarthy describes amusingly on p. 102). Here, though, she is bitter rather than playful as she reflects on the inexorable passing of calumniating time. Following Polly's firm action (which in the film also refers to Polly's closeness to, but not dependence on, her father), Lumet reveals Helena, off her balcony now, in a lotus position with her Hindu guru during a telephone conversation with Kay. Lumet thus also places Helena structurally in closer affinity to the confused Kay than to the progressively self-defining Polly. Lumet further visually suggests this impression in an apt two-shot of Kay and Helena following Lakey's return from Europe with her lover. As Helena's painting looms ominously over the group, Kay looks purposeful but agitated, while Helena, seated on a piano bench holding her wine glass, appears aristocratically composed yet purposeless, born to a consummate knowledge of the forks yet unable to summon the power of choice to use her fine attributes. As the film begins with Helena's helping others, so it concludes with the class secretary in reasoned command of her environment but not of herself, establishing who shall go to the cemetery in whose car. Lumet's camera closes in on Helena in the back seat of her vehicle, listening in memory to the offscreen reiteration of her inspiring words in the valedictory address, the ironic class song reminding her of her lack of dedication to purpose, her settling for indolence, as the line of black cars enters the cemetery.

Polly is, with Lakey, the member of the group who refuses to foreclose her dreams; in contrast with the others, she seeks self-knowledge and self-definition, both in work and in her relational life. A rather modest girl in college, a good if not brilliant science student, she is content with her hospital career and emotionally supports her unstable but loving father. Very keen psychologically, she is prepared to risk a premarital relationship with the kind but ultimately self-deluded Gus (Hal Holbrook). She is equally decisive in ending the affair when she realizes Gus's essential passivity. Lumet follows McCarthy's description of Polly's character closely, interspersing her increasing growth

with others' gaps in knowledge and will. From her generative beginning in the film's second sequence, in which Polly and Helena run to
Polly's (but not to Helena's) father, Lumet reveals Polly's unusual
capacity for sympathy and love, often in bits of action original to the
film. At Kay's reception, Lumet cuts from the odious Norine to Polly's
steadfastly defending her choice of refreshment to a bothersome man.
Lumet's usual mastery of suggestive, realistic visual detail also appears
later in the sequence when, at Harald's proposing a toast to the Class of
'33, Polly is the first to rise. As the group sees Lakey off to Europe, Polly
asks her date also to go with her on a boat someday, and in a very quick
cut (as the well-wishers descend the ramp) Lumet catches the man
dismissing her vitality with a summary wave of the hand.

The director makes adept use of his own father, Baruch Lumet (a
memorable Mendel in *The Pawnbroker*, as well) as the kind, kibitzing Mr.
Schneider, to draw from Polly her fondness for the socially marginal
and unusual person. Self-determining, Polly resembles E.A. Robinson's Cliff Klingenhagen as she tastes the bitter cherries on Kay's cake
at Pokey's wedding, manifesting Lumet's frequent theme of the pain
and risk necessary in achieving change and growth. She is seen alone
doing the dishes, instead of mingling with partygoers whose superficiality bores her. Significantly, Polly and her equally honest fiancé are
the last people shown with Kay in the scene before her fall from the
window; as Kay kisses them, congratulating them on their engagement, Lumet's shot of her back as she goes toward the window to
ponder her sadness contrasts with the emotional wholeness of her
friends. In the film this "quiet type . . . who knew everything" (10)
telephones Kay just before the accident, realizing her friend's agitation
at listening to war news alone. With Lakey ever the closest to the body,
she dresses the corpse before the funeral ceremony. Gaining in confidence as she loves and is loved by the wise Jim Ridgeley, she is
nonetheless independent of him and a woman of her own, unlike the
female characters in the popular "feminist" films mentioned at the
beginning of this chapter who achieve their identity or happiness
centrally through the agency of a man. Unlike her sorry sisters, Polly is
comfortable with the insight of Alfred Adler that dependence is the
root of all feelings of inferiority.[7]

Lumet subtly renders the character of Lakey, the wealthy and
sophisticated art historian who, as in the novel, is physically absent
through much of the action, yet in the film is a living and vital presence
whose independence of mind and spirit infuses the entire action with
dignity and grace. Lumet's glimpses of her in the film's first two
sequences show her serenity and self-possession, hinting at a self-

determination that is ampy fulfilled as the narrative progresses. At Kay's reception, Lumet quickly cuts to Lakey's deftly fending off Harald's hand on her rear in a shot so swift that it is barely perceptible as Lakey's avoidance of the unwelcome. Lumet and Kaufman's adroit camera positioning continues in the rice-throwing scene at the subway, done mostly in fast intercuts except for a slow close-in on a softly crying Lakey in black suit and black bowler, mourning Kay's loss as well as celebrating her hoped-for happiness with Harald. Lakey's emotional integration is revealed further in her relation of Kay's "truth game" to Dottie and Dick Brown. In the novel the information is presented through an omniscient narrator representing the group's opinion through its collective memory (13). But Lumet discloses the story solely through Lakey: she both chides Kay in absentia for the unconscious cruelty of the game and simultaneously implies its cause in Kay's deeply rooted insecurity. Lumet's having Lakey impart this information to the inconsiderate Dick confirms her opposition to such people not because of their sexual difference from her but because of their emotional callousness and lack of moral sensitivity.

While McCarthy centers Lakey's independence in her lesbianism itself, Lumet reveals a human being emotionally and intellectually supple regardless of her specific sexual orientation. In the film, her sophistication lies in what E.M. Forster termed an interior, rather than a social, aristocracy. In depicting Lakey as somewhat kinder toward Kay than in the novel (14), Lumet makes her lesbianism a subtler aspect of her motivation than McCarthy does. Lakey in the film is more morally admirable in openly loving Kay even though she recognizes that doing so will not engender a directly sensual reciprocity. And Lumet further humanizes Lakey's character after her return from Europe with the baroness. In the novel the group is united in opposing Polly and Jim's plan to have the manic, loving Mr. Andrews live with them, but in the film Lumet represents both the baroness and Lakey as happily approving the idea. This brief scene during a telephone conversation between Polly and Lakey unites both women in having taken a responsible position regarding their sexuality and domestic status; only Polly and Lakey among the group have gained mature womanhood, have fully come to be, because both have integrated with their chosen sexualities.

Nowhere is Lakey's confidence and moral self-determination more evident than in Lumet's conclusion. Whereas in McCarthy, both Lakey and her lover attend Kay's funeral, Lumet shows Lakey seated alone: this shot is less sentimental than the scene in the novel, because Lakey realizes that in times of crisis in the lives of her college friends she must share the burdens alone and not oppress the baroness with emotions not a part of her experience. While in the final section of the novel (368-78) McCarthy didactically spells out Harald's and Lakey's emotions in relations to Kay and lesbianism, Lumet's vision is less obvious and more mature. In the film, Lakey does all the driving, is in command all the way to the cemetery, and does not grant Harald his last verbal stand in the bar. She does not need to take "revenge" (377) on Harald nor place him in a position where she must oratorically defend lesbianism. Their confrontation occurs more spontaneously, and an alternative sexual preference seems more a natural aspect of life, as the emotionally defective, despicable Harald self-destructs of his own compulsive momentum. Lumet directs Bergen's suave, controlled performance superbly here; she is neither self-conscious nor disdainful in her contained contempt for a man who has wasted Kay's potential, whereas she would have nurtured it. Perfectly blending serene happiness with tenderness toward Kay's memory and her own aesthetic memory of Kay's physical perfections, Lakey describes her to Harald in natural terms appropriate to an art historian. Unlike the novel, which describes Harald at the last, leaving Lakey in anger and heading back to New York, attempting to justify his moral failure, Lumet shows Lakey continuing on. Coolly driving her red sports car—the one note of color and life in the death procession—Lakey keeps her responsibility both to her friends and to fantasy, secure in her choices and resolutions, with Polly the sole emotional survivor of the group at the cemetery, whose gates wait for her as if in tribute and slowly close on the deaths of the rest of their dreams.

That Kind of Woman: Levels of Insecurity

Lumet's third film, *That Kind of Woman* (1959) is an adaptation of Robert Lowry's story set in World War II America, "Layover in El Paso," which was published in a volume of Lowry's war stories, *The Wolf That Fed Us* (1945), and anthologized by Charles A. Fenton in a 1957 collection of the best stories of that period, which included stories by Faulkner, Ellison, Mailer, Styron, and John Horne Burns.[8] In his 1946 war novel, *Casualty,* Lowry wrote, "Life for each man had become a menial thing."[9] This anomic condition indeed prevails among the major characters in Lowry's brief fiction. A slangy, cynical omniscient narrator makes several references to lonely bored soldiers and other passengers aboard a crowded train en route east from Los Angeles, "gone mad with the fury of the war" (67). A young, inexperienced soldier named Red, on his way from his California army base for a brief furlough to his small hometown in Tennessee, encounters, with his sailor drinking pal, Georgie, a somewhat older, more experienced woman, Kay, traveling with her constantly smiling friend, Boots. Kind but naive with women, Red quickly becomes infatuated with the flirtatious Kay, although the casually wise narrator indicates that Kay is a fickle woman incapable of intimate emotional relationships. She reveals her selfishness and egocentricity by demanding shrimp cocktail in the dining car when the war-rationed train contains scant fare for the soldiers. "This is one of the reasons I just *hate* the war," Kay says. "You've got to *wait* and *wait* and *wait*" (70). At a layover in El Paso, Kay and Boots suggest that the two men stay with them in their apartment, mainly financed by Kay's support from a wealthy former husband. Georgie, usually referred to in his mythic role as the Sailor, murmurs to Red as they talk in the dark, "I never did get home on a leave yet. . . . I tried about three other times, but I never make it; I always get into something like this. It ain't bad, though, they got a good set-up" (75).

For the next day and a half Red is tantalized by Kay, who alternately encourages and discourages his sexual advances and forsakes him twice for other lovers. Despite many diversions such as drinking, bullfights, and movies, Red becomes more lonely and guilt-ridden, knowing that his poor farm family, having sent him money for his furlough home, will be saddened at his absence. Finally so unhappy and guilty that he gets drunk and beaten up by another soldier in a barroom brawl, Red loses everything but his railroad ticket home. Struggling to free himself from Kay's apartment, he resolves to catch his train. But fate leads him to the wrong train, one bound west instead of east, and he ends almost where he started, fingering the empty rifle shell in his pocket that he had promised to bring home to his brother, rationalizing that mailing it home will serve just as well. The story concludes with some soldiers offering Red a bottle and commiserating at his returning from a furlough, as he turns aside so they cannot see the bruised side of his face.

Lumet's version of Lowry's story truly makes, in the Bazinian sense, a new and original work of art. *That Kind of Woman* catches the transience of life during the mid-1940s in America, particularly the hopelessness of the minor pair of "lovers," corresponding to Georgie and Boots, but the film reaches beneath the surfaces of Lowry's tough-edged sentimentality to find, through a far different set of events and circumstances, deeper levels of spiritual and moral issues similar to those that concern Lowry. The result is a film that could have been a mere soap opera in another director's hands. Lumet and screenwriter Walter Bernstein's story of a beautiful kept woman who chooses ultimately her love for a poor rural soldier over the wealthy sophisticate who offers her marriage and stability rises considerably beyond stereo-typed melodrama. Turning Lowry's story into a seemingly ordinary love story, Lumet examines potentially trite material in a manner at once even harsher and more compassionate than the story and creates one of his finest and most universal existential representations of human responsibility and the dignity inherent and necessary in per-sonal choice. In so doing, Lumet adds to his considerable reputation as an actor's director, drawing forth superior performances from support-ing players as diverse (and typically excellent) as Jack Warden, Barbara Nichols, George Sanders, and Keenan Wynn and eliciting incredibly fine portrayals from Sophia Loren and Tab Hunter as the lovers.[10]

Even in the credit sequence Lumet reveals that his adaptation will focus upon his conception of the character of Kay (Sophia Loren) and of her friend Jane (Barbara Nichols), as the two curvaceous women walk alongside a train, the Silver Meteor, leaving Miami for New York City in June 1944. Lumet's quick pace underscores the transitoriness of experi-ence for the people on the platform, who say goodbye to their loved ones in a setting fraught with wartime anxieties. The credit titles flash on and off the screen quickly, and Lumet abruptly cuts to Red (Tab Hunter) waiting by a telephone booth for his army buddy Kelly (Jack Warden), while Kelly contacts one of his numerous, yet ephemeral, women. As Kay and Jane hurry along the platform, Lumet positions them in an angled relationship to the train; as Red and Kelly climb aboard barely in time, Lumet shoots the train angling off sharply to right frame, with Kay's smiling face visible in a window. In the first shot of the men on the train, a child is shown dropping an ice-cream cone on Kelly, while visible in the background is a sign: "The Farm is a Battle-ground Too." Adding to the uncomfortable atmosphere, Kay, just before boarding, is greeted sardonically by Harry (Keenan Wynn), who says with a leering irony, "So glad you could make it, doll," suggesting his position of emotional supervision over her. It emerges that Harry is employed by a very wealthy man (George Sanders, known mythically only as The Man), who has managed to secure for the women a cramped compartment aboard the wartime train, and that Harry will function as their overseer during the trip north. Once aboard, Kay offers her friend the lower berth, saying, "I can sleep anywhere." Harry responds with another leering laugh. At this, Kay slams closed a suitcase that lies open beside her facing Harry, a visual gesture suggesting that her ample sexuality is not available to him, while also indicating her superior sensitivity to Kay in Lowry's story.

Throughout the film's early sequences, Lumet establishes Harry's ambivalence toward Kay, as Harry at once desires her yet ridicules and scorns her for being a kept mistress. The sexual atmosphere becomes electrically charged—unusually so for a thematically serious American film of this period—as Kay teases Harry for not serving in the war, for not making anything essential (in reality, for having been spared as a result of working for the wealthy capitalist). Harry replies, "You make anything," as Lumet frames him dominated visually by Kay's curved, thrust hip as she stands tauntingly over him, attempting to exercise what psychological control the situation will allow her. Her vulnerability is underscored aurally, however, as, a moment later, Kay can only attempt to assert herself by playing dance music on her portable radio even louder than the music Harry is listening to. But Lumet chooses to focus upon her essential strength, even early in the film: while she threatens Harry's position with his employer if he does not soon secure them a place in the club car, her guardian sometimes reacts to her with a yearning that is more than simple lust, though he but dimly realizes this. As the perennially sweet but lost Jane cries over having lost another boyfriend, a Marine, Kay lectures her friend, urging her to appreciate that the men they are going to next are rich and need not, therefore, be "nice," while she languidly plays solitaire to ease her boredom.

If the two women are contained spiritually by the circumstances of the war, then Red and Kelly are next shown by Lumet to be similarly constrained on a material plane. Boris Kaufman, famed cinematographer of several of Lumet's early black-and-white films, shoots the men enshrouded by shadows in an enclosed space between railroad cars, playing dice. Lumet brings the camera in very close on Kelly as he wins a large sum from a sailor and reveals Kelly's penchant for unconsciously needing to lose emotionally, as a fight nearly breaks out when Kelly decides he wishes to stop playing in the game. Inside the door separating the playing space from the next car, Kelly leans against the door with a freshly scrubbed Red, counting his winnings and carelessly throwing out a one-dollar bill ("How'd that get there?"), which Red hurriedly scrambles to pick up. But as Kelly ostensibly celebrates, Lumet frames him cornered between the wall and ceiling of the car, foreshadowing his self-defeating behavior later in the film. Kay is similarly driven by her emotions, which are sometimes healthier than Kelly's. When a slight, cerebral young soldier (played by John Fiedler, in an amusing development of the story's PFC who studies *A Critique of Pure Reason*, p. 72) attempts a romantic approach to Kay while Red and Kelly are also getting acquainted with her and Jane, Kay rejects him. Lumet skillfully reveals Kay as more emotional than rational in her reactions to life: even though she considers herself a rationalist, she has deeply rooted emotional needs that she will satisfy, if with difficulty, by the film's end.

As Kay and Red become known to one another, Lumet visually comments upon the varying levels of lacking self-knowledge and insecurity that will entrap most of the characters. In deep background, while Red and Kelly are introducing themselves to Kay and Jane, Lumet reveals a sailor, framed by two railings of the bar at which he is drinking, seated and seemingly oblivious to his surroundings. The sailor provides a marked visual correlative to Kelly and Jane, who certainly are trapped throughout by their lack of self-understanding and awareness. While the outward appearance is full of conviviality, as Kelly continues to drink and relieves Harry of his seat, flashing a V sign and making corny jokes like a military Willy Loman, beneath the fun Kelly begins to turn sour with self-contempt, threatening the cerebral soldier for no apparent reason. The slender young man is reasoned, yet not heeded: Kelly, Harry, and Jane are terminal losers because of their traditional self-ensnarement by habit and ignorance; and Kay, despite Lumet's revealing her quick glance at the man's watch she wears on her wrist, will come perilously close by the end of the film to destroying her happiness through repression of her fundamentally sound human instincts. Only Red, the rural Vermonter distinctly different in character from his counterpart in the literary source, seems emotionally free among these people. When the sultry Kay begins to tease the young man, who is twenty-three but appears even younger, that he is not old enough to take a drink, Red reveals his emotional strength and maturity, leaning down into camera over her and saying with a soft, but strong, kindness, "I'm old enough to do anything."

Red's mature contrast with the others is sustained as Lumet cuts to a medium shot in the club car, Red watching Kay steadily as Kelly, now very drunk, describes the strange fearlessness of parachuting. The intellectual young soldier ascribes this phenomenon to the difference in visual perspective, which impels Jane pathetically, and tellingly, to ask what "perspective" means. Moments later, Red helps Kelly sober up by putting wet towels around his head; all the while Kelly bitterly scorns his friend as a "hero," the kind of soldier who dies easily because he risks too much. Looking up at the younger man, Kelly drunkenly assails him so that Kay will hear: "You just point him at whatever'll kill him and he'll do the rest all by himself." A cut to Kay's reaction suggests her ambivalence toward Red, a blend of tending toward her habitual manipulation with a developing sympathy and admiration. While helping Kelly, Red towers over him with the wet towels, kindly silent, smiling gently, understanding Kelly's fear, his distaste at not considering himself much of a hero, sympathizing with Kelly's insecurity at the intellectual soldier's subtle heroism. And Kelly, drunk as he is, fears for his friend's safety in the company of such an experienced and possibly manipulative seductress as Kay. Well before Leslie Fiedler and the Newman-Redford axis, Lumet presents a sensitively wrought study of heterosexual male bonding and companionship, as, through his words that he "hates that look," Kelly reveals his deep caring for his friend.

After an amusing interlude as Kay begins to yawn and the intellectual soldier assures her, as he sidles in from frame right, that it is simply caused by a lack of oxygen, Kay, dispensing with such rationality, induces Red to take her out on the platform for some air. The darkly lit scene and the typically Lumetian enclosed space betoken the forthcoming honesty of their exchange. Asked his astrological sign, Red replies that he is a Leo. "Brave soldiers, but foolish ones," she replies. Her suave response engenders only slight contempt from the young soldier, who feels that astrology is foolish. Suddenly Kay angrily snaps that "the stars may as well control us as anything else" and adds that he, like most Americans, is just a naive youth. Kay has made a significant, if unconscious, revelation here that she feels out of her own control, that some form of externally imposed control seems to her a donnée in life. Then, just before Red kisses her, she speaks of Kelly's being all alone and says that this condition gives her "chills." Not returning his kiss, Kay slowly walks to the far window of the platform, turns to him in shadows and, with the metallically harsh sound of the train's wheels louder in the background, tells Red that she is the mistress of "a very rich man." Contrary to her expectation, given his youth and the sexual standards of the times, Red is not stunned. "*I* know what you mean," he says quietly, and Lumet shoots him coming into close-up toward her, as he leans down over her and says softly, "It's your life if that's what you want." A splendid long reaction shot reveals that her attempt at a tough facade is beginning to break down. Lumet then cuts to ever-isolated Harry coming out to the platform, cut off even further as Red leads Kay into the club car to dance to the radio music, leaving Harry with the coat that he had just used to shield Kay from the cold.

In a short, wordless scene, Lumet gradually closes the camera in upon the couple dancing to "I'm in the Mood for Love." Kay's face discloses that she likes the emotions she is beginning to feel. But she also fears these incipient emotions; suddenly, she pleads a headache and departs quickly, as Harry throws Red's rolled-up coat at him so hard it nearly knocks him off balance and also leaves. Kelly tells Red,

"You looked great, kid, she put wings on your feet," but Lumet tempers this mythically heroic reference with the next shot. Viewed through the legs of a chair placed upside down on a table as the place is closing, Kelly pleads with Red, "Don't try to understand, just go after her; if you try to understand, you won't have time for anything else." Kelly's plea reinforces the visual image of self-entrapment despite the elements of truth in his words, and Lumet echoes Kelly's antirationalism with Jane's clichéd attempt to soothe Red's disappointment over Kay's sudden and unexpected departure: "Kay's moody sometimes, it's her Latin temperament." Lumet then cuts to Harry taking Kay back to her compartment. As she enters the door, then turns to face Harry and the camera, Lumet shoots down at her over Harry's right shoulder, emphasizing the fragmented emotional condition of her supervisor who needs to be more to her, caregiver rather than caretaker, perhaps lover. Kay can only stare back at him with surprise, then disgust, before she slams the door in his face. Harry stares at the closed door for several seconds; then, perhaps identifying her look with what she may feel for The Man who sponsors her through him, Harry trails off sadly to his compartment. The sequence ends with Red's knock at her door, and he and Kay kiss passionately as the camera completely circles their heads to the background sound of light jazz drums. The complete camera movement, with the synchronous sound representing the ultimate musical freedom, visually represents the totality of Kay's feelings for Red—at least to the extent that she can admit them at this point—and the vitality of these emotions in sharp contrast with the fragmented emotions Lumet has represented in the other major characters.

The kiss dissolves into a long shot of the train pulling into New York the next morning. Ascending the stairs of the station, Kay completely dismisses Red, as Lumet's camera comes close in on his face, rapt with feeling for her, over the truncated image of her disdainful shoulder. Having about convinced herself that her brief flirtation is at an end, Kay is now in her sponsor's city, and the next cut to a magnificent New York home confirms her as another among The Man's possessions. But as Kay enters a sumptuously furnished room, she is still humming, perhaps unconsciously, the melody to which Red and she danced the previous day. Sitting in a chair, she languidly picks up the telephone to thank her benefactor for an expensive necklace, but more for his card that tells her he wishes to see her that evening. "That's in the future—it's always more exciting," she says, subliminally indicating her boredom; Kay needs ever to live in a future, for the present is for her usually too painful to bear easily. This need is again visually revealed by Lumet in the next shot, as Kay, standing by a table, throws down her accumulated mail sharply, then stares off into right frame for several seconds.

In the next brief sequence, Lumet contrasts Red's solid strength of character and rural values with the shallower world represented by The Man's practices and standards. Eating with Kelly in a cheap café, Red thoughtfully considers the rifle shell he has brought with him as a gift for his younger brother in Vermont, its empty functionlessness perhaps reminding him of Kay's dismissive treatment of him that morning. Kelly is once again solicitous of "the kid," playfully stuffing an onion into his mouth (just after trading defensively rough repartee with a tough-looking WAC) and trying to ease Red's anxiety over Kay's rejection. Immediately thereafter, Kay is represented as instinctually closer to Red's values than to those of The Man's surroundings, as she consoles and advises Jane, who is soon to become again a sexual pawn, this time for an elderly general. The two worlds then collide, as Red comes to her unannounced. Kay girds herself for all that Red is hurt by; Lumet shoots her walking toward the tracking camera, then turning and sitting, before coming at Red with her own accusations of his childishness in giving in always to his feelings. "It's easy to feel, it's like going to a party," she declares; life to such people is "just the taste." Feeling that she is capable of distinguishing between her actions and her emotions, Kay says that Red is a child for not dividing the two. Angry yet controlled, Red replies, "I don't like what you do here." Maturely, he continues to try to follow what he feels and believes.

Red is willing to undertake a reasonable risk by continuing to pursue Kay despite the differences in their values. Lumet's next carefully selected details show the correctness of his instincts: as Harry enters the room, Kay lays her hand tenderly on Red's face and asks him to go home. In the background a distant foghorn sounds, a symbolic correlative to Lumet's film of O'Neill's *Long Day's Journey into Night*, suggesting the unbidden return of the repressed. The two soldiers leave, Kelly's V sign to Harry offering a silent support of Red's confident smile that Kay does not really mean what she says. Outside the house, the two men walk into the glare of The Man's headlights, as Kelly sardonically laughs, "If you got a car like that and a house like this I guess you got a boat and a seaplane. Probably sell 'em in sets." Lumet's lights, more subtly than Lowry's occasional didacticism (67, 74), symbolize the cold gleam of truth in Kelly's observation on class and power in 1940s America, made and sustained by wealth, buying their way out of serving their country during the war, and seeing that beauty sells itself to them.

The restaurant scene shows in microcosm Lumet's skill in accomplishing much in a slight romantic tale. The director's sometimes leaden, off-pitch handling of comedy (*The Wiz, Stage Struck*, and parts of otherwise artistically excellent films such as *The Hill* and *Bye, Bye Braverman*) is sprightly here and is well integrated with variations on Kelly's earlier sociological critique. Jane's elderly general, at dinner with Kay and The Man, observing Kelly and Red entering the expensive restaurant, says, "I just hope they can afford it! Fine looking boys and well trained, too, you can depend on that." (When Kelly sees the menu prices, he cracks, "Now I know what we're fighting for.") In one of her strongest scenes as the pathetic Jane, Barbara Nichols comments on her newest boyfriend, "He's not bad at all for a general, he's not fat and he's got a nice smile." Earlier, complaining of the uncomfortable train, she had asked the general, "Can't you make the trains run smoother?" Nichols's winsome loser reminds the viewer of Lumet's frequent thematic attraction to Tennessee Williams's fugitive kind. In the powder room with Kay, Jane continues, "He's got such a nice smile he must be nice all the way through." Kay replies cynically, "Be happy with the nice smile."

In this episode George Sanders is his smooth, unctious best as Kay's cold-eyed, manipulative patron, recapitulating the motifs of the previous scene. Just before Red and Kelly enter the prestigious restaurant (the latter limping comically to gain entry), Lumet's repeated close-ups of Kay imply that The Man, despite his urbanity, is less generous to her with his time than with his finacial support. As Kay introduces everyone, her benefactor, observing Red's infatuation with Kay, shrewdly observes, "One should never feel sorry about being pleasant, only about being kind." Lumet's reaction shot of Kay is revealing, as she seems confused by The Man's game into wondering if her feeling for the young soldier was, after all, merely kindness. In a thematically significant interlude outside the powder room, Red confronts Kay with Rodriguez's charge to Nazerman in *The Pawnbroker*, that Kay fears self-knowledge, that she is in danger of living inauthentically in regard to her feelings; indeed, he seems even more concerned at this potentially deadly failing in her than with her selling of herself monetarily. After Harry tries to assault him and Red wins the fight, the youth angrily leaves, but not before throwing money for the dinner and the champagne on Harry's prostrate form, supplementing by gesture the personal integration indicated verbally. The sequence closes as The Man warns Kay of the difference between a "fever" and real feeling, saying that the former could lead her to act against her "interests." As she pleads to be excused for the rest of the evening because of a headache, her patron icily reminds her to guard her health: "I don't like to see you ill."

Lumet's most arresting visual sequence in *That Kind of Woman* rivals any in his films, as a distraught Kay walks home alone following the evening at the restaurant. Like several of Lumet's most memorable sequences, it is without language and almost without sound, its artistry eventuating through cinematic composition and technique that reinforce the literary, humanistic values and meanings of Lumet's composition. A mannequin stands in a department store window, viewed from high angle; it is dressed in a beautiful white party gown, and though it occupies only the right half of the frame, the mannequin dominates the composition of the shot, as Kay walks slowly into the left half of the frame to observe it. Its right hand is raised, its head is cocked a bit to the right; the eyes, somewhat askance, seem to look down at Kay, the face appearing about to speak. Then Lumet executes his most precipitous camera movement in the film: the camera pans to the left to focus close in upon Kay, still from slightly above her. Like a lost child, perhaps with Red's primitively stated yet perceptive truth, "You're all dressed up, got no place to go," reverberating in her memory of the evening, Kay now stares at the lifeless mannequin, which seems to be suspended in a kind of vague warning. Lumet continues the pan until the camera again focuses in upon the mannequin's face and body from medium range at low angle but from across Kay's right shoulder, at once fragmenting her and yet implicating her inescapably in the outer world of the lovely, dead figure, crowned by a glittering chandelier.

Lumet's fine shot removes Kay from a position of control and egotism to one of acute vulnerability; yet at the same time it ironically places this morally fragile woman at the center of her experience, making her visually responsible for it as for much of her unhappiness. As the thing she stares at quite literally has no place to go, neither has Kay, for by her emotional dishonesty and failures of courage, she has created a doll-like shell as her self, externally glamorous but internally empty. Like many of the other characters who fascinate Lumet— Nazerman, Groteschele, the passive jurors of *12 Angry Men*—Kay fails to engage the hurtful world as it is and thus degrades her self, reduces her humanity. For Lumet's world is not one of Berkeley's relativism, so popular in much of the consumerist art of Lumet's own era: the director's firm, but not harsh, vision of humankind assumes that we move as if upon Melville's great, mysterious ocean, that while we are terribly responsible for creating our own life-meanings, we cannot change the nature of the ocean merely by wishing or fantasizing it so. Kay—and we—are at the center of our experience, but we must deal with the world-as-is with realism and integrity if we are morally and psychologically to survive and to enjoy our experience. Kay's emotional inauthenticity and attempts at self-deception lead her only to stare into the terrifying whiteness of a moral vacuum.

Kay continues to stare into her blankness for a full ten seconds before she slowly walks off, the sound of asynchronous light jazz drums reminding her of what she has lost. Lumet's camera remains for a few seconds more upon the mannequin's white vacancy as Kay walks out of its controlling frame. Lumet ends the sequence with a surprise, as Kay stops short at the sight of Red waiting for her on the steps of her house. They embrace, but in a dissolve, for the director refuses to leave us with a falsely romantic view of Kay's predicament. The embrace will have meaning only if Kay can choose to act upon its future implications. It, too, will be for her a lifeless blankness unless she can endow it with meaning through moral choice and action.

Such actions can be undertaken only with great difficulty. Kay and Jane decide the next morning that they will enjoy one day with Red and Kelly before Red's train departs for Vermont at 8:45 in the evening. She wants the way she feels with Red for a day but is resolved not to give up her material security for feelings of love. While the final third of the film is overly attenuated, with some sentimental moments, as Red and Kay argue overmuch about whether or not she will go with him that evening, Lumet effectively captures their day in Central Park, as Red persists in his reasoned arguments to persuade Kay to leave The Man.[11] After one happy meal, Lumet dissolves on a shot of a group of nuns, their life of professed spiritual sacrifice visually symbolic of the choice Kay is considering. At a stream, she wades after a child's boat, after Red tells her about losing boats as a child. She inspects her drying shoes as they continue their discussion; the shoes are Cinderella slippers of possible deliverance for her. Red corrects his grammar at one point to impress her, changing *me* to *I*; this detail will gain significance as Red and Kay leave the stream's edge to walk, and Lumet shoots their departure through gnarled tree branches. In Red's reasoned arguments, he is ironically more free in his feelings and imagination than Kay, whose twisted emotions are those of one who indeed feels controlled by the stars. At dinner at a small Italian restaurant in the Village, Kay admits the source of her fear, her immigrant origins that allowed her to find employment only in a factory until she entered her relationship with The Man. "It takes great strength to live with your kind of love," she adds sadly. Her courage slipping, she plays games with Red, trying to use his strength instead of her own to induce her to be with him, and angrily Red slaps her arm away when she reaches for him during this interchange. As their day ends at the railroad station, Red tells Kay that she will like Vermont even though it's cold; when she will not tell him to go away without her, he tells her he will wait at the station until the train leaves.

Kay returns to the house surprised to find her benefactor waiting for her; it emerges that he has never before done this. Lumet's effective direction of Loren and Sanders in this scene discloses implicitly that their lives together have not been sordid: he is a man of accomplishment and taste who obviously respects her. Fearing that he will lose her to the younger man, he awaits her, seated and reading; he lies, saying that he is trying this evening to take extra time for this pleasure, given excessive pressure lately from his business. Lumet shoots Kay's entry to the house from a very high angle, visually reinforcing her indecision and vulnerability amid The Man's material wealth by enclosing her within a separate plane of space, as she is visually walled in between the door she entered and a stairway railing in foreground for ten seconds. Kay's psychic enclosure is echoed by The Man's own fear, as he admits to her his need for this reading room with concrete evidences of his own individual accomplishments, separate from a house that he says has generally depressed him because of his emotional estrangement from his family in childhood. That he is really telling her that he has been able to give love only with great difficulty and that he fears losing her to Red becomes apparent when he speaks against her "Young Lochinvar," again warning her tenderly against kindness. "Because it isn't really an emotion, you know, like love or hate, it's an excuse, like guilt, to be used as a sort of permission so that you can keep doing what you don't really want to do."

Lumet here reveals his abilities in set blocking and intrashot montage, as The Man leaves his chair and crosses in front of Kay, who is seated in rear frame. While she is framed there entirely by curtains, his lack of psychological integration is suggested visually by the images of status and success that frame him, particularly by the sporting trophies atop his head, and by the fact that his back is turned toward her, as he reminds her of their physical pleasures together. Moving toward the fireplace and a position facing but far from her, he speaks: "He has so much to offer—youth, courage, faith; he seems too innocent to be rich even by inheritance. But then in the dark all men are equally rich or poverty stricken. And we get along rather well in those delicate areas where it seems important for a man and woman to get along." Though none but his family had ever touched the house before, he offers to redecorate the place, symbolically authorizing her entry into his family.

His offer of marriage, financial wealth, tradition, name, does not include love directly but implies it. Kay sees that he needs, perhaps loves, her. This partial humanization reminds Kay, and the viewer, that The Man is no villain but, like most characters in Lumet's world, is an incomplete, human sufferer.

Lumet explores levels of insecurity in Kelly and in Jane before Kay can cast off her denial of reality and reach for what she needs most. Working out her conflict at one remove, Kay induces Kelly to ask Jane directly to stay with him. He manages this, assuring Jane that he can win enough money at poker anytime to support them. But Kay has taught her too well, and Jane, although caring for him, refuses; instead she will go to Washington to become the part-time mistress of the elderly general. Sadly, Jane does not recognize that Kay, having received evidence of feeling and commitment from both her men, is beginning to lose her hold on fears that still imprison Jane. Visual barriers separate Kelly and Jane as he asks her to marry him, though they are physically close to one another in the scene. Kelly mechanically plays "Chopsticks" at one point in their parting. And at the station where Red waits, trying to care for Kelly in his disappointment, it is apparent that Kelly will drift through the remainder of his leave chasing women in an endless succession of booze joints in Atlantic City. He denies his feelings of isolation with "I've got 'em lined up from here to Jersey," before Lumet's camera pulls back from him and he is lost in the crowd. Kay tries to mend Jane, but Jane sees that this is the end for her, especially when the war ends. "Everybody likes a good time, but nobody likes to marry one." The soft sound of jazz drums is heard again as Jane, realizing all she has lost and will lose, persists in denial, bitterly muttering as she leaves, "Don't let the good times stop," though she knows the war that brings her pleasure brings death to countless others. Jolted into decisiveness, learning that there is time still to catch up with Red's train at 125th Street, Kay leaves, returning everything The Man has given her, even her purse. Lumet's camera is above and behind him on the stairway as she gently touches his hand, knowing his hurt at losing her is real, before she runs from the house. A structural repetition ends the film: Kay extends her hand into the left of the frame toward Red's face, as he sits in the train disconsolate with the thought that he has lost her. Following a pan left to her face and Red's grasping her in mute thankfulness in the jostling car, a close-up to her face reveals her increased knowledge through suffering, her awareness of all that she has given up, and of more that she has very nearly missed.

Lovin' Molly: Psychological Aspects of the Archetypal Female

Lumet's one venture into the cinematic world of rural regionalism is *Lovin' Molly* (1974). Usually an interpreter of the harsh urban vision in contemporary American life, in his adaptation of Larry McMurtry's 1963 novel, *Leaving Cheyenne,* Lumet transfers to the Texas plains his vision of tragic choices that lead to unhappiness and moral stasis. In so doing, Lumet toughens the sometimes sentimental aspects of McMurtry's regionalism. Less interested than the novelist in details of cowboying and rural local color, Lumet pulls together the main strands of the novel's life—the unconventional forty-year relationship between McMurtry's eternal female, Molly Taylor, and her two central lovers, Gid Fry, a sensitive and kind but repressed and guilt-ridden Puritan, and Johnny McCloud, Gid's best friend and his emotional opposite, a freewheeling cowpoke less concerned than Gid with always establishing right from wrong. For Lumet, the center of the action is Molly, magnificently portrayed by Blythe Danner. More poignantly than in McMurtry's novel, Molly becomes in the film an emblem of Lumet's frequent theme of the emotional carnage caused by a failure of the imaginative use of reason, of the adult to think and act like an adult. While this free spirit is in many ways admirable to Lumet, her unconsidered and impulsive "choices"—she is never seen using her mind or thinking of much except her menfolks—combined with the harsh circumstances of the Texas environment in which she and her lovers live, cause much pain to several people, setting in motion a chain of events that affects in significant ways every character in her world.

The film begins as, over the credits, four freeze-frames appear of life in Bastrop, Texas, where Lumet filmed on location. A country road winds off through trees (through which we will last see Molly in a freeze-frame concluding the film); a rider on a horse is seen beneath trees by a lake in deep rear frame; Gid (played by Anthony Perkins) leans back on his plow, with his father (memorably played by Edward Binns) in the background, planting; and a lone horse grazes on a hill in rear frame. These four brief shots compress much of the realistic action and mythic depth in the film, for they convey both the loneliness of Molly's lovers, isolated from her spiritually by her adolescent decision to marry Eddie White because of her subliminal need for him to occupy the exploitive role in her life formerly filled by her ignorant father, and Gid's part in the emotional chaos of their lives caused by his ill-considered adherence to his father's work ethic-dominated nature and values. Thus Lumet introduces us to the basic action and themes while honoring McMurtry's regional setting; yet he does not sentimentalize the action through adherence to McMurtry's hazily articulated metaphor of "leaving Cheyenne" that provides the epigraph to the novel but has little to do with the psychological dimensions of the action. McMurtry explains the book's title thus: "The Cheyenne of this book is that part of the cowboy's day's circle which is earliest and best: his blood's country and his heart's pastureland."[12] This sentiment trivializes the major importance of the novel's action, because the "blood's country" has little to do with the flawed choices made by Molly and Gid that lead to their unhappiness. While McMurtry in his epigraph suggests that these choices are made for them by the circumstances in which they live, Lumet as usual in his films will have none of it: characters suffer in his work largely because of choices they make or fail to make, by the presence or absence of conscious control and moral will in their lives. While McMurtry's *Cheyenne* eventually declines to the soporific level of "Terms of Endearment," Lumet's vision of the novel's action is more tough-minded and more truly heightened to the level of tragedy.

Lumet's film is divided into three parts, equivalent to the action in the novel. Gid narrates the first part, which shows the lovers in their twenties. Molly narrates the second, as the lovers have come into their forties during the World War II period. Johnny (Beau Bridges) narrates the final section, set in the mid-1960s, when the lovers are in their own sixties, if little wiser. In the first section, Lumet emphasizes the essential conflict of greatest thematic interest to him, that between the life force Molly represents and the destructive instinct in both Molly and Gid that will doom their love. Lumet reveals character through action in the first sequence, in which Gid takes Molly from the schoolhouse on voting day for what he thinks will be several hours of kissing in the fields. As Gid insists that he is her man, Molly replies, "I think I'm too silly for you. Why you ain't even as silly as Johnny, and he isn't as silly as me." As she speaks, Lumet photographs her from a slightly high angle, as if to suggest that while the words of this undeniably attractive, free-spirited earth woman place her in a morally superior position to Gid's excessive carefulness and ethical stiffness, she too mistakes "silliness" for moral flexibility and maturity. While throughout her life Molly admirably remains true to the immediacy of her feelings, this present-tense nature of her relationship to her world gives insufficient attention to Gid's strengths: his search for a moral order, for an ethical center that, while sometimes repressive and excessively cognitive, does search for depths and reasons beneath mere appearances. Molly rarely accepts or sufficiently considers the value of Gid's kind of love.

Further, the irony of Lumet's camera placement here emphasizes Molly's vulnerability to men, to the ceaseless flow of her affections and desires. Lumet holds the shot as Molly says, of the "silliness" of her beaus, "Eddie's the only one who is." While typically Gid fails to understand the significance of this to Molly, Lumet's film foreshadows effectively (and more subtly than the novel) Molly's susceptibility to insensitive men who, lacking Gid's or even Johnny's awareness, will cause her to destroy much of her happiness.

Lumet is also subtler than McMurtry in not telegraphing Molly's attachment to her cruel father as the source of so much of the misery she will cause Gid by her thoughtless marriage to Eddie, a crude, at times sadistic, roamer. As Gid's romancing is interrupted by Johnny's trick of Ikey's arrival with his mule, Lumet reveals Gid standing, on principle, wishing neither to hide nor to be seen kissing Molly. Lumet positions Gid and Molly at middle distance, as seen from the rear; as Gid stands, back arched, tense yet proud, Molly sits with her face turned toward frame right with a look of quiet sadness. While a lesser director would have exploited these emotions with intercuts of the potential lovers, Lumet is content to record the scene as a single fact of nature, nature that binds all the characters, their weaknesses and strengths, into itself, into time, as the camera continues to hold them in the middle distance two-shot. Finally Molly stalks off, angry with Gid's inflexibility; she lacks the awareness to see the strength behind his insistence upon principle and his deep love for and admiration of her. She dismisses him: "You just ain't very silly, are you?"

The scene in the fields, in which Molly next upbraids Gid for his conventionality in insisting that sex and marriage always be equated, is similar to the novel but for one important exception: Lumet photographs Blythe Danner from behind as she strips completely and walks slowly into the water to swim. McMurtry has complained of this in a *New York* article, but the shot is not sensational and merely shows us how natural Molly feels about her body and the innocence of her act in this natural setting.[13] As Gid guiltily looks around to see if they are observed, saying, "I know what's right and what ain't," she calmly and purposefully strides into the water. As Lumet cuts to a low-angle shot of the perplexed young man, we see that Gid is confused by the eroticism of her act, and that it is precisely Gid whose immaturity about the erotic, natural life causes him to attribute pornographic content to merely socially uninhibited behavior.

Lumet catches very well the ambiguity between Molly's life force and the pathology of her attachment to her brutish father. In the next major sequence, Gid stops by Molly's house to take her to a dance and finds her sobbing, her eye blackened by her father. Molly identifies her own pathology by warning Gid: "Don't you dare say a word against my Daddy, he wouldn't have done it if I hadn't been so mean." Lumet does not probe this statement, although neither in the novel nor in the film's action is Molly ever mean to anyone. It seems not in her nature. Rather than exploring the sensationalistic aspects of her neurosis, Lumet simply accepts it: the next scene shows Gid trying to make up to Molly for his denial of himself earlier by leading her to the bedroom. In one of the film's finest moments, Lumet shoots up at Gid from behind Molly seated on the bed, as she calmly unbuttons his shirt. Again, any pornographic aspect is absent; Lumet is most interested in the play of emotions upon Gid's face as he stands above her, tenderly kissing her hands. Rare in American films, Lumet's *Lovin' Molly* is an erotic work about human intimacy, love, and sexuality, not a pornographic film or one solely about sex. After Gid and Molly have made love, again Lumet does not load the scene with psychological exposition, mercifully omitting Gid's line in McMurtry, "But Dad is the boss of me, I guess" (55). This astute psychological director prefers to intimate and to suggest rather than to pummel the audience with the tangled problems of both of these lovers.

Lumet is faithful in content and style to McMurtry's episodes of Molly's adjustment to her father's death, except that Gid is more in character in the film, chastely lying atop the covers while comforting Molly after her father has drunkenly killed himself by accidentally downing lye, while in the novel he lies in bed with Molly. This may seem a small point, but McMurtry sometimes sentimentalizes his major male character by having him sexually blow hot and cold, so to speak, as the narrative effect demands. Lumet keeps Gid perhaps less emotionally sympathetic, but truer to the neurosis—and winsomeness—of his native character. Lumet also adapts faithfully McMurtry's moving scene of the death by suicide of the seriously ill Mr. Fry, with the significant exception of the last lines of section 17, after the ritual funeral by Gid and Johnny and their turning free of the old man's white saddle-horse, as Gid intones to the reader, "Sometimes when I'm doing the chores early in the mornings, I wonder if Dad and that old pony aren't still out there, maybe, slipping around through the misty pastures and checking up on the new calves" (125), as bathos, too, runs free again on Idiot Ridge.

The conclusion of Gid's narrative in the film is similar to that in McMurtry's novel, except that the writer resents Lumet's insertion of a scene showing Gid and Molly birthing a calf just after the sequence in which the lovers pledge to have a child.[14] In this scene, Gid drags the calf, roped by its hooves, out of its mother's womb; Molly then raises her arms over her head as if in celebration of the new life and gently kisses the calf's head. While McMurtry complains that real-life Texans don't carry on like this down on the farm, Lumet here seems to be trying to extend the book's tedious realism into another artistic level, by showing Molly, whom he often presents in a less sympathetic light than does McMurtry, positively as an affirmative life principle, an archetypal force, as the Lawrentian earth mother recognizes triumphantly the appearance of new life and of human life to come. Significantly, in the film this action immediately follows Molly's words to Johnny, returned from his cowboying with old Grinsom: "Half the time I eat alone." Molly's most positive trait, according to Lumet's interpretation of the novel, is her connection to the deepest and most mysterious wellsprings of life, of the earth. Her aloneness, which she dimly recognizes in this scene of the film as a consequence of her own unwise choice of a marriage partner, is a self-ravaging condition; by inserting a nonrealistic sequence celebrating Molly's celebration of even animal life, Lumet returns her to the organic connection that makes her happiest, most spiritually fulfilled. McMurtry's objections here show a curious absence of awareness on the youthful novelist's part of art's potential to generalize experience, to pass from realism to symbol in order to lift the audience beyond mere local color to a more spacious representation of the human condition.

Lumet's final sequence in this section—the Gid narrative is by far the longest in the novel—shows Molly surrounded by earth imagery, dropping her buckets and walking toward the visiting Gid from some distance, then slowly beginning to turn around as she walks, already larger with their child. As she shows him her increased size, she also compliments Gid's new land purchases. Hair wild, her work shirt half off, she hugs him, saying, "I am so proud. . . . I am so glad that the first one is yours." As Gid rides away, Lumet positions Molly in the rear right half of the frame as she watches him go. Then Lumet shows Gid turning halfway and bowing low, saluting Molly with his hat while still astride his mount. Just before the dissolve into the second section, however, Lumet pulls the camera slowly upward and back, placing Molly in a dominant yet vulnerable position to the land, her feet together and slightly pigeon-toed, sensual but almost slatternly as Gid disappears to the voice-over of McMurtry's fine close to this section: "I never rode off from Molly in my life that I didn't want to turn around and go back a dozen times. She always stood right where you left her as long as she could see you. . . . I felt Molly was just as permanent as my land."

The Molly section of *Leaving Cheyenne* is titled "Ruin Hath Taught Me," a reference to Shakespeare's Sonnet 64. While the novelist does not spare his audience in his lengthy explanations of Molly's sufferings, her reaping of the mistakes of her marriage to Eddie White, Lumet more subtly suggests these consequences in his film adaptation. The novel spells out her needs to "do for" men (167), to have "somebody I could let my feelings out on," and we are even subjected to a scene in which Cletus Taylor uses his daughter as a sexual mannequin to instruct his son about the physical mechanics of the sexual act (180-85), thus establishing, in case we have not already absorbed the information, Molly's utter domination by her father. Lumet wisely omits the incredible scene in which Mr. Fry confesses his sexual hunger for Molly, a revelation that seems introduced for sensationalistic effect and to be unrelated to either's characterization earlier or later in the action (203-4). Missing also from the film is the sensationalistic ploy of Gid and Molly's son Jimmy writing a confessional letter home from the South Pacific about how he has been so embittered by learning that he is their illegitimate son that he has become a homosexual. Such melodramatics are generally of little interest to Lumet; here he strengthens his adaptation by leaving out the less mature aspects of McMurtry's novel.

Lumet gains verisimilitude by the fine make-up work on the three lovers in the last two sections of the film done by make-up artists Robert Laden and Reggie Takley. Molly and Gid seem believably aged into their forties and, by the last section, well into their sixties. The combination of Danner's superb performance and Lumet's keen direction seems perceptibly to age her: her neck seems withered, her entire frame thinner, and Gene Coffin's period costumes further advance her at least into a chronological maturity. As Johnny helps Molly unload packages from the car she has bought "to last her for life" and they talk of the fate of the two sons (the second is Johnny's) in the war, Lumet enhances the atmosphere of natural, easy carnality that distinguishes his adaptation of the novel: the two old lovers sit on the porch and fondle each other openly and casually as they speak of their different levels of being "crazy," Gid crazy over his land, Johnny over his cowboying, and Molly "just plain crazy." As she takes his face in her hands, then rubs his sore leg with linament, Johnny fondles Molly's rear as she fondles the arm fondling her. It is easy to see why Lumet's film was not among his more popular box office successes, for the natural, unforced eroticism of even such casual scenes in the film creates a mood of such tenderness and unsentimental compassion that American audiences seeking jolts of titillation were bound to be disappointed.

Lumet also employs subtle visual correlatives to enforce the meanings in this section of the novel. As Molly stands in her bedroom before the mirror, finally beginning to be aware of her "silliness" at marrying Eddie, Lumet frames her cornered in an angle of the mirror. Although this technique is not used as often in *Lovin' Molly* as in such earlier films as *12 Angry Men* and *Fail Safe*, Lumet's occasional "cornering" motif suggests the self-entrapment brought on by these frequently admirable people throughout the often unhappy courses of their lives. Lumet then flashes back in Molly's mind to her vision of having sex with Eddie while they viewed themselves in the mirror, according to Eddie's fetish. She remembers her father's prophetic and unintentionally ironic words: "Dad said if I married to marry Eddie, he'll never have more to his name than a fancy automobile, but at least by God he drinks and he'll treat you like a wife ought to be treated." The next sequence underscores Molly's psychological limitations, as she receives the postman's notification of the death in combat of her older son. At home, as she says, "What's life going to leave me, Gid?" Lumet depicts the aging lovers in four fine silent shots: at the table, from a sharp high angle; on the porch swing, from a slightly low angle, seemingly drifting through time; at the living room table playing dominoes; and finally and most memorably, in Molly's bed, with Gid staring at her for a very long time. The following morning, Gid decides to leave Molly permanently because of the adverse social reaction upon his granddaughter of the community's gossip concerning his continuing extramarital affair with Molly (he has long since married a shrewish woman after Molly's marriage to Eddie). Lumet frames the lovers within thick lines of flowered wallpaper strips, as if to isolate them from each other (and Gid from himself); this framing is similar to a framing motif used by the director in his adaptation of O'Neill's *Long Day's Journey into Night*.

The concluding shot in the Molly narrative is one of the film's best. As Gid comes back to Molly's house with a tiny puppy for her to raise, Lumet shows the aging lovers on the porch as the day grows perceptibly darker. Molly's voice-over confesses her urge to reach out and offer Gid the human contact he desperately needs but still, after all the years, feels uncomfortable with and her finally mature decision to postpone her incessant desire to nurture to help him abide by a choice that emotionally has cost him so much finally to make. Lumet holds Molly and Gid in mid-two-shot, gradually tilting down from a slightly high angle to a level exactly even with his characters, showing us an extended foreground of the space of the front yard, distancing the lovers both from us and from the world of nature as they gradually gain some growth from the controlling world of their compulsive emotions toward a more loving and more rationally commanded level of feeling. As the darkness increases, Lumet in the same shot shows Molly seated alone in the gathering darkness, accompanied by her voice-over of McMurtry's fine lines at the end of the second section of the novel, of her menfolk rising before her as in a vision, her father and her husband drunk, her elder son looking away, perhaps thinking of school, her son by Johnny laughing, and Johnny grinning and lazing. "But Gid was lookin' at my face, and wishin' he could put his hand on my hair."

The briefest section in both the novel and the film is Johnny's narrative from the year 1964, as the lovers are now in their sixties. As Gid and Johnny work, Gid falls from high atop his windmill, at work until nearly his last breath, victim of a sudden heart attack. As Johnny gets him into his car and frantically drives toward town and the hospital, sobbing and trying to hold Gid's hand, Perkins has his best moment in the film as, leaning into the corner of the seat and the door (and the frame), he says his final words: "Oh me, Johnny, ain't this been a hell of a time," more in wonderment than in sorrow. Lumet depicts Johnny stopping, sobbing, and responding to the angry honks from the car behind him in a long high-angle shot. Johnny gets out of the car, pleading "What's the hurry for?" now that his friend is dead.

Lumet almost literally adapts McMurtry's moving and splendid ending of the novel, as Johnny and Molly, after one final night of lovemaking, discuss marriage and decide that they are just not the marrying kind, but that doesn't mean he shouldn't come over for supper every night if he wants to. As Johnny drives off, his mind turns to the voting day forty years ago when he used Ikey and his mule to trick Gid out of precious time with Molly. As he dreams of how "the bloom was really on the peach" that day and of his regret that he hadn't brought a Kodak that morning, "so I could have got a picture of Molly while she was sitting in her blue and white dress on the schoolhouse steps" (298-99), Lumet ends the film with its most memorable shot: as Johnny drives away Molly stands in deep frame, watching him pull away, and Lumet slowly tilts up on her and pans across her from left to right. He then cuts to a stand of trees, also panning left to right through the trees, from an extreme view of the right side of her face and shoulder as she leans on the porch of the polling place that day forty years ago. As Johnny's voice-over continues, Lumet's camera moves slowly through the trees, then closer toward Molly, as she sits on the schoolhouse steps, smiling. As he concludes the novel's final lines, the camera is now close in upon her and ends in a freeze-frame of the smiling mythic woman, as yet not wise and suffering, ironically less the earth mother than she will grow to be when her men are either old or dead. Lumet's *Lovin' Molly*, while one of his least overtly visual and publicly celebrated works, is one of his most mature and moving films about the continuing human dialectic of passion and meditation, the life of earth and the life of mind.

Chapter Four

Lumet at Zenith: In the American Film Pantheon

Few film directors manage to create twenty major works during a career, much less during a career that is still in progress, the director yet in late middle age. In any assessment of the most artistically important of Lumet's major films, films that may rightfully be placed among the culture's landmark creative achievements, persuasive arguments can be advanced for the inclusion of such relatively recent films as *Daniel* and *Prince of the City*, and perhaps for such earlier works as *The Group*, *The Sea Gull*, and *Dog Day Afternoon*. Four films, however, clearly stand beyond doubt among America's great films, excellent in the union of theme and cinematic form, in superb direction of actors, in the depth, sometimes even profundity, of psychological, social, and moral meaning. *12 Angry Men* (1957), *Long Day's Journey into Night* (1962), and *The Pawnbroker* (1965) are regarded as major work by previous scholarly commentators on the director's career, and as I hope to demonstrate here, *Fail Safe* (1964) is an as yet unacknowledged American classic. These films testify to Lumet's substantial accomplishment, each melding form uniquely with meaning to reveal Lumet's consistent thematic concern with the dynamics of family and social life; the importance of a rational, personal responsibility for the existence of a humane social order; humankind's propensity for self-delusion and flight from its best self; the immense difficulty of achieving self-knowledge and awareness; and the ubiquity of meaningful suffering that lies at the heart of life.

In these four films, Lumet uncompromisingly considers the depths of human desolation in the manner of the great tragedians of other genres, finding memorable visual correlatives for the inevitable human penchant for illusion and failed self-development and creating some of his most imaginative wordless sequences. The final sequences of these four films are among the most visually and thematically arresting in American cinema. Together the four films represent the apogee of Lumet's continual concern with problems of moral responsibility and with the necessity in the contemporary world of personal authenticity. With Karl Rahner, the distinguished German philosopher, Lumet seems to seek his God by an unremitting passion for reality: his frequently existential tragic humanism seems ever to be centered upon our individual choices, commitments, and responsibilities, or upon our decisions to avoid them. Perhaps a suitable epigraph to his cinematic pantheon would be these lines from Joyce's *Ulysses*: "*If Socrates leave his house today he will find the sage seated on his doorstep. If Judas go forth tonight it is to Judas his steps will tend.* Every life is many days, day after day. We walk through ourselves, meeting robbers, ghosts, giants, old men, young men, wives, widows, brothers-in-love. But always meeting ourselves."[1]

12 Angry Men: Toward an Imaginative Use of Reason

12 Angry Men (1957), Lumet's first feature film after seven years of outstanding television productions, stands to this date as one of his most thematically rich and cinematically evocative films. Treating typical Lumet concerns such as the necessity for personal responsibility if democratic processes are to survive, and the tendency for humanity's illusions, guilts, and prejudices to endanger its legal systems *12 Angry Men* goes beyond the well-intentioned "message picture" to make a remarkable cinematic statement about the nature of the limitations of the American jury system and of the American democratic process itself.

Reginald Rose's screenplay (expanded considerably from his 1954 teleplay) treats the jury deliberation in a murder trial of an eighteen-year-old minority youth accused of the premeditated killing of his father. We do not hear or see any of the trial itself beyond the judge's direction to the jury. Nor do we witness the boy on trial except for one wordless view of him near the beginning of the film. Lumet is uninterested in the legal attack and defense system, in the sometimes pyrotechnic emotional displays by both counsel and witness in American courtrooms. On the contrary, as is so frequent in his films, Lumet here is far more interested in human character, in the nuances of the ways that people make up their minds about things (or think they do), than in the more obvious spectacle of such legal melodramas as *Kramer vs. Kramer* or *And Justice For All*. Almost all of *12 Angry Men* takes place in one small room, a jury room in which sit twelve ordinary men, chosen at random by a human institution that entrusts them with a decision that determines the future of a human life. To all but one of the jurors (all but two of whose names are never known to us), the boy seems clearly guilty as charged on the abundance of circumstantial evidence, and the jury's responsibility seems obvious: they must put a guilty man into the electric chair, despite his youth and the impoverished environment from which he has come and that may well have contributed to his alleged crime. But Juror #8 (Henry Fonda), a soft-spoken architect in his outside life, is not certain that the evidence is sufficiently clear or ample to establish beyond reasonable doubt the boy's guilt. To the surprise of almost all the other eleven jurors—and the anger of a few who feel that the case is so clear that they should be permitted to go about their business—Fonda insists that the case be discussed for a while, that a little of their time is called for before a terminal decision is made regarding a human life.

For the approximately one-and-one-half hours of the film (congruent with the elapsed time of the jury's deliberations), Lumet reveals the processes of thought and feeling of the twelve men as they grapple with the facts of the case, facts that seem to become less clear, more elusive, the more carefully they are reflected upon. Ultimately neither they nor we ever conclusively know the young defendant's guilt or innocence. To Lumet the boy's eventual fate, important as it is, is less significant than the ways in which it affects the minds and sensibilities of the twelve chosen to decide that destiny. Lumet's legendary skill with actors is evident even in this early film, as all the jurors—even those with smaller speaking parts—emerge as recognizable human beings with whose conflicts and weaknesses we can identify. Though a cross-section of middle-class and lower-middle-class New Yorkers, they are individualized by Lumet's unobtrusive yet sharply probing camera eye, sometimes seen from behind Fonda's shoulder as the man of deliberation and reason attempts to argue some jurors out of their prejudices and to persuade others away from their unconsidered conformity or fear. Several of the jurors (John Fiedler, Edward Binns, Martin Balsam, Jack Klugman) are "average" men, some more intelligent and reflective than others, who wish justice to be done. Yet their natural tendency to follow others leads them often to defer to the ill-considered judgments of the impatient and careless (Jack Warden, Robert Webber), the intemperate (Ed Begley), or the deeply conflicted (Lee J. Cobb). Pivotal to the decisions and conflicts of these less self-realized jurors is the juror played by E.G. Marshall, whose greater insight and intelligence sometimes is as endangered by his own preconceptions and illusions as by the dogmatism and prejudice of those more fearful and dependent than himself. An "expertly fashioned" actor's picture, 12 Angry Men reveals "individuals exposed as being ridden by fears . . . and an aversion to analytical thinking."[2]

At a sociological level, clearly Lumet's film reflects strong concern with the constituent parts of a living democracy, as the wiser and more emotionally stable jurors must responsibly lead those men with less self-awareness and self-knowledge than they, if democracy is to have any chance to work fairly and justly. Though the film contains little doctrinaire preaching on the subject of democracy, the audience is led to respond favorably to those jurors—Fonda, Joseph Sweeney, George Voskovec—for whom reason and the liberal vision of the world and of humankind are paramount. Nowhere is Rose's screenplay more subtly eloquent than in the scene in which Voskovec, an East European immigrant watchmaker now proud of his American citizenship, berates Warden, the successful marmalade salesman, for casting a crucial vote thoughtlessly, in simple indifference and haste, so that he can get to his baseball game on time. Whenever Voskovec speaks of democracy, he does so simply, out of the harsh experience of a man who has seen, another political system up close and has found it wanting. He insists that if people are to govern themselves and their social relationships fairly and reasonably, then they must be guided by principle. As he forces Warden for the first time to state his convictions for casting his vote, to ask questions of himself, Lumet frames Voskovec coming toward Warden's seat in an extremely tight close-up, but with the camera tilted only slightly up at the watchmaker, as if to minimize the European's "heroism" and to make him less important than the convictions for which he stands. The subtlety of this low-angle shot in an emotionally heightened scene underscores visually the fact that though Voskovec may regard Warden with contempt, he does not consider himself—nor does Lumet consider him—intrinsically superior to the all-American baseball fan.

Earlier in the film, as a few of the jurors take a break from the sometimes angry debate, Lumet's meditative camera follows Fonda and Binns to the washroom, where Binns, an earnest working man who honestly disagrees with Fonda, states his conviction of the boy's guilt. After a critical comment about the irrationality and unfairness of some of the jurors who support his own position, Binns says, "I'm not used to supposin', I'm just a workin' man, my boss does all the supposin'." Yet he calls Fonda back as Fonda is about to return to his seat in the jury room: "But supposin' you do talk us all out of this and the kid really did knife his father?" The well-intentioned juror misses the point, of course, that the jury system exists at least as much to protect the innocent as to convict the guilty. Holding Binns in steady midshot during this brief scene, Lumet suggests more, however, than the intellectual vacuity of this decent man; he emphasizes the fact that those who do not exercise their imaginative faculty, who do not "suppose," make weak cogs in a social system based supposedly upon the imaginative use of reason. That this sequence takes place in the most mundane location of the film underscores the basic importance of the theme of democracy in 12 *Angry Men*; here its "hero" shows a penchant for fastidious cleanliness. It is not the character of Juror #8 that Lumet celebrates in the film, but rather the man's reasoned use of principle.

Lumet visually enhances his concern with the workings of the liberal democratic system early in the film, when, having walked into the barren, sultry jury room, Warden and Binns manage, with a difficulty emblematic of the film's action, to raise the window together. Moments later, Robert Webber, a slogan-spouting advertising executive in private life and one of the least sympathetic of the jurors, happens on the democratic idea that the eleven jurors convinced of the defendant's guilt present their reasons in turn, in order to attempt to convince Fonda of the rightness of a guilty verdict. But the four-minute, word-less opening sequence of the film most impressively and succinctly represents the principles of reason and liberalism that 12 *Angry Men* upholds. After an establishing shot of the city courthouse, Lumet's camera tilts very slowly upward toward the building's four framing pillars; a huge lamp hangs down from the exact center of the frame, at the top of which is seen a motto carved in stone: "Administration of Justice is the Firmest Pillar of Good Government." Against the background sound of city traffic noise, Lumet cuts to an equally slow downward tilt from inside the courthouse, from a large chandelier at ceiling level down to the center cupola, again precisely framed between four inner pillars. Pausing at the level of the second landing, the camera observes five people passing slowly near one another from several directions and converging at a point directly beneath the hanging chandelier. Their carefully orchestrated passage, reminiscent of the balletlike passing sequence in Welles's *Magnificent Ambersons*, offers a symmetrical arrangement that parallels the carefully framed backdrop against which they move. By his formal composition and intrashot montage, Lumet suggests a tone of almost classical stateliness and rationality for the forthcoming action. The extraordinarily leisurely camera movements, featuring but one cut in almost four minutes and ending in a slow tracking shot to the outside of the courtroom where the boy's trial is being conducted, imply that the course of human justice is glacially slow and that only the classical values of ordered, reasoned, meditative inquiry will possibly defeat the irrational preju-dice that we are soon to see dominating the jury room. Typically, Lumet's cinematic technique does not call attention to itself here, but its union with the film's thematic and moral meaning reminds the film viewer that the purpose of technique in any art form is less for spectacle than for serving the thematic values of the work of art itself. Rarely a pretentious, self-conscious artist, Lumet here reveals, quite early in his directorial career, that his central aesthetic interests lie in joining as closely as possible artistic content and form into a mutually integrative web of meaning.

Part of the subtext of that meaning throughout 12 *Angry Men* is the significance of personal responsibility if a just, civilized order is to continue and flourish. A central concern in many of Lumet's films— *Prince of the City, Serpico, Q & A, Power, Running on Empty, The Verdict, Fail Safe*—the responsibility of the individual is especially pertinent in 12 *Angry Men* in the characterizations of Fonda, Voskovec, Sweeney, and Balsam. Fonda risks censure and ridicule by all his peers on the jury for his initial stand: "Well, I guess we talk. . . . it's not easy to raise my hand and send a boy off to die without talking about it first." Throughout the first half of the film, he continues to risk the sneering disapproval of Warden and Begley and even the implied violence of Cobb, whom he goads and satirizes on occasion to try to show him his own potential for violence that subconsciously prejudices him against the youthful defendant. Fonda occasionally pontificates on personal responsibility (one of the film's few aesthetic weaknesses), but a more subtly crucial sequence involving the theme concerns Martin Balsam, the jury foreman. Trying to organize the proceedings, he is called "a kid" by Begley. When he challenges Begley, saying that someone has to chair the jury, and asks him to take the first chair, Begley promptly backs away from assuming the responsibility. When Webber, trying to smooth over the rift, denies the importance altogether of the principle of jury leadership, Lumet cuts to Balsam seated twisted in his foreman's chair, in extreme close-up right profile, with Warden's offscreen, unintentionally ironic condolence, "You stay in there and pitch," emphasizing Balsam's feelings of powerlessness and disgust. After Fonda attempts to salvage something of his pride and of the group's order, Balsam is again shown, face turned away from the jury table, saying, "I don't care *what* you do," resignedly chewing his nails.

Shortly after this, Fonda gambles on a second ballot—this one secret—and Sweeney, the oldest member of the jury by many years, changes his vote.[3] As Lumet cuts down-angle at him to stress his function and not any sense of self-importance, Sweeney speculates about chance and possibility and defends Fonda's motives for standing heretofore alone against the group. But as he speaks, Warden insults the old man by leaving the table for the men's room; as Sweeney remonstrates against this indignity, Fonda says softly, "He can't hear you, he never will." Here Lumet interweaves, as he does often in the film, a motif of fathering that becomes an important visual correlative to the theme of the necessity for personal responsibility in an increasingly depersonalized, bureaucratized world. The boy is on trial for the primal crime, the murder of the father, the crime that Freud posits as underlying most feelings of guilt and so much human misery. Throughout his attempt to induce fairness and reason among the jurors weighing this alleged crime, Fonda—and to a lesser extent Sweeney, Voskovec, and Marshall—become fathers to the other jurors, disclosing to some of them to some degree, at least, the sources of their irrational responses to the issues in the trial. Lumet, always sensitive to psychoanalytic motifs in his films, enhances the dramatic and visual power of 12 Angry Men through the use of these motifs.

Our first image of fathering (aside from a brief glimpse of a man carrying a child in the silent four-minute sequence that opens the film) is hardly reassuring: Lumet cuts from the opening sequence to a close-up of a bored-looking judge instructing the jury on the law of pre-meditation in murder. As the judge concludes his comments, saying, "You're faced with a grave responsibility, thank you, gentlemen," his right hand props up his cheek as with his left he reaches for a glass of water. We sense that, although he is languidly adhering to the forms of the law, he is ignoring its spirit and thus setting a poor example for at least some members of the jury. (Lumet at this point pans slowly over the jury panel for the first time: Warden and Cobb seem not to pay any attention to what the judge says.) As the jurors leave, Lumet stages one of his memorable sequences in the film: shot from over the right shoulder of the defendant (John Savoca), we see the twelve jurors file out toward the jury room. Some look back at the boy nervously, but Webber just flips his lapels to cool off while idly glancing at the youth, his mind obviously made up, his guilty vote cast before he reaches the jury room. Lumet then cuts to an extreme close-up of the defendant's face, an unforgettable image that Lumet holds for twenty seconds. He is a boy, looking younger than his eighteen years. He is perhaps Mexican or Puerto Rican but is quite light-skinned (soon after this shot, the bigot Begley will rant that it is not surprising that "these kids" murder their fathers). Most memorable are the boy's eyes. They stare out at the courtroom, not angrily, but passively, whether all-knowing or uncomprehending we never know. For the final seconds of this shot, Lumet gradually superimposes the defendant's face over the empty jury room where his judges will decide his fate. As the superimposition occurs, his eyes are sharply downcast; the entire shot is from a slightly high angle as if to accentuate his vulnerability at the hands of these fathers.

As the men mill about waiting to convene, Binns approaches the men's room door to summon Sweeney, then helps him into his chair, treating the elder with the respect that he will show him throughout the film. Sweeney does not fulfill the father role psychologically until Fonda's courage and determination—which initially place Fonda in the role of father to Sweeney—enable the older man to assume a leadership role when he changes his vote to not guilty. Particularly interesting is Lumet's handling of the relationship between the Fonda-Sweeney axis and Juror #3, Lee J. Cobb. Cobb, who has driven his own son from him because of his barely suppressed violence many years before, is the juror most in need of fathering. He is also the most irresponsible, since he seems unable to exercise rational judgment in dealing with an issue that calls up dimly realized personal associations for him that are highly charged with subliminal energy. Cobb runs a messenger service, and early in the film he hands his card to businessman Marshall, saying that he "started with nothing." His occasional turning to Marshall for reassurance, particularly when his emotional gaps have been exposed by Fonda or Sweeney, suggests that Cobb himself has experienced an unfortunate relationship with his own father that has soured him to the extent that he has become dictatorial and unforgiving in most of his human relationships.

One of the subtlest camera movements in the film occurs as Marshall gives his opening arguments against Fonda. Cobb, having finished his statement to the group (which concerned the old man who testified that he lived in the room beneath the scene of the crime and heard everything), walks slowly around the table toward the slowly backward-tracking camera and toward the water cooler, looking intently at a small photograph—we learn later that it is a picture of his estranged son. Marshall's voice offscreen says that he feels it is not the jury's business to go into the reasons why the defendant "grew up the way he did." At these words, Cobb, now in extreme close-up, looks up sharply from his son's picture. Though he says nothing and the camera almost immediately shifts to another juror, Lumet swiftly etches the first touching of the film's rawest nerve. Moments later, as Marshall discusses the exhibit murder weapon—a switchblade stiletto—the camera tracks slowly, following Marshall back to his seat at the table. Just at the instant when Marshall recounts that the defendant allegedly had another fight with his father, Cobb alone of the other jurors is visible in deepest frame behind Marshall.

During the episode in which Fonda attempts to disprove the testimony of the old man who said he heard the crime committed in the room above his, Sweeney movingly attests to the old witness's possible motive for testifying, leaving unspoken his own fears of his existence as a forgotten, unknown old man. As Cobb berates Sweeney for his sympathy to the old witness, Lumet cuts to Sweeney twice in reaction shots that key Binns's defense of Sweeney, whom Binns is beginning to appreciate for enlightening him. Binns threatens Cobb, reminding him that he "ought to treat an old man with respect." Sweeney continues with an argument that gets at the heart of why Cobb and the other jurors who possess minimal self-understanding have such difficulty in acting responsibly: he argues that the old witness, because of his loneliness, his need for a moment in the sun, might have come to believe his own story. Lumet for the first time treats a theme he returns to again and again in his films: human beings' propensity to delude themselves, to become so immured in their illusions that they come to be bound by them, even to the extent that they lack awareness of their self-induced imprisonment.

In the latter half of the film, Cobb becomes increasingly isolated from the rest of the jurors because of such psychological unawareness. After Fonda goads Cobb into rushing at him in an attempt to show Cobb how close to the surface are his impulses, Lumet isolates Cobb from the group so completely that he is out of the frame, as the rest stare into a seemingly nonexistent plane of space. Moments later, as Cobb tries to regain lost prestige with the group by giving a demonstration of how the angle of the knife's descent could have been down and in even allowing for a seven-inch height difference between the murdered father and the smaller son, he unwittingly becomes son to Fonda's father. In one of the film's tensest moments, Cobb approaches the camera (Fonda's point of view), slowly raises the knife from a stooped posture, then quickly starts his hand downward. Lumet switches to a two-shot, and Cobb slowly drops the knife into Fonda's breast pocket. While seemingly he has gained status and relieved his emotional blocks by this thought-murder of the father, Lumet's visual irony catches Cobb reducing his stature considerably below that of Fonda, metaphorically as well as physically. Cobb's performance here as throughout is superb; his voice breaks as he says, "Nobody's hurt . . . down and in, down and in." But Lumet holds the two-shot long enough for the calm Fonda to repeat his words, thus emphasizing Fonda's own superior role in the tortuous process of teaching Cobb self-awareness and, with it, social responsibility.

Lumet elicits superior performances from all the members of his

cast, both individually and as an ensemble. Balsam speaks movingly of
the joy he gains from his high school coaching job, Klugman of his
nurture in the city's ghettos. Lumet's skill and care in extensive rehearsals produces a gem by Voskovec. When Webber patronizes Voskovec
by his suggestion that the finest watchmakers come from his part of
Europe, Voskovec's courtly, barely discernible little bow perfectly ironizes the ad man's unconscious penchant for consistently adopting the
jargon and hypocrisy he publicly scorns. Webber's performance enhances the motif of the imprisoning power of self-delusion; at the start
of the jury's deliberations, he adjusts his collar and tie carefully, as if he
thinks he is at a meeting of account executives. This self-proclaimed
liberal amuses himself during his debate with games of tic-tac-toe and
polishing his sales pitch for his company's newest breakfast cereal; his
unconscious and cheapened liberalism is the focus of Lumet's most
sustained visual satire in the film.

E.G. Marshall's performance is one of the film's most compelling
and restrained. The enlightened, rational, responsible conservative is
Fonda's most formidable adversary, for in him Fonda does not oppose
undue prejudice or a careless mind. Juror #4 is a highly educated,
judicious, and cultured stockbroker; he is convinced of the boy's guilt
primarily because the boy cannot remember what he did after his father
allegedly struck him twice on the night of the murder and because of
the testimony of a woman who said she saw the killing through the
windows of a passing elevated train from across the street. In another
of Lumet's superior visual presentations in 12 Angry Men, Marshall,
ever the composed WASP, wearing his coat and tie through the oppressive summer heat even when a sudden storm forces the closing of
the windows, is challenged by Fonda to remember his own movements
of the last four evenings. Although Marshall calmly replies to Fonda's
questioning that even under great stress he could remember exactly
what he was doing at any recent time during his past (and thus he
implies that the boy from an underprivileged class should be able to
remember, too, if he were innocent), Fonda finds details that Marshall
cannot recall, albeit the stockbroker's life is a comfortable one, with
little stress.

The sequence begins with a cut to Fonda over Marshall's right
shoulder—a frame that Lumet uses often in the film to accentuate the
cramped existential space people sometimes have for the working-out
of problems and dilemmas. Then Lumet cuts down to Marshall over
Fonda's left knee and elbow, a shot that seems to trap Marshall by
further reducing the space in which he must think and try to remember. As he struggles to recall the title of a movie he saw a few evenings

back when he was completely relaxed, Lumet frames Marshall against the window upon which the rain beats. During cuts between the two men, the wooden sill below the window in deep rear frame passes behind Marshall just at his neck, suggesting the distancing of his cognitive faculties from his abilities to empathize with the traumatic emotional condition of a boy who has been seriously underprivileged since early childhood. Fonda, however, is completely framed by a door far behind him, suggesting his greater emotional spaciousness and psychological integration. Further, Lumet gradually increases the sound of the rain driving against the window during his cuts to Marshall and the background windowsill in this sequence, as Marshall learns from the wiser juror something of the difficulty—particularly for the less-privileged classes—of containing life's mystery, its constantly changing impressions, into comforting fixities. As Marshall makes these discoveries, Lumet's final extreme close-up reveals a single bead of sweat forming on his forehead.

At other points in the film Lumet uses the jury room window and its connotations of psychological spaciousness as a backdrop for other small learning experiences in the jurors' paths to greater self-knowledge and responsibility. Early in the film Webber comments to Fonda as both stand at the window that, even though he has lived in New York all his life, he never realized the Woolworth Building was exactly there. When Begley, the bigoted garage owner, after demeaning Balsam for trying to conduct the jury's discussions according to principles of order, gains a glimmering of awareness that he fears the responsibility of acting as foreman, Lumet positions him at the window. Fonda gazes out the window as he gambles on a second, secret ballot, hoping to find at least one ally in his fight for the boy's life. Just as the thunderstorm breaks late in the film, Balsam and Fonda close the windows, and Balsam gives his moving speech about the joys he gains from his coaching work.

Director of photography Boris Kaufman, one of the most distinguished cinematographers in black and white and Lumet's most frequent cinematographer through the middle sixties, praised Lumet's "fine and sensitive . . . feel for camera-work" in an article dealing with the great difficulties of making the film dynamic given such a small working space. (Other than the opening sequence, and the final sequence as the jurors leave the jury room, the entire film takes place on one set—the cramped, barely furnished jury room, "a room no larger than an average hotel room.") Lumet and Kaufman decided to take advantage of the cramped space by making the sense of confinement an integral part of the visual mood. As the film's tensions mount,

Lumet changes lenses to give the effect of crowding at the table over which the jurors argue. The lighting gradually grows darker as the thunderstorm approaches and as issues and men reach a breaking point. During the long take as the men first enter the jury room—to that point, the longest single continuous take in Kaufman's career—Lumet introduces the psychological characteristics of the jurors as they mill about the room and bump into one another. Revealing gestures (Fonda's meditative tapping of his fingers as he stands at the window) and casual comments (the frustrated Begley's cynical comments about the defendant, Warden's clichéd talk about baseball) that seem irrelevant to the case presage the inner nature of the combatants, twelve men, said Boris Kaufman, "whose backgrounds, attitudes, problems, and reasons behind their decisions had to be shown photographically as well as in the dialogue."[4]

Critics such as Andrew Sarris have often criticized Lumet for literary "pretentiousness" yet he has steadfastly refused to consider film as a wordless medium, while at the same time adhering to the principle that, as Kaufman has said, in "good cinematography the camera should never distract the audience from the basic theme and never move without justification."[5] In a *New York Times* interview, Lumet spoke with typical brio about his distaste for the self-consciously "tricky" film. He said that he vetoed having a glass top on the jury table to allow trick camera shots and added: "Some people have suggested that the picture needs jazzing up. For instance, somebody had the idea that we should explain that all the regular jury rooms are occupied and have this in the basement, where we could show the exposed pipes and maybe the furnace in order to provide pictorial contrast. But we threw the idea out." Speaking to the actors during rehearsal, Lumet commented: "There's going to be no artificiality in this. You are going to be the whole picture. This is not a tract. This is not a pro-jury or anti-jury thing. It's . . . about human behavior. No glass table tops. No basement room. Just you and the fullness of your behavior."[6]

As this remark indicates, Lumet's union of cinematic technique with literary and thematic moral meaning precisely defines his directorial significance. Lumet may not always move the camera in ways that call immediate attention to his technique (thus his low ranking in Sarris's 1968 hierarchies), yet his frame is rarely static but usually full, busy with life's detail and flow. Though the camera work is seldom spectacular, its controlled movement is subtle and filled with the movement of human event. Some critics habitually and impressionistically criticize Lumet for weak visuals and overdependence on dialogue and for an insufficiently personal vision.[7] Lumet creates all his own frames and shots, and he has done so since the beginning of his directorial career.[8]

The greater depth of characterization and theme in Lumet's finished film when compared with both versions of Reginald Rose's play indicates Lumet's originality.[9] For instance, Lumet represents the character of Juror #9 (Joseph Sweeney) as stronger and more emotionally durable than Rose's original characterization of him as "long since defeated by life and now merely waiting to die" (114). As directed by Lumet, the foreman (Martin Balsam) is far more sensitive and aware of ambiguities than is indicated by Rose's original depiction of him as "impressed with the authority he has . . . petty . . . dogged" (113). Lumet's direction of Cobb (Juror #3) brings out in full the messenger service owner's latent sadism barely hinted at in the play. The memorable shot of the defendant's face in extreme close-up for twenty seconds has no correlative in Rose's play; likewise, Lumet's brilliant early visual presentation of the hall of justice is absent in the play except for a bare reference to the play's judicial setting in the expanded version.[10] Most crucial, however, is the deletion in the film of the sentimentality that now and then surfaces in the play. Early in the action when Sweeney remonstrates against Begley's bigotry (120), Lumet omits reference to this flowery passage: "Somehow his [Fonda's] touch and his gentle expression calm the old man. He draws a deep breath and relaxes." Gone as well in the film is Rose's unnecessarily sensational episode in which Juror #3 advances upon Juror #8 at the end of the play with the exhibit knife as if to stab him, and Juror #8 grabs the knife. Lumet also mercifully omits the closing close-up of "a slip of crumpled paper on which are scribbled the words 'not guilty.'" Indeed, even the longer version contains but three references to any sort of camera movement or technique.

12 Angry Men also reflects a strain of persistent liberalism in Lumet that is out of fashion among many of today's academic intellectuals and critical writers. Lumet has never favored radical-chic style or content in his films, and his strong penchant for meditative psychoanalytic themes has also not endeared him to the film critics' establishment. Nowhere does the film defer to, for example, Webber's shallow liberal view that the American judicial system is a perfect institution. Lumet's films are much like the basic themes in this film: the evidence is to be respected; theory is less trustworthy than the particularity of each instance of reality as the characters perceive it. Lumet refuses to make films that as a group easily fall into categories. Of course, facile categories and theories make headlines, and so the Godards gain more fame than the Frankenheimers, even though work without such theoretical embellishment may possess the greater excellence. Given Lumet's strong commitment that the technique must suit the theme of the particular work of art, his cinematic style has received much less attention than it deserves, and certain recurrent motifs and themes throughout the oeuvre have been unjustly ignored.

But although Lumet is an "old-fashioned" liberal committed to looking at themes of personal responsibility and to looking at each situation on its own terms, he refuses to give his audience what some liberals did in the 1950s: the comforting illusion that there are relatively easy answers to complex questions. (See the ambiguities and unresolved situations at the end of *Prince of the City*, Lumet's 1981 crime film, as we are moved both to applause for and hostility toward the police informer played by Treat Williams.) All Lumet offers us in *12 Angry Men* is that, given the preponderance of irrationality in this society in the 1950s (as perhaps best represented by Warden and Begley), the liberal and humane solution represented by Fonda is just possible on a limited basis, case by case. As in Emerson's time, democracy is still an individual, personal concern with no easy answers, just the necessity of hard work and patience to combat the chicanery and ignorance all about us. This great theme—distinguishing Lumet's work from *12 Angry Men* and *Fail Safe* through *Serpico*, *Prince of the City*, and *Running on Empty*— is, of course, no more fashionable in the age of Godard than it was in the day of Emerson. As the *Time* review notes, "The law is no better than the people who enforce it, and . . . the people who enforce it are all too human." [11]

Perhaps Lumet's fine conjoining of theme and visual technique is most evident in the film's final sequence, as Cobb caps his wrenching performance by admitting his frustration and sorrow over his past treatment of his son, tearing up the boy's picture and sobbing out the final "not guilty" that will clear the defendant on the existence of a reasonable doubt of his guilt. Lumet shows Cobb against the window of reality, of flux and change, as he cries out his symbolic confession. After Fonda helps Cobb put on his coat as the jurors get ready to leave, Lumet shows the anonymous jurors—with the significant exceptions of the film's prime fathers, Fonda and Sweeney, who momentarily introduce themselves—slowly coming down the steps beneath the columns seen in the opening sequence and one by one going their own ways, some across the street into a park opposite the courthouse. Cobb, the last one down the steps, walks very slowly, glancing at Fonda, who disappears into frame right. Cobb is boxed in by the two rows of stair railings in frame left, as if made partially aware by the events of the trial that he has far to go to reach the serene spaciousness of the park across the street into which the others have blended.

Long Day's Journey into Night: The Flight from Self-Knowledge

Concerning the process of adaptation from literature to film, American film director Eleanor Perry said: "It seems to me two things are extremely important in [adaptation]: one, a really deep empathy with the material, the author's theme, intention, and view of life; and two, an unblocked imagination which is able to flow freely from the original source, playing, embroidering, ornamenting, extending, and, in the most successful adaptations, even enriching the original material."[12] Graham Petrie called Lumet's *Long Day's Journey into Night*, because of its "intelligent and restrained use of cinematic resources . . . Lumet's best film, and one of the greatest films of the past decade." British critic Robin Bean, also writing a few years after the film's 1962 release, commented that *Long Day's Journey* was "probably the most brilliant adaptation of a play. . . . it is a purely cinematic interpretation of O'Neill's work. [Lumet] uses his camera to intensify the atmosphere evoked by the author's dialogue, examining in minute detail the character, feelings and reactions of the Tyrone family; each hesitant glance or slight movement having a very special purpose."[13]

In a *New York Times* article, Lumet underscored Perry's theoretical insights, while providing his own attitudes toward literary adaptation and especially about his involvement with O'Neill:

What makes *Long Day's Journey* a film rather than a photographed stage play is a fifth character . . . the camera. It is the camera with its revelations, definitions, and meanings of its own. . . . I don't understand why film must be one thing. . . . [French directors] accuse me of loving language and of trying to impose it on the screen. . . . There are certain pieces of material that are better revealed in silent pictorial concepts and there are others that are revealed in language. Language should not be ruled out as a part of a film technique. . . . My only criterion for what constitutes a film is, "Does the film tell *that* story better, and more revealingly, and more movingly than any other medium can."[14]

In an interview with Dale Luciano some years later, in which he spoke of both *Long Day's Journey* and of his celebrated 1960 television production of *The Iceman Cometh*, the director reaffirmed his respect for O'Neill's artistry and, while defending the necessity to sacrifice little of O'Neill's length because the fulfillment of tragic themes requires time for full development, also again implicitly defended an equally valuable kind of film language:

I find O'Neill a great writer. "Great" in the classic, total, historic sense of the word. . . . People are so used to finger-tip experience, and a lack of a really profound revelation. They're impatient, they think it can come quickly. Well, in many instances, it can't. It's so often like life, and O'Neill is like life. It has to go around the same circle four times, but all the time it's like an awl which is biting deeper and deeper into the wood each time it goes around. It's not going around on the same level, [but] on one level deeper until, finally, something bursts within the play. For that, all those repetitions are needed. You need them in *Iceman*, you need them in this.[15]

The executors of O'Neill's estate chose producer Ely Landau and Lumet to make *Long Day's Journey* because of their confidence that the filmmakers would respect O'Neill's text, based upon Lumet and Landau's triumphant "Play of the Week" production of *Iceman*. Lumet's concern with discovering and revealing in his major films the recesses of human experience is apparent in this early work, starring Jason Robards, Jr., as Hickey and Myron McCormack as Larry Slade. *Iceman* presaged many of the cinematic techniques in *Long Day's Journey*, particularly compositions emphasizing the characters' choices of self-entrapment. One of Lumet's initial revelations of Hickey shows the salesman, usually from the rear, almost dancing along the bar as he brays to Harry that he has stopped drinking; Lumet shoots him from high angle and counterpoints his hasty movements with much slower camera movements in the opposite direction. The discontinuity of rhythms suggests at least that Hickey, eventual death-bringer, is not his usual convivial self. More than once when Hickey pretends to dispense happiness, Lumet frames him dimly on one side by an empty coatrack that is nearly as tall as a man though it is far in the visual background, and on the other side by darkness. Near the end, as Hickey reveals his guilt, Lumet tightly frames him within bannisters and by a chair in front of him that blocks out his legs. As the visually reduced lecturer regales all with tales of his supposed love for his wife, Lumet shows flowers in a bowl on the piano near Hickey's face. He repeats this framing after Parritt reveals a guilty complicity. Lumet, of course sole director of photography here, creates a memorable final scene involving Hickey, as the bums take delight in his ostensible craziness as their newest self-delusion: the director pans from Hickey across them all, slowly, the camera rising slightly until it is just over Hickey, then panning very slowly over the group before returning to Hickey's ironically dominant position.

Equally does Lumet cinematically reflect the play's themes as regards other major characters. Early on, as Larry declares that truth has little bearing on the reality men must live, we can see his hand through a clear, empty bottle. The terribly free Larry, no less than Hickey, is presented as visually pinned between wall borders in deep rear frame even while he powerfully denounces Hickey; as Larry challenges Hickey's ostensibly newly won peace, the ambiguity of his nothingness and his existential freedom is suggested by Lumet's framing him backed by total blackness. When Larry draws an admission from Hickey of his wife's death by murder, Lumet reveals in a well-composed shot Parritt (Robert Redford) far in rear frame, between the two men, just before Hugo wakes up, seen through chair slats in a long-distance shot. Earlier Lumet also links Parritt to the play's general theme of guilt in a shot that positions the youth directly between Hickey and Larry with Oban, the remnant of law and reason, at the far rear. Visual ironies multiply here: the law is a drunk, and Parritt is helpless between two derelicts, one lost in an illusion of his competence, the other a spiritual father who cares more for humanity than he is able to admit, yet who cannot help Parritt, though he beseeches Larry for aid, until he can throw off his own penchant for self-delusion. All end finally in self-delusion excepting Larry, who alone does not join the now-"happy" throng that pours booze on the hapless Hugo (Sorrell Booke) as he lies on the floor, recently awakened but now poured back into oblivion.

In transforming to film O'Neill's other great American tragedy on the abdication of moral responsibility, Lumet also remained quite faithful to the original source. Lumet used no screenwriter, choosing to leave the dialogue virtually intact, with the excision of approximately twenty pages of the play's 165-page length. Shooting the film in only thirty-seven days, at a cost of merely $435,000, Lumet began with a three-week rehearsal period for his magnificent cast of Katharine Hepburn, Ralph Richardson, Jason Robards, Jr., and Dean Stockwell—the four would win an ensemble best-acting award at Cannes. Lumet told Robin Bean of initial difficulties between Hepburn and himself:

It was just *the* best cast for the film. . . . Everybody was our first choice. When I met Kate, I couldn't have disliked her more, and I imagine she felt the same way about me. Ely Landau sensed this . . . [and] said, "Well, let's get somebody else." I said, "No, what ever hell it is going to be it is going to be worth it, because she is the best person in the world for that part." And of course it didn't turn out to be hell at all. She's a great, great woman, and it wound up just as happily as anything ever could.[16]

Then, unusually, the director shot the entire film in sequence out of his respect for the play's integrity. Lumet is rare among contemporary

directors in his insistence that the actors conceive their roles in terms of
the entire film, and he invests much time on all his films discussing the
characters and the ideas of the work with the actors. In fact, Lee Bobker
says, "A kind of creative collaboration . . . takes place."[17]

Lumet observed in an interview that he departed from the famed
stage version's emphasis upon the male characters to stress the significance of Mary Tyrone as the moral center of *Long Day's Journey*.[18]
Frequently during his directorial career, Lumet has been attracted by
the characters who are loners or outcasts, often because of an inability
or disinclination to make courageous moral choices: the Anthony
Perkins character in *Lovin' Molly*, the desperate Treat Williams character
in *Prince of the City*, the mythic Sophia Loren figure in *That Kind of
Woman*, and, perhaps most memorably, Nazerman in *The Pawnbroker*.
There exists throughout Lumet's films a theme similar to the concern
expressed by John Gardner in his fine book *On Moral Fiction*: "Art
asserts and reasserts those values which hold off dissolution, struggling to keep the mind intact and preserve the city, the mind's safe
preserve. Art rediscovers, generation by generation, what is necessary
to humanness."[19]

In his film of O'Neill's tragedy, Lumet seems especially interested
in representing Mary's life-denying flight from the human community
into what ends as a complete regression into the past, into total withdrawal from choice, from responsibility. While he is always compassionate toward Mary, and to all the haunted Tyrones, he relentlessly
reveals that her flight can have only the most sorrowful of consequences. Lumet created several technical strategies to represent
Mary's character as different from those of her men.[20] Lumet's lens plot
for the film included a plan for increasingly longer lenses to be employed in photographing Mary, in order to isolate her gradually from
her surrounding world by a loss of depth of field and clear focus on
background objects. Lumet commented to me, "If you look carefully at
Long Day's Journey—which is used in film schools for its skill in use of
lenses—you'll see that as the film went on, I used longer and longer
lenses on Hepburn, and wider and wider lenses on the other three, so
that she became more and more isolated, whereas the reality of the
room kept imposing itself more and more on the other three, the reality
of the place, the reality of the time." Further to dynamize the space
occupied by Mary in the film, Lumet shoots Mary from progressively
higher angles as the film progresses, diminishing her in size as she
loses contact with the world around her. Lumet's editing principles
also emphasize Mary's thematic prominence: she is shot in long takes,
some very long.[21] Unlike many of the strong women characters in the

Lumet canon, such as Lindsay Crouse in *Daniel*, Maureen Stapleton in *A View from the Bridge*, Christine Lahti in *Running on Empty*, Ali Mac-Graw in *Just Tell Me What You Want*, and Blythe Danner in *Lovin' Molly*, Hepburn's Mary Tyrone is the most memorable weak female character in Lumet's work. In fact, Lumet's film presents Mary in an even more unsparing and harrowing light than O'Neill's drama does. In Mary's characterization, Hepburn's superb realization of her, and Lumet's memorable cinematic compositions and camera placements dedicated to revealing her, Lumet enriches and, in the Bazinian sense, multiplies by the cinema the O'Neill play.

One of Lumet's most prominent variations from the play is the opening sequence. Instead of introducing the Tyrones through a visual depiction of O'Neill's opening scene set in the living room at 8:30 in the morning, with *"sunshine com[*ing] *through the windows"* and with intimations of the destructive behavior to come in faintly testy innuendos, Lumet suffuses the early minutes of the film with intense sunlight, moving the opening action outdoors and downplaying the family members' irritation with each other in a sequence that is more emotionally subdued.[22] As André Previn's sad, strident piano accompanies the credits, a blazing sun dominates the left half of the frame. It dissolves into the opening shot of the porch of the house, partly in shadows, as if to represent the darkness beneath the shining exterior of the Tyrone's lives this sunny August morning. The almost unbearably bright light during the film's opening moments not only sets a stark contrast for Lumet's famed last shot of the family completely lost in the darkness of the following night but also offers a hint of their familial and personal potential on this new day, as four highly intelligent, financially secure, and basically loving people prepare for an outdoor breakfast on a morning that betokens brightness and promise.[23]

Only part of O'Neill's first several pages of dialogue is retained; most notable during Mary's opening gentle teasing of Edmund for sleeping late is Lumet's carefully continued interplay of light and shadow, as Tyrone's shadow—not the man himself—is visible in frame left while Mary coddles her younger son. To complement the motif of a hidden shadow across these seemingly sunny lives, another shadow is visible, that of a tree behind Mary in frame right and also behind Edmund as he comes out to the porch to meet his mother. As Mary fusses over Edmund, Lumet cuts to a reaction shot of the older son, Jamie, staring, lost even in this light, foreshadowing the strong theme of rejection by his mother that forms such a dominant part of O'Neill's play. Mary's first words in the film concern her fear that Jamie might be staring at her, followed by what will be her frequent concern about her misplaced glasses and her fear that her hair may be mussed. Lumet's early focus on Mary's deep-rooted insecurity about her appearance advances the thematic focus upon her human weakness. Associated with her initial wordless actions of babying her son, Mary's other anxieties suggest a motivation of withdrawal and regression that will become more pronounced as the film continues, and we recall psychoanalyst Alfred Adler's telling of the Arabic tale that all drug addicts want to go to the same place. As the family members strive to talk gaily and to deny their pain, Lumet again departs from O'Neill's stage directions by showing Tyrone and Mary walking, left to right, on the porch of the house. The sons walk in the same direction, but they are separated into another plane of space by the heavy porch railing.

As an argument looms over Jamie's twitting his father about his last night's snoring, Mary suddenly leans toward frame left, walking backward, flourishing her hand theatrically, as if to wave away the incipient arguments that she is not emotionally strong enough to address. The sons listen to her forced laugh, separated from their parents in spatial plane, much in the manner that Hitchcock's lovers in *Notorious* move in different planes, suggesting deep emotional estrangement. Just as Edmund angrily accuses his father of criticizing Jamie again and as all four are almost out of the frame and are turning the corner to the yard, Lumet allows us a bare second's glimpse of Jamie. He stares at Edmund, bitter despite (and because of) his younger brother's defense of him, knowing that his mother will favor Edmund for his charity and that he himself will be pushed yet further away from his mother's attention. Thus in a brief sequence that depends comparatively little on O'Neill's dialogue, Lumet brilliantly introduces the psychological complexities and ambiguities of a family that, though it outwardly walks in light, has already started the long day's journey toward darkness.

After a lull in the hostilities, Lumet again underscores, even more than O'Neill himself, the compassion with which he regards these emotional derelicts, through a subtle gesture on the part of Tyrone. When the father again begins to upbraid Jamie for his laziness, Edmund disgustedly leaves the family group and goes inside the house, coughing as he goes. Rather than following O'Neill's stage direction— *"Tyrone looks after him angrily"* (26)—Lumet reveals Richardson lamely stretching out a hand toward his son, not seeming to know why things are going so badly between them again. Here, however briefly, Lumet alludes to one of his dominant tragic themes, the difficult human task of achieving successful understanding or communication with others and a concomitant self-knowledge and self-understanding. This gesture begins Lumet's second major sequence of the film. As Mary begins to repress the uncomfortable facts of the gravity of Edmund's tubercular condition beneath the illusion that he has merely a "summer cold," Lumet twice photographs her from a slightly elevated angle, and Hepburn's fingers again begin their nervous little dance around her mouth. Lumet does not condescend to Mary by shooting her from the steep high angle that he uses to present Jamie in this sequence, but rather lowers Mary gently, echoing her own grace of movement. As Jamie says, "The Kid is damned sick," Tyrone's knee slides into the left portion of the frame, gently nudging Jamie, urging him to suppress this fearful truth for Mary's sake. Often in Lumet's films we see only fragments of people's bodies and gestures, as if to emphasize the spiritual and emotional fragmentation so prevalent among the characters. This device is especially prominent in *12 Angry Men*, another film in which the characters' personal tragedies are made greater by the fragmentary portions of reality they allow themselves to experience, or to acknowledge.

Mary's vulnerability is heightened in the next shot: Lumet cuts to the men from behind Mary, then pans across her, placing her in bottom frame, seen from low angle, as Tyrone dominates frame center, trying to explain away Edmund's disease. Lumet further increases Mary's vulnerability by then cutting to a close-up of her face from slightly high angle, with shadows playing on the porch behind her, as if to suggest her gradual, inexorable disintegration. At this point, Lumet makes a slight but significant change in O'Neill's dialogue. Instead of O'Neill's "What is it? What are you looking at? Is my hair—?" (27), Hepburn says here, at a markedly slower and more poignant pace, "Is my hair— coming—down—or something?" Now Lumet blocks Richardson plunging to his knees, and the camera follows him down to Mary's feet on the grass as he tries to praise her: "The healthier you get, the vainer you become." The camera movement seems to include Tyrone in Mary's vulnerability and emotional chaos. Even in her weakness and misery, Mary is here visually focused as the thematic center of Lumet's vision of the drama. Struggling to assert control, Mary rises, saying, "But I did truly have beautiful hair once, didn't I, James?" As she comes up, Lumet frames her in one of the most evocative and original images in the film: a tree on each side of her, whose branches hover overhead to form an arc, she is momentarily organically connected to her world. Her men are complimenting her, and she half-believes them, while still aware of the irony that Tyrone "isn't a great actor for nothing." She is also about to enter the house to direct the preparation of dinner. This is one of Mary's strongest moments, its poignance heightened by the director's cinematic skills.

In the next sequence, Lumet makes the only major change in O'Neill's play during the film, apart from the opening scene, by cutting almost all the argument between Tyrone and Jamie in the middle of act 1. Much can be learned about a director's adaptational style by considering what he chooses to omit: by curtailing this lengthy diatribe of recriminations and accusations between father and elder son, Lumet both abbreviates a subtheme that is rather repetitious in O'Neill's play and, more important, focuses on Mary and her inexorable withdrawal from her family and from reality. Significantly, the only section of this conversation Lumet includes is Jamie's admission to his father of Dr. Hardy's conclusion that Edmund has consumption. While the men attempt to deal with this harsh reality, Mary begins to regress: Lumet next cuts to the living room, where again Mary pampers Edmund, subliminally aware of the gravity of his illness, at the start of what corresponds to the end of act 1 in the play.

As Mary talks on about her hatred of Tyrone's summer house and her feeling of inferiority compared with the Chatfields, who have more "presentable" houses, one remembers Lumet's astute psychoanalytic insight, expressed in a *New York Times* interview, that Mary attacks others in her family before she senses they are about to attack her, thus attempting to displace her sense of inferiority and specifically her guilt over the coming resumption of her drug addiction. Alfred Adler called this game "safeguarding through aggression," and Mary devastatingly employs it against Jamie, causing him untold guilt and depression.[24] Here, as she plunges to the depths of self-hate and self-abasement with the exclamation "It would serve all of you right if it was true!" (47), Lumet shows her for the first time framed within clearly visible, thick lines of wallpaper. Lumet underscores this sense of barriers by an extremely fast pan as Mary begins circling the room agitatedly muttering about her sense of aloneness. Momentarily the camera pauses, as Mary pauses in her ceaseless flight from herself, and pins her for a moment, framing her exactly within the borders of two window frames. Then the sequence ends as Mary again circles the room, the camera relentlessly following her, as Lumet finds a fine visual equivalent within the room of O'Neill's closing stage directions to act 1: *"Her long fingers, warped and knotted . . . drum on the arms of the chair, driven by an insistent life of their own, without her consent"* (49). Needing desperately to live in the past, to forget all her pain and failure, Mary looks up the stairs longingly as she cautions Edmund to get out of the house for some fresh air. The camera again bears in upon her from behind and above, then pans right to left as she runs left to right to the bottom of the stairs, suggesting the dissonance of her emotions.[25] Mary then runs up the stairs to the renewal of her doom.

After a dissolve to suggest that time's pace will now begin to change for Mary, Lumet opens the film's next major movement (act 2) with emphasis upon Jamie's suffering as a result of his mother's withdrawal. Shortening the expository lines concerning the sons' gradual discovery that Mary has been left upstairs unwatched for too long, Lumet employs cinematic resources to heighten Mary's central speech in act 2 on the alleged determinism that she feels is at the heart of human events. Referring to Jamie, she says, "None of us can help the things life has done to us. They're done before you realize it, and once they're done they make you do other things until at last everything comes between you and what you'd like to be, and you've lost your true self forever" (61). As Mary sits beside Edmund, again coddling him and teasing (and humiliating) the ignored and terribly aware Jamie, Lumet reveals Jamie in rear frame, immobile for fifteen seconds. Then the camera tracks very slowly in on Jamie into an extreme close-up of him, at which point he turns away from it, utterly isolated and defeated, as much from his mother's withdrawal from the community of the family as from his realization that she rejects him in favor of the younger Edmund. As if to underscore Mary's emotional exclusion of Jamie, Lumet cuts to Mary again hugging Edmund, but from a position three-quarters behind Jamie's left shoulder. Abruptly he cuts to an extreme close-up of Jamie's crushed expression as Mary slowly says, "Yes, the only way is to make yourself not care," and he fully realizes that she is beginning to be lost to them again.

During this sequence Lumet subtly underscores Jamie's sense of estrangement more than O'Neill does in the drama. Although O'Neill depicts Jamie in stage directions looking out of the window, Lumet frames Jamie visually centered and caught between rows of shelves on the living room wall. Then as Jamie displaces his frustration upon his father by becoming angry that the family must wait for Tyrone's arrival before they can begin to eat lunch, Lumet positions Jamie partially in the dining room framed off from the rest of the family both by the heavy wood of the entryway to the rear sitting room and by his more distant plane of space, just as at the start of the sequence Jamie was visually separated from Edmund by the rocking chair he had set in motion as he sat elsewhere in the rear of the frame. The director emphasizes Jamie's psychological and spiritual estrangement by cutting to a subjective shot from Jamie's eye level of Mary visually encased between the heavy frames of two living room windows, in the blank space between them. The emotional effect of this composition of spatial confinement is, like the scenes in *Fail Safe* in which Henry Fonda discusses on the hotline the possibilities of nuclear engagement with the Soviet premier, unusually stifling and oppressive. Lumet's intent here seems to be, as in *Fail Safe* and in certain scenes in *The Offence* and *The Pawnbroker*, among other films, to express through oppressive visual and scenic design what Fritz Lang realized in *M*.

This effect is sustained as Lumet lengthens the time it takes in the play for Jamie to confront Mary with the mirror and the proof, expressed in her eyes, of her renewed addiction. As Lumet's camera rises behind Mary to Jamie's eye level, Jamie slowly walks toward it and her as he demands that she observe her eyes in the mirror. Lumet now shoots Jamie from a slightly low angle, tightly framed by the entryway to the room and the harsh angles of the room's corner. Edmund also slowly comes toward Mary from the rear of the frame to see if Jamie's suspicion is correct, and Lumet's camera bears relentlessly in upon Mary's face in its hauntedness, almost cutting Edmund out of the right of the frame. Though Edmund is not involved physically in the action in O'Neill's play, Lumet stresses the consequences of Mary's choice of passive disengagement from the human family through her opiates by showing Edmund grasping her face, staring into her numbness, and looking away, defeated. As Tyrone pours drinks and says lamely, "Here's health and happiness," soon after this, Lumet quickly cuts to a point in back of him, with Jamie staring at his father in wordless incredulity at his vacuous false cheer, his attempted repression of Mary's precipitous decline. Lumet again shoots the three men, bonded in their common rejection by Mary Tyrone, all three visually enclosed within the blank space between the two heavy window frames, with Tyrone visually bound between the dining room entryway and a heavy cabinet in deep rear frame.

The first scene of O'Neill's second act ends as both Tyrone and Jamie move toward the stricken Mary. Lumet isolates the two men in separate planes of space, with the father for a long moment blocking our view of Jamie, a cinematic suggestion that it is Jamie whose psychological existence is most threatened by Mary's disengagement and the frequent aggressions that occur between them. As Mary notices Edmund's glass filled with liquor, she connects his suspected tuberculosis with that of her own father. In the play, she suddenly retracts this awareness with the recognition that covertly she has admitted that her favored son is gravely ill. Unable to face this, like most instances of reality, she stammers, "But, of course, there's no comparison at all . . . *is there?*" Lumet adds the final two words to O'Neill's line to stress Mary's poignance and helplessness in the face of truth.

For act 2, scene 2, Lumet continues to employ all his spatial resources to heighten the tragedy of the haunted Tyrones, utilizing "composition, lighting, camera angle and movement within the deliberately confined space of the film to create a dynamic cinematic space that is charged with emotional meaning." [26] After Tyrone receives Dr. Hardy's telephone call with the news of Edmund's tuberculosis, he walks strickenly back into the dining room; but the telephone's huge black mouthpiece continues to dominate the frame's foreground, a visual equivalent of the recurrent foghorn that calls those lost in illusions back to reality. As Mary again attempts to retreat up the stairs—stairs that O'Neill does not show us—Lumet forces us visually into connection with them, as does Hitchcock in *Notorious*, employing them as a visual symbol to suggest the brokenness, the fall, implicit in the human condition. Whereas in the play Mary simply disappears through the unused back parlor, Lumet compels us to engage the stairs. We never see upstairs, for Lumet is uninterested in the sensationalistic technical aspects of Mary's injecting herself; rather his concern lies, as it does frequently in his films, in visually confronting us with the moral choices involved in human action—in this case, in self-abasement and self-humiliation.

Even as her husband pleads with her, Mary again and again hurts him with her rasping about her disappointment at this house, the cheap doctors, and on and on. By expressive use of close-ups, Lumet heightens Mary's realization of how she hurts her husband—and how she needs to. Hepburn's face is a memorable collage of contorted, conflicting feelings, an unspoken expression of how cowardice and circumstances have continued to doom them to hurt one another, and ceaselessly to regret it. Her husband sits back, ashen, and she raises a hand to her mouth in this film of delicate, miniature acts that have the most terrible significance for the tortured who must experience them. After this recognition, Hepburn raises a hand tentatively toward Tyrone as she sighs, "I'm *sorry*, dear," and drifts away. Lumet's direction of Hepburn's gestural language of tentative self-accusation and pleas for forgiveness is, as throughout, superb. His omission of much of the accusatory harangue between the three men that occupies several pages of text in favor of gestural nuances provides further evidence that Lumet is more interested in the subtlest aspects of emotion in O'Neill than in the occasionally florid and theatrical dialogue of the men. Concerning his justifiable fame for his skill in close-up photography, Lumet said, "Images do not only mean 5,000 head of cattle, a sunset, scenery and still frames. For me, photographing a human face that is *saying* something profound is as much cinema as a chariot race

. . . It is my deep hope that putting *Long Day's Journey* on *film* will reveal facets and profundities of that play and those characters that could never be caught in any other medium." [27]

Lumet makes a minor, but significant, departure from the play's text in the next sequence. He moves the action briefly to the porch as Mary laments her lack of friends and she and Tyrone talk of another foggy night coming on. Lumet obscures Mary by shadows as she says that tonight she won't mind the fog. As Mary and Tyrone sit rocking on the porch swing, Lumet finds another visual equivalent of their circular, repetitive cycle of ambivalent intimacy and flight from intimacy. The porch setting is distinguished by cinematographer Boris Kaufman's brilliant grays and shadows. Lumet commented to me that "with Boris, the director of photography for most of my early black and white films, it was the *richness* of the black-and-white gradations. He could get more tones into black and white than a lot of cameramen with color. On a scale of one to ten, going from white to black, Boris would get in a *hundred* shades, whereas another cameraman if he was marvelous would get ten. He had extraordinary sensitivity about light." [28] The brief scene on the porch allows Lumet different metaphors to express Mary's conviction that people are just passive pawns in life's game. Realizing that she centrally lacks will and courage to try to deal with her pain, Tyrone says gently as Mary rocks back and forth, "It's you who are leaving us, Mary." Then she almost disappears within the house, except that her hand is visible momentarily on the door jamb. She comes part way out to flirt with her husband, again revealing her insistent need for approval. Lumet closes this sequence, too, with a dissolve as a further indication of Mary's deepening state of addiction soon to come.

In one of the film's most memorable images, Lumet opens the next sequence (act 3) with a shot of the empty top of the stairs, into which flutters Mary's ethereal left hand, like a fragment of a ghost; then her body fills the top of the frame, pressed between railings. As she staggers down the stairs half-way, the foghorn sounds in the background, a sound Mary hates because "it keeps reminding you and calling you back." While O'Neill begins the third act immediately with Mary's and the servant girl's dialogue, Lumet suspends their talking together until after this visual image of Mary's utter desolation, a visual and an ironic correlative of her lament just previously, "Mother of God, why do I feel so lonely?" During her scene with Cathleen, Lumet repeatedly divides her off in separate spatial planes from the girl. Although Mary attempts to breach her defensive notions of class superiority by offering to have Cathleen drink with her, Lumet reveals the ultimate ineffectiveness of this empty gesture by keeping the girl at extreme frame right, sometimes almost out of the frame, illustrating Mary's isolation. Throughout the "conversation" with Cathleen, Mary really talks to herself. Drunken, she finally topples out of her chair in the rear of the frame. Lumet ends act 3 also with a dissolve, as Mary expresses the hope that she will accidentally take an overdose of the drugs and be destroyed, without of course having to take moral responsibility for her action, for "the Blessed Virgin would never forgive me, then."

In the early parts of act 4, Lumet continues through intrashot montage, particularly spatial restrictiveness, to emphasize the dividedness among Mary's three men. While this section is effective, Lumet is somewhat less visually imaginative in the treatment of the men alone than when Mary is present. Since the men do gain a very limited sense of self-knowledge and Lumet frequently in his work is attracted by the refusal to face reality as the primary base of humankind's unhappiness, it may be that the scenes with Mary most fully engage his cinematic energies. Nonetheless, each of the three men gains stature and sympathy in Lumet's presentation. During Edmund's long talk and partial reconciliation with his father, Lumet reveals him at one point visually cut off at the hip line, symbolically emasculated in relation to his father, by a large, empty wicker chair dominating near frame. Lumet thus implies that the family's incessant self-absorption and recriminations may doom Edmund as effectively as his tuberculosis, despite Tyrone's being shown standing on a table in the center of the room to turn on three lights in an attempt at generosity and emotional flexibility, as well as perhaps to defeat the guilt born of his impoverished, dark childhood. At one point, as Tyrone wonders where his elder son is, his shadow is thrown upon the wall by a light from beyond the house, and the truth of the lighthouse's beam that crosses the window behind Edmund serves as a reminder both of his sons' immurement in the father's fame and of his personal dominance. Unlike the play, as Tyrone grumbles to Edmund about his memories of childhood poverty while offering to send his son to a more expensive sanatorium and reminisces that the great Booth once approved his acting style, Lumet's film shows the old man in shame turning out the lights he had formerly and with such flourish turned on, subconsciously blotting out the praise he needed and so needs now. Not only the young men are in his shadow.

Stockwell's colloquial, unoratorical Edmund, a more vital force than the other men, nicely balances his father's orotund pronouncements as he sits in the dark. Like Tyrone Edmund is a fog person, and he shares the occasional lighthouse beams with his father. And Robards's magnificent Jamie, returning drunk for the confrontation with his brother, in the film, unlike the play, is seen (like his father) standing on the table to light the lamps. Revealing his hatred for his father, Jamie is backgrounded by his shadow, just as his father has recently been. Also unlike the play, as Jamie dimly links the relationship of Fat Violet to the object of his longing look up the stairway, Lumet shows the brothers conversing as they lie on a couch faced in opposite directions, Jamie warning his brother against his need someday to undermine and destroy his future and echoing his own self-image as he refers to his mother's corpselike state as she descends the stairs.

Indeed, the closing sequence is one of American film's great moments. As Mary, far gone into the past now, enters in her wedding dress and drifts through the hall into the dining room, then into the sitting room where the three men sit at a table, Lumet pans slowly to center her from the viewpoint of her sons' backs. She circles them, not acknowledging now their touches, not even Edmund's. Lumet cuts to her seated, dreaming of being a nun, the camera significantly positioned behind Jamie. With a little light on Mary and less on the others, Lumet moves the camera very slowly back from a close-up of Mary as she begins her memoir of Mother Elizabeth's doubt about her entry into the convent when she was a young girl. The camera continues its backward movement, then pulls upward, over them all, as Mary speaks only to herself.[29] Finally the pinpoint of lighted area is a minute part of the frame, surrounded by total blackness, as if to symbolize Mary's total regression from this world into another. And as she grows smaller, so do the men who love her. The only faint reality is an occasional light beam from the lighthouse, crossing the windows in deep background. Then, as Mary begins the play's closing lines, "That was in the winter of senior year," Lumet sharply and jarringly cuts to an extreme close-up of Mary's face, now leaning down into her left hand. She begins, perhaps, to admit that she married because of romance and illusion and passivity rather than because of a commitment to Tyrone: "Then in the spring something happened to me. Yes, I remember. I fell in love with James Tyrone and was so happy for a time." Then the camera returns to its long-view vantage point, and Lumet's meditative eye ends the film staring at the spot of light that contains them all, now, until even that light is dimmed. All we can sense is the thin ray from the lighthouse at the successive windows, and then we hear the foghorn, as one last beam tracks along the floor, barely revealing the Tyrones. Mary's will to oblivion brings her to the end of night.[30]

In an interview in 1962, Hepburn praised Sidney Lumet's direction of her, even though the relationship between them at the start of the rehearsal period had not been overly friendly. "It's the best thing I ever did." Commenting on the moral dimensions of the play, she said, "Oh, how O'Neill knew our misfortunes and our dreams. . . . The saddest thing that happens to the human animal, I think, is to be unrealized. There will be old people in the audience who feel that life has gone by them."[31]

Fail Safe: The Final Game

A few weeks before the release of Lumet's *Fail Safe* (1964), Stanley Kubrick's better-known *Dr. Strangelove* appeared, a film, like Lumet's, also on the subject of nuclear devastation. But *Dr. Strangelove* is quite different from *Fail Safe* in tone and approach, as Kubrick emphasizes the absurdity, dark humor, and even the beauty he finds in nuclear destruction. For over two decades, it has been insufficiently appreciated how morally numbing and intellectually superficial is Kubrick's artistic response to the tension between human responsibility and fallibility.[32] By his condescending burlesque of the ultimately terrifying subject, Kubrick desensitizes his audience, allowing us the easy response of laughing away a horror about which, his film implicitly alleges, we can do nothing anyway. So we might just as well sing along with Vera Lynn as the final bombs descend that will end all human social structures, ideas, passions, and dreams. Kubrick's shots of sanitized, "beautiful" nuclear explosions that end the film to Lynn's voice-over are distressingly cynical: they celebrate life's ultimate horror as a mere game, a pastime that appeals to our spirit of fun, and thereby circumvent our deepest capacities for thought and feeling. What is so unfortunate about Kubrick's attitude in *Dr. Strangelove* is the subtle derogation of his audience, the director's assumption that we are so spiritually impotent, so frightened of nuclear destruction, that we cannot dare to let ourselves think or feel about it directly or honestly, that instead we need only the drug of unconsidered laughter to deny the prospect of incipient nothingness.

The reactionary nature of such a vision of the human condition is obvious; less noticeable on first viewing are the film's easy targets of satire, from Keenan Wynn's bumbling stooge to the great god Coca-Cola and Peter Sellers's President Mutley, whose inane responses to crisis equally assert the abdication of human responsibility for human errors and failure, since all our leaders are fatuous imbeciles and thus their followers must also be. Even Sterling Hayden's memorable performance as the paranoid officer whose sexual insecurities lead to the politically unauthorized sending of the bombers to Russia misleads the audience unconsciously to generalize the causes of horror to cartoonlike figures and thus thrusts the responsibility upon the most facile of targets. The director's thematic vision does not encompass outrage that might prompt audience exploration of such a considered study of the subject as physicist Freeman Dyson's *Weapons and Hope* (1984). Such a contemplative, reasoned response is rendered unlikely by a film that continually exploits its audience's most adolescent responses, from the usual guffaws at Hayden's "precious bodily fluids" to the broad mannerisms of Sellers's stiff-armed Nazi guru in the closing war room scenes and George C. Scott's braying general's commandeering of the Lord, which confusingly imply that the bombs may be launched as a result of oversexed as well as underconfident militarists. The film's imagery suggests that a lack of human control and command totally define the human situation, from Sellers's mechanical celebration of his Fuehrer to Slim Pickens's cornpone ride on the weapon that begins the final extinction. And as Dr. Strangelove's final mine shaft fantasies turn increasingly sexist with his suggestion for official amusement during the long postholocaust cooling-off period, more thoughtful members of Kubrick's audience may recall Eliot's somber warning that "Humankind cannot bear very much reality."

Lumet's *Fail Safe*, on the contrary, forces its smaller audiences to confront the visual and moral results of one day of American nuclear strategy in the seconds before the explosions over New York City. His film makes emotional and intellectual demands upon us, reveals characters who are not mere pasteboard figures, but people about whom we care enough that their deaths, or those of their loved ones, make a significant impact upon us, disallowing Kubrick's more comfortable Brechtian distancing. As in his films from *12 Angry Men* to *Prince of the City*, Lumet's *Fail Safe* refuses to evade the moral center of complex human and technical issues. The film is among Lumet's finest in its presentation of characterization, visual imagery, and narrative pacing, and in its thematic insistence that humans must face the seriousness of—and accept responsibility for—exactly what we most fear and thus what we most should attempt to change. Rather than taking the escapist route that mass death is funny, Lumet's film forces us closer to the nothingness that must inevitably follow nuclear holocaust. Lumet's reasoned, humanistic approach to the subject of nuclear war is too sophisticated to remain content with Kubrick's sophomoric repose in the idea that all military men are mad ghouls. Lumet's realization that life's imponderables, mechanical slips, accidents, and slight failures in human attention and communication may cause the final Armageddon more closely coincides with scientific and political analysts' concerns that accident and fatigue, as well as dimly understood beliefs, are now, as so often throughout history, humankind's central enemy.

Lumet emphasizes the psychological and moral aspects of human crisis even more prominently in the film than Eugene Burdick and Harvey Wheeler do in the solid and suspenseful popular novel. Instead of the novel's detailed, well-observed opening chapters on White House Russian translator Peter Buck and the preliminary events in the Omaha War Room, Lumet begins his adaptation with the events in chapter 5 of the novel. The film's beginning concentrates upon General Black (Dan O'Herlihy), the officer most suspicious of Pentagon war policy and throughout the action the most sustained, rational military presence against the philosophy of nuclear overkill. Immediately following the flashed white title "New York City, 5:30 A.M.," a long establishing shot from an extremely high angle reveals a bull entering a bullring, running left to right before pausing in center frame; then a close-up shows it looking from side to side, having come very close to the camera. As in the novel's vision of General Black's recurrent dream, we hear the noisy, swelling roar from the crowd in the arena, but only in the film is added the growing, incessant whine and scream of jet engines that will grow nearly unbearable by the end of the sequence, overcoming the human cheering, obliterating all other sound. The bull charges madly from right to left, the camera among the spectators still above him; as he skids almost into the camera just beneath Black his movements seem at once frenzied and yet somehow remote-controlled. Lumet cuts to General Black in the stands, the right half of his face bathed in a bright white light. As the whine of the engines increases, the scene becomes more ominous: an unseen matador begins to lash and flay the bull, which stares at General Black. Fast cutting continues—there are thirty cuts in this hypnotic and splendidly paced sixty-five-second section, perhaps Lumet's finest opening sequence—as Lumet shows General Black, horror-stricken, leaning in a wind that seems to propel his body toward frame left, while six other spectators in straw hats and flowered shirts smile, enjoying the spectacle below them. While in the novel Black knows that the others are his military associates, Lumet indicts irrationality generally as the co-conspirator in the bull's victimization. The director next cuts quickly to the tortured bull in a close shot of the side of its head and massive body, its features now indistinguishable from its mass, similar to the last aerial view Black will see of New York, city of his human victims at the film's end.

As in the novel, neither we nor Black can see the identity of the matador, who now bears in from above the bull and rams the sword home several times. Each time the bull's head seems to respond in recognition; each time Black's face shudders as though he himself has been stabbed. Until the bull finally falls, each shot of Black shows his face surrounded by a grayer background. Finally his face, bathed in white light, is framed totally in blackness. The crowd now invisible, their cheers completely subsumed in the excruciating roar of the engines, Black gasps for breath, his eyes closed. But the bull demands to be seen, to be acknowledged, as Lumet's camera probes its dying hulk, seeking out its eyes, which are fixed upon Black. Then Lumet cuts directly to an extreme close-up of Black's own eyes, which now are but dark hulls, though the remainder of his face is as brightly lighted as before. Abruptly Black awakens sweating, as the jet scream abruptly ceases. The man of reason is thrust into a real world, where the consequences of military decisions in which he daily participates will have a terminal effect upon a particular segment of those whom the dream bull symbolizes.

Following the dream episode, one of the most surreal sequences in contemporary American cinema, Lumet does not utilize the mass of novelistic material in chapter 5 treating Black's social and graduate school background, his training under Professor Tolliver, and his meetings with Betty, his future wife, and Groteschele, his future military antagonist. Gone also are the Blacks' didactic speeches on nuclear policy at Senator Hartmann's party. Instead, Lumet concentrates upon the moral and psychological effect of the terrible dream on the rational, technological man. First, in silence the titles appear on the screen; all but the film's title are edged in white, but hollow, so that the mise-en-scène emerges visible through them. Just as Black will insist on every truth he sees during the terrible day to come, the camera finds his own ravaged face, through the titles, the wild eyes desperately seeking out his sleeping wife, then his children. The children's room is redolent of his own profession—a hanging Air Force Academy pennant, suspended model planes, pictures of aircraft. Black covers the son in the top bunk bed and does not awaken either son as he smiles, having restored order to his world, but he leaves the room only after a quick glance back in at them.

Following this episode, Lumet includes a scene completely original to the film between Black and his wife; their interaction here reveals not only Black's human stature but Lumet's artistic sensitivity, compared with many contemporary directors, in the handling of mature scenes of love and attachment between developed human beings. As Black dresses for his meeting in Washington, he says that he had "the dream again. It always ends at the same place. . . . sometime I'm going to see that matador, find out who he is. And when I do that's it, that's the end of me." As he approaches her bedside, they discuss his possibly resigning his commission to dispel the dream. Betty (Hildy Parks) suggests a romantic lunch together, which they haven't enjoyed for months. She is a woman in her forties, enormously attractive through her very warmth for him, her considerate awareness of his need to protect her and the children yet his concomitant need to continue work he considers crucial. At her suggestion of a day off, he comes toward her again: "In the middle of the week, that's immoral!" he responds to her subtle blandishments. Black himself is less attractive physically than in his humorous self-deprecation throughout the interchange. Bending over her, he smiles warmly, "You got me, you can get anything." The couple look at each other for a few seconds, then, as one, draw toward each other in an intense, devoted, and passionate kiss and embrace that is rare in American films: Lumet captures true *eros* between a physically average, middle-aged married couple whose passion for each other is very deep because of their expression of commitment as well as physical desire.

Gradually he rises from her and with soft urgency says, "I don't know what I'd do without you," sensing both her appreciation of his previous teasing and her gratitude for his awareness of her fear. Reaffirming their love, Betty says, "You wouldn't do very well, but there's no chance of that, is there?" "None at all," he replies, barely audible but with great tenderness, sensing her intimation that a possible change in his career might betoken a change in his personal life as well. The short scene concludes with a cut to Black, but from inside his closet from the unusual point of view of his official uniforms; he takes one that shows his one-star general status and quietly leaves. In a film about the possible triumph of reason and sacrifice in human affairs for the unfashionable purpose of the common human good, the quiet, yet sexually charged, scene between Black and his wife acts as a metaphor for the film's moral concerns. Here are no clashing bodies, but a conjoining of two mature loving persons. Such a joining occurs frequently in Lumet's films, whether between man and woman, as in *Lovin' Molly* and *Stage Struck,* or between man and man, as in *Dog Day Afternoon* and *Prince of the City,* revealing Lumet's stature as one of the few contemporary directors whose aesthetic vision is sufficiently mature to make interesting the less sensational aspects of human sexual connectedness. The scene's final shot re-emphasizes its moral resonance, showing Black in the air, flying a small plane to Washington for his meeting at the Pentagon. Pensively he looks down at the skyline of his beloved New York. The Empire State Building, which will become his target some hours hence, appears most prominently in his line of vision.

The next sequence in Lumet's film involves Walter Groteschele (Walter Matthau), in the novel "the earliest of the brilliant group of mathematical political scientists that developed after World War II, a group which later included such as Henry Kissinger, Herman Kahn."[33] In a well-condensed version of material in chapters 5 and 7, Lumet and screenwriter Walter Bernstein introduce Groteschele's concept of a winnable limited nuclear war, as the cold warrior entertains a posh Washington late-night cocktail party crowd with his positions on how the expected loss of a mere one hundred million Americans could perhaps ensure that American "culture" could emerge a "winner" in such a war. The novel presents Warren and Betty Black's remonstrances against Groteschele's sophisticated lunacy, including General Black's menacingly predictive comment, "I have the awful feeling that we are reconciled, both we and the Soviets, to mutual destruction. We are now rallying our different logics to support our identical conclusions. We will probably both get the results that we want" (99). Lumet, however, does not have the Blacks present at the party (which ends the same early morning that Black flies into Washington), allowing their viewpoint to be spoken by a less eloquent congressman. The film thus heightens Groteschele's chilling authority, in a sense seducing the audience with his artful arguments toward a subliminal worship of death, in sharp contrast with the Blacks' respect for *eros* and imaginative sympathy reflected in the previous scene. In the film, Groteschele affirms his narrow technocratism in words not in the novel: "I'm not a poet, I'm a political scientist who would rather have an American culture survive than a Russian one." While Groteschele next speculates for the crowd's delight upon who would survive after the carnage, Lumet shoots him at long range, directly beneath the statue of a white eagle, from behind the white shoulder of a glossy young socialite, Ilsa Wolfe (Nancy Berg), who seems fixated on his every word.

These visual ironies associate the nuclear propagandist with unconscious forces of patriotism and sexuality, and the remainder of the episode reveals, somewhat more credibly than the novel, the need for power and control that seems to drive Groteschele toward the thesis that, as the film's action unfolds, leads toward the inevitable horror of the concluding events. The party ends, and Groteschele finds Ilsa seated in his car. In the novel, Groteschele, stimulated by Ilsa's fascination for the power his technical expertise lends him, spills out his ruthless need to salve the knowledge of his own death by his games and fantasies of "the power to take everyone else with you" (124). Lumet's scene is less melodramatic and sentimental than the novel's. The convertible pulls away, viewed from a very high-angle shot through the leafy branch of a tree, but there is not to be the sexual motivation of the book. Groteschele's power fantasies cause him to project onto Ilsa his own neurotic needs, accusing her of wanting to salve her fears of death by pushing the final button that would "carry the mob with her" but so fearing such an act that she seeks instead the thrill elsewhere in a strong person who is not afraid. Instead of the novel's slap across Ilsa's face as Groteschele's punishment of her carnality, the action in Lumet's film is part of Groteschele's shifting of responsibility for his horrific visions upon her. He dimly understands her awareness of his need to make death "an entertainent" and perhaps cannot accept the game he seems doomed ever to play, buoyed by the acclaim and celebrity his military mind games bring him. Lumet's scorn for such celebrity-obsession, vividly conveyed in *Dog Day Afternoon*, among other films, is here heightened by Groteschele's revealingly vindictive hiss, "I'm not your kind," at Ilsa as he strikes her. The Pentagon theorist's false pride and his need for illusions to sustain his self-esteem, if still rather broadly presented by Lumet, contrast pointedly with the integrated personalities of General Black and the president, who, together with saner Soviet officials, will shortly attempt to undo the technological madness that has resulted in part from Groteschele's barbaric theories.[34]

These theories have taken concrete form in the giant Strategic Air Command War Room in Omaha, where, in chapter 2 of the novel, the reader meets General Bogan, his deputy, Colonel Cascio, and two visitors, Congressman Raskob and Gordon Knapp, president of Universal Electronics, who are present this day to examine, respectively, the efficiency and public cost of the gargantuan military machinery. While these characters and their setting are important throughout the novel and the film, Lumet significantly alters the ordering of the material, concentrating immediately upon Colonel Cascio, a relatively minor character in the novel, and assigning thematic prominence to the colonel's emotional background. In the book, Cascio's feeling of familial disgrace is presented through Bogan's random memories amid the presentation of his more socially respectable family background.

Lumet, however, immediately reveals in the "Omaha, 5:30 A.M.," sequence the complexity and terror of the war room through Cascio's demeanor and reactions, emphasizing the great significance of the human factor ever present in any consideration of atomic technology. Lumet shows Cascio (played by Fritz Weaver, in his first feature film performance) against the ominous backlighted shadows of the SAC instruments, separated from the camera by three levers. Under obvious emotional stress, he dials the telephone with excessive force, responding to the call of a drunken parent. Directly he makes an innocent airman a target, ordering him to button his shirt before the general sees him, symbolically expressing the repressions that drive him throughout the film.

Lumet devotes the remainder of this scene to Bogan's memory of his deputy's humiliation over Bogan's accidental discovery of Cascio's alcoholic parents; much of the action is original to the film and dramatizes convincingly Lumet's central theme of the catastrophic results of human irrationality. Driving to Cascio's sign-out address because he suddenly needs him, Bogan unexpectedly finds his subaltern in a slum tenement. Lumet's visual mastery of street scenes is evident here as Bogan (Frank Overton), seeking the correct address, enters a frame composed of a dirty gray background wall along which a line of shadow descends from top left to bottom right, along his head's path as he stoops to try to locate Cascio's name. Bogan stands, pensive, in the lighted portion of the frame; then Lumet cuts to a shot in back of the general, his arm touching a wire leading to the superintendent's buzzer. The wire is broken, and Bogan stands for a moment, feeling it. It is a splendid metaphor both for the lack of human connectedness Bogan is soon to observe when he enters Cascio's building and for the flawed technological connection in the machinery supervised by Cascio that will bring destruction to millions at the film's conclusion. Lumet next cuts to a hellish basement—the harsh lines and angles of the shot evoke Carl Theodor Dreyer, an early Lumet influence—and frames Bogan with trash cans and overhead pipes on his way to a dim apartment.[35]

As Bogan enters, Cascio is visible in rear frame, pouring contents from a liquor bottle into a sink. Bogan stands embarrassed, as Cascio's parents mouth clichés at his arrival. A crucifix is visible on the rear wall behind the bed, where the mother sits in a drunken stupor as the father hovers over her. Grabbing another bottle as he reluctantly leaves with Bogan, Cascio must listen to his father's shouted parting insults at his son's alleged elitism in being a military officer. Outside, Cascio almost forgets military protocol, nearly escaping into the car ahead of his superior officer, and once inside he can manage no extended communication with Bogan, despite the general's sympathetic attempts to divert his attention from his humiliation. Cascio's predilection for defensiveness and repression will later cost the Americans precious minutes in their attempt to help their Soviet counterparts stop the wayward American Vindicator bombers headed toward Moscow. One of Lumet's finest visual images in the film occurs just after both officers enter their car: as they drive away, Lumet's camera, at the level of the car's hood, reveals the street seeming to veer downward as a drunken, shabby man lumbers along. He glances for a second at the garbage can outside the door of the apartment building into which Cascio hurled his father's final liquor bottle, but he does not see the bottle and blindly passes on. This irony silently recapitulates Lumet's gathering imagery of the tragic lack of vision that so often crushes humankind in his films. Cascio has followed a difficult path out of his ghetto at too sharp a cost; still a victim of forces and pressures he dimly understands, in a military society placing insufficient value upon self-knowledge, the colonel will contribute his insecurities to a technological and human madness that, in a few hours, will nearly destroy civilization.

Lumet continues his focus upon the human element in the technological equation in the "Anchorage, 5:30 A.M." sequence, conveying the scientific information on the Vindicator bomber squadrons (68-75, 133ff.) through the character of Colonel Grady, who does not appear until nearly half-way through the novel, under somewhat altered circumstances. Grady (Edward Binns, a frequent member of the Lumet stock company of fine actors) whiles away the time with another older pilot playing pool until the start of their flight shift. Grady longs for earlier times when "you knew you were flying an airplane, not the other way around, like with these things"; he also complains that the young Vindicator crews are tending to facelessness, losing the individuality so crucial to him in flying and in war. "Open them up, you find they run on transistors," he says, and Lumet cuts to a group of young fliers in a gray barracks recreation room, sitting smoking, riffling magazines, eerily resembling one another as Grady has said. To Grady's lament that each time he goes up he must fly with a different crew, that these men "may be good at their jobs but you don't know *them*," his companion replies, "That's policy, Grady, it eliminates the personal factor." With everything now so complex, "you can't depend on people the same way." Just at this point the grating whine of jet engines that was heard over General Black's dream in the film's first sequence begins, and shown in a sharp low-angle shot, Grady asks his friend a question that the latter cannot answer: "Who *do* you depend on?"

Lumet's next cut delivers a possible answer: the last young crewman casually flips his jacket over his shoulder as the group goes out to the bomber squadron, as though disengaged from his action, removed from the implications of the next shot. The sequence ends with a cut to serial shots of six Vindicator bombers taking off in the early morning light, their snouts like arrowheads splitting the air, reminiscent of Hemingway's "mechanized doom" in *For Whom the Bell Tolls*, but of course far deadlier technologically than the planes of the earlier generation. They leap mechanically into the air toward frame right, and with the takeoff of the third, fourth, and fifth Vindicators, Lumet's camera hones progressively in on the bombers, intensifying their demonic energy and frightful power.[36] Accompanying the three fast cuts to the Vindicators is the sound of the screaming noise of their engines, contemporary machines in the garden that, in a few minutes and by accident of men and another machine, will be launched past the failsafe point toward the Soviet Union.

In addition to providing information concerning General Bogan and Colonel Cascio, the novel's long second chapter amply details the technological complexity of the Omaha War Room, the seemingly routine activation of its machinery by an unidentified blip on the SAC big screen, the officers' unqualified confidence in the infallibility of the fail-safe system (supposedly allowing only automatically transmitted information to the Vindicators through a fail-safe box in each plane activated only by presidential authorization), the unnoticed short-circuiting of a condenser in the fail-safe activating mechanisms, and the sudden discovery, after the UFO blip on the radar screen has been revealed as simply an off-course commercial vehicle, that one of the bomber groups has flown past its fail-safe point and is headed into the Soviet Union. Lumet, in the film's next major sequence, continues his emphasis upon human factors behind the technological accident leading to the unauthorized unleashing of the Vindicators. The people's representative, Congressman Raskob (Sorrell Booke, also featured prominently in *Bye, Bye Braverman*), probes General Bogan for information on exactly who is ultimately responsible for the momentous decisions that could be made in the war room, and Lumet's camera underscores Raskob's fears with visual correlatives that intensify both the gathering suspense and the director's moral concerns. As Bogan praises the sophistication of the SAC nerve center, the satellite spying devices, and the nuclear weaponry aboard each Vindicator, Raskob demands, "Who controls them?" while they, Cascio, and Knapp approach the screen, coming down a concrete stair sectioned into four enormous wings. Shot from sharp low angle as they descend, the four men seem crucified by concrete and steel; heavy blocks of metal and stone loom over them from every angle in the huge room. To Raskob's fear that the machinery "might get ideas of its own," Knapp can only reply, "Those are the chances you take with these systems. . . . it's in the nature of technology." Of the men present only the congressman foresees that the machines may "create situations" they have been designed to manage, and he later forces their designer, Knapp, to acknowledge this.

As Bogan attempts to reassure us that double checks are enforced on every machine in every situation, just at the top of the frame, inauspicious in deep background, Lumet reveals four gleaming machines, ominous Langian images whose whirring tapes may prompt Raskob's crucial question, so often implied throughout Lumet's work: "But who checks the checker? Where's the end of the line, general? Who's got the responsibility?" At his words, Lumet's camera poses a grim answer: behind Raskob is a gray wall whose sole visual detail is a computer diagram. After Bogan and Knapp hastily and simultaneously say, "The President" and "No one," before exchanging uncomfortable looks Raskob sums up: "The only thing everyone can agree on is that no one's responsible." By now the apparently routine UFO has been sighted, and six minutes must elapse before the Vindicators reach their fail-safe points. Throughout this scene, Lumet's fairness and balance are demonstrable, for Raskob's liberal view is not left unchallenged by other ominously relevant visual evidence. General Bogan reminds watchers of the big screen that all across the Pacific Ocean many Soviet submarines sail, each armed with nuclear warheads, the closest a mere fifty miles off San Francisco's coast. Immediately following Raskob's charge concerning human responsibility, the director cuts to the head of a V-shaped table in the Pentagon briefing room, where soon Secretary of Defense Swenson, another of the film's reasoned men, will be seated. The camera is aimed at the apex of the V, the position of Swenson's officially designated responsibility, but the wide part of the table extends out toward the camera as if to suggest another, more public, area of responsibility.

Here General Black, even before it is discovered that Group 6 has flown past fail-safe, argues with Groteschele at a briefing session that the concept of limited nuclear war is lunacy, that the mad logic of their war games has only increased the complexity and power of war technology beyond human power to oversee it. Despite pressure from Groteschele that Black is a "military dove, press would be interested," Black insists, "There's no such thing as a limited war anymore. . . . once those hydrogen bombs start to drop you won't be able to limit a

Sidney Lumet in command of his collaborative craft, at work on the set of his 1986 film *The Morning After.*

All film stills are reproduced courtesy of the Museum of Modern Art Film Stills Archive, New York.

Above, the naive assistant DA (Timothy Hutton, left) and the violent cop (Nick Nolte) stand in ironically equal oppression beneath heavy visual structures in *Q & A* (1990).

Opposite, the psychiatrist (Richard Burton) heals the deeply disturbed youth (Peter Firth) in *Equus* (1977).

The door between the agent (James Mason) and the suspected spy (Simone Signoret) is a symbol of betrayal and isolation in *The Deadly Affair* (1967).

The possibilities for intimacy are tenuous and demand risk as Val (Marlon Brando) cups the face of Lady (Anna Magnani) in *The Fugitive Kind* (1960).

This carefully arranged ensemble scene in *The Group* (1966) includes Libby (Jessica Walter), far left; Priss (Elizabeth Hartman), sixth from left; Lakey (Candice Bergen), sixth from right; and Kay (Joanna Pettet), third from right.

Separation in closeness:
Molly (Blythe Danner)
and Gid (Anthony Perkins)
in *Lovin' Molly* (1974).

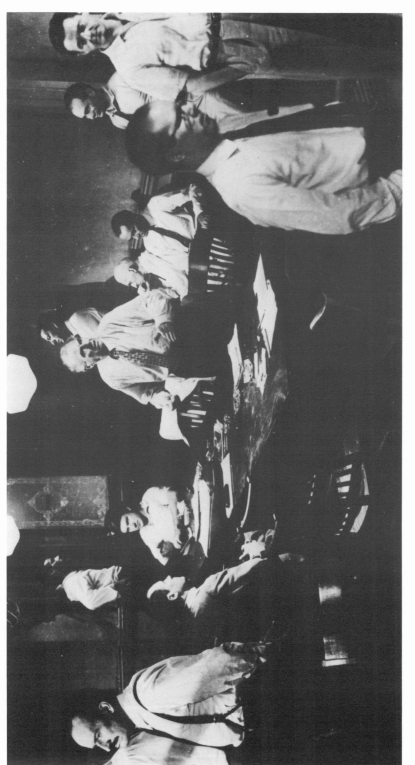

Lumet's skilled lighting and group composition are evident as eleven jurors distance themselves from Ed Begley's racism in *12 Angry Men* (1957).

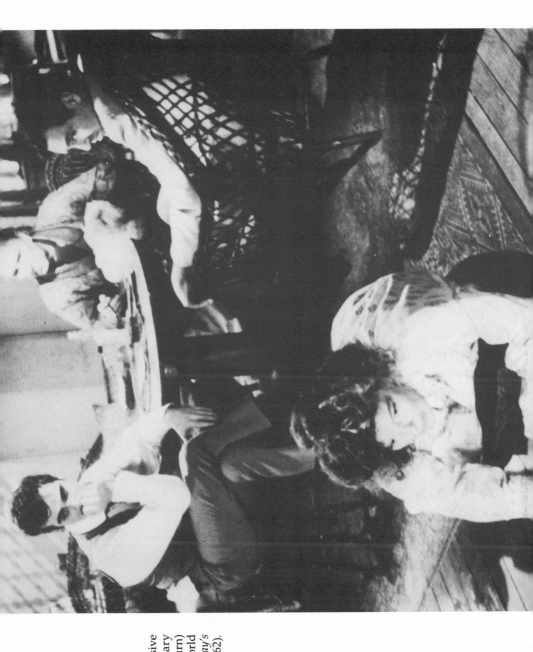

This typical, oppressive high-angle shot shows Mary Tyrone (Katharine Hepburn) denying the shadowed world of her men in *Long Day's Journey into Night* (1962).

Above, extreme close-up reveals the ultimate existential responsibility as the president (Henry Fonda) tries to avert nuclear war in *Fail Safe* (1964).

Opposite, backgrounded by others among the city's victims, a grieving Nazerman (Rod Steiger) is brought to life by the sacrifice of his assistant Jesus Ortiz (Jaime Sanchez) in *The Pawnbroker* (1965).

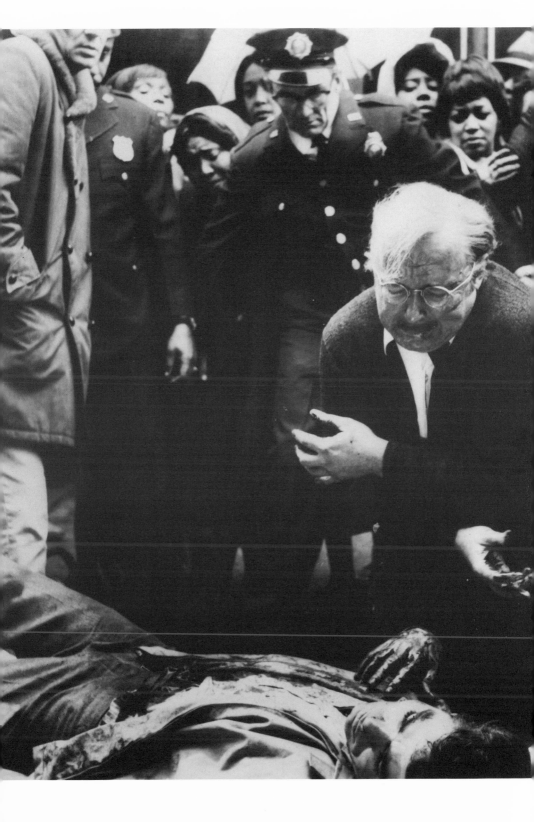

The lyrical visual structure and background setting of *The Sea Gull* (1968): from left, Masha (Kathleen Widdoes), Nina (Vanessa Redgrave), Arkadina (Simone Signoret), and Sorin (Harry Andrews).

A wry Morroe (George Segal) approaches the sadness of wisdom in *Bye, Bye Braverman* (1968).

Lumet's long shot provides a metaphor for both struggle and inhumanity in
The Hill (1965).

Artful lighting on Peter Finch as the mad TV prophet suggests the blended satire and farce in *Network* (1976).

The detective-informer (Treat Williams) runs everywhere and nowhere, pursued by his guilt, in *Prince of the City* (1981).

damn thing." Here Defense Secretary Swenson, physically crippled (only in the film) but the emotionally resilient final adviser to the president in crisis, will sift the arguments and subtly support General Black's counsel of reasoned and temperate action toward the Soviets for the goal of preventing universal nuclear devastation.

Perhaps Lumet's most interesting and suspenseful alteration of the novel is that, until almost half-way through the film, no one knows that the bombers have gone beyond U.S. control, whereas this information is definitely conveyed to the president a sixth of the way through the novel. Such structuring allows the director to build suspense to an unusually heightened degree; but more important, it gives Lumet ample room to represent character and idea, to allow, indeed even to force, emotional and intellectual responses in his audience, particularly through the actions and opinions of General Black. In the next scene, again in the Omaha War Room, with two minutes now until fail-safe, the still routine readiness preparations of Bogan and his staff begin to arouse trepidation in everyone present in the room. Continual sharp low-angle shots of the big screen and its images seem to engulf the characters, and the audience, in the very technology that will mislead them, foreshadowing Black's direst fears. As Bogan seeks calmly to explain to Raskob and Knapp that the unidentified blip is probably simply an airliner blown off course, the suspicious Cascio, long inured to social humiliation, constructs yet another war game, supposing that the UFO is really a Soviet rocket very much on its intended course. Suddenly all are relieved as the big screen flashes the words that the UFO is, indeed, an off-course commercial aircraft. But Lumet holds the shot of the full-scale board for several seconds, revealing the entire world littered with blips, images of potential destruction.

Lumet now cuts to Colonel Grady and his crew, poised at their fail-safe point. In the novel's ninth chapter, Grady is centrally occupied, before the jarring signal activating his fail-safe mechanism, with reverie about the aesthetic grandeur of the Vindicators and his feelings of personal mastery and satisfaction at flying what will probably be the last humanly operated SAC bomber. But in the film, Lumet continues to examine the personal factors underlying the imminent mechanical failure. The youthful copilot, Thomas, attempts to repress and to conceal his feelings of anxiety as the experienced and more personally integrated pilot tries to ease him over the morning's prolonged holding at fail-safe point. Thomas even feels he must apologize: "I was just calculating fuel, sir," he says, as he looks at Grady with distaste and Lumet's camera holds the copilot at a low angle. Grady, by a sharp glance, expresses silent disbelief at Thomas's lack of emotional involvement in their flying and his insecurity at what he must consider the older man's temerity in broaching human feelings. Grady asks how the rest of the squadron is doing and, in a veiled disparagement of another senior airman, Flynn, the pilot of the Vindicator carrying decoys and evasive-action equipment, Thomas replies that all are in proper formation, "even Number 6." Grady praises Flynn as "half man, half bird," in a kindly, unstated contrast with the cool Thomas and with Sullivan, the equally emotionally removed navigator. This reference will become symbolically important near the film's end when, with terrible irony, only the imaginativeness of the senior "seat-of-the-pants" pilots, Grady and Flynn, can manage to accomplish the destruction of Moscow.

Lumet's compressed settings and Gerald Hirschfeld's closeted camera work in the Vindicator episodes effectively convey the mechanistic aspects of the emotional atmosphere in Colonel Grady's cockpit.[37] Lumet employs a similar motif, to reveal rigid military command procedures, in the war room when, suddenly, a circuit blows in the master control box's fault indicator. As Bogan has been directing Cascio in the simplest military routines, Cascio now ritualistically orders a subordinate to replace the control box component. In Grady's cockpit, the blown circuit, uncorrected by the new component, sets off the fail-safe mechanism. He cannot get through on any radio frequency to the war room because, as the Soviets later admit, one of the new Soviet war games, a special jamming device, has that morning been successfully tested against all SAC bombers at fail-safe points. As in The Hill, Lumet in this scene reveals his continuing interest in the ways that human mechanisms deny spontaneity, unnecessarily stunting organic responses to the world. As the fail-safe machine mistakenly determines human destinies, Thomas pointlessly continues verbal rituals "by the book," and Grady reaches a bandaged hand into his flight jacket for the top secret orders, bound with an absurdly official-looking ribbon, that disclose Moscow as their target. In marked contrast with the previous mechanical behavior, Grady, held by Lumet in extreme close-up for five seconds, pauses, his eyes closed, enduring the emptiness of command's responsibility, before giving the order to approach and penetrate Soviet airspace.

Lumet's next major sequence introduces Buck, the Russian translator (Larry Hagman), and the president (Henry Fonda), far later than they are encountered in the novel. While the events in the subsequent action are quite similar to those in the novel, this section reveals the director's ability to render visually interesting material that occurs in

circumscribed space. Before Buck and the president enter the elevator
that will take them to the emergency war room containing the telephone hot line to the Soviet premier, Buck must show a Secret Service
man a small scar on his wrist to prove his correct identity. All bureaucratic procedures must be followed, even though Buck is the only
person who can possibly save this situation by his power of astute and
sensitive communication, work that must begin very quickly. Then he
and the president step into the elevator and the doors close behind
them. Lumet frames the two heads from the rear in a close-up two-
shot, then cuts to an extreme close-up of the back of the president's
head against the background of the gray steel elevator door in front of
him. Enclosed but not trapped by his cramped environment, the head
turns to the right, and the president greets Buck, whose taut face is
seen in side view: instead of the casual greeting in the novel (60),
reminding the reader of their meeting in chapter 1, Lumet's president is
direct, yet not urgent, "Hello Buck, how's your Russian today?" underscoring subtly this day's crucial need for human excellence, sensitivity
to nuance, and professional responsibility at the highest level. As they
descend to the war room beneath the White House, Lumet shoots the
president in left frame, just after two rapid intercuts to his translator's
understandably nervous countenance, as Buck removes his glasses
and rubs the sides of his face. Lumet holds for several seconds the shot
of the president's face, however, so that we can clearly see its reflection,
faint but visible in the surface of the gray steel door. It is a time when, as
in many of Lumet's films from 12 Angry Men to Q & A, if humans are to
have a chance for survival, they must come face to face with themselves
and must assume ultimate responsibility.

The room that the two men enter is not clearly described in the
novel, but Lumet's president makes two immediate references to its
hellish aspect. Lumet has seldom used confined space to better effect:
the emergency war room is stark and gray-walled, sparsely furnished
with a desk on which sits a communication system and over which
looms an oppressively large speaker. The room seems unusually
sharply angled, containing at least five corners that, at various times,
will exert maximal cinematic pressure upon the president. (Fonda's
character is never given a name, other than that of his titular social role,
although in the novel the national leader is a thinly veiled representation of John Kennedy.) A low-angle shot of the president against one
wall and a corner with two shadows of him visible against the wall
accentuates both his isolation and the gravity of the responsibility he
faces. At a telephone call from General Bogan in Omaha, Lumet's
camera glides in a slow pan right to left from behind the president onto

the emergency war room's big screen. Then the camera pans around to face him, with the useless communications equipment in the dominant position in the foreground at frame left, separating him from us as he is told that no radio contact is yet possible with the Vindicators. He demands "Why?!" as Lumet shoots at a sharp high angle down at the telephone over the president's left shoulder to the big screen whose images increasingly will dominate him.

Lumet now cuts to an extreme close-up of the telephone, the wire leading into it clearly visible like the broken wire earlier handled by General Bogan, as he hears Bogan's admission that he does not know why. The director increases the emotional pressure with the next sharply low-angle cut to the president, pressed in between the overhead speaker and the telephone system that visually cuts him off at chest level as he demands of Bogan whether it is possible that the fail-safe system may be giving the Vindicators a false go signal. When he learns that the sound of his voice can bring back the planes only within the next five minutes, so well have the airmen been drilled in a fail-safe procedure designed to defend against the enemy's trying to imitate the president's voice in a crisis, the camera tilts upward to regard four large machines, with lights in the form of a cross above them, and settles on the big screen showing the Vindicators significantly beyond their fail-safe point. As Bogan informs the president that the final hope is to have the accompanying fighter planes at fail-safe point ordered in to attempt to shoot down the Vindicators, Lumet cuts to an extreme six-second close-up of the president. He asks, "Who gives that order?" His eyelids flick upward as Lumet holds him in another prolonged close-up, listening to Bogan's inevitable response.

After General Black convinces Swenson and the group at the Pentagon that the only alternative to widespread nuclear holocaust is to advise the president to order in the fighters, the president so orders. His decision is rational in view of the fact that the Soviets must be made aware that an accident has occurred and that the United States is trying to correct it; but he also realizes that if the fighters, barely faster than the Vindicators and presently far behind them, are to have any chance of catching them, they will have to use afterburners, thus expending all their fuel and guaranteeing the pilots' deaths in the Arctic Ocean. Lumet's camera follows the president to a corner of the room by a couch, where he stands silent, held for several seconds, hands down in front of his body, pressed visually into the corner by the speaker above and by the couch below and even by a briefcase that hems him in from lower left frame. The emotional cost to the president of this decision is also revealed by a contrasting shot in Omaha of Knapp, the designer of the big screen's technology, enraptured at the sight of the images of the fighters' formation turning perfectly following the president's decision. Congressman Raskob stares at Knapp in disbelief, but Lumet also reveals the cultural inevitability of what Knapp represents: as Raskob stares, he is framed by a computer diagram and one of the machines on the wall. Lumet's comprehensive vision continues in the next brief scene as the men in Omaha and the Pentagon attempt to assess the causes of the crisis and probable Soviet reaction and response. It is Knapp (in Russell Collins's fine performance, among many splendidly conceived minor roles directed by Lumet in the film) who, with Black, proposes the most sensible view of the dilemma's cause. His voice mixed with adoration and fear, Knapp admits that the probable mechanical failure was bound to happen, because humans cannot always control machines. "The machines work so fast, they are so intricate, the mistakes they make are so subtle." General Black has official and technical evidence for the basis of his disturbing dream.

The complete absence of a musical background to Lumet's *Fail Safe* is nowhere more effective than in the brief scene of the fighters, flaming out one by one, firing their missiles in futility, too far away from the Vindicators to accomplish their mission, and falling like mechanical birds on extended wings, arching gracefully into the ocean. In a terrible long silence, Lumet cuts separately to Black, Bogan, and the president, as the fighters' images flicker out on the big screen. Lumet cuts to Swenson at low angle as he gently says to the president (in lines not in the novel), with understatement typical of the four central men of reason, "The fighters have not succeeded, they have gone down into the sea." In one of the film's most memorable compositions, Lumet cuts sharply down-angle to a despairing president, now seated, nearly crumpled into the couch, cornered by grayish walls and, in frame right, by what appears to be a metallic electrical fixture suggestive of the form of a clock, with black markings near what would be twelve o'clock were it a timepiece. To frame left appears a large wooden frame in another corner of the room angling in upon the president, the pressures upon him nearly unbearable as he listens to Black offer the military opinion that, according to many earlier studies, one or two of the Vindicators will evade Soviet defense and get through to bomb Moscow.

Lumet uses a similar framing device to one he used in *12 Angry Men* when at one point Fonda is framed within a door outline, to accentuate the president's integrated sense of responsibility and command as he decides the time has come to use the hot line to talk to the Soviet premier. His instructions to Buck to strive to translate not only content

but also nuance, tone, and emotions seem almost didactically to reinforce Lumet's theme of the necessity of clear and rational communication among reasoned human beings if the world is to survive. Lumet's
president, however, unlike the character in the novel, makes the advis-
ing ironic; the president, perhaps fearing that the young translator will
come apart with fear, adds casually, "It's big but it still depends on what
each of us does . . . history lesson number one."

The president removes the large, cumbersome hot-line telephone
from the desk and unbuckles it, as Lumet shoots the action from low-
angle, the telephone looming out at us so that it visually diminishes the
president in size, though he is positioned slightly above it in the frame.
The composition emphasizes at once the distance and separation the
contraption places between the national leader and the camera and the
significance of such communications devices upon our destinies. Then
in tight two-shot, with the greater amount of light upon the telephone,
the two men set to work, attempting to convince the premier that the
technical crisis is not part of a general planned attack upon the Soviet
Union. While Lumet's powerful scene of the initial hot-line conversation closely follows the novel's action, some additions further
illustrate his emphasis on the theme of the necessity for and inevitable
isolation of responsibility. After the president concludes by giving the
premier the information that Moscow is the Vindicators' target and that
one or two of the bombers will most probably reach the city, Lumet
shows him quietly pouring a glass of water for himself, then pushing
the water tray over to Buck. He does not pour the harried translator a
glass; in Lumet's stern, yet dignified, conception of the novel, that is
the tired Buck's own prerogative and responsibility. Silent, the two
men are shown in their awful isolation, the president against a blank
wall, the translator against a corner; then Lumet holds them in two-
shot, at a sharp high angle.

The suspense is heightened by Lumet's change in making the
premier speak through Buck's own halting, nuanced translation: Buck
must translate for both men while enacting as best he can the tone, as
well as the content, of the premier's statements and feelings. (Larry
Hagman, a competent actor throughout his career, defines his finest
performance, as have other actors before and after him, under Lumet's
careful and sensitive direction.) The president, in responding to the
premier's demand for proof of his sincerity, lest Soviet generals persuade him to launch a retaliatory ICBM attack on the United States,
suggests that the difficulty in his communicating with the Vindicators
may lie in some special Soviet radio-jamming device. In distinguished
close shots, Lumet cuts to and holds an extreme close-up of the presi-

dent's mouth as he says with great urgency, "Is it *possible, could* it have happened?" and then cuts to another close-up of the president's left eye and left ear with the telephone as he awaits the premier's gradual, grudging admission of the radio jamming that morning.

Dialogue not in the novel supports this visual emphasis upon means of communication necessary to humankind's continuance. As Buck whispers to the president that he overhears the premier's generals demanding that he not reveal the existence of the radio-jamming technology, the president sharply retorts, "We're paying for our mutual suspicions, Mr. Chairman. . . . We can't afford not to trust one another." As the premier admits the existence of this new war game that even he did not know about, the president pleads, "Why *this* time?" The premier lamely replies that the Soviet computers told them that this American approach to fail-safe might underlie a real attack plan. As the president convinces him to lift the jamming device, the premier, now subdued and sorrowful, finishes, "Probability, the law of averages . . . they have their own logic, it is not . . . human but it is positive, so we listen." Such binary thinking has been so instilled into the minds of the Vindicator crews that, when the jamming is lifted, the president cannot convince Grady to listen beyond a few seconds to his plea to return to base, and the likelihood increases that Moscow will be destroyed.

Lumet swiftly moves through the novel's final sixty suspenseful pages, heightening visually, as well as by some additional material, the novel's subjects and themes. The premier accepts the president's offer of a special telephone line from Omaha's SAC headquarters to the Soviet Union to assist Soviet defenses in trying to shoot down the remaining Vindicators. As the president contemplates the difficulties this will cause among the generals in both countries, Lumet's camera pans behind his left shoulder, showing Buck at the end of a table that now seems much longer than before. This change in lenses reinforces both societies' almost insurmountable difficulties in achieving adequate understanding with one another. As a telephone link is completed that includes the Soviet ambassador at the United Nations in New York and the American ambassador in Moscow, the president reminds Black, his college classmate, of the Abraham and Isaac legend they learned in chapel, ordering Black to a nearby airbase where instructions will await him. Black seems to sense what will be demanded of him when the president casually asks if Black's beloved wife is now in New York. Huskily pledging his ultimate obedience, Black abruptly leaves for the airbase, even before the camera can record the event: Lumet shows only a shot of the door swinging upon the

dreamer who will soon know the identity of the matador. For this—
though he realizes that his own wife is presently in New York—is the
president's final necessary play in the game: if Moscow is destroyed,
then he will order Black to drop from his SAC bomber nuclear warheads equal in number to those that have decimated Moscow upon
New York City. Both world leaders will know of the mutual destruction
by the shriek of their two ambassadors' telephones melting from the
heat of the blasts. The Soviets will have incontrovertible proof of the
Americans' sincerity, and complete world annihilation can be avoided.

Lumet faithfully adapts the novel regarding Omaha's cooperation
with Soviet generals in attempting to destroy as many of the bombers
as diminishing time will allow, including melodramatic additions of
Groteschele's stereotypical reactionary rantings and Colonel Cascio's
descent from fantasies of humiliation to paranoia under the strain of
divulging American military secrets, rare instances of excess in an
otherwise brilliant film.[38] A fine variation depicts the final conversation
between General Bogan and his Soviet counterpart, General Koniev,
as they work together to down the last Vindicator. Ironically, the
ground bureaucracies of both sides are more efficient than either's
military technology, for aides immediately provide each general with
the other's dossier. As they wait on the telephone, they fall to remem-
brances of their mutual enjoyment of walking in London and of the
city's history, moments before two of the world's great cities, with their
histories, are to vanish. As Bogan turns the pages of the dossier to
pictures of Koniev's wife and children, he cannot bear to ask their
present location. Lumet also adds an effective brief scene involving
Colonel Grady's wife, who begs her husband to turn back during his
scheduled call-in to Omaha just prior to reaching the target. But her
plea that there is no war, that nothing could force her to lie to him, falls
upon a mind so well trained that it is closed even to her; Mrs. Grady,
desperate, stares beseechingly at an aide standing next to her in the
war room while she talks. Grady's eyes close in pain, but then his rote
training causes him to quench the emotions he so wants to trust and to
snap off the radio. His wife's last utterance is an anguished, wordless
scream in recognition that modern military civilization's repression of
the instinctual causes the barbaric to rule. The scene ends with extreme
high-angle, desolate shots of Bogan, then of Buck and the president.

Lumet's major changes from the novel in the last two sequences
rank the film's conclusion among the director's most distinguished. In
the novel, the Soviet premier, after ordering his missiles to stand
down, attempts to alleviate both his guilt and his portion of the responsibility for the probable slaughter of millions of innocent people, and

he and the president agree that no human beings are to blame, except for placing too much trust in computerized systems. Suddenly the screech of the ambassador's telephone in Moscow signals the destruction of the city, and General Black acts on the president's order to sacrifice New York—"A chance, the only chance, for peace" (283). Then Black poisons himself with his suicide kit. The novel ends with the president's official commendation of his friend's valor and "supreme conception of duty to his country and to mankind" (284). Lumet's conclusion is less comforting and conclusive and, therefore, free of sentimentality. As is usual with this director, his meditative eye, almost without compromise, pauses upon and considers the starkest implications of his premises. In the film, the president and his translator make idle talk to stave off insanity while they wait, hoping that Soviet defenses will bring down the remaining Vindicator in time to spare Moscow. As the premier calls in, announcing that he has ordered his ICBMs to stand down, Lumet's camera hones in to a side-view close-up of the president's face, then Buck's. Their faces are in darkness, except for traces of light at the edges of their communicative eyes and lips, which shortly will be used to seek the most unpalatable truths. After the premier says, "And yet this was nobody's fault, no human being did wrong, no one is to be blamed," the president snaps out a demurrer to the bureaucratic shuffle: "We're to blame, both of us. We let our machines get out of hand. . . . what do we say to them, Mr. Chairman, 'accidents will happen'? I won't accept that. . . . men are responsible, we're responsible for what happens to us. Today we had a taste of the future. Do we learn from it or do we go on the way we have? What do we do, Mr. Chairman? What do we say to the dead?"

As the president's words begin, the camera begins a very slow pan left, and both the president's face and Buck's become more frontally visible, suggesting the enormous responsibility that must be carried by both men for the imminent destruction they have allowed to happen. This president is no Boy Scout; he sees uncompromisingly that he is responsible just as much as anyone. The subtle camera movement, the lighting, and the translator's visual replacement of the unseen premier emphasize the necessity in political affairs for continually clear and courageous seeing and speaking. The nervous voice of the American ambassador and the sudden screaming of his melting phone as the Vindicator finally destroys its target makes indelible the necessity for the prompt removal of the barriers erected between the two countries. And Lumet's next camera movements clarify the necessity for mutually shared political responsibility, as he cuts quickly from the president's horrified reaction to Omaha and then the Pentagon, with

identical swift pans over the desolate Bogan and his staff and then over
Swenson (whose wife is also in New York this day), Groteschele, and
several officers and staffers. Lumet finally cuts to the president, head
bowed to the left, the hot-line telephone hanging listlessly in his hand.
The harsh shriek of the burning phone in Moscow continues through
these rapid visual movements, then ceases suddenly.

From the stillness of General Black's bomber cockpit, after he
receives the order to drop the bombs and releases his crew from the
horror by accepting total responsibility for flying the plane and releasing the warheads, Lumet visually echoes Black's ten-second count-
down to the bombing. He cuts to a panorama of New York from Black's
bomb scope, and then to a series of ten flashes of moving, vital life in
the city: two lovers in Central Park; a children's group at the Bronx Zoo,
with a little black girl sprinting joyously across the seal pond; two taxi
drivers arguing about a small accident; a Hispanic dancer shimmying
to the music of a group of bongo percussionists in Spanish Harlem,
with a young woman beside her watching closely; a sharp low-angle
shot of a priest talking to an elderly couple in front of St. Patrick's; two
little girls frolicking on a cement city playground amid traffic noise; a
Park Avenue doorman walking a poodle on the curb in front of his
building; a black man and a bald white man conversing in front of a
Times Square discount store; two eight-year olds, one white, one
black, looking at each other on a street on the lower East Side; and
pigeons on a pavement in center city. With seconds to go, Black stabs
his finger on the poisoned needle before releasing the bombs. In a
gutteral moan as if in his dream, he speaks to his wife and realizes that
he is the destroyer, having allowed himself, despite his doubts and his
reasoned questioning, to serve a senseless technological war machine
and is now to be used by it, however heroically, against the vulnerable,
the defenseless, to perform the ultimate avengement of such systems
upon feeling, humanity, life itself.

Lumet ends *Fail Safe* with a stunning reiteration of the images we
have just seen of this pulsating life, without sensationalism and without Kubrick's evasive techniques, as the audience is forced visually to
experience the ceasing of human life. The bomber poises directly atop
the Empire State Building. Lumet cuts to a three-second shot of the
pigeons nibbling, then, as one, alerted to something ominous, beginning to take off, fluttering upward amid a loud noise of rustling wings,
surrounding unnoticing humans, until a freeze-frame stops their flight
in silence. The director then uses nine swooping zoom-shots (now a
visual cliché, but little used in the mid-1960s) of one-half second each,
catching the nine enactments of human passion, love, and dignity in an

instant of precious, terribly fragile life before an almost instantaneous freeze-frame, as in the background the faint sound of an engine's roar emerges. The lovers smile at one another, his hand gently around her waist; a seal just begins its leap into the zoo's pool; a taxi driver poises in midshout at another; the Hispanic dancer is joined by the formerly watching friend, arms upraised, now sexually vibrant, entering the dance; the matron raises her hand to shake the hand of her priest; the little girl's cry of joy as her head is thrown back, the other's arm around her, is abruptly truncated; the poodle just begins to raise its head a trace to the right; the background of the store reveals the word PLAY to suggest the moral idiocy of what is just about to happen; in extreme close-up the black boy's eye gazes at the white boy. Then Lumet cuts to all-dominant whiteness, blankness, with complete silence, and then to all-encompassing blackness, as the whine of the Vindicator's jet engines is heard over the incessant cheering of a crowd, as at a bullring. By celebrating life without sentimentality in all its tenuousness, by suggesting the possibilities for human reason and dignity amid ignorance, incompetence, and meaningless carnage, Lumet heightens and intensifies the novel's implicit concern with the tragic nature of the human condition.

The Pawnbroker: The Insistence of Memory

In any consideration of Lumet's finest literary films, critics generally think that his 1965 adaptation of Edward Lewis Wallant's 1961 novel, *The Pawnbroker,* occupies a high place, because of Lumet's handling of themes concerning the Holocaust and of his directorial skills in integrating characterization, societal ironies, visual symbolism, and the ambiguities of time. More loosely adapted from its literary source than such films as *Lovin' Molly* and *Long Day's Journey into Night,* Lumet's *Pawnbroker* perhaps surpasses Wallant's excellent novel in its realistic and expressionistic representation of the personal costs of repression and self-delusion, of the harrowing price that must be paid by people who attempt—albeit through the most understandable of motives—to become less than full human beings. Through his shaping of Morton Fine and David Friedkin's sensitive screenplay and his memorable direction of Rod Steiger's luminous performance as the psychologically scarred Sol Nazerman, who has lost everything he loved to the Nazi death camps and now can feel involvement with nothing, Lumet creates from a superior novel an independent work of cinematic art that stands, with *Long Day's Journey, Fail Safe,* and *12 Angry Men,* as one of the director's most distinguished literary cinematic achievements.

Lumet's variations from the novel in the opening stages of the action (corresponding to Wallant's first two chapters) significantly indicate his intent to create a separate artistic work, though, typically of Lumet, one fully respectful of the spirit of the original. Wallant's narrator opens the novel in Nazerman's present—the late 1950s—telling us of the heavy crunching of Nazerman's feet as he plods along the Harlem River toward the pawnshop and of the observant "small, skinny Negro" who thinks, "that man *suffer!*"[39] before the pawn-broker's entrance into the shop, his first conversations with his assistant, Ortiz, the initial entry of the lost souls of the city's streets who seek cheap dreams for their oratorical awards and blasted table radios, and Sol's angry confrontation with exploitive and dependent suburban relatives. These early chapters end with Nazerman's hoped-for escape to his "cool, immaculate bed" (28) after the narrator's observation "The shop creaked with the weight of other people's sorrows; he abided" (25).

In contrast, the film opens with a silent sequence, shot in slow-motion, set deep in Nazerman's past. Two small children run through a field, the boy's hands reaching for a butterfly. Their lovely young mother walks away from a stream, toward a picnicking elderly Jewish couple, waving and seeming to call out to her husband (a much younger-appearing Steiger), filled with love for her family and her children's innocence. Almost unnoticeable amid such peace, however, are the leaves of the tree above the young woman's head as she waves; blowing in the breeze, the leaves of the bottom branch almost engulf her. The young husband comes toward her and toward the camera, grabbing the children up in his arms and swinging them around and around until suddenly the boy's face reflects a look of fear.[40] Just before the boy's reaction, Lumet shows the old man in medium deep frame, separated from us by strands of high grass that create a well-defined and confining plane of space. At the boy's reaction, Lumet abruptly stops the slow-motion, cutting to the old couple, their chessboard and tablecloth seeming to run downhill and out of the front of the frame, their vulnerability accentuated by the slightly low camera angle that ironically undercuts the audience's typical association of authority connected with such up-angle shots. Through these wordless intro-ductory actions and camera placements, Lumet sets the film's tone as one of steady movement downward from expectation to disillusion-ment, from Nazerman's apparent security toward his pressing aware-ness of the immanence of his past.

The film's next sequence continues Lumet's marked departure from the novel, as the director quickly cuts to the present day: from a long establishing shot we observe a suburban scene with eleven identical houses, all yards fenced off in neat geometric designs, and Nazerman seated lifelessly on a lounge chair in one of the many backyards. As the camera slowly tracks in on Nazerman, he is sharply framed at four angles by the fence post behind him, a telegraph pole to frame left, a steel utility pole in front frame, and an almost leafless tree in frame right, caught, as we will soon observe, by the economic trap he has built himself in his effort to separate himself from life and human feeling. The ensuing scene with Nazerman's dependent relatives echoes much of the action in chapter 2 of the novel, except that Lumet sets it outdoors. By moving the action to the backyard, the director does not merely "open up" this section of the novel but ironically suggests that these comfortable suburbanites will gain little benefit from proximity to the natural world because their behavior is so conditioned and ritualized. As Nazerman's sister-in-law, Bertha, offers him a lemonade and a section of the *New York Times* in preparation for her extortion of yet more money from him for the family's hoped-for trip to Europe, the camera angles sharply down on the pawnbroker, isolating him in a corner at the left of the frame. Soon afterward, "Uncle Sol" is framed from above by four sets of telephone wires as well as four additional sets of wires at the top of the frame, and, a moment later, as Sol spurns both the drink and the newspaper, his head seems pressed in by the harshly angled steel tubing of his chair. Nazerman seems as if lost in a dream, oppressed by his family yet cut off from them, as from the neighbor seen watering his grass in the distant background.

As Lumet satirizes the bourgeois depths to which the sacrifices of the Holocaust have fallen, there seems yet some hope in the younger generation of Nazerman's relatives. Nazerman's nephew, Morton, more prominent in the novel than in the film, is revealed here as estranged, like the pawnbroker, from the rest of the family, as he sits on the fence near Sol, teased by the family for his interests in art and painting. Morton's sister, Joan, though she listens to bland popular music on her transistor radio and fantasizes about the Danish modern furniture she wishes to buy for her impending marriage, emerges as more sensitive here than in the novel. She taunts Morton's art, and then, in a scene only in the film, flaunting her physical charms at the camera, steals her brother's paintings of nudes and runs by Nazerman's chair, showing her uncle the pictures. While she seems to possess only a realistic aesthetic sense (she comments, "Don't you know, Morton, girls just aren't built that way?"), Lumet suggests her real motive as Nazerman puts his arms up over his head when she runs by him, as if to ward off the visual sexuality she offers her uncle. Joan may sense Nazerman's isolation from humanity and attempt subtly to stimulate him back into some sort of response. This surmise gains probability as, in a scene original to the film, Bertha mentions the approach of the twenty-fifth anniversary of Nazerman's marriage to her lovely sister Ruth, and Joan testily reminds her mother that "Uncle Solly knows how beautiful, Mother; he was married to her."

At this, Lumet makes his first two of four jarring intercuts to the pawnbroker's past, as Nazerman's long-dead wife (the comely dark Ruth of the wordless opening sequence) appears in two staccato flash shots beneath the tree, which each last but one-fifth of a second onscreen and are each juxtaposed to Sol's reactions to Bertha as she insensitively repeats her comment about the approaching wedding anniversary. As Bertha describes Ruth's beauty, the third flash cut lasts only a second, but the fourth lasts just a tenth of a second, visually suggesting Nazerman's subliminal need to repress the memory of Ruth's beauty, even of her existence.[41] Yet Lumet makes the pawn-broker more sympathetic than his family because of his realism in some things: as Bertha and her educator-husband attempt to connive him into financing their trip to Europe and apostrophize the Continent with clichés about its "charm" being lent by age, Nazerman sar-castically refers to its atmosphere as "rather like a stink." Just at this point, Joan, a rare organic force in his family, struts provocatively into the camera with her coffee, allowing us to see only Nazerman's right arm and leg. Not only is the pawnbroker cut off from sexual feeling, but his bourgeois family, save Morton and occasionally Joan, separate him further through their affectation, wanting more to "do" the Old World than to see it as Nazerman considers it really to have been.[42]

Lumet defers until the film's third major sequence the social and moral stink in which Nazerman spends his days. Over the film's credits, the director shows the pawnbroker driving to Harlem to begin his day's work. Backed by Quincy Jones's apt jazz scoring, Nazerman drives through the grainy seaminess of Harlem: black men lounge purposelessly in front of bars, a man carries a window that reflects the detritus of the streets, dirty sidewalks, old newspapers filling curbs, garbage cans. The camera shows the streets from the viewpoint of Nazerman's darkened face, observing storefronts filled with old sneakers and old coats and oppressive building structures, like the elevated train tracks, that form such a prominent visual part of the film's final sequence. Parking in front of a fence on 119th Street, Nazerman walks toward the camera in a very long shot, past a litter-filled field, toward the shop, shot from high angle as if to emphasize his ironic status as an unconscious victim in this scene of social victimiza-

tion. Nazerman, slumped slightly, walks along the compressed corridor of the street, pressed in by the dirty buildings, their top edges
angling back toward rear frame making even narrower the path Nazerman has chosen to walk, accompanied only by the sound of the
continual rattling of the elevated train at frame right. Shading his eyes
from two small black girls who also move toward us, as he touches his
glasses we see no wedding ring on his left hand.

Lumet's silent title sequence is one of his most memorable studies
in human desolation. Nazerman shares this isolation, as Wallant underscores in the novel, with the people of the streets whom he exploits
through his pawnbroking business, though he cannot yet understand
this. Lumet captures this effectively at the end of the title sequence, as,
cutting to one of the apartments across from the elevated railway, up
the street from the pawnshop, he shoots over the shoulder of a middle-
aged Hispanic woman down at the street. In deep frame Nazerman
slouches slowly toward the shop just after the train has passed in that
direction. Lumet's fine compositional detail associates Nazerman with
the mechanical object: the pawnbroker is framed by the building and
the elevated railway, and through the bars on the woman's window
just to her left; in deep frame Nazerman seems fenced-in by two light
poles at the end of the street toward which he proceeds. The director's
depth composition reveals Nazerman as a man apart and yet unwittingly in relationship to the flow of street humanity to which the
woman is solidly joined. As this scene continues, the woman is revealed as the long-suffering mother of Jesus Ortiz, Nazerman's assistant; to her Ortiz vows his intent to leave a life of petty street crime
for a "strictly legit" job in the pawnshop.

It is only after these sequences establishing Nazerman's isolation
and pursuit by his past that Lumet returns to the material in the novel's
first chapter. The director shows Nazerman, described by Wallant as "a
man with no allegiances" (7), in relation to Ortiz, who is ambitious to
please the pawnbroker and to learn his trade, and to the two young
men trying to pawn, respectively, the old oratorical trophy and a
worthless radio. But Lumet visually reveals both the pawnbroker and
the street youths as victims of their sociopsychological environment:
both master and man are shot through layers of wire screening. In fact,
Lumet's first shot of Nazerman shows him, from slightly high angle,
seemingly trapped by his barred windows behind the counter. Jesus
Ortiz is also frequently so revealed, as if to emphasize the shared union
of the street's victims. As the pawnbroker summarily dismisses his first
morning customer, the young white man with the oratorical award,
Lumet shoots Nazerman backed also by wire framing. The film's

narrative thus visually reinforces at several places the cage of Nazerman's experiences.

Lumet makes significant additions to the novel in the episode involving Nazerman's second visitor that morning, the heavy-set, older black woman, Mrs. Harmon, with her eternal bric-a-brac to sell, committed to laughter, believing "mightily in salvaging what you could" (16). In the film the episode is both funnier and sadder than in the novel, as the old woman, conscious of the absurdity of her bearing two large candlesticks for the examination of a man who she knows will regard them with barely concealed indifference, assertively enters the pawnshop wailing, "Man the lifeboats, heah I am agin." Lumet shoots her from slightly high angle, as if rooting her amid the clutter she rummages in. Bent over and burdened, Mrs. Harmon can still find humor in the debasement of the pawning process: "Each time it seems the boat's gettin' deeper and deeper into the water." Then pausing with a look at Nazerman, she says quietly, "Ain't it a wonder a body stay afloat as long as it do?" commenting indirectly on her awareness of the pawnbroker's own tenuous station in the ghetto of his mind, trapped among his own victims. As she speaks her final lines from the novel, in departure from the shop, "I see you again, Mistuh Nazerman, that for sure. Take care now, hear?" Lumet shows her completely enclosed by the heavy door frame she will depart and reenter by, again and again. But she is morally a victor in comparison with her overlord, for her mind is so concentrated on his welfare as she leaves (unlike the novel, she does not smile; her face in extreme close-up is stern but pitying) that she forgets both her pawn ticket and the two dollars she has extracted with such difficulty from Nazerman.

The director omits the short scene from this part of the novel involving Leventhal, the Jewish policeman who vaguely threatens Nazerman for suspected illegality in his pawnshop business. Rather than Wallant's uncharacteristically blatant implication of a partnership in crime among the people of the streets, even fellow "landsmen" (13), Lumet reveals dramatically the stasis and moral emptiness of this ghettoized world. In an important variation from the novel's structure, Lumet moves the first sequence involving the aspiring intellectual, George Smith, to a point immediately following Mrs. Harmon's departure into the street. In contrast to the street noise, carrying with it the sense that endless streams of dead-ended people come to the pawnshop with pitiful scraps of their lives and dreams, Jesus Ortiz proudly announces that he wants to catalog every item of merchandise in the store in three cross-indexed lists, in order to learn his trade well and to be of greater value to Nazerman. But as Smith ritualistically enters the enters the shop on the pretext of repawning the same lamp repeatedly, in hopes of connecting emotionally with another learned man in conversation, Nazerman appears in a separate plane of space from Smith and from Ortiz, who both needs and cares for him. The pawnbroker is seen within the innermost compartment of his office, enclosed completely by wire partitions. Lumet depicts Nazerman as emotionally disconnected from Smith, who, in Wallant's novel, manages to evoke momentary sympathy from the pawnbroker, albeit perhaps merely because "their talk created a small, faintly warming buzz in the pawnshop" (50). In the film, the sad old man, ably revealed by Juano Hernandez, is simply Mr. Smith, whose vain attempts to sustain conversation with the pawnbroker in order to provide a slim interval of light in his deadened days are met only with cold indifference.

Speaking haltingly throughout the scene, Smith slowly enters the shop mumbling about Herbert Spencer, an apt philosopher to underscore the determined aspects of these lives, as shadows from the mesh wiring of Nazerman's screened counter gate cross both his lamp and his face. Smith pauses for breath after almost every phrase, partially because of his decrepitude, but centrally because his mind strains for adequate expression of his desire to talk to the educated Nazerman— formerly an instructor at the University of Cracow—about his newfound learning. Lumet builds sympathy for Smith in part by omitting Wallant's details of Smith's nightly fantasies of pederasty (48, 199-200) but, more important, by employing the character to reveal the intensity of Nazerman's need to avoid intimacy with anyone. In lines absent from the novel, Smith mumbles pleadingly, "From time to time, I like to drop in here, Mr. Nazerman, because a man gets hungry for talk, good talk." Ignoring his need, Nazerman merely bounces his marker on the pawn ticket in exact syncopation with Smith's words, measuring the time until his hoped-for departure. Significantly, after marking the pile of pawn tickets before him, Nazerman puts them on the pointed spike that will release him at the end of the film from his moral neutrality. As Smith glances up periodically in hopes of gaining Nazerman's interest, the shopkeeper just sips his milk—with a napkin wrapped around the glass so that he cannot feel the moisture. In one of Lumet's most distinguished close-ups, Smith finally leaves, having accepted a pittance for the lamp, mumbling, "Two dollars will be quite all right. I apologize for talking so much, Mr. Nazerman . . . forgive me?" as the shadows from the mesh of Nazerman's cage cross his face.

Near the end of this day in the pawnshop, Nazerman receives the usual telephone call from his boss, a racketeer who employs Nazerman as front man for the purpose of laundering syndicate money. At this point in both the novel and the film, the pawnbroker does not yet know the extent of the mobster's operations. Wallant's novel treats the racket boss, named Murillio, as an icy, removed cipher, albeit a vicious one; throughout the novel he is a menacing, but typed, character of the Italian mafioso. Lumet significantly changes the character, at once rendering him less trite and using him to reveal further Nazerman's relentless retreat from humanity. While Murillio sounds like a "recording" (26), Lumet's racket boss, Rodriguez, a black man, played with savage energy by Brock Peters, is an animalistic force beside which Nazerman pales. During the telephone conversation, Rodriguez orders the pawnbroker to sustain yet a further loss as a cover for the mobster's various enterprises. Lumet shoots Nazerman behind double sets of wire mesh within his inner office, walling him into another plane of space from us as well as from Rodriguez, whose total enterprise—and its sustaining profits—Nazerman does not want to face. Just as Nazerman resists Mr. Smith's calling him "Professor," reminding him of his former days in Europe, so Rodriguez's use of the term so upsets him that he incurs the mobster's displeasure by hanging up on him at one point.

Lumet also uses color imagery artfully in this scene to underscore visually Nazerman's need for withdrawal. He shows Rodriguez in his apartment headquarters, decorated from floor to ceiling in white. An obsequious white subaltern places his master's phone calls. Rodriguez is dressed in an expensive, immaculate white robe. His flight from his own racial identity in favor of a false class identification parallels his moral withdrawal; while on the telephone with Nazerman, Rodriguez sits in a white chair, separated from the source of light at the rear of the frame by a white screen, reminiscent of the barriers within the pawnshop that continually place Nazerman in a different spatial plane from the rest of humanity. As Rodriguez will later show Nazerman, the pawnbroker does not wish to know the true nature of the black mafioso and therefore does not allow himself to realize how closely he shares in Rodriguez's moral absence through his emotional numbing.

Lumet also changes the sequence of the novel's action in regard to Marilyn Birchfield's entrance. Wallant introduces the social worker later in the narrative, after Ortiz has spoken to Nazerman of his dreams of advancement in the pawn business. But in Lumet's film, Miss Birchfield, whose awkward innocence is well realized by Geraldine Fitzgerald, enters immediately after Nazerman's telephone conversation with Rodriguez. While her verbal pleas to Nazerman for his financial support of her neighborhood youth group are similar to those in the novel, Lumet's backgrounding of the scene heightens his vision of the novel. As Miss Birchfield tentatively reveals her own loneliness and isolation through her words about the needs of the street children, a group of young blacks and Hispanics enters to redeem their musical and percussive instruments. Lumet shoots them through a maze of the shop's wire meshing as the social worker attempts to convince Nazerman of the importance of caring for people's future, visually dividing the group from Nazerman's concern. Receiving their instruments, they begin slowly to play, their conga rhythms growing louder as Nazerman rails at Miss Birchfield's innocence in trusting people. He reminds her that minorities consistently take advantage of him with solicitations for nonexistent charities. "With this experience, I say why not you?" he asks. Nazerman's ubiquitous cynicism infuses the streets with a miasma that disallows the possibilities of change, even for these youths whose music celebrates that drugs and crime have not yet claimed them. As Nazerman routinely gives Miss Birchfield money simply to rid himself of her intrusion on his privacy, he ignores the potential liberation she could provide him. Lumet visually endorses this potential at the beginning of the scene, by first shooting the social worker from a point at the level of, and behind, Nazerman's work counter, upon which sits a pen pointing at her as she enters. Marilyn Birchfield will, indeed, eventually bring Nazerman closer to the ultimate realization that he is inescapably joined to all isolated people of his ghetto.

And Nazerman is certainly implicated in some of the terrible actions of the more dangerous people among his clientele, those men who have become hardened to a degree beyond that of the comparatively innocent street musicians. In the novel, the initial entrance of Tangee and his henchmen occurs shortly after the departure of the young drug addict, with the "terrified, twitching face of a jackal" (18), who tries to pawn his worthless radio. But in the film Lumet introduces the three hoods as if to dissipate Marilyn Birchfield's innocence, as well as that of Ortiz, who is trying to become the ideal stock boy to escape his life of petty street crime. Jesus joyfully exclaims, "Right now I feel special bright and special willing," as he rides on the shop's wheeled dolly, climbing toward the top clothes rack as it simultaneously moves toward the camera and toward the opening door at lower frame left through which the hoodlums enter. The sharp reaction shot of Ortiz, looking down at the recent past he wishes to escape, is from a very low angle; but ironically, though it seems to place Ortiz in a position of dominance, it really indicates his vulnerability. For the hoods enter the pawnshop in one of the most terrifying shots in Lumet's films: Tangee, followed by Buck and Robinson, strides in pushing a power lawnmower, running full speed, which they attempt to convince Nazerman to accept in pawn even though the machine is obviously stolen property. Lumet's camera held at floor level, the machine grinds right toward it; the movement and the screeching sound continue unrelentingly for twelve full seconds, while Tangee croons (in lines not in Wallant's novel), "Blades shiny and sharp, cut grass to the skin, last a lifetime, Uncle."

The scene's tension increases as the hoodlums—including the brooding Robinson, whose face looks like a bleached skull—exert escalating pressure upon the pawnbroker to accept the stolen merchandise. Lumet uses the scene for more than frightening effect, however; he suggests through it how inextricably Nazerman is bound up in the widespread corruption of his world and the victimization of so many classes of its people. Though in the novel Nazerman emerges sufficiently self-possessed to agree to seven dollars for the power mower, in Lumet's vision he is browbeaten into parting with more money. Shadows from his counter gate cross his face and also Ortiz's frightened countenance. As is so often true in Lumet's films, cinematic technique is well allied to his particular theme: Tangee's "last a lifetime, Uncle," a revealing commentary on the gangster's power to begin to mow down Nazerman's encrusted resistance to human feeling, is spoken as Lumet holds the shot slightly angled to the left so that we can see the hoodlum himself overwhelmed by the low ceiling of the shop pressing down upon him. Even Tangee and the brutal Robinson—significantly a Caucasian in the film—are victims here, despite their apparent possession of power and the destructive technology of the street jungle, dwarfed by the circumstances that grip them all. Tangee's resonant phrase is an inadvertent use of the sort of catchy advertising lingo employed by the majority culture to enslave his race and class. Tangee, menacingly yet humorously portrayed by Raymond St. Jacques, kisses his right little finger, raising it in mock scout's honor, as he bids goodbye. "We be in again, Uncle," he says, smiling warningly at Nazerman and underscoring all the forces recapitulated in these images. He forces Nazerman's beginning realization that he is subsidizing the very criminal group that he scorns to Ortiz throughout the film, that Rodriguez subsidizes all, from pawnbroker to street criminals and victims, and that Nazerman cannot escape his inevitable connection to this corruption and to the very nature of the humankind he scorns.

The tension in Nazerman's mind between the ubiquity of evil in his world, his need to block out this reality, and the incessant inroads memory must make upon his attempts at self-numbing is reinforced after Savarese's visit to deliver Rodriguez's laundered syndicate money. Nazerman suddenly recognizes the desire on Ortiz's face as the youth watches his boss deposit the money in the safe. Just afterward, Nazerman stops the youth from removing the calendar page showing the date September 29—Nazerman's wedding anniversary. Ortiz, like all youth, wants time to hurry onward, boasting to his surrogate father that he will be in very early on Monday. Nazerman needs to keep time still; over soft flute music, he closes the shop for the weekend, his figure (except for his head) encased in the shadows in which he spends his days. Moving slowly, he checks windows, doors, and safe, keeping the calendar as it is. He changes to his outdoor eyeglasses, turns off the lights according to the routine of many years, and goes out to the dark street. Here Lumet cuts to a close-up of the top half of Nazerman's face as he looks back through the window to the calendar, before his eyes drop and he begins to walk down the wet street toward his car.

As Nazerman walks past women lounging in doorways, he passes a fenced vacant lot in which a gang is beating a young black man. He seems not to notice the violence; but over the asynchronous sound of barking dogs some streets off, Lumet cuts to a two-tenths-of-a-second flash cut of the booted feet of a man and a dog running. Nazerman cannot control his memories, and the flashes become longer in duration: a concentration camp guard and a dog chase down a prisoner whose hands claw at barbed wire, while, in the present reality, the black youth runs toward the camera and leaps at the chain fence, trying to climb it to escape. Lumet now cuts exclusively to the past, as a younger Nazerman, head completely shaved, watches in horror as the dog gnaws at the screaming prisoner and the guard beats him senseless. The hideous screams of the camp prisoner coalesce with the screams of the young black victim as Nazerman enters his car, making no protest to the current atrocity. As he prepares to drive away, Lumet's camera, passing the right side of Nazerman's face, reveals a middle-class black couple strolling by the vacant lot, oblivious to the young man's beating. Without preachment—the beating of the black youth is held in longshot throughout—Lumet suggests not only the decline of American urban life into mindless violence but also the withdrawal of the middle class of many racial backgrounds from its less fortunate and victimized brothers. This subtheme is important especially to the character of Jesus Ortiz: interspersed with the scene described above are images of Ortiz and his girlfriend, Mabel Wheatly, planning their route out of the ghetto toward his business success. Ortiz's treatment of Mabel is interesting; heading up some stairs at one point, Ortiz declares imperialistically to her, "All you gotta do is be around when I go like this," wagging his finger at her. Throughout the early part of the film—especially in this original sequence—Lumet reveals the mutuality of destructive forces that will eventually lead to young Ortiz's death. Tangee, and Rodriguez in a more significant way, are joined in greed and manipulation that establish a system making the violent end of the youth inevitable. And Nazerman supervises Jesus' training to become a member of this system.

The nets begin to tighten around Ortiz in chapter 5 of the novel, as he and Mabel go to a dance hall and there meet Tangee and his gang, who seek entry to Nazerman's safe. Lumet introduces this episode in a scene original to the film that enhances the atmosphere of impending doom. An aging, corpulent dancer is seen in long shot as Ortiz and Mabel enter a squalid nightclub. Her feet barely move; the routine shufflings seem endlessly repeated, without desire. As the couple enters the club, Lumet frames them on the left by the dancer and on the right by a mirrored reflection of the dancer's spectacle, as in a Renoir-like hesitation shot the two pause in the aisle while talking to acquaintances, momentarily hemmed in by identical images of corruption. As Ortiz and Mabel take seats at a table, Tangee and his friends sit on a level above them in the next tier, heckling Ortiz about earning so little money since going straight. "It's a chicken business," says Tangee, tempting the youth to divulge the amount of money in Nazerman's safe. Robinson, the most violent of the hoods, has no woman with him at the club; the women with Tangee and Buck are stretched out, drunken. All contrast with the abundant sexuality of Mabel (Thelma Oliver) and her obvious emotional attachment to and admiration of Ortiz. Despite Mabel's passionate defense of their plan to make their money honestly through starting slowly in a business of their own, the hoods' heckling goads Ortiz into the bragging admission of the large sum of money in the pawnshop safe. Just as Ortiz makes this important, and self-revelatory, admission, the jaded dancer—seen at a third level beneath the two tiers above—rips off a wig, disclosing beneath the facade a female impersonator. The cheapness of the scene—its directness and blatantly vulgar background music are rare in commercial American films of the period—serves as a visual correlative to Lumet's concern with the false appearances and the dubious sexual and moral realities omnipresent in the street world.

Lumet places Nazerman's visit to Tessie Rubin, original to the film, immediately following the female impersonator's nightclub revelation, suggesting the similar superficiality of this relationship. The pawnbroker and Tessie, the wife of the pursued camp prisoner whose image Nazerman recently attempted to repress, live only in the sad memories of their past. Lumet wisely omits Wallant's obvious satiric indictment of the greedy collector, Goberman, to concentrate upon the emotional emptiness of Tessie and Nazerman's relationship. Partially supporting Tessie's family, too, because of her husband's death in the extermination camps, Nazerman mechanically engages in sexual coupling with Tessie during his weekly visits to her in her father's home. Lumet intercuts their arid lovemaking with the avid animality of Ortiz and Mabel as they passionately plan their future together; in a scene with unusually blatant eroticism for an American film of the mid-1960s, the lovers talk of Mabel's wish to engage extra lovers apart from her arrangement with Rodriguez's brothel to secure the necessary money for Ortiz to begin his own legitimate business. Mabel's ecstatic statement "Oh, honey, I'll go in with you, we'll be partners" expresses their passionate sharing and also contrasts with the emotional distance between Nazerman and Tessie, who lie together disconnected spiritually. Nazerman's hand wrings the pillowcase next to Tessie's face, his head is buried in the sheets, and the only sound is the ticking clock. In one of the film's most visually arresting brief shots, Lumet introduces this extension of Nazerman's desperate numbing in the sequence's first view of the home. In the deep background from Tessie's kitchen we see the head of her old father, Mendel (memorably portrayed by Lumet's father, famed Jewish actor Baruch Lumet), his voice railing against the intrusion of Nazerman's living death into their house. Lumet's careful depth composition shows in deepest center frame the old man's head as but a spot of light, yet clearly visible through the expanse of space separating him from the camera. Mendel seems imprisoned in two frames of space, both by the kitchen window and the window framing of his own room, as he equally laments his own aging and illness and despises what he considers the degradation of his family life since Tessie exists not with her husband but in Nazerman's "land of the dead." Yet another victim of Nazerman's indifference and moral passivity, he is so reduced in size that his life-affirming values seem in danger of annihilation.

Again varying the novel's sequence, Lumet next reveals Ortiz trying to fix the calendar on Monday morning in the pawnshop. As Ortiz is solicitous of Nazerman, the pawnbroker's mind flashes momentarily on his dead son from the early slow-motion sequence of the child's reaching out for the butterfly. This establishes quickly, but implicitly, a filial connection, just as it must covertly exist in Nazerman's mind. But Nazerman immediately represses his feeling for Ortiz, as he must repress all human bonds. Lumet shows this trenchantly in the following sequence as the young junkie (a Caucasian instead of a black youth in the film) attempts to pawn his worthless radio and, in frustration at Nazerman's impassiveness, screams anti-Semitic invectives at him. Lumet's pawnbroker remains impassive; neither the youth's harsh racism nor his terrible vulnerability can touch Nazerman. Nor can Marilyn Birchfield move him as she enters the shop at this point, attempting to reach out to Nazerman by apologizing for the discord at their first meeting and suggesting that they have lunch some afternoon in the park. She places her hands tentatively on the wire screen between them as she speaks, but its shadows line and cross her face. Her touching the screen makes her analogous to both the assaulted black youth and the concentration camp prisoner, Rubin, who attempt to claw beyond their spatial planes toward different kinds of freedom; the Harlem streets victimize her as the camps victimize Rubin and Nazerman, but, as occurs so often in Lumet's vision, there is even less remedy for these victims than for victims of external oppression. Immediately, Lumet reinforces this imagery as a young, sallow, pregnant blonde woman enters the shop to attempt to pawn a worthless engagement ring she believes to be a diamond, as Marilyn looks helplessly on at her degradation. While Nazerman dismisses the young woman, a tenth-of-a-second flash appears on the screen of hands held up upon barbed wire. Gradually the shots extend in duration; camp guards pluck rings off fingers, and, some hands missing fingers, most shake as they offer up to the brutal guards what little they have. Outwardly Nazerman is unmoved at the girl's pathetic cry, "He said it was real," and as Marilyn backs out of the shop silently, the pawnbroker can only murmur at her, in a dead tone, "Wednesday, Thursday, whatever you like."

In the novel, Wallant sets Nazerman's great speech on the skill of the Jews in business near the end of chapter 3, as a response to Ortiz's yearning to follow in the path of his uncle's business success in Detroit. Excellent as the lines are, they are dissipated in Nazerman's closing cliché, "Is it not simple? My whole formula for success—'How to Succeed in Business,' by Sol Nazerman" (52), and in Ortiz's wordy, anticlimactic statement, "I can't hardly wait for tomorrow's classes. . . . You all heart, Solly, all heart" (53). Lumet gives the passage greater dignity by placing the memorable lines just after Marilyn's departure into the dark street in the rain and by significantly changing the conclusion. Cars proceed slowly up the stark, gray avenue as Ortiz saunters into the shop, casually asking the pawnbroker to teach him the essence of his trade, ending his request with the question "How come you people come to business so natural?" Whereas in the novel Ortiz says "Jews" (51), in the film the youth says, with less consciousness and therefore less malice, "people." Master and man are further brought closer by Lumet's shooting them during the introductory portion of Nazerman's speech in very low light, reminiscent of the stark street we have just witnessed. For one of the first times in the film, both characters are presented in medium two-shot, yet still partially separated into different spatial planes by a wall panel in deep background. The visual effect implicates ever more gradually these two lives, as the bitterness of the words Nazerman utters reveals, to us and to Ortiz if not yet to himself, the insistence of the memories the pawnbroker increasingly finds difficult to hold at bay.

While the director has commented that, in retrospect, he might have preferred James Mason to Steiger in the role, granting the latter's magnificent performance, because Mason could communicate icy remove and moral coldness even better than Steiger, here Steiger's verbal and physical muscularity well convey the volcanic force of emotion that Nazerman continues to possess, though deeply laid under a decade and more of repression and denial.[43] As Nazerman intones, slowly and quietly at first, the history of Jewish trial and suffering, the motif of the passage, more than in Wallant's novel, becomes centered in the lines "All you have is a little brain, a little brain and a great bearded legend to sustain you." Lumet increasingly closes in on Nazerman's face, at a slightly low angle, and bathes the face in light up to the upper half of Nazerman's forehead as he speaks the word *brain*, more often than in Wallant's passage. At this point the words begin to tumble out, as Steiger's delivery grows increasingly rapid; in Lumet's film, unlike the novel, Nazerman includes Ortiz in his racial memory, calling him "my friend," as he tells of the endless instinctual process of selling and self-denial. But the shattering conclusion of his speech in the film both includes Ortiz as covictim and expresses for the first time, if with dim consciousness, Nazerman's rage at the genocidal horror fallen upon his people and upon himself. His words on victims' gradual self-victimization come closer to home than in the novel, as he cries, "You just go on and on and on repeating this process over the centuries, over and over, and suddenly you make a grand discovery: you have a mercantile heritage, you are a merchant, you are known as a usurer, a man with secret resources, a witch, a pawnbroker, a sheenie, a muckie and a kike!"

At the word *sheenie*, Steiger's voice becomes deeper, thicker, more outraged, and more bitter. At the word *kike*, a single low piano note hangs for six seconds. Literally he refers to the junkie's racist invective a few moments before, but psychologically he acknowledges his well of suffering for the first time. It is a beginning for Nazerman, and Lumet subtly indicates this structurally by placing the scene in about the middle of the film's narrative. And Ortiz, in all his simplicity, has some realization of the significance of what has occurred, as, at first stunned, then smiling in admiration, he says quietly, "You really is some teacher, Mr. Nazerman. . . . you really is the greatest." Both an indictment of and a prayer for his people, Nazerman's "lesson" emerges unconsciously as a lament for the human condition, including latently Ortiz and his future mythic suffering for Nazerman, as well as Marilyn, the white junkie, and the sallow, pregnant girl. The pawnbroker has considered these people the swill of the streets, but now they gradually begin to coalesce into the aging Jew's own suffering.

Lumet's next sequence reinforces the ambivalence between Nazerman's emotional unlocking and his need for repression. From the more responsive Ortiz's admiring lines in the previous scene, the director cuts immediately to his mother's shabby tenement apartment, as the youth, immersed in the kitchen bathtub, talks to his mother in Spanish as she prepares dinner. There is no need for subtitles to reveal the easy communication and love between them. Trying to help her with her English, he repeats over and over, "I am a good boy," and they both eventually convulse in laughter at her difficulty with the strange sounds, their hands clasped. In contrast with this scene of emotional union, Lumet cuts to Nazerman and Tessie at the card table, as in the background Mendel continues to regale them, particularly Nazerman, who he feels is a "living dead man." While Mendel has too many lines that repetitiously embroider the notion of Nazerman's psychic freezing, the visual detail and composition more ably underscore the literary theme: at one point, as Nazerman rises from the table to go to Mendel's room to give him medicine, Mendel proclaims, "I was in Auschwitz too, I came out alive," and Nazerman throws down his cards. But his eye catches one that he cannot seem to release just as the old man says, "You came out dead"; the card seems momentarily to adhere to his hand. While the card is never shown, the fast detail tellingly suggests the passionlessness that enshrouds the pawnbroker. Out of his guilt at emerging alive when so many died in the camps, Nazerman financially superintends several people. But Mendel realizes that he does so at the cost of his own emotional death: as Nazerman must pour Mendel's medicine back into the bottle amid the old man's maledictions, Lumet shoots him with his back to the camera, a few feet out of Mendel's room, framed in the room's doorway, almost in a freeze-frame.

Lumet's next sequence begins with Nazerman seated on a bench near the pawnshop. Marilyn Birchfield walks up, expecting to meet him for their prearranged lunch, but finds that he has forgotten it and there is nothing for them to eat. While Wallant structures this meeting at the end of chapter 13 and in chapter 14, as the two leave the pawnshop together, Lumet typically darkens the scene both situationally and visually. (The film also omits the temporarily renewing boat trip they share in chapter 21.) As she speaks, he stands, centrally backgrounded by the increasingly harsh sound of the ever-passing elevated train. Visually Lumet divides them into two distinct planes of space, even though they stand near each other: a tree looms between them in deep background, and though boys play in the distance, the building lines are sharp and angular. During their conversation, as Miss Birchfield tries to establish emotional connection with Nazerman, Lumet increases the social worker's personal suffering from that in the novel; not only has she been lonely because of her appearance and her shyness, but a deeply loved young husband suddenly died of an unexplained heart stoppage. The cruelty of Nazerman's utter rejection of her suffering and consequent heightened loneliness underscores his primary need to isolate himself from human feeling and community.

He moves away from her to a bench opposite; she follows him, offering a sandwich, which he shuns. In lines even more bitter than Wallant's he both scorns and insults her: "*You* have found out that the world is unjust and cruel; well let me tell you something my dear sociologist, that there is a world different than yours, much different and the people in it are of another species!" As he substitutes the more general word *people* for Wallant's *emotions* (146), Lumet quickly cuts between the two characters, visually isolating them from one another, and Nazerman glowers over Miss Birchfield at one point in center frame, terrifying her while degrading her suffering as being nothing in the scheme of the world's madness and evil. While much of Nazerman's dialogue in the interchange is similar to that in Wallant's novel, Lumet and the screenwriters significantly add a passage, as the pawnbroker proclaims his lack of desire for even vengeance: "I have escaped from the emotions, I am safe within myself." Humiliating her further by saying that people like her prevent his gaining that "peace and quiet," he ends in deadly, slow tones: "One more thing; please, stay out of my life." These words, only present in the film, and delivered by Steiger with a slight pause between each word, elicit a reaction shot of Miss Birchfield's numb stare. Backgrounded now solely by black children lounging in a doorway and an alley visible deep in the distance, she silently gets up and, beaten, walks away.

The gradual proximity of Nazerman to his repressed feelings comes a step closer in the next scene, original to the film, as Rodriguez's henchman, Savarese, enters the shop and tears off the calendar page to reveal the correct date, demanding that legal papers be signed by Nazerman. The pawnbroker replies with a barely controlled roar, "No papers get signed today," covertly revealing for the second time the press of circumstances that will thrust him back among the living. Trying to repress these uncomfortable feelings, the pawnbroker refuses Ortiz's offer of help with his coat, as the early morning light in the pawnshop throws the shadows of the wire screen over both their faces, branding both with a shared incipient fate. Just then Mr. Smith enters, yet again seeking human connection through the educated Nazerman's approval, stuttering out vaguely formed ideas of Socrates' influence on the drama. While in the novel Nazerman manages some compassion for Smith (108), Lumet's protagonist completely dismisses Smith's pitiable condition. As he stammers and searches his empty pockets for the excuse that justifies his presence in the pawnshop, Nazerman says harshly, "Just for once in your life try to be rational and think exactly what you came in here to pawn." Smith must only reply, "Nothing . . . I had nothing to bring." His thin voice trails upward as he backs out of the pawnshop; "I will miss talking to you," he says, as shadows cross his eyes very slowly, closing them off to Nazerman and to us.

At Smith's departure, Nazerman demands of Ortiz what makes such "scum" exist, ignoring the fact that, although Smith's words are slurred and his thoughts disconnected, he at least tries to give ideas shape and voice—he attempts, unlike Nazerman himself, to fulfill his limited capacity for being alive. Ironically, Nazerman does not yet possess sufficient consciousness to realize that his fascistic rejections of feeling confirm him as akin to the oppressors who have destroyed his happiness. As the pawnbroker attempts to convince the religious Ortiz that street people like Smith are "rejects," Lumet shoots them far apart from one another at extreme ends of the long rear corridor of the pawnshop and also photographs Nazerman here in a close-up at a sharply high angle, revealing him as the specimen "creature" he conceives Smith to be. In answer to his assistant's question if he believes in God, Nazerman delivers his important speech from the novel (114-15) on money as life's ultimate value. The youth's face noticeably hardens at his boss's cynicism; a single shadow of a bar on the front screen bisects his chest, and the shop safe is clearly visible behind him. Ortiz's decision to betray Nazerman to Tangee and his gang is more heightened in the film than in the novel (116): Nazerman concludes his lines on money, saying, "That's what life is all about. . . . Money is the whole thing." As he speaks, unconsciously urging his assistant toward criminality, Lumet frames Nazerman at a low angle against a deep

background of hanging suits and coats that Ortiz has recently cata-
loged, the shells of cloth seeming to weigh down upon him in reflection of his emotional vacancy. A single jagged note from a trumpet
pierces the emptiness of the shop's interior.

Down a long tracking shot of Park Avenue past 111th Street, Ortiz
now rushes toward his doom, searching for Tangee to plan the robbery
of Nazerman's safe. Unlike the novel, in the film Ortiz first seeks out
Mabel in the Park Hotel; she protests that she will get the money he
wants through giving "private sessions," lest he become ruined in a
criminal life. In a visual reversal of the nightclub scene involving the
female impersonator, Mabel pulls him toward the bed in her room
while pulling off her prostitute's wig in an attempt to rid both of their
lives of the inauthenticity she fears. But her effort does not matter.
Shouting "I'm gone to get it and fast, " with a prophetic import he does
not foresee, Ortiz dashes next toward the camera up a long, narrow,
imprisoning stairway toward the pool hall where Tangee, Buck, and
Robinson inevitably await him. Wallant sets this scene in the relatively
innocent arena of a cafeteria, but Lumet's grainy pool room is a place
where Ortiz is dominated by his past and his needs as much as by the
other conspirators. As Ortiz grabs a cue to attempt an attitude of
dominance over his situation, he insists that he will be the one "to call
the shots" and that there must be no use of guns; but each time he
asserts this to the languidly smiling Tangee and leans into the camera
in right frame in supposed emphasis, Lumet frames his head partially
by his own angled pool cue, shooting him from a slightly low angle so
that the grimy ceiling of the place continually presses him downward.

In another of the film's fine tracking shots, Mabel rushes across the
street toward the pawnshop, held in extreme high angle to accentuate
her vulnerability. She dashes along the littered streets, dodging people
and cars, against the incessant rattle of the elevated train crushing
down upon the street's victims. Mabel's coming to Nazerman is one of
the film's outstanding sequences. Her visit makes clear to Nazerman
that a major source of his own support from Rodriguez comes from
prostitution, a fact that will weigh almost unbearably upon his memories from the extermination camps. In the novel, Nazerman learns this
information through a chance comment from Ortiz (112); Lumet heightens the discovery, again increasing the weight of the pawnbroker's
victimization by revealing it as shared with that of a person Nazerman
dismisses. Reaching the shop just as Nazerman prepares to lock the
front door, Mabel first offers him a locket gained from a customer in a
private session, reminding him that she will be severely beaten if her
boss discovers she has been seeing clients independent of his control.

As Mabel attempts to gain Nazerman's sympathy, Lumet shows the two poised in the doorway in front of the screen door Nazerman has opened a little as a tacit agreement that he will not inform on her. But Nazerman can accept little more emotional risk than this; as Mabel mentions Rodriguez by name and Nazerman suddenly realizes that both the girl and he are supported by the same corruption, he simultaneously must face the burden of Tessie's telephone call announcing the end of her father's long illness. Lumet moves this incident from its unemphatic position in the novel (192): Nazerman retreats from both women as he goes deep into the shop behind two walls of screens to deal with Tessie's emotional needs. Cruelly telling her that his money will also pay to get Mendel buried, his harshness toward Tessie seems a projection of his guilt at Mabel's searing revelation. Nazerman is more and more being forced by circumstances to see feelingly the interlinked corruption that binds most lives in this environment, and he cannot bear that Rodriguez controls, and that he himself profits from, so much evil in his world. Ironically, his dismissal of Tessie's needs is but a more cruel variant of his cynical advice to Ortiz a few moments before. And as Nazerman verbally assaults the sobbing Tessie, asking, "Where do you think your money comes from?" he does not realize that soon, in his confrontation with Rodriguez, that lesson will be driven home to him with a power he no longer will be able to deny.

But Nazerman must first relive one of the great horrors of his life in the camps. One of Lumet's most significant changes from the novel is his marked compression of Nazerman's gradually surfacing repressed memories: to this point in the film's narrative, three extended dream or daydream sequences from the novel have been reduced into a few instantly repressed, staccato flashes from Nazerman's memory. But Mabel's desire to earn money quickly for Ortiz's needs prompts her into a sudden offer of her body to Nazerman after the conclusion of his conversation with Tessie. His head cupped in his hands to drive away the sight of Mabel's nakedness, Nazerman experiences progressively longer flashes of the terrible day in the camps when a guard forced him to watch the rape of his wife by a Nazi officer. While in Wallant's novel, this memory (168-69) occurs separate from the scene with Mabel (184-85), unleashed in a dream after Nazerman has heard his sister-in-law and her husband making love, Lumet renders the memory more horrifying to Nazerman both by associating the experiences with Mabel and by increasing the degradation of the present incident. The provocative whore, unlike Tessie, represents the very archetype of carnality, and she is more graphic in her inducements in the film than in the novel.

As Mabel croons, "Look, look," to Nazerman, he sees a one-tenth-second flash of Ruth, then gradually longer scenes of rain in the camp; many prisoners being herded along, women into a separate building; and himself, with his head shaved, forced to watch the women filing into the barracks. We hear the sounds of the rain seconds before the initial flash cut to Ruth, as the buried memories come slowly back out of the years of his repression. Amid the cries of the prisoners, a man in Nazerman's group sags to the ground and is forgotten. As Mabel continues, "Look, look, don't cost you nuthin' to look," he must watch the victimization of his beloved Ruth. Lumet's tracking shot moves slowly up the corridor of the Nazi officers' barracks, showing the women being carefully washed, one sitting with an officer and seeming to enjoy herself. The camera glides with insidious slowness left to right from one room to the next, until it stops at the room where Nazerman's wife sits, waiting for her brutalization. Lumet cuts to the window through which Nazerman is forced to watch, before the guard thrusts his head through the glass to allow him a better look. We view him in extreme close-up, as in the background Mabel's plea—the only sound—soothingly continues. Ruth is seated on the edge of her bunk, stripped naked, and her composed beauty compels her husband to flash back within the memory to her image as she stands beneath the tree in the meadow at the beginning of the film. Suddenly Lumet crosses Ruth's body with the back of a Nazi officer standing in her doorway. At this point the camera pulls back, isolating Nazerman in center frame as he rises, barely under control, his face contorted with pain, and goes toward the black prostitute, covering her nakedness with her coat and stuffing money into her hand as she rushes from the shop. Trying to hold in the pain, clenching his left hand to his face in horror and building rage at the thought of Rodriguez's superintendence of Mabel's corruption, Nazerman, in extreme close-up, cries out hideously like a hunted, wounded animal. The sound expresses not only profound suffering but also an increasing awareness that Nazerman himself is emotionally embedded in Ruth's and Mabel's mutually degraded victimization.[44]

Nazerman's visit to Rodriguez in his apartment to protest the source of his earnings immediately follows the encounter with Mabel and the resultant memory of his wife's rape. It is thus better psychologically integrated into the film's structure than in Wallant's novel, where it haphazardly follows Nazerman's unsuccessful lunch with Miss Birchfield and precedes his dream of the rape at the end of chapter 15. In Lumet's vision of the work, the pawnbroker comes to his employer knowing fully why he objects to getting his money from the proceeds of Rodriguez's brothel. The novel presents the mobster as a stereotypical villain, his eyes "the pale-gray color of slush . . . a translucent, light-conducting texture rather than a color" (157). In the film Rodriguez achieves greater emotional and perhaps moral stature than Nazerman. He does not require a gun, as in Wallant's novel, to threaten his employee. At the beginning of the scene, Lumet's camera, behind Nazerman's shoulder, pans around the room, concentrating on the powerful Rodriguez's feline movements as he paces toward Nazerman. Resplendent in his white robe, Rodriguez compliments Nazerman's education, admitting his own lack of formal learning by saying, "You're a welcome change of pace for me." When Nazerman objects to receiving money from the whorehouse "because it's money that comes from filth and from horror," Rodriguez looms over him until the pawnbroker is almost completely in his shadow. Throughout the scene, however, Nazerman's glasses intermittently reflect the overwhelming light that seems to emanate from everywhere in Rodriguez's all-white apartment, so that he appears to possess no eyes. As the mobster accuses him of really knowing "that's what it is, Professor," that he has long been in the "middle of one big whorehouse, right in the bosom of the world!" Nazerman's face becomes taut with mute horror. The shrewd Rodriguez guesses that there are many things Nazerman does not allow himself to know: "Are you that kind of man, Professor, the kind that doesn't want to know about things, feel about things, are you that kind? That makes you *nothing!* You give me a front and I give you money, so don't hang up on me, *Professor!* "

Lumet here shoots Nazerman over Rodriguez's right shoulder from high angle as the mobster grabs Nazerman's sallow face in his huge right hand and screams down at him, "Look at me!" the pawnbroker completely in his power. Then Rodriguez backs away from the sobbing Nazerman, insistently pointing his finger at him as he sits across a long table from him, ordering him to sign the necessary papers for laundering the syndicate money. The pawnbroker's voice now a broken whisper, Lumet now shoots four fast intercuts between the two men as Rodriguez insists that Nazerman give him a clear, controlled yes to his demand. Following each repeated, menacing "Yes?" uttered by Rodriguez, Nazerman manages a more audible, if progressively more abject, reply, until "Yes, yes, yes, oh yes" pathetically emerges from his slumped form. The humiliation complete, Lumet's last view of Rodriguez shows the racket boss ascending the stairs in rear frame: Rodriguez emerges as morally superior to his employee, for he both increases Nazerman's awareness of his condition and possesses the capacity to confront the moral ugliness enveloping them all. Lumet's direction of Steiger here keenly reinforces these themes: the actor's face appears literally to break apart during the mobster's shaming of him, his eyeless gaze a mere system of reflectors, his uncontrollable facial muscles a fine visual equivalent for his continual retrogression in emotional control paralleled by his gradual moral reintegration at the film's conclusion.

One of Lumet's most outstanding and original contributions to his adaptation of Wallant's novel is Nazerman's Walpurgisnacht episode following his departure from Rodriguez's apartment. After the mobster's ironic parting words, "Happy dreams, Uncle," the initial section of the sequence is wordless, as Lumet cuts to the lights of cars and street lamps, out of focus, and Nazerman staggers into their surreal presence in the left of the frame. He seems lost in the frame, off to the side; viewed from slightly low angle, his tie askew, Nazerman is overwhelmed by the huge, dominating structures of buildings he shambles past. All the detritus of the city and its "rejects" loom at him: a dilapidated movie house and café, all-night bargain stores, black people hurrying past him in the littered street. A huge concrete structure behind him towers over his silhouette; in a shot worthy of Fritz Lang, Nazerman is then framed by three skeletonlike girders whose sheer weight and volume seem both to hem him in and to crush him. Expressionistically, Lumet makes it appear as if Nazerman is plodding uphill on a city street that seconds before appeared as perfectly flat. Overwhelmed by the power of materiality, of which he earlier so calmly lectured Ortiz, Nazerman seems to sense the buildings moving toward him as he walks aimlessly. He crosses a street slowly, walking toward a huge apartment project, his face harshly cornered by an extreme low-angle shot. Surrounded by three huge white concrete pillars, he staggers into Miss Birchfield's lobby. He is dwarfed both from above and, by Lumet's variation of lenses, from below as he stares at the long brass rows listing the tenants' names. The camera tilts in on them; like the endless list of names of the European dead they seem to annihilate his ability to respond to them. As Nazerman stumbles toward the elevator, he is framed by the heaviness of three unusually wide formica pillars in the antiseptic lobby, as the elevator door closes with agonizing slowness behind him. At Miss Birchfield's floor, he emerges into a grave-narrow hallway, down which he stares momentarily as, at her door, she bids him enter. Entering her apartment speechless, shot from behind, Nazerman wanders toward her terrace window, framed by the early dawn light, then stands dazed by the view of the day's awakening life below him. Seldom is Lumet's strength in visual composition and intrashot montage more effective: Nazerman, finally seated out on the balcony, is seen framed by harsh angles of wire fencing. As he begins talking to Miss Birchfield, cars in very deep background move continually behind his head, their movement indicating the life he so needs to deny.

When she asks why he came, he pathetically replies, "I felt I needed to be with someone," adding that suddenly in the past few days he has begun to feel afraid. "It's been a long time since I felt . . . fear," he says, but her word *anything* almost cuts off his final word. Sensitive as Miss Birchfield is, she does not understand Nazerman's overriding need to repress fear. In one of his most memorable lines original to the film, Nazerman attempts to explain: "No, no you don't understand. . . . it's just that there have been memories that I thought I had pushed far away, words that I thought I had kept myself from hearing, and now, now they . . . flood my mind. Today is an anniversary. . . . I didn't die. Everything that I loved . . . was taken away from me . . . and I did not die. There was nothing I could do. . . . Strange, I could do nothing." Just before the pawnbroker begins to speak of his loves, Lumet frames in close-up the left side of Nazerman's face, while in deep center frame he shows the smokestacks of factories, appearing like a more contemporary version of Nazerman's cities of the dead. As he concludes the words above, Nazerman rises slowly and walks resignedly toward the corner of the balcony. The latticework shadows from the balcony railing fall across them both. Marilyn also slowly rises and stands beside Nazerman for several seconds as he stares bleakly out, before she decides, wordlessly, to reenter her living room. He seems almost content here; having thus cut himself off from responsibility for having been unable to do anything in the past, he seeks as well to make himself immune from action and involvement in the present. Further, he cuts himself off from former as well as present pain by attempting to justify his incapacity in the past through abdicating responsibility now.

Lumet visually and almost soundlessly gathers together these ideas in one of the great shots of his career: over a modulated cello refrain repeated from the end of Nazerman's lines on the balcony, Marilyn seats herself, back to the camera, in a chair across from the couch beside a glass coffee table, her arms crossed against the early morning temperature, as though holding herself against Nazerman's emotional coldness and pain. Nazerman enters from the balcony and sits across the table from her. Lumet holds them in two-shot, separated by the vine on the table and by the balcony railing behind it; the camera behind them removes any sentimentality from the next action. Slowly, Marilyn raises her left hand, reaching out toward Nazerman across the table, without turning her head toward him so as not to embarrass him or overtly infringe on his privacy. Her hand hangs in the air for several seconds, almost touching the vegetation that separates them. But incapable of reciprocation, Nazerman just sits there dully, unmoved and unmoving. Shot from slightly low angle, Marilyn's hand, unmet, falters and then drops to the table top, as the pawnbroker slowly rises and walks out of the room, pulling the door softly behind him.

Nazerman's horrors have only begun this night. Lumet abruptly cuts to a racing subway train entering an underground station. Sitting down in the subway car, the exhausted Nazerman catches the eye of an onlooker, an older man, possibly Jewish, who watches him only absently, perhaps because there is nothing else to look at. Nazerman at once moves from this seat, unable to bear even this casual glance. As he moves away he turns and looks at the back of the man's head as if to establish control over him. Leaning against a pole, he notices another passenger, a light-skinned black man, and again cannot meet a casual look: if he interacts with them even slightly, he may fear losing them. The glances of the riders remind him of the stares of previous passengers, whom long ago he could not help. Ironically Nazerman is only dimly conscious of this perception, for he has placed himself in a psychological situation in which he cannot help these who continue to suffer. Gradually, Nazerman's eyes travel up and down the crowded subway car, and Lumet intercuts very quickly to flashes of passengers in another car—on a train from the past. These cuts extend in duration as the car becomes the cattle car loaded with concentration camp victims. As the images become unbearable, Nazerman rushes toward the front of the car in an attempt to escape to the next car, accompanied by the train's shriek echoing the memory of the screams from his past suffering.

The car of memory into which he rushes, from which he cannot now escape, is the completely packed Auschwitz car; his son David is on his father's back, slipping inevitably down toward the floor filled with excrement as his father cannot move even enough to lift the boy upward. Here Lumet shifts Wallant's dream sequence (37-38) to a more dramatically effective place: rather than a dream following an argument with his mendacious relatives, Nazerman's vision assumes greater conscious significance in the subway. The horror of his memories amid his conscious attempt to escape them forces them into his present awareness, leading more closely to the ultimate acknowledgment of the ubiquity of human suffering that constitutes Lumet's vision of the novel, and perhaps of human experience. As Nazerman struggles to adjust his position enough to save David from sliding down to the slime-filled floor of the car, yelling to his wife that there is nothing he can do since the bodies are packed together so tightly, the screaming whine of the train becomes the loud squall of a child in the death car. Powerless, Nazerman now cannot stem the flow of his long-repressed memories. All about him Lumet reveals the pile of degraded bodies, their clothes torn, their faces covered with filth. All about him is agonized crying. Again he screams out to Ruth, paralyzed not only with fear but also with guilt at his enforced inaction, at the fact that he survived such horror. Suddenly the awful vision stops, and Nazerman hurtles out of the subway car onto the platform. The screaming continues in his mind as he stands mute, his hands cupping his head trying to wall out all that he has reexperienced. In an evocative repetition of the motif of Marilyn's reaching hand, Nazerman's left hand helplessly goes out toward the train as it slowly leaves the station. Lumet ends this sequence of appalling horror with quick intercuts to the film's opening scene as David, dying in the train of Nazerman's memory, is seen in earlier memory, reaching his hands out for the elusive butterfly in the lovely meadow.

Nazerman's final progression to a fully shared humanity comes more quickly in Lumet's vision than in Wallant's. While in the novel (chapter 22) the pawnbroker begins to lose his hold on the shop's finances after the river outing with Marilyn, Lumet's Nazerman begins to invite Rodriguez's vengeance immediately after his night journey. Nazerman gives more money than required to several customers, while still repelling Ortiz's repeated attempts to care for him. "I'm a student to you," pleads the youth, and Nazerman icily replies, "You're nothing to me." As Nazerman repeals his former close accounting perhaps to escape the guilt he increasingly allows himself to feel, he further punishes himself by rejecting his young assistant's concern. In the novel, blatant Christian imagery accompanies Ortiz's decision to go ahead with the robbery of the shop (238-39), but Lumet handles this decision more interestingly, visually depicting the boy's self-immolation through images familiar to him. Seen through a hand-held camera, suggesting the tenuousness and volatility of his life, Ortiz rushes down the street in search of Tangee; he passes a group of blacks stealing the tires from a Cadillac and others dealing drugs, through hordes of the poor milling about in markets who nearly crush him in their multitude. He is first viewed through the window of the pool room where the robbery previously most strongly tempted him, framed in and dominated by the elevated railway's oppressive structure; then the camera shows him from behind as he dashes down the street beneath the train—in the very place where the ambulance will, too late, come for him at the end of the film.

Lumet does not sustain the novel's sentimental intimation of a doubly Christian sacrifice. His vision, as always in the major films, is uncompromising and thus more powerful and true. When Ortiz locates the hoodlums, he insists that there be no guns, not out of compassion or charity, but because "I'm worried about Jesus Ortiz." The orthodox Christian solution provides no answer for Ortiz in the film, as the pawnbroker's assistant rushes up darkened stairs to discover his mother at a Catholic chapel above a funeral parlor. Just before we see his guilt-ridden face sliding out of frame left, Lumet encloses him as he ascends the stairs, gradually vanishing up from the camera's view even though supposedly he runs toward his God. Nor does a simple religious solution appeal to the director in regard to Nazerman, for, before the church scene, Lumet cuts to the pawnbroker in the shop from a very high angle, behind two rows of bars, and holds the scene there for several silent seconds. The final shot of this sequence likewise does not lead to a comforting conclusion: Lumet replaces Wallant's flashes of the central characters in chapter 25 just before the robbery with one silent scene of Robinson, the most violent hoodlum, whose shot will kill Ortiz. Lying in bed, with his harmonica in his mouth, he casually stares at pictures of muscular male models, tapping their nipples four times with his gun barrel to the beat of his own twisted melody. The suggestion of the inevitability of violence's connection to psychosexual aberration—daring for American commercial films of this period—presages the price that must be paid for Nazerman's psychic liberation.

The final sequence of Lumet's *Pawnbroker* is a monument in the history of American film. Nazerman, his face bloodied by Savarese and Rodriguez just previously, watches as Ortiz and his three henchmen enter the pawnshop by various doors to surround him. Gazing dazedly around the shop, Nazerman fixes momentarily upon the butterfly collection recently sold him by an elderly black man. The collection forces upon him the unwelcome memories of peace at the film's beginning, but as well the unwitting victimizing of the butterflies by his son and his children's vulnerability as they turn into the gunsights of the Nazi soldiers who long ago intruded upon his peace for the first time. Here Lumet speeds up from slow motion the rhythm of the film's opening scene; now Nazerman experiences the death of all illusion, as the horror that will let him live begins to rush in upon him. As the memory of the Nazi soldiers' siren fades away, Nazerman confronts the present criminals, perhaps resignedly anticipating his own death.

Seeing his master endangered by Robinson's gun, Ortiz leaps toward the camera and the opening in Nazerman's work counter, pulling the gangster's gun around into his own stomach as the gun discharges beyond Robinson's intended will. From an extremely high angle, Lumet's camera shows the dispersing of the gunmen and the wormlike crawl of the mortally wounded youth as he inches toward the door, separated from us by the wire screening of the counter. As a crowd gathers in front of the store, surrounding Ortiz, who has inched out through the door, Lumet closes in on Nazerman's unbelieving face, contorted at the horror of a repeated violence from which there is no escape. Above, black people lean idly out of their tenement windows; one is Ortiz's mother, who suddenly realizes the figure lying crumpled on the pavement. Another thin, desiccated old woman peers out of her window, unsurprised at the ritual. Nazerman seems to ooze out of his posture toward the street, almost limping, nearly stung into feeling; then his pace increases, and he reaches Ortiz and holds his head. Nazerman's right hand becomes bloody as he holds Ortiz's right hand, filled with his own blood from grasping at his wound. Ineffectually he tries to comfort the boy's face with his left hand and almost succeeds in cupping Ortiz's face in his hands, but it slips out of his reach as the boy dies, having screamed out, "I said not to hurt you, no, not to hurt you." In a sharp, low-angle, extreme close-up, Lumet shows Nazerman's face twisted with pain, the mouth opening wide, forming into a scream that never quite approaches sound (we hear only the wail of one lone trumpet). Then the ambulance arrives, and Nazerman walks slowly back into the shop.

Lumet cuts quickly to yet more of the street victims high above, leaning out of their windows, before he reveals Nazerman, slumped against his work counter, feeling with increasing pace and intensity the insistent memory of all the people whom he has exploited and denied, whom he has perceived as mere scum of the streets like the husk who is being carried into the ambulance. Flashes of Tessie, Mr. Smith, old Mendel, the blonde pregnant girl, Miss Birchfield, Mrs. Harmon, the oratorical award winner, and finally Ortiz well up before him.

Rather than Wallant's depiction on the novel's final page of Nazerman saying goodbye to his dead (279), Lumet forces the pawnbroker to face both his memories and the pain of the living. Significantly, Quincy Jones's jazz score accelerates quickly at this point, as the cycle of those Nazerman has hurt flashes ever more rapidly in his memory. In a close-up of the left side of his head and his left hand hovering near the metal office spike that has held his pawn tickets, Nazerman slowly raises his hand. With the deliberation of a man finally driven to know and to feel real things despite his horror of them, he slowly places his left hand upon the sharp spike and drives it far down. Lumet cuts to an extreme close-up of Nazerman's face and neck from a slight low angle; the neck and facial muscles quiver with the terrible pain, but the face gains a look approaching exaltation, release. His eyes open, his gaze up, he has no words now: there is only a quick cut of the maimed hand coming off the spike. Typically, Lumet refuses to sensationalize the shot with any show of gore. For the occurrence is a profoundly spiritual one for Nazerman; Lumet shows this silently when the pawnbroker gasps, obviously beginning to learn how to feel again, as the background jazz score sustains an almost unbearably high note.[45]

Then Lumet cuts to a low-angle shot from Nazerman's back out to the street crowd surrounding him, then to Nazerman wandering dazedly out the door, under the three balls of the storefront, into the rattle of the elevated train and the milling black people. In a low-angle frontal close-up, Nazerman looks back at the shop and then at his bloody right hand, the hand that has touched Ortiz and not the hand that he maimed. He begins slowly to walk through the crowd, as the now buoyant, pulsating jazz score again begins. Tentatively he turns a corner and leans momentarily against the wall of a bar. Then, as the camera gradually pulls back into a medium long-range shot, Nazerman manages to continue into the human throngs of the street, until he is visually lost, but morally found, in the flow of people, joined again with the cycle of humanity.

Chapter Five

Comic Misconnections and the Universality of Loss

One of Lumet's most appealing attributes as a director has been his career-long penchant for seeking to develop and to grow as an artist by working with various genres and types of cinematic literature. He has frequently commented upon his own felt weakness in directing effective comedy. Not content, as other important directors might have been, with such hallmark films as those discussed in chapter 4, nor with his acknowledged mastery of the films of sociological import, addressing crime and the gritty urban tragedy, Lumet has also attempted to develop his skill in films lighter both in subject matter and approach, working to correct what he has considered a weakness or incompleteness in his talent. Sometimes he directs a film with the central purpose of growing beyond his previous level of achievement in that art form, of trying to improve upon a perceived artistic limitation. Indeed, perhaps the central reason why Lumet remains critically underrated lies in his refusal to conform to audiences' preoccupation with directors who make one kind of picture, to his society's expectation of artistic specialization. Ranging from the flawed romances, *Stage Struck*, *Garbo Talks* and *The Wiz*, to the more satirical *Network* and *Just Tell Me What You Want*, Lumet has continued to attempt to impart a greater gaiety of spirit to his direction of comedy.

His two most successful comic films from literary sources, despite some weaknesses that the director himself acknowledges, are his 1968 films, *The Sea Gull* and *Bye, Bye Braverman*. In these, Lumet balances his consistent concern with social and psychological themes with a keen empathy for the comic aspects of human frailty, a sense of the ambiguities underlying human desolation, and an emphasis upon visually lyrical characteristics of the undeveloped and unrealized character. As Chekhov's sea gull is an apt symbol for the director's fine adaptation of premodern disappointment amid attempted liberation, so is Holly Levine's red Volkswagen an appropriate symbol for modern humanity's disorientation in and disconnection from the natural world.

The Sea Gull: The Comedy of Compassion

Cleanth Brooks and Robert B. Heilman write that it was Chekhov's genius "to observe compassionately the necessary mixture of strength and weakness in man."[1] Beneath the events and characters in all Lumet's major films lies a consistent concern for the ambivalences and ambiguities of human character and actions and a compassionate stance toward humankind's weaknesses and failings. Such compassion underlies the power of some of the director's finest representations of character: the loners of *Dog Day Afternoon* and *The Deadly Affair*, the pathological in *The Offence* and *Equus*, the frustrated in *Lovin' Molly* and *Long Day's Journey into Night*, and the futile of *The Group* and *The Fugitive Kind*. Lumet is nowhere stronger than in his depictions of complex, multifaceted characters, so it is not surprising that he was attracted to the lonely, suffering, winsome characters in Chekhov's great tragicomedy, *The Sea Gull*. Rather than following the older, more famous translations of Constance Garnett or Stark Young, Lumet used a recent translation by Moura Budberg for his film, making few, but significant, additions to the play that competently capture the comic charm of Chekhov's bumbling characters while maturely revealing the somber tone and the tragic implications and results of the characters' actions.

Before Chekhov's opening with the conversation of Masha and Medvedenko near the stage where soon Konstantin's romantic play will be presented, Lumet's wordless opening credits sequence expresses in tableau the ineffectually placid disconnectedness of the aristocratic Russian family on the weekend country estate of one of its members. Arkadina (Simone Signoret), the family's center, lies upon a hammock, with the lake in the background. The camera observes from above the actress in her yellow dress amid cushions as she looks at the trees, her face in bluish shadow. Her lonely, doomed son, Konstantin (David Warner), dressed in black, gazes off into the distance, and coming through the trees toward them, Nina (Vanessa Redgrave) walks, dressed in soft white, with her right hand upon her hair. The leisureliness of this prerevolutionary scene is heightened by Lumet's slow pan right to left to a horse and rider caught between Sorin's country house above and its reflection in the lake below, as the rider approaches the camera through the trees. Lumet next shows the old house and a slow close-in to Trigorin (James Mason), with Arkadina at the dresser observing him, then he slowly pans over estate workers and staff down a hill toward Konstantin working on his stage, and thence to a field where, beneath a tree, Masha (Kathleen Widdoes) and Medvedenko (Alfred Lynch) embrace. As the two speak the play's opening lines concerning Masha's habitual unhappiness and the schoolteacher's poverty and unrequited love for her, Lumet's additions accentuate Masha's loneliness. Unlike the play, in the film we see the couple embrace, then rise and walk, parted by trees as if to suggest the young woman's spiritual distance from the ardent Medvedenko. In a strikingly original manner, Lumet shows Masha, the steward's daughter, walk into camera, from low angle, and take snuff: Lumet's pan, right to left following Masha, speeds up somewhat as she takes the snuff, then slows pace as she resumes her walk.

Lumet lightens the action as the couple comes to the stage and encounters Arkadina's brother, Sorin. Portrayed superbly by a favorite Lumet actor during the middle 1960s and 1970s, Harry Andrews, Sorin emerges as Chekhov's voluble, frustrated, and unhappily retired civil servant. Reflecting Sorin's emotional openness and casual approach to the world, Lumet offers here a lovely, airy shot of the stage against the backdrop of the lake and the oncoming darkness, as Sorin and his nephew, Konstantin, discuss the youth's bitterness toward his mother's rejection of him and his art. During Konstantin's long diatribe, Sorin hovers above him, watching as though Konstantin were a part of the theatrical performance to come, chewing at his cigar. Andrews's jaunty performance well suits the lightness of the new Budberg translation here, revealed by a brief comparison between Lumet's choice and the standard Garnett translation. As Konstantin describes his eventual nemesis, the popular writer Trigorin, to him, Sorin says,

[Budberg] I must admit, dear boy, I'm rather drawn to literary men myself. There was a time in my youth when there were two things I wanted passionately. To get married and to be a man of letters. But I did neither, no indeed. It would be nice to've been a mediocre writer, even, you know.[2]

[Garnett] Well, I am fond of authors, my boy. At one time I had a passionate desire for two things: I wanted to get married, and I wanted to become an author; but I did not succeed in doing either. Yes, it is pleasant to be even a small author, as a matter of fact.[3]

Lumet gains our compassion for Sorin as the Russian rambles along in an informal style but yet reveals his modest artistic pretensions in such phrases as "literary men" and "man of letters."

One of the reasons for the success of Lumet's adaptation of *The Sea Gull* is its simultaneously artful balancing of the comic and the serious.[4] Sorin's amusing reactions to Konstantin's speeches do not completely offset the terrible pain suffered by Arkadina's son, whose felt rejections will end in his suicide in the film's final image. As Konstantin resentfully scores his mother for her selfishness and stinginess, her disdain for her son's work and preference for only sentimental and popular art that will increase the fame of an aging actress, Lumet holds him in sharp low angle against the sky and the trees, prefiguring his kinship with the things of the natural world that the artificiality of his mother's world will soon snuff out. Kneeling beneath his uncle and picking flower petals as he decides yet again upon the reality of his mother's lack of love for him, Konstantin at once expresses an underdeveloped personality and a view of art maturer than that of the veteran actress. Lumet once frames him by tall trees in deep background as the youth excoriates the vulgar conventionality of the age of Arkadina's theater. As he expresses his preference for nothingness rather than the present stale artistic forms, he walls out the lake and the trees by suddenly raising the stage curtain, predicting his ultimate dissolution with the sea gull by referring to himself in a low whisper as "the only nonentity. What am I? Who am I?" Yet the sound of an unseen rear curtain's flapping loudly in the breeze wittily balances this potentially tragic scene, as Konstantin points out the superficiality of Trigorin's writings.

Nina's sudden flustered arrival to act in Konstantin's philosophical drama, a brief respite from the father who closely guards her, is accompanied by Nina and Konstantin's warm embrace and a fine reaction shot of Sorin smiling at them, against the moving stage curtain upon which shadows of the leaves move about. Expressive of the old man's past dreams, the shot is also a visual correlative for Chekhov's theme of the evanescence of social classes and of all mortal things. Nina expresses her fear of her father, and Sorin comforts her, slapping her rump playfully (original to the film), a foreshadowing that another older man will exploit her insecurity and vulnerability more profoundly than the harmless Sorin. And Konstantin's kiss and his declarations of love for Nina are met centrally by her request concerning Trigorin's age.

Lumet reveals his frequent concern with psychological enclosure as Polina (Eileen Herlie), the wife of Shamraev, Sorin's steward, and her true beloved, Dorn (Denholm Elliott), the superficially wise doctor, begin their walk toward the stage. Their long walk through the trees begins with both enclosed spatially on a porch between the railing and the house, in shadows. Polina's solicitous concern for Dorn's health and her displeasure in his attraction to Arkadina's status as a famed stage actress reveal her love for him, which, like so many loves in the drama, is to be unrequited. As Arkadina begins already to dismiss her son's vision of a new art, Lumet suddenly cuts to Nina, all in white, her head peeping up out of a hole in the stage, ready for her opening speech from Konstantin's play. The author teeters in front of the curtain like life's inconclusiveness itself, then hops off. As the curtain squeaks down, up into the frame floats Nina, the white billowing spirit of art and the world soul. To her "Cold, cold, cold. Empty, empty, empty. Terrifying, terrifying, terrifying" speech, Konstantin reverently and silently mouths the words of his lifelessly idealistic play. Masha responds hopefully, while Polina attempts to put her arm around Dorn and then withdraws it. Arkadina, already bored, cracks a nut loudly. As the black-garbed, red-eyed devil figure lumbers toward the lovely world soul, the lake reeds blowing behind Nina, Arkadina's carping eventually enrages her son, who stops the play and angrily runs off into the woods, bound by his mother's ceaseless rejection of him and his aspirations. As Arkadina begins her fine scene of renunciation of the "new art," Lumet's camera reveals Masha in deep background, between Arkadina and Sorin, her back to them as she faces the lake; then Lumet visually juxtaposes the downcast young woman to a white swan just before she rushes off to search for her beloved Konstantin, who does not return her love.

Lumet says that he considers Simone Signoret's performance as Arkadina as one of the finest in his films, despite her French accent that distressed some of the film's early reviewers. "She's fabulous for that part; that *is* Arkadina." [5] The actress's superior performance is nowhere more effective than in the sequence in which she ridicules Konstantin and his art, employing the occasion of the play and her son's angry departure to show off her still-striking beauty and coquetry while defending her own popular art against the threat of his less conventional precepts, thus also attempting to secure the dying culture she both loves and needs against the oncoming incursions of a new century. Called Jupiter by Dorn, Arkadina is at once the supreme center of the family galaxy, a wise commentator on falsely motivated art, and a jealous, selfish woman. Lumet's choice of the new Budberg translation heightens Arkadina's vitality and spirit, even when measured against the Stark Young version, which is livelier than the Garnett. Arkadina calls her son "a capricious, conceited boy," and Sorin answers softly, "He only wanted to give you pleasure." She replies,

[Budberg] Did he really? But he didn't choose a normal play, did he? He merely forced us to listen to this decadent, nightmarish nonsense! I'm perfectly willing to listen to nonsense for a joke, but this is some kind of pretension to new forms, a new era in art. It isn't, in fact, a question of new forms, but of a nasty temper.

[Young] Yes? I notice he didn't choose some familiar sort of play, but forced his own decadent raving on us. I can listen to raving. I don't mind listening to it, so long as I'm not asked to take it seriously; but this of his is not like that. Not at all, it's introducing us to a new epoch in art, inaugurating a new era in art. But to my mind it's not new forms or epochs, it's simply bad temper.[6]

Lumet's camera also honors Arkadina's ambiguity. Strutting about as she judges her son's art mainly according to her own standards of normality, Arkadina soon walks, followed by the camera, to a seat by the lake, with Trigorin following her. Admitting that Medvedenko's plea for theatrical realism is just, she asks, "Don't let us talk about atoms and plays anymore. It's too perfect a night for that. Listen, someone is singing. Ah, it's lovely." As she evokes memories of better days from the past across the lake, she simultaneously regrets her cruelty to "Kostya," calling out to him into the woods, and flirts both with Trigorin and Dorn, in an action original to the film looping an arm casually over each admirer. Lumet concludes the sequence with a series of shots of three other female characters, occupying separate planes of space, that echoes Arkadina's basic isolation and loneliness. First, a close-up shows Masha rushing off behind Polina to search for her beloved Konstantin, then a pan left to right ends holding on Polina, disclosing that her beloved Dorn is not with her now, and finally Nina is observed in deep background just before her fateful meeting with Trigorin, coming through the stage curtain's white sheets toward the camera.

Lumet reveals his compassion for these people whose efforts to reach each other and some meaning in life nearly always just miss connection and fulfillment in graceful character blocking, especially in the material that concludes act 1 of the play. Nina meets Trigorin as Redgrave gives a perfectly timed little curtsey; as Arkadina also fawns on the writer, the usually masterful Dorn looks hurt and suddenly asks that the stage curtain be lowered so that the dark night does not appear so fearful. The stolid Shamraev (Ronald Radd, the captain in Lumet's *Iceman Cometh*) of course misses all their subtle play of emotions and brags of the singing prowess of a man from the local church choir. Nina fears she must appease her father and depart, and the loving Sorin cups her chin, urging her to stay, near her dream of going upon the stage. Yet she runs off up the hill, her white dress just visibly moving lyrically upon the green. Then the family walks slowly back to the house in groups, crossing each other in a Renoir-like dance with Medvedenko trailing behind. As if to show Konstantin lost in his abstractions, Lumet then shoots the dark youth from the rear emerging from the woods and approaching the stage and the waiting Dorn. As the doctor kindly tries to help the muddled Konstantin, Lumet accentuates the older man's literary ignorance and vulnerability by shooting him from high angle as he stands on the nearly dark stage, vainly attempting to locate his own feelings in admiring Konstantin's play in unintentionally comic declarations, while behind him stands a crudely painted stage flat of eddying waves. "But what, what I wanted to say was you've chosen a subject from the field of abstract ideas. That was the right thing to do because a work of art has got to express a great idea. Only serious things can be really beautiful." In a beautifully lighted shot Lumet next shows Masha running in search of Konstantin, her dark black dress even darker than the woods, reaching her love just as he, paying scant attention to Dorn's words, runs off in search of Nina. Once again, the sometimes foolishly wise Dorn has an opportunity to offer wisdom to the lovelorn Masha, as she confides in a father figure to substitute for the obtuse Shamraev. Shadows gradually cover Masha's face as she lays her head on the shoulder of a man who can only offer the remark "Everywhere such a lot of love. H'm. It must be the sorcery of the lake."

Lumet continues in the middle section of the film to explore the mysteries behind the characters' loneliness and frustrated dreams, faithfully adapting the material in the middle two acts of the drama and using grace of movement, camera work, and even color to draw forth Chekhov's ideas and themes. When Arkadina plays croquet on the lawn by the lake, her spiritedness, compared with Masha's usual blackness of dress and demeanor and Dorn's withdrawal in white-suited philosophizing, is captured in the blazing yellow of her gown as she knocks Dorn's ball almost into the lake. One of the film's loveliest compositions occurs as Sorin, limping, with Medvedenko and the wheelchair hovering nearby, joyfully brings Nina into the group, temporarily freed from her tyrannical family. Nina sits at the center, surrounded left to right by the consoling Sorin, Arkadina, Medvedenko seated on the ground, then Masha and Dorn, all backgrounded by varying shades of green in the woods behind them. As each argues positions inconclusively, Sorin, clutching his dwindling life as he does his cigar, seems most vitally in possession of his illusions. Then, as Arkadina lies back in her hammock, Nina does also, her head and feet facing the opposite way from the older woman whose profession she so soon will emulate.

Lumet varies the sea gull episode somewhat, visually emphasizing the foreshadowing of Konstantin's death as well as of Nina's emotional paralysis through her future relationship with Trigorin. Just after Polonia is passionlessly given the flowers she begged from Dorn, Lumet cuts to Nina running through the woods along an aisle of two confining lines of trees toward the camera, and then he follows her left to right until she almost runs into Konstantin who, unlike the drama, in which he lays the freshly killed sea gull at her feet as he announces his imminent suicide, instead thrusts the bloody sea gull out toward her at the level of her face. Lumet then holds them in separate close-ups, as Konstantin accuses her of coldness to him and of despising his play, talking more to the shadow of his mother than to the real Nina. Her face in shadows, Nina attempts to respond to him with a wisp of hair in her mouth. "You've become so irritable lately. You talk in a strange kind of way, well, in symbols. This sea gull, too, is apparently some kind of symbol. Well, forgive me if I don't understand you. I'm probably too simple to understand you." While in the play Nina lays the dead gull on the seat, in the film Konstantin hurls it away as he derides "my own pride that sucks my life's blood away like a snake!" At the final word, Lumet cuts to Nina's face looking toward the lake where Trigorin walks with a book; she runs down the road toward the writer, recognizing Konstantin's lifelessness but tragically failing to see Trigorin's. Into the shadows she goes, where during her talk with Trigorin she will come upon the sea gull and throw it near the place where Konstantin will eventually end his life. Lumet draws a performance from Mason that embodies moral coldness itself; Trigorin here is not simply the slightly meandering writer of the play, but a figure of potential menace, who, during his long speech concerning the writer's life and pain, circles Nina three times, codifying, already using her, sardonically bitter rather than just filled with self-doubt. In Nina he finds a gull so eager for celebrity and glory that she will, indeed, condemn herself to dwell "alone with the hateful knowledge of my own imperfections."

Lumet respectfully, if in a somewhat static manner, adapts the material up to the lapse of two years in the action, including Trigorin's weak-willed submission to Arkadina's flattery designed to lead him away from Nina and his accidental encounter with the girl before his departure that will lead to their brief, unhappy affair in Moscow after Nina leaves her cherished lake to begin a career on the stage. Lumet effectively visualizes the decline of all the characters to a state resembling Masha's description of herself: "Maria, who belongs nowhere and lives on this earth to no purpose." As the consequences of their lack of self-recognition and vision become more serious than amusing,

Lumet's compassionate comedy becomes a sensitive cinematic study in human desolation and eventual degeneration. When Polonia and Masha cry separately over Dorn and Konstantin, who has become a successful writer, the director instead focuses upon the loneliness and rejection of a life force, Medvedenko. Now Masha's ignored husband, he persists in seeking confirmation by repeatedly saying goodbye and pathetically reaching out in turn for the hands of his wife, his mother-in-law Polonia, and Dorn, receiving but a perfunctory nod from each. As Sorin and Dorn continue their cyclic conversation on unrealized goals and death, the ill Sorin pleading in favor of life and Dorn, at a low angle, visually cornered into the ceiling, counseling acceptance and forgetfulness, Lumet's camera pulls back very slowly behind the back of Masha's head to include them all, stopping again behind Polonia to view the group in their vulnerability. As Konstantin relates the sad story of Trigorin's abandonment of Nina following the death of their child and her lack of stage success, Masha watches his sadness from out of her own, and at his mention of Nina's signing her letters Sea Gull, Lumet closes in on a two-shot of Dorn and Konstantin, suggesting some complicity, some recognition on the older man's part. When Arkadina and Trigorin enter just before their autumn card-playing ritual, Lumet frames Arkadina, who will admit that the lotto game is boring but necessary to pass the time, from low angle in a confined space between the wood beams. As the cardplayers begin, Lumet's camera tilts slightly once again to include all the frustrated and exhausted, the camera over Masha's left shoulder and, of course, the irrepressible Arkadina facing into the camera at the center of the frame.

Masha plays most vigorously of all the cardplayers, as she must listen to Trigorin's bored dismissal of her love's lifeless literary efforts. When Konstantin sees that Trigorin has not even read his work after pretending to praise it, he enters the card room and kisses his mother both more passionately and tenderly than in the play, Arkadina still facing into the camera. As Konstantin departs for his final meeting with Nina and then his pistol, Lumet cuts to the reflective Dorn, his shadow visible to frame left. Trigorin of course wins the card game, caring no more for this victory than for the sea gull he had two years before asked Shamraev to preserve for him. Lumet shoots the final meeting between Konstantin and his beloved in the woods and draws from Redgrave a performance of superb ambivalence, heightening both Nina's achieved spiritual endurance through suffering and her great difficulty in maintaining emotional control as her repeated references from their innocent past to the sea gull interrupt her story, sometimes rendering her voice and face nearly inhuman, birdlike in the dark light. While she sobs the opening lines of Konstantin's play, confessing to him her continuing obsession with Trigorin, Lumet's camera remains in close-up upon him. Nina hugs him, but without giving the love Konstantin needs to prevent his dissolution. At the sound of the pistol's discharge, Lumet cuts to a long shot from where the body lies to Dorn, walking toward the place from the house, a more starkly realistic ending than Dorn's quiet urging of Trigorin to get Arkadina away from the estate. Lumet's conclusion visually emphasizes the finality of Konstantin's act and its effect upon all his eroded companions, as he pans around the card table, stopping one by one to observe the players, from the silent Arkadina to the finally stunned Trigorin. Dorn enters the room, and all look at him as the stricken Masha numbly keeps repeating lotto numbers. Lumet successfully adapts Chekhov's "tragedy of attrition" in part because of the director's career-long fascination with individuals who waste life and ignore opportunity, with sensitive, melancholy strivers who move through evocative, lyrically rendered atmospheres. *The Sea Gull* contains sympathetic instances of characters "rusting away in disuse, eventlessly stalemated, or permanently dislocated," and the director establishes cinematically effective means to memorialize their pathos.[7]

Bye, Bye Braverman: Death and Sympathy

Lumet observed in an interview, "I've always felt guilty about *Braverman*. . . . I don't think I did it well enough. I know a lot of people like it, and *I* like it, but it's very imperfect, it's very uneven. . . . You feel the director's insecurity with comedy, a lack of command of a certain level of comedy . . . the light comedy edge that was missing from *Stage Struck*. . . . A little irony, a little laughter wouldn't have hurt it; and I've been aware of that lack for a long time." An adaptation of Wallace Markfield's undeservedly forgotten 1964 novel *To an Early Grave, Bye, Bye Braverman* (1968) may not meet its director's own high standards for his work and does, indeed, contain some excessively broad sequences and heaviness of treatment in certain scenes. Lumet's frequently lyrical film, however, represents his first major attempt at comedy and successfully transmits at least some of the manic spirit of Markfield's novel. At the same time it adds substantially to Lumet's reputation as an explorer of sensitive psychological and social issues as well as of the novelist's "mother and father of all sorrows," humankind's fear of death and the perhaps equal sadness at early expectations and dreams gone unrealized.[8]

Markfield's first novel treats one day in the life of four third-string

New York Jewish literary intellectuals, during which they attempt, with humorous and satiric sidetracks, to attend the Brooklyn funeral of a fellow early middle-aged writer and critic, Leslie Braverman, dead suddenly of a heart attack at age forty-one. Termed by Stanley Edgar Hyman "a small comic triumph, the sunniest novel about death that I know," *To an Early Grave* memorably depicts the literary endeavors and petty games of the second-generation Jewish *Commentary/Partisan Review* crowd.[9] It includes frequently hilarious urban Jewish speech rhythms and dialogue, pointed anecdotal humor ("I had a very, very bitter and tragic life. They put it on television, it would crack the tube" [170]), and perceptive characterizations of the four pseudointellectual but basically good-hearted travelers who, each in his own way, comes to terms with his life while in search of the elusively deceased Braverman. The most sympathetic searcher is fund-raiser and occasional minor writer, Morroe Rieff, who by day's end can cry not only for his friend but, more important, also for himself. His two colleagues closest in age, Barnet Wiener and Holly Levine, both overrate their intellectual status and accomplishments and really are most attached to their adolescent preoccupations with B movies and pop culture slogans and heroes. The fourth, late-fiftyish Felix Ottensteen, a writer of minor articles for Jewish newspapers, comes earliest to a realization of the finality of Leslie's and all death, and his "rhetoric about Jewish woes is a relief from the culture-faking of the rest of them."[10] Markfield, also the author of the 1970 novel *Teitelbaum's Window*, forges a fine serio-comic vision of the growth toward limited understanding among this group of lower-middle-class Jews in which satire is balanced by affection.[11]

Lumet's problems in adapting the novel included the excellence of its detailed ethnic Jewishness, its rhetorical and anecdotal excesses, and the frequently forced and overextended humor and topical and period allusions. There are so many in-jokes in *To an Early Grave* that they tend to swamp the novel's moral and mythic resonances; Stanley Edgar Hyman succinctly expresses the novel's greatest problem in the title of his review-essay "Jewish, All Too Jewish." Lumet and screenwriter Herbert Sargent effectively remove much of the sometimes funny but extraneous material to concentrate upon the more universal human comedy at the heart of the novel.[12] To deepen the action and its implications beyond Markfield's ethnic regionalism, Lumet removes early material in the novel concerning Morroe's father's business failures with a candy store and the split and eventual reconciliation between Morroe and his father. Also excised are Morroe's memories of his mother's death, the argument between Holly and a Jewish cab driver after their cars collide (in the film, the cab driver is black), the episode between Felix and the lady in the candy store following Morroe's discovery that they have arrived at the wrong funeral, and the humorous but very long section in which the group assembles with Inez Braverman at the proper cemetery for mourning amid an almost interminable tally of the mourners and their varied backgrounds. Lumet additionally widens the scope of the themes by omitting such topical New York references as Morroe and Leslie's dispute over Morroe's decision to forsake the Village for the higher status of an uptown address, and the character of Toego, Markfield's didactic complainer, who at the beginning and the end of the novel establishes blatantly the hardships caused in the city by creeping inflation and human insensitivity. Further, the director condenses the novel's abundant zaniness and wordy anecdotes: gone in the film are such elements as material on Felix's background, Wiener's con on Brucie Siskind (the newly annointed editor of *Portent*), Morroe's fantasies of Miss Social Welfare and of the departed Goldie Bromberg, and the cemetery fantasy with a strange old Jewish pretzel lady. As Hyman complains, the ample humor and pace of the novel frequently are overwhelmed with wordy passages.[13] Morroe, for example, in a moment of dejection, invokes the intercession of Leslie's spirit:

I am no big intellect. I am no bargain. I watch too much television. I read, but I do not retain. I am not lost exactly, but still I am nowhere. I am the servant of no great end. I follow the recommendations of the *Consumer's Research Bulletin*.

But do me this favor, anyway. Keep them off. . . . They wait deep in the dark. They put in my mouth the taste of darkness. They set grief and despair upon me like savage dogs. They give me queer feelings, they get me all balled up . . . they will rip me with tooth and claw. They will throw me from awful heights. . . . They will put me in a grave. (136-37)

Lumet extends the moral implications of sometimes overlong and overly wordy scenes while sustaining the novel's fine local habitation through the direction of splendid performances that thoroughly embody the Jewish charm and lexical humor of Markfield's daffy characters and events. He draws scintillating performances from George Segal as Morroe, Jack Warden and Sorrell Booke as Barnet and Holly, and Joseph Wiseman as Felix. He also expands the importance of the novel's marginal female characters, so that Inez Braverman emerges as a dynamic force, represented by Jessica Walter, and Zohra Lampert deepens the significance of Morroe's wife, Etta. Lumet also heightens the roles of three minor characters by directing good (if not altogether thematically successful) performances by Alan King as the rabbi and Godfrey Cambridge as the cab driver; he also adds a short but amusing scene featuring Anthony Holland—who brightens the comedy in *The Anderson Tapes*—as Max, Felix's errant son.

Lumet's credits sequence underscores his vision of the novel as a meditation upon youth's losses discovered in early middle age. While the novel opens with Morroe's reiterative dream of a past failure preventing his voyage on a huge ship of knowledge, Lumet's film first reveals Morroe as a pensive young boy, seated on a horse in 1930s New York, a floppy cap astride a sad smile, as we hear in the background a drum roll, a whistle, and the soft moan of a calliope. Over the credits, all in lowercase, Morroe and his friends launch into the circus of their lives; Lumet cuts from a close-up of Morroe to a freeze-frame of a lonely, red-headed Barnet on a merry-go-round, before the machine begins, like his life, to move him around, with just a little jerk at first, until the camera pulls back and the boy is obscured by a passing horse and wagon loaded with old mattresses. Avidly reading comic books while dressed in their high-top black sneakers and knickers, the two boys are next seen in front of a candy store, surrounded by images of beloved licorice balls, orange Jujy Fruits, and Sky Diver kites, until they are again caught in freeze-frame, just as was Barnet by the horse and wagon. As the chums are to be caught for years in the experiences of childhood, a physically mature Holly is next seen among a gymnasium audience, cheering Barnet as he leaps for a basket and is held in freeze-frame. Lumet next cuts to a Village movie house, where Barnet gets tickets for *Shoe Shine* for Morroe, Holly, and himself, and holds that shot also finally in freeze-frame. Felix, too, will be fixed in his youthful dreams as Lumet concludes this sequence with gestural humor: his three younger friends approaching him, Felix stands before a crowd, orating in the rain in praise of Norman Thomas's Socialist candidacy. Waving his arms with such enthusiasm that his right arm sweeps so far around the left of his head that it almost encircles it, he, too, is held in freeze-frame.

Omitting the novel's details of Morroe's meeting the Bravermans and of their literary parties and existential talks, Lumet in the following sequences, most of them original to the film, introduces the four intellectuals in their present middle-aged lives. First Morroe begins to face his ambivalence concerning his move recently from the Village for a more secure life in fund-raising on the Upper East Side. When he receives Inez's telephone call about Leslie's sudden death, Morroe at once romanticizes Braverman's "Russian energy" and bemoans a never-to-be-repaid small loan he made to Leslie. Lumet visually shows the potential here for both the serious and the comic: while Etta reminds him unsparingly of his attraction-repulsion to his youthful bohemian life, Morroe is framed by a bare, white wall as he buries his face in his washcloth; yet a moment later, the director reveals Morroe's improved material status, showing him brushing his teeth with a huge electric toothbrush. In the novel, Etta remains silent after a mild quarrel as Morroe leaves for Braverman's funeral, but Etta is more sympathetic in the film. Despite her complaint that her husband is acting the stooge for Inez—and for people, generally, at the mere hint of a need—she is shown in close-up, seated on the bed, as she faces her husband in the bathroom while he shaves. Gently she says, "Morroe, do you know why you're going?" and Lumet cuts to Morroe at the word *why*. His face lathered in side-shot, he pauses in midstroke at this but does not look at his wife. In a close-up of her looking with tenderness at him, her voice dropping on the last two syllables, Etta says, "If you find out you'll tell me?" Framed by Morroe's numb stare at his wife from the bathroom, Lumet cuts to the first of his humorously revealing fantasy scenes in *Braverman:* after a policeman's finger pushes the bell of the Rieffs' apartment and a decisive Morroe enters informing Etta of her husband's death, Etta, garbed in a gossamer negligee, floats about the flower-filled room, accompanied by lush background music. Walking toward her husband's typewriter, she dissolves in tears into policeman/Morroe's sturdy arms: "His books, his notes, look, this will never know his touch again. . . . This morning, I didn't squeeze his orange juice."

We first see the present-day Felix as Lumet cuts to a deli on the Upper West Side, where Felix has breakfast with his whining, pseudointellectual son, Max. Directing the superb Wiseman with both tenderness and satiric bite, Lumet reveals the staunch old liberal's ambivalence toward his son, who bitterly complains, in preparation for borrowing yet more money from his father to finance his formal education, that he suffers such drains upon his creativity from the burdens of his office job that he cannot write poetry. Felix acidly reminds Max of past generations of writers who worked in shops fourteen hours a day, still finding time for poetry and energy for starting revolutions. The youth replies that it is not his fault if there are no more revolutions needing to be waged, and Felix withers his son with a stare: "I'll mail you a list." In this scene, Lumet perhaps reveals a reason that his films have not gained greater cachet among certain critics: while the director favorably presents true intellectuality where he finds it (General Black in *Fail Safe,* the courageous architect-juror in *12 Angry Men,* and to some extent Nazerman and Mr. Smith in *The*

Pawnbroker and Dysart in *Equus,* as well as Felix in *Braverman*), he ruthlessly mocks the fakery, pomposity, and disingenuousness of many pseudointellectuals. Young Max, like Groteschele in *Fail Safe,* Trigorin and Konstantin in *The Sea Gull,* and, to some extent, Dobbs in *The Deadly Affair,* is caught up in abstractions at the expense of intelligent approaches to them, to say nothing of passionately lived life. After his father comments on the themes he has located in Max's poems, the young man unctiously and condescendingly explains the finer points of literary criticism to the old Socialist: "I was mocking, satirizing the poet's attitude toward industrial society." Max follows up immediately with his wish that his father finance his Ph.D. studies. Max's nastiness finally provokes Felix into slapping him with the admission "I wasn't too crazy about your mother and I liked you even less," before Max makes a miffed, running exit from the scene. While Lumet will typically balance the issue by gently satirizing Felix's overzealous support of Israel throughout the film, here Felix emerges as the most sincerely intellectual of the four searchers for Leslie Braverman.

Perhaps the most hilarious of the four realistic scenes involving the four major characters is the introduction of Holly Levine and his prodigious writer's block. Lumet's depiction of Holly's compulsive style of intellectual endeavor, coupled with the writer's adolescent attachment to his pop art cult heroes, is his richest satire in the film. Outside Holly's Lower West Side writer's garret, neighborhood adolescents attempt to despoil his precious red Volkswagen—though scorned by Felix as a "legacy from Hitler," later the film's most famous icon for an illusory lyrical freedom. Inside, clad in a cream robe with orange trim, Holly stands imprisoned by other possessions, his large white telephone, his camel hair bed pillow, the implements on his desk in perfect order. As the master prepares to write, Lumet's camera stares at the blank page: no words appear. Although Holly ostensibly uses his typewriter, we next see him frenziedly cleaning all the shavings from his pencil sharpener, brushing every shaving from his immaculate desk, and then sharpening all his pencils before he repeats the sharpener-cleaning procedure. Following another shot of the still-blank page, Holly polishes assiduously with Windex every surface of his glass desktop; as he does so, the camera catches in the background by his bed a giant poster of the Phantom fighting an enormous tiger, the caption "Whew" echoing the eternal adolescent's dismay at his present struggle. Now Holly moves everything on his desk, cleaning beneath it, then seats himself to renew the assault, lighting his cigar with a large silver lighter. Rubbing his hands together vigorously, peering again at the insistently blank page through his horn-rimmed glasses, Holly slowly types and speaks for posterity: "Certainly, Professor Gombitz's essays—gathered together for the first time—yield pleasure of a kind." In a superior comic performance, Sorrell Booke smiles smugly, slightly twitches an eye, and, tilting his cigar at a rakish angle, softly murmurs, "That's nice, very nice." He reflects with a contented smile on the first word in his sentence until he begins to worry that word, a scowl clouding his cherubic countenance until he becomes the embodiment of a contemporary Oscar Wilde on style, preparing to dedicate yet more hours to taking a comma out again.

We meet another writer manqué as Lumet cuts to "barnet weinstein on the lower East side" (not Wiener as in the novel), frolicking in bed this Sunday morning with the lissome Myra Mandelbaum (Phyllis Newman), both backgrounded by Barnet's colorful wall poster of "The Big Musical Hit, Earl Glenn and His Rosebud Girlies." Ever attached to his mother, who delights in referring to Myra as Mary Murphy, Barnet defends her to Myra with such proclamations as "She's crazy about you, with her own hands she grinds top round for your stuffed cabbage" and accuses Myra of "Bronx cunning" as symbolized by her Helena Rubinstein compact, for her refusal to stay over after they have made love sixty times. After a tiff the lovers finally return to bed, Barnet in his electric blue pajamas lost in his adolescence as he looks starrily upward and coaxes her, "And who will write the definitive piece on Lawrence?" Her predictable response aids his gentle bondage to boyhood.

Lumet's final original scene in this early sequence returns to Morroe as he journeys to the Village to attempt to console Inez Braverman. In Lumet's initial shot of Morroe on the bus, we can observe behind the glum fund-raiser a tired workman on a rear bench, a person truly beset by life's harsh circumstances, less fortunate than the four well-meaning but passive intellectuals whom Lumet sympathetically spoofs. Surrounded visually by a striking red and blue plastic bus interior, Morroe strives to compensate for the sympathy he himself needs by extending it uninvited to fellow passengers, some of whom are angered at his interference, especially as he identifies for a comic book reader the villain in a Dick Tracy episode and ruins the experience for the disgruntled passenger.

The heavy-handed treatment of at least three major scenes in *Braverman* weakens the film's comic impact. The episodes involving Godfrey Cambridge's long-winded turns as an improbable cab driver who collides with Holly's precious red Volkswagen as it carries the four friends toward what they hope is the funeral, and Alan King's rabbinical orations over the bier of a corpse who, to the tired searchers' dismay, turns out not to be Braverman's, both today are criticized by Lumet himself as excessive and labored.[14] Similarly lacking the comic deftness of other parts of the film, notably Lumet's fantasy scenes involving Morroe, is the overly protracted scene of Inez hosting Morroe, who comes both to comfort Leslie's widow and to learn the location of Braverman's funeral. As in the other two more literally adapted episodes, some of the visuals and slapstick business are amusing: backgrounded by a billboard proclaiming "Happy Motoring," a chubby, out-of-shape Holly challenges the huge black cabbie to conflict by karate; much funnier than the lumbering Cambridge is the work of Jessica Walter as the voracious Inez, as she breezily greets Morroe, "Hi, baby," squirming her tight-fitting black mourner's sheath into a director's chair in the Bravermans' crowded, professionally bohemian apartment.

Inez skewers the naive Morroe's illusions about his friend with the revelation that she and Leslie were about to divorce because of his continual infidelities and unsanitary habits. Ever loyal to Leslie as a "creative person," Morroe allows, "Believe me, no one ever said Leslie was the cleanest person in the world." But the very bravura of Walter's performance slows the film's pace as, becoming lugubrious over her husband's clothes and his professed devotion to Morroe, she starts kissing her visitor, throwing him on the bed and entangling herself with him. As Morroe vainly attempts to free himself, Inez's child, to whom she has earlier described Leslie as "a pornographer . . . versatile, sweetie," reenters, asking solemnly, "How do you spell pornographer?" Inez then rises, saying acidly, "Later, sweetie, I'll read some to ya," before she rushes out, giving Morroe only the sketchiest directions to the funeral parlor. Beyond its humor, the scene significantly excises from the scene in the novel Morroe's unsuccessful attempt to weep after telephoning "the boys" about Leslie's death (102). Lumet's version of the story will defer so substantial a realization of suffering until the conclusion and will then share with Markfield the expression of that suffering.

One of Lumet's most successful scenes depicts Morroe's meeting with Barnet in a Manhattan park after he has informed the others of Braverman's death. The director extends this scene from that in the novel (100-102), retaining some of the humor while emphasizing, with the addition of a surrealistic passage, Morroe's gradual discovery of sorrow. The camera pans across the park to a street in the background where the beginnings of the process of life's sadness are visible in the squalling of a baby, gently being rocked. Suddenly, the man-child Barnet appears, singing loonily, "Down in the Village they're starting the day, Morroe Rieff calls you I'm caught in the ha-a-y-y," ending in falsetto. A moment later, as Morroe reflects that Braverman was only forty-one at his death, the camera pans right to left to a railing separating a left side-shot of Barnet in rear frame from a right side-shot of Morroe in front frame, suggesting visually the separateness from some of our fellows and from childhood inevitably brought on by the gaining of experience and of years. After Barnet jokes about Braverman's unique brand of integrity, Lumet cuts to a building in the background, and Morroe begins to fill the nearly empty frame, recalling that Braverman "could spend two days over a sentence." As Morroe slowly grows in awareness of the human condition, Lumet conveys the inevitable pain accompanying such recognition by visually positioning him so that a pointed iron railing stands just at the level of his chest. Barnet also praises Braverman's great attachment to the printed word (echoing Lumet's own similar respect), expressing sorrow that he "was all alone at the end."

As Morroe begins to demur that Leslie "was stopped in the middle," Lumet cuts momentarily to a surrealistic episode. Morroe flashes back in his mind to the bus ride on his way to seeing Inez: now the driver, he sees in the rearview mirror the two passengers whose routines he disturbed by his kibitzing. One speaks of a recently dead Morroe: although he worked in fund-raising, his "writing was getting sort of popular." Lumet immediately cuts back to Morroe in the park, as he says to Barnet that it is easier to die in life's beginnings: "In the beginning you go out sure of yourself. Because in the middle, good or bad, you know maybe where you're going and you want to see it through. To die then is not too nice." Morroe's poignant words coalesce with screenwriter Sargent's "Braverman Theme," which is sung over the opening credits and whose wordless melody recurs at key points in the film, reminding the audience of humankind's responsibility to endow each moment with significance as long as we continue in life's dance.

Lumet's comic touch deftly balances the seriousness of the scene by having the boys agree that to die in midflight is akin to departing before the end of a Hitchcock movie. They proceed to discuss the merits and demerits of several such films. At this point Holly, in driving beret, arrives in his red Volkswagen; the others park him in too tightly, and the first of what will be the day's substantial damages is inflicted on Holly's prize, a mechanical correlative to the personal gaining of wisdom that will occur. The three men are next framed inside a typically Lumetian cramped space as they attempt to allay their fears of death with amusing repartee concerning former pop heroes, old commercials, and related trivia. Booke is especially brilliant here, as with utter aplomb he recalls such minutiae requested by his friends as the identity of the Green Hornet's driver and the names of Daddy Warbucks's protectors. "A little room, please. A person could die in here," Morroe protests to Holly, and the boys, led by Holly, segue into "in its entirety, the theme song from the Fitch Bandwagon." Lumet's use of the Fitch theme is more amusing than Markfield's Wheaties/Jack Armstrong theme (113). Also faster in tempo, it provides both splendid harmonic singing by the trio and a more staunch and thematically relevant defense against their fears:

> Laugh awhile,
> Let a smile be your style.
> Use Fitch Shampoo.
> Don't despair,
> Use your head, save your hair,
> Use Fitch Shampoo.

The bald Holly ("Yul Brynner shaves his head, I'm authentic") leads them to ever-grander flights of zaniness, as he croons, "Once again, from the beautiful Astor Roof, overlooking fabulous Times Square, in the heart of glamorous Manhattan, it's time for the Meshugenah Melodies of Holly Levine and His Music Machine, for your listening and dancing pleasure."

As he leads the small group in song to dispel the insistent present in favor of the fantasies of the past, Holly also leads the foursome in his Volkswagen along the tortuous route to Braverman's funeral, and Lumet shoots the blazingly colorful yet vulnerably small automobile from hundreds of feet above in the most spacious aerial sequence in his career to that time.[15] With Sargent's opening theme jubilantly backgrounding them, the minute yet humanly significant quartet (Felix has joined them) passes many neighborhoods, funeral homes, cemeteries, rabbis, at times almost lost in relationship to elevated trains and bridges, blending into life's constant variety, as Lumet retains from the novel Barnet's enraptured evocation of Whitman's "hungry-hearted manswarm" from the poet's paean to Brooklyn (120). Just before Holly arrives in Brooklyn and Barnet delivers his celebration visualized by shots of old neighborhoods superimposed over the new, Lumet cuts to Morroe's fantasy of Etta's confronting her husband's cemetery monument, crafted by Morroe as the stonecutter, on which the final f is missing from the name Rieff. Morroe the carver attempts to convince Etta that if she approaches the stone always from the right, a hastily added-on letter will appear in balance, and he will not be forced to carve the name again in its entirety. Etta muses, "Poor guy, nothing ever went quite right." To the carver's argument that "perspective will even it out," Morroe the traveler daydreams that his wife will reply, "Why not, he was stuck with his life so he's stuck with this." Her hair blowing across her lovely face shrouded by her black rain hat, Etta concludes with a terrible question, "Who's going to notice?" Lumet ends the sequence with a cut to Morroe's saddened countenance in Holly's festively colored car.

Following the two strained comic scenes involving the incident with the cab driver and the Alan King episode (to which Lumet adds an amusing Morroe fantasy in which Morroe himself is the sole mourner as a rabbi eulogizes him), the director introduces a humorous silent sequence in which the four continue their mythic quest.[16] Morroe runs across freeways seeking the correct funeral parlor, Barnet peers hopefully into a passing hearse, and the group investigates a Spanish mission, then passes by the sea and, with droll contrast, a Chinese restaurant, in front of which Holly bolts his food while Morroe makes yet another telephone call. Eventually, they locate the correct cemetery just as Braverman is being interred. Lumet reveals Morroe and Felix walking past rows of gravestones, emphasizing the scene more than Markfield in order to heighten Morroe's attempt to convince the others and, most important, himself that those who lie beneath the stones really have a connection to those who walk above them. Even Felix's humane rationalism resists this concerted a connection with the dead as he ironizes, "Excuse me, Mr. Dale Carnegie, go enjoy yourself, talk to them, mingle."

Morroe's journey among the gravestones is one of the memorable scenes in Lumet's films. Adapted from the Markfield passage (196-97), Lumet's version is less didactic and specific, and his Morroe is more tentative than the novel's as the fund-raiser wonders how to address the dead and what to tell them of the new world they have lost. Lumet's film omits such overtly symbolic lines as "My life isn't really connected to anything," "Your names and mine at the foot of one page," and "I get very little personal mail." Visually lost at first among the gravestones, a more hesitant Morroe sounds the plaints of universal humankind:

Well, folks. What can I tell yuh? You're all so smug in your certainty. Well, let's see. . . . Uh, everybody seems to have good taste. But still not in grave markers. . . . The big department stores have gone down hill. . . . Children don't think death is impossible for them anymore. Air pollution's very big. Infant mortality is down, suicides are up. . . . You can't get a good egg cream any-

where. And laundries ruin your shirts (sighs). Teenage girls are pretty, boys are
ugly but smarter. It looks like there'll always be war veterans. Newspapermen
know more than government people. . . . I don't read, uh, Blondie and Dag-
wood anymore. . . . Uh, housing developments are bigger. Planned commu-
nities are all over the place. The doctors have invented things that could've kept
some of you alive a little longer. I, I, I don't think you missed too much. Not
really.

Lumet's visual accompaniment to Morroe's speech acts as an apt
thematic correlative to the verbal meanings. Morroe is first seen walking in a great circle as he wonders what to say; then Lumet pans right to
left into an extreme long shot of Morroe, with the camera first moving
past him as though having difficulty locating him, then backing up to
isolate his dark dot amid the white stones. As he continues to speak,
Morroe gradually approaches the camera, alternately walking toward
frame left and then tacking toward the camera, reflecting his ambivalence toward life and death. He speaks his final two sentences as
he moves into extreme close-up, shot from high angle, and leans on a
gravestone.

After Lumet cuts to Leslie's burial, he adds the penultimate fantasy
sequence in *Braverman*, one of the film's funniest wordless moments.
As Morroe watches his friend's end, he fantasizes about his own funeral, a self-burial. With no dark paint available, Morroe must make
do, and he steals yellow paint with which to paint his coffin. After
digging his own hole, he tries to insert the coffin, but it sticks and he
attempts to maneuver it by climbing part way inside. After he nearly
gets stuck in his predicament, a strong wind blows the top off, and
Morroe must then extricate himself and chase it down. Finally, once
again he steps into the box, pulls the top over himself as far as he can,
leans his arms out to shovel dirt on himself and of course is stymied,
Keaton-like, with a semiparalyzed, foolish expression. Without dialogue, Lumet's visual and gestural humor creates a fine existential
symbol of self-destructive, self-mocking, yet self-renewing man, trying his best to bury himself, yet kept alive by his own paradoxes, his
own motion.

In the film's final sequence, Lumet concentrates and compresses
Markfield's material, more subtly deepening the novel's theme by
again focusing upon Morroe's coming to ultimate awareness of the
"mother and father of all sorrows" (255). Following Morroe's self-burial
fantasy, Lumet cuts to the four sadly and silently driving home. Barnet
is deposited at a telephone booth, where he can call his mama about
cooking her pea and barley soup for the boys on a night when he hopes

they can all see a Randolph Scott film festival. In the film, the others depart from the eternal boy more abruptly than in the book (244-46), and we last see Barnet, still hugging his youth, leaning out into the street after the disappearing car. Felix's departure also occurs more abruptly than in the novel (246-47), as Lumet cuts from Barnet's forlorn form to the car dropping Felix at the curb, then isolates the older man from the rear as he crosses the street, unlike Barnet not trying to push away thoughts of death. Holly is the last to leave Morroe to his solitude, and the director eliminates the humorous aspects of their parting in the novel (248-52) to emphasize Holly's intimations of death in the damage done during the day to his Volkswagen. Morroe, ever the mensch, assures his friend, "It's not bad. Honest. You'll see." Lumet catches Holly in close-up, muttering, "Yeah, we'll talk." He drives off, and Morroe watches Holly pull away in the dusk.

As Morroe enters his home, Lumet omits the sentimental business in Markfield of Morroe's trying unconsciously to protect himself and Etta from death by spreading insect repellant on both their bodies. His love and appreciation for her—she has made Jello for him and even offers to put bananas in it—is less overt, as he lies down on the bed. Lumet shoots Morroe from slightly low angle, accentuating his fragility by visual contrast with normal audience expectation, his head close to the camera. As he says, "Listen, you don't know what a day I've had," the director cuts to Morroe's final fantasy/memory of himself as a boy on life's threshold at the beginning of the film. After a medium-speed zoom into the boy's thoughtful face, Morroe the saddened man turns onto his left side and begins to weep. Instead of Markfield's closing lines, "And he began to cry freely and quietly" (255), Lumet's meditation on death and sympathy concludes more poignantly, Morroe's body faintly shaking from the force of his sobs. As Etta watches over him from rear frame, the sounds of a loud whistle and a calliope slowly resume the theme that begins the film, echoing Morroe's lost boyhood, when promise, still unfulfilled and unalloyed, lay ahead and all seemed possible.

Chapter Six

Major Films from Nonliterary Sources

In addition to the fourteen films from literary sources that compose the major part of this study, Lumet has directed at least half a dozen important films from nonliterary sources that reveal much of the visual and formal artistry of the major literary films and reflect many of their important thematic concerns. Along with the recent *Power, Q & A, Family Business,* and *Running on Empty,* the earlier *The Hill, The Offence, Dog Day Afternoon, Prince of the City,* and to a somewhat lesser degree *Serpico* and *Network,* demonstrate the director's frequent interest in crime and the significance of moral action as well as the individual's coming to understand present realities through deeper engagement with the past. From nonfictional sources or original screenplays, these six films reflect Lumet's attempt, consistent with that of his major literary adaptations, to transcend the welter of sentimental romance and fantasy that George Lucas and his followers have brought to film over the past decade or so, to create intelligent, rigorously rational, and formally disciplined films that deal seriously with issues of moral and social importance in contemporary America. While *Serpico, Dog Day Afternoon,* and *Network* possess some of the commercial appeal necessary for sustaining the career of even an experienced and successful director in our era of increasing celebrations of the trivial, Lumet demonstrates in all six films his successful endeavor to surpass the minimalist ephemerality that inundates the culture toward the creation of cinematic art, and thus to endow with literary quality, depth, and, at best, even universality, such real-life stories as Ray Rigby's in wartime North Africa and Frank Serpico's and Robert Leuci's on the streets of New York City.

The Hill: Ambiguities of Order

Few films so powerfully explore the ambiguous area between moral system and moral anarchy as Lumet's *The Hill* (1965). Made just after *The Pawnbroker, The Hill* is based upon screenwriter Ray Rigby's autobiographical play about his experiences of imprisonment in a North African military detention camp during World War II. The desert stockade is run by Regimental Sergeant Major Bert Wilson (Harry Andrews, directed by Lumet to a performance equaling his brilliance in *The Sea Gull*), a decent man who, under the Iago-like influence of a sadistic subordinate, Staff Sergeant Williams (Ian Hendry), becomes enslaved and his ostensibly fair and rational system of justice destroyed by his overzealous, misunderstood enforcement of the king's regulations and a growing obsession with his own legalistic conceptions of power. Victimized by the system and ultimately annihilated by it are a rebellious prisoner, Joe Roberts (Sean Connery), the most forceful combatant of Williams's malice and Wilson's gullibility, and other British soldier-prisoners such as Stevens (Alfred Lynch), Watson (Jock McGrath), and Bartlett (Roy Kinnear). Yet equally its victims are Wilson and his staff, as Roberts snarlingly realizes during an interminable inspection when all must stand in a midday sun: "We're all doing time, even the screws." Failed self-understanding imprisons all here, even the sensitive and educated medical officer (Sir Michael Redgrave) and the ineffectual, sensual camp commandant (Norman Bird), until the final carnage at the film's conclusion violently sweeps away all misconceived ideals of order, as well as all humane vestiges in the system.

Lumet first experienced filming in Europe while directing *The Hill;* it was shot in the desert near Almeria in southern Spain and at MGM's Elstree studios in England.[1] The film's central symbol of the system's dehumanization, a thirty-five-foot rock and sand hill used by Wilson for continual punishment climbs to establish prisoner discipline, was laboriously constructed on the set and inclined on a sixty-degree angle. Lumet for the first time used British actors whom he would feature prominently in later films: Kinnear memorably portrays another petty criminal in *The Deadly Affair,* and Ian Bannen, who plays the concerned staff sergeant Harris in *The Hill,* is excellent as the suspected child molester in *The Offence.* Of the splendid classical actor Harry Andrews, Lumet commented: "When you get that kind of training, and get the actor onto a realistic level, it's brimming over, you can't contain it, everything is so rich; I've never used him in the leading part, but always just under the leading part, and to have that *weight* going for you in a supporting part is just magic." Lumet early saw Sean Connery's fine potential as a serious actor being underutilized in the James Bond role and related his use of Connery to a continuing interest in improving his directorial skills in comedy:

When people saw Sean doing Bond, they thought that was just flip, easy stuff, but that's one of the hardest kinds of acting, only a real actor can do that. People always assumed Cary Grant was no actor at all, just a personality. It was always a pity to me that Grant got frightened off by the commercial failure of *None But the Lonely Heart*. I'm sure that Grant would have been a marvelous dramatic actor, and I'd always felt that about Sean. God knows, after *The Hill* I felt there was almost no telling where he'd go.

Lumet also used *The Hill* to extend his continuing experimentation in visual technique.[2] Noting in an interview that "for me there was always an emotional difference in lenses," he added that he always chooses his visual field in conjunction with the choice of lens "for the sake of what will happen to the field," referring to the distortions in visual field toward the end of *The Offence* when Sean Connery's detective experiences his world as twisted and shattered by his emotional compulsions as he walks up the police station corridor. In *The Hill*, Lumet gradually shortened the lenses from 25mm during the early part of the film to 18mm "for everything we shot, close-ups, wide shots. . . . I kept wanting it greater and greater depth; the shorter lens gave the faces greater and greater distortions." Using such techniques, Lumet distorts the planes of Andrews's face at the end of the film and establishes a visual correlative for the soldier's disintegrating sense of power, as what he imagines as a rationally imposed order crumbles into savagery and madness.

Throughout the film, Lumet's alert visual sense heightens a script that is sometimes forced and strident—as in the Ossie Davis anti-imperialism comic relief scenes. The opening shot of *The Hill* shows a tottering figure struggling Sisyphus-like up the camp's eternal torment until he falls backward in exhaustion into front frame, the British flag visible near him. Frequently interested in themes and situations of psychological impressment, Lumet uses landscape or interior imagery that suggests containment less often in this film than in, for example, *The Pawnbroker* or *A View from the Bridge*. In the early scenes as Wilson verbally harrasses the new prisoners on the spiritual benefits of discipline, Lumet's camera is usually steady, motionless as it surveys the open space and implacable heat of this prison, accentuating the tedium of life in the camp. Subtle details far from the camera reveal much not expressed in words: as Wilson approaches the sadistic new staff officer for the first time, he is momentarily framed beneath an arch, a visual intimation of the character flaw Williams will exploit to destroy his superior officer. Williams's emphasis upon appearance rather than reality immediately becomes evident as the camera catches him buffing the shine of his shoes on the backs of his socks as he awaits Wilson's approach. Wilson's vulnerability to the system's militaristic sexual repressions is clear as Roberts disparages the ridiculously inadequate medical examination given by the cowed medical officer with the question "Where are you sending me, to a stud farm?" and the sergeant major is uncomfortable as Roberts disrobes for the examination.

Williams continually harrasses Stevens, the physically weakest of the prisoners, with climbs up the hill that strain the man's constitution beyond endurance, ultimately to result in Stevens's death. Roberts at one point attempts to divert the sergeant's hostility by starting a dirt-slinging fight, ending with rare healthy laughter as all the afflicted prisoners tumble down the hill to Williams's insistent screams. In one of the film's best long shots, suddenly two military policemen appear from the opposite side at the pinnacle of the hill, silently confirming the irrational absurdity behind this type of military authority. In the following sequence, Williams, not burdened by his kit, attempts late at night to scale the object of punishment. Failing, he is confirmed in his hostility toward the prisoners and toward Wilson. Later that night he and the sergeant major have a drinking contest during which Williams begins the process of reducing the decent but inflexible Wilson to his own bestial level. He exploits the sergeant major's lonely involvement with his authority that will not permit him to heed Roberts's and Harris's warnings; Wilson so identifies with his regimentation that he disallows criticism of even the most brutal segment of his machine. As Williams increases his competition with Wilson in disciplining the prisoners, the sergeant major hardens in his adherence to legalisms; standing the injured Roberts in the sun, he circles him screaming, unconsciously projecting his own impotence, "You'd be lost, lost, unless someone was shouting an order at you."

In the film's penultimate sequence, Lumet's camera reveals Wilson's disintegration as Williams undermines what is left of his authority. Pulling in and to the right onto his ashen face, the camera also frames the sergeant major within the cell corner as he pathetically tries to protect order by shielding his sadistic assistant. A shadow vertically bisects Williams's face as he threatens the medical officer with blackmail over the prisoner's death. Moments later Williams nearly drives the sergeant major to violence: in a superior shot, Willams now becomes Wilson's visual center instead of the humane Roberts, and the camera looms down into Williams's triumphant, satanic smile while his superior officer circles about him. Lumet's implication that psychological and thus moral control have now passed to the forces of irrationality predicts the final scene's complete deterioration of all order and humanity. The amoral Williams, perverting even his own new authority, drives prisoners to insane violence that, while consuming him, also condemns them to a stark future. The film's pessimistic ending reveals the crippled, helpless Roberts screaming to stop the violence, over-whelmed finally by the imagined sounds of his perpetual imprison-ment and by reason's abdication to the powers that must then inevitably replace it.

The Offence: The Repression of Disorder

No film in Lumet's canon is more uncomfortable to watch than his relentless *The Offence* (1973); yet none shows so strikingly how the director can confront the most controversial and horrifying themes without resorting to gratuitous violence or sensationalism. Perhaps lines from Eliot's "Sweeney Agonistes" introduce most compellingly the theme of *The Offence:*

> I knew a man once did a girl in
> Any man might do a girl in
> Any man has to, needs to, wants to
> Once in a lifetime, do a girl in.[3]

Detective Sergeant Johnson (Sean Connery), a veteran of twenty years in investigative police work, has stored unbearable memories of the hideous sadism, violence, and inhumanity he has been forced to witness through his grim duties. But he has continually repressed these horrors, never having discussed their effects upon his in-creasingly morbid psychological state even with his wife, Maureen (Vivien Merchant), with whom he has a mutually unsatisfying emo-tional intimacy. His current case involves the search for an unidentified child molester already suspected of three crimes; as the film opens a fourth assault occurs upon a young girl, Janie (Maxine Gordon), and an early middle-aged man, Baxter (Ian Bannen), is taken into custody. Johnson, having already shown behavioral signs of identifying too closely with Janie's assault and with the search for the child molester, becomes obsessed with Baxter's guilt, although Baxter has been picked up by police simply wandering about the city in a dazed condition. Johnson takes command of Baxter's interrogation, and as the two talk at length, the detective realizes through the suspect's goading his own latent complicity in the crimes continually assaulting his mind and with the criminals he pursues. Their shared guilt—Baxter over his homo-sexuality, Johnson over his long-repressed sadism—results in Johnson's almost orgiastically beating Baxter to death, before the detective comes to see all that he has repressed. As William Avery observes, in murdering Baxter, Johnson symbolically punishes himself. Stephen Farber notes that the film "has a fierce honesty that distinguishes it from all the other police movies that are in vogue today. What makes this film unique is the psychological depth with which it dissects a cop's inner life . . . [his] anguish as he perceives his close symbiotic relationship wih the killers, sadists and psychopaths he hunts."[4]

Scripted by John Hopkins from his similar play, *The Offence* was, like *The Deadly Affair*, shot on location in London; Gerry Fisher, who directed the cinematography for *The Sea Gull*, directed its splendidly gloomy photography. As in *The Hill*, Lumet adeptly directs some fine British actors, drawing excellent performances from Connery and Bannen; "The last scene between them," said Lumet in an interview, "is some of the best acting I've ever seen in the movies." Lumet also provides roles for luminaries Merchant and Trevor Howard; Howard plays the superior officer who investigates Johnson. The director was attracted to the project because of his interest in character studies and in individuals' conflicts between their present lives and the encroachment of their pasts, and he provided in an interview a keen example of the commercial dangers that await directors who pursue such themes: "The film was released in the U.S., it played seven days in New York, and I don't think United Artists spent $3000 advertising it; they had no faith in the picture, and when it got marvelous reviews they decided they had to be right so they didn't support it. . . . they're embarrassed at having been wrong, so in order to prove they're right they're just as happy to let it collapse commercially, to justify the way they opened it."

The Offence does reveal aesthetic weaknesses, despite its excellent acting and fine symbolic camera work. While Hopkins draws the psychological issues well, the plot is contrived and melodramatic and the dialogue sometimes florid. Richard Schickel rightly noticed the repetitiousness of the film's structure, and the events do not provide a sufficiently probable objective correlative for the film's symbolic themes.[5] (Baxter is never charged with any crime; Maureen does not seem sufficiently neurotic for a long-term marriage to such a Freudian case study as Johnson.) But Lumet provides superb visual correlatives for the psychological themes, especially for the destructive moral and societal effects of denial and repression, in which he has a consistent interest. And considering the horrific nature of the film's subject, Lumet's direction is notable for its tact and taste. *The Offence* contributes well also to the director's development of a cinematic style astutely evocative of his concerns with psychological conflict.

Lumet has expressed his admiration of Teinosuke Kinugasa's *Gate of Hell* (1953), widely considered one of the best color pictures in film history, especially for Kinugasa's use of various shadings of whiteness.[6] In *The Offence*, Lumet suggests varied emotional nuances through his employment of a young girl's white raincoat and stockings, the white walls of the interrogating room, the oppressive sameness of the building structures (sometimes white) that tower over Johnson as he returns to his apartment block following his beating of Baxter, and Johnson's tormented flash-memories of victims' savaged bodies. The film opens with complete whiteness, a Melvillian moral void, gradually dissolving to a bufflike whiteness through the slow-motion sequence in which Johnson's beating of Baxter is first discovered by other policemen. Then the camera reveals intense white light coming from the ceiling as Johnson begins to recognize the horror of his act; this color progression is approximately reversed at the film's conclusion when Johnson more fully comprehends the gravity and meaning of his murder of Baxter.

In full-color sequences, Lumet's visual technique also expresses theme. An early wordless sequence shows the police hunt across a field where Janie was last seen; a tractor is ready to dredge a nearby pond as the police team, shot from the culvert, begins to move off down a hill in the coming darkness. As the flashlights progress, Lumet shoots the left side of Johnson's face passing the the gnarled branches of trees. Suddenly at a seeming hunch, Johnson breaks from the crowd of searchers, comes through some bushes, and from low angle snaps off his flashlight before coming upon the frightened Janie. Kneeling over her and tenderly enfolding her in her coat, he smiles down at the girl a little too long. As the others' lights discover them, Johnson suddenly looks up, frightened, then slightly lowers his eyes. Lumet ends the sequence with a cut to Johnson from the rear, the low angle revealing the mass of police searchers approaching him from above, as if to reinforce his sensation of guilt. The impersonality of Johnson's work, despite its terrible emotional cost, and the anonymity he increasingly feels are well evoked as, following his return to his apartment block, the detective is momentarily framed within a gray steel elevator before he walks to the wrong apartment door, prior to the scene with his wife. At the conclusion as Johnson gains deeper insight into his crime, Lumet pans slowly around from the back of the detective's head to a view of the left side of his face. The camera movement supports cinematically Lumet's remark concerning a continuing thematic preoccupation: "I think most of the pictures were about a conflict in what you are. What you are is no longer working for this moment and the hell that that causes."[7]

Serpico: "Who Can Trust a Cop Who Don't Take Money?"

In the winter of 1975, two years after his courageous police career ended with a nearly fatal gunshot wound following his testimony on widespread New York City Police Department corruption before the Knapp Commission, Frank Serpico wrote "A Letter Home" from his European anonymity to the *Village Voice*. He talked about his own conflicts of conscience in a voice that makes clear why Lumet was attracted to making a film based on Peter Maas's popular biography of Serpico.

Today people ask, didn't you know what [police work] was like? . . . I heard vague rumors about envelopes, you know? . . . You just don't become a cop once you take the oath. They start to mold you. . . . That's the part that started rubbing me the wrong way. Maybe it was my conscience that was bothering me, because either you face up to your conscience, or you go along with the system . . . and then there's no turning back. . . . I'd like to think [conscience] was always there. I'd like to believe it exists in everybody. It's just a matter of listening to it.[8]

Serpico (1974) resembles many of Lumet's films in its concern with an outsider, a rebel who opposes what the individual considers a corrupt system in an attempt either to improve the institution or, through rejecting it, at least to salvage his or her own reasoned concept of dignity or morality. Win Sharples, Jr., writes that *Serpico* follows in the tradition of such cinematic exposures of sociopolitical systems as Constantine Costa-Gavras's *Z* (1969) and *State of Siege* (1973) and Gillo Pontecorvo's *The Battle of Algiers* (1965).[9] Certainly Lumet throughout his career has been drawn artistically to films about people of principle and conscience, from such male protagonists as General Black in *Fail Safe*, the architect-juror in *12 Angry Men*, the 1960s revolutionary in *Running on Empty*, the iconoclastic television anchor in *Network*, the courageous Latin teacher in *Child's Play*, and the attorney in *The Verdict*, to similarly independent female protagonists like the heroic farm woman in *Lovin' Molly*, Bones in *Just Tell Me What You Want*, Polly and Lakey in *The Group*, and the rationally anarchic Estelle Rolfe in *Garbo Talks*.

Andrew Sarris and Tom Allen have commented that Serpico "is a Lumet tone poem on New York police corruption that hints at the symphonic stature to come in *Prince of the City*."[10] The film covers eleven years (1960-71) in Serpico's police odyssey, beginning with his induction ceremony and family life, through many episodes in the young policeman's exposure to the ubiquitous police corruption in the Bronx, Manhattan, and Brooklyn. Serpico attempts to establish an emotionally satisfying personal life with a woman, reads, and conducts and unconventionally liberal after-hours life in the Village. He struggles to avoid obsessiveness over his ideals while remaining committed to them, and he becomes frustrated and gradually disillusioned at finding few colleagues or superiors who even share his desire for integrating police work more closely to people's needs on the city streets, much less his passion to reverse widespread police bribe-taking. He eventually resigns from the force after his testimony and serious injury. Lumet does not glorify Serpico but frequently depicts the emotional costs of his zeal by showing his increasing isolation and alienation. At the same time, Lumet underscores the humorous aspects of "Paco's" character by drawing a subtly balanced tragicomic performance from Al Pacino, whose portrayal was widely hailed and brought him an Academy Award nomination as best actor.[11]

The making of *Serpico* sorely tried Lumet's legendary stamina and pragmatic resourcefulness as a filmmaker. Producer Dino De Laurentiis fired the original director, and Lumet "came in six weeks before the shooting was to start. There were 107 speaking parts to cast, 104 locations to choose," and the script—which was to garner Waldo Salt and Norman Wexler an Oscar nomination—was only in draft.[12] Visiting from Europe, Frank Serpico sat in on script conferences and contributed ideas, and through Lumet's noted openness to collaborative contributions to his films, the actors were allowed to do some improvisation of scenes. Since the film was shot in the hottest summer months, difficult winter scenes, including defoliated trees and simulated visible breath, had to be staged. Associate producer Roger Rothstein praised Lumet as "a tremendously organized director" who possessed the "ability to get everybody together" and managed to do as many as thirty-five set-ups in a single day.[13] Lumet was pleased at the very necessary cooperation of the New York Police Department in making the film: "I'm not apologizing for corruption, but they had their code, and it's painful for them, that kind of a movie. . . . it should be painful for them. But I shot in four live stationhouses with their work going on at the time. The NYPD were wonderful." Cinematographer Arthur J. Ornitz, photographer for such fine films as Ralph Nelson's *Requiem for a Heavyweight* (1962) and John Cassavetes's *Minnie and Moskowitz* (1971), who had worked with Lumet in 1971 on the director's thoughtful caper film, *The Anderson Tapes*, praised highly Lumet's artistic control and direction: "A cameraman is only like the first fiddle in an orchestra. The director is the conductor."[14] Given the nature of the crime film genre, Lumet's customary avoidance of excessive violence is evident, but Lumet said that the difficulties in getting the film made were artistically beneficial: "It's all up there on the screen, all the intensity."[15]

Lumet's skill as a director of themes involving urban street realism, shown to good effect throughout his career from *A View from the Bridge* to *Q & A*, helps give *Serpico* its energy, anticipating Lumet's soon-to-follow *Dog Day Afternoon* and *Prince of the City*. The film's nearly silent opening sequence discloses an almost unconscious Serpico, a bullet hole visible just under his left cheekbone. Lumet then cuts from the front of the car to the barely visible silhouette of his head, pressed back on the seat. Serpico's increasing vulnerability as the film progresses is echoed by his flopping hand over the orderly's shoulder, seemingly disengaged from him, as he is carried into the hospital. One of his few loyal supporters, Inspector Sid Green (John Randolph) stands over him, and Lumet reveals Serpico's left hand entering the frame to grasp Green's in what is for the young cop a rare human connection. As Serpico's memories begin, Lumet bathes the mean streets in blinding light while the neophyte gropes toward comprehension of the city's fathomless corruption and betrayal. As he refuses to take bag money, his Bronx colleagues meet with him in a park; distantly visible is Yankee Stadium, with its associations of the heroic Babe Ruth and Lou Gehrig. Visually Serpico is centered: the men walk up the hill to curse him and down again to isolate him, leaving him standing by a tree.[16] Lumet shows Serpico, his isolation nearly unbearable, at target practice. The target figure moves inexorably at Serpico in the half light, visually dominating the policeman, who is shown in silhouette. Set up in the Brooklyn narcotics bust, Serpico must make his way through refuse even on the tenement rooftop. Lumet cuts twenty-eight times in the riveting twenty-second sequence of Serpico's shooting, his fellow cops not reacting until the drug pusher's pistol blast has hurled Serpico down on his back in the filthy hallway.

But Lumet balances the urban blight with tender, often amusing scenes of Serpico's world. As he celebrates his entry into his dream career in his Italian neighborhood, Serpico playfully reverses his new official cap like academic regalia. When he outgrows his old neighborhood, his unsentimental farewell scene, all in Italian dialogue, with his mother (Mildred Clinton) who tries to press money upon him that he does not want, represents for him rare human warmth. In his scenes with Laurie (sensitively played by newcomer Barbara Eda-Young), he is humanized even as he becomes more preoccupied by his moral quest. At one point near the end of their relationship, he sulkingly refuses to come to bed, preferring to stand in near darkness feeding nuts to his parrot, then to himself. When the couple parts, Laurie runs down the street, not at all glamorous, but slightly waddling, rendering the scene more realistically poignant. At the conclusion Sid Green helps him pack up his apartment, and Serpico at the film's end is seated on a wharf, Lumet's withdrawing camera isolating him against the side of a huge ship, a dead end street sign visible at frame right. But over the final credits, Lumet shows him walking slightly uphill among a crowd, thoughtful, having survived, having accomplished something, if not enough to suit him; the Knapp Commission predictably convicted only low-ranking police officials. The ending confirms the high price of rebellion, but it also symbolically celebrates its value and the value of a sensitive, angry man's outrage at the society's increasing passive acceptance of mediocrity. The ending anticipates Frank Serpico's 1975 warning from Europe: "There isn't any man on a white horse who's going to make it good for us. It's either we make it good, by ourselves, and for ourselves, or we may as well forget it."[17]

Dog Day Afternoon: The Contemporary Urban Absurd

Throughout Lumet's career, critics have identified him as a maker of excellent "New York films," even as the creator of a standard for films about New York City in such works as *The Pawnbroker, Bye, Bye Braverman, The Anderson Tapes,* and *Prince of the City.*[18] In a discriminating review of *Dog Day Afternoon,* Jack Kroll wrote, "Lumet's strong feeling for New York, seen even in such piffle as *Stage Struck,* produced in *Serpico* the best film about that city in many years and drew from Pacino a performance that was almost a mythic incarnation of metropolitan chivalry. . . . in a film that at least glancingly captures the increasingly garish pathologies of our urban life."[19] In fact, Lumet plumbs beneath the surfaces of urban absurdity in the film to explore such issues as the complex relationship between violence and media attention to it, the forces that drive the urban desperate to crime, the electric energy of the metropolis, the edge between the city's image as dream-giver and death-bringer, and contradictions within homosexual and heterosexual relationships. *Dog Day Afternoon* concentratedly covers fourteen intense hours during a ninety-seven-degree day, August 22, 1972.

On that day, as reported in a magazine article by P.F. Kluge and Thomas Moore concerning actual events and imaginatively elaborated in a splendid, Academy Award-winning original screenplay by Frank Pierson, three young men ineptly try to rob a branch bank in Brooklyn. Nothing works for them: the youngest accomplice gets scared and departs early in the proceedings; the leader, Sonny (Oscar nominee Al Pacino), a former bank clerk, has misestimated the money currently in the bank (just $1100); and Sonny's main helper, Sal (John Cazale), also a Vietnam veteran, gets his gun out too soon. An alarm is tripped and suddenly the would-be robbers find themselves surrounded by half the Brooklyn Police Department and soon the FBI. Sonny's life is further complicated by the hostages in the bank, by Sal's mercurial personality, and by trouble with the bank's air-conditioning system, his parents, his conventional wife, the corpulent Angela, and their two children, and his homosexual wife, Leon (Chris Sarandon), whose sex-change operation the heist was intended to finance. While the ravenous media create reality as they report it, Sonny tries to arrange for a jet to fly them to a foreign country (the ignorant, doomed Sal can only suggest Wyoming). Sonny negotiates with police out on the street to the adulation of the crowd, as he in turn manipulates their celebrity worship and thus ironically contributes to the escalation of the madness. Finally he suffers the collapse of his dreams with Leon's withdrawal, Sal's killing by the FBI, and his own capture.

Commenting on the insanity, comedy, and pathos of the story, Lumet remarked insightfully on a character type that intrigues him: [Sonny is] "enormously talented, but he has no place to put it . . . the way he manipulated the crowds, the way he reacted to a situation for which he was totally unprepared. . . . He has tremendous energy and imagination and—I know it sounds funny to use this word about Sonny—but, like Frank [Serpico], he has dedication."[20] Lumet has consistently shown interest in the idealistic, committed, psychologically complex loner/rebel in his films, but in *Dog Day Afternoon* he attempted to limit psychological analysis of his protagonist in favor of simply presenting him as a participant in his melodrama. In one of the director's most astute self-criticisms and self-evaluations of his own continued attempts to expand his artistic powers, Lumet said in an interview with me that "more and more, I want to explain less and less." He continued,

One of the things that thrills me about *Dog Day*, we never went into *any* background, but it was there, you knew it all. I learned that from Chekhov when I did *The Sea Gull*—there is no exposition, you never know who Konstantin's father was; it is so marvelous not to know much about Masha. . . . I had been brought up in such a tradition of psychiatric explanations for everything, and tend to that myself . . . but one of the reasons you understand so much about what Al does in *Dog Day* is because we inject it in the performance, in the non-verbal text. . . . Also, you get ashamed of what you can do well, about melodrama. . . . that's where the critics affect you; they make you feel guilty over what there's no need to feel guilty about, and thus your work does not get any better. . . . Now I am not only not ashamed of melodrama, I want to get back to it, like every four movies . . . because it's very important the more introspective you get, the more self-involved, to get back, like a ballet dancer, to the bloody bar, first position, second position, third position . . . get right back to basics, shake yourself up. Because it's good for the drama, it's good for the more serious work.[21]

Because of Lumet's flexibility in his approach to the film, he not only succeeds in his stated aims of making a melodramatic plot serve serious, thought-provoking drama but also achieves a more spontaneous level of comedy, a lightness of touch he had sought since his perceived inadequacy in *Bye, Bye Braverman*. This confidence with comedy would show clearly in his next film, *Network*. Lumet's ease makes possible the film's balancing of the many contrasts and tensions of subject and theme, and the combination of his typically urgent social critique with streetwise humor and understanding earned his second Academy Award nomination for best director. (*12 Angry Men, Network*, and *The Verdict* also earned Lumet Oscar nominations for direction. He shared an Oscar nomination for best screenplay for *Prince of the City*.) Paul Bailey noted Pacino's far superior direction by Lumet than by William Friedkin in a 1980 film, *Cruising*, which also concerned homosexuality; Lumet's treatment of the subject, Bailey said, was characterized by "disinterested understanding," Friedkin's by "a morbid, and far from disinterested, fascination."[22] Lumet aptly blends the sequences of Sonny's bisexuality into the film's general concern with the contemporary absurd; the result makes Sonny more human, not freakish. The depictions of Sonny's mother and of Angela approach stereotypes of the "smotherer and the shrew," but the scenes with Sonny and Leon are models of gentle humor and tact.[23]

When Leon (skillfully depicted by Sarandon in a performance that earned him an Oscar nomination for best supporting actor), still groggy from drugs, is brought from the mental hospital to talk by telephone with Sonny, he is seated by the Feds in a barber chair, still in his bathrobe. Then the crazy Sal remonstrates to Sonny that the media is also labeling him a homosexual. But Leon and Sonny's talk is dignified, despite the societal environment. Loving but unsentimental, Sonny at one point explodes at Leon's self-pity, "I'm with a guy who don't know where Wyoming is, you think you got problems!" They talk about their relationship honestly; Leon's less courageous decision to return to the hospital is treated by Sonny nonjudgmentally, despite the horrendous pressure he is under. As Leon hangs up, Lumet reveals Sonny staring at Sal, a poor if brave substitute for human community. As night comes and the Gay Pride supporters cheer him on from the street outside, Sonny looks sickened, disappointed at their converting his chosen sexuality into a celebrity carnival show. As he dictates his will to the head teller, his generous and sensitive treatment of his loved ones of both sexes brings to this uneducated, resourceful, and lonely man, leaning against a wide pillar as he speaks, a fragile but considerable stature and dignity.

Lumet's opening shots of the city's majesty and sadness establish a visual context in which the film displays its thematic contradictions. After a sanitation crew is seen clearing a heavily littered street, Lumet reveals the dream of Manhattan in the background, across a cemetery; the next shot is to the would-be robbers' car, with a one way sign visible behind it. As Sonny becomes more and more the captive of the media blitz, he courageously attempts to turn the imprisonment to his advantage psychologically in scenes that contain some of Lumet's best street theater. Officer Moretti (Charles Durning) approaches the bank via a wide semicircle in a fine shot across Sonny's shoulder, as he stands waiting ambivalently in the doorway. As Sonny tries to reach accord with the sympathetic, tough officer while fanning the crowd to his support, a shot from a helicopter reveals the few yards of turf in front of the bank over which he exercises a psychologically powerful, but politically and physically precarious, control. Paying for pizzas with marked bank money, Sonny watches his new stardom trickle down, as the pizza boy (Lionel Pina) etches his place in media history, clapping Sonny on the back and leaping for joy with one of the best comic lines in Lumet's canon, "I'm a fuckin' star!" as he bows deeply to the crowd's roar. But as Sonny and his hostages drive toward the airport and a chance at freedom, the same mob beats the police car as they stream along the route, all coherence gone in the director's distinguished vision of the "crazy collage of contradictory elements that increasingly make up our public reality." [24]

Network: Crime at the Top

Lumet's concern in Dog Day Afternoon with the destructively symbiotic relationship of a media gone amok and its social supporters/victims is a major theme in his darkest comedy, Network (1976). Ostensibly about television's increasing propensity to confuse the news with show business, the film also offers a satiric vision, as Vincent Canby notes, of "what television *might* do if given the opportunity."[25] Lumet and screenwriter Paddy Chayefsky, awarded an Oscar for best original screenplay, use television as a metaphor for the growth of a megacorporate state that progressively dehumanizes and makes passive the individual. Allan Wolper, interviewing Chayefsky, wrote: "To research [*Network*], he watched lots of television. He watched television news people audition for their roles. He waits to see if I catch that key phrase. Audition. 'It's not how smart they are, but how they look, how they sound,' he laments. 'They're models.'"[26]

Chayefsky, who mastered realism in his 1950s plays, *Marty, The Bachelor Party,* and *The Middle of the Night,* also developed satiric skill in his screenplays for *The Americanization of Emily* (1964) and *The Hospital* (1971), which he uses well in his story of lunatic crime in "the upper depths" of the national media.[27] Unlike previous films about the media, such as Jack Conway's *The Hucksters* (1947) and Elia Kazan's *A Face in the Crowd* (1957), *Network* adopts a frenzied surrealism and a driving energy in its attack on the greed and hypocrisy of network executives. Howard Beale (Peter Finch), aging news anchor of the UBS Network, about to be dismissed for low ratings, informs his audience that he will commit suicide on the air. Allowed by sympathetic, Ed Murrow-like news executive Max Schumacher (William Holden) to do a farewell show, Beale unexpectedly attacks the television media as "bullshit" and is yanked off the air. But voraciously ambitious programming executive Diana Christensen (Faye Dunaway, like Finch a recipient of the best-acting Oscar), thrilled at the publicity, convinces superiors to put Beale back on the air as a soothsayer denouncing the hypocrisies of the time, to be accompanied by co-opted radicals on the "Mao-Tse-Tung Hour," who can now "stage their heists before a slack-jawed mass audience."[28] But Beale then has a mystical experience that persuades him to use his show to denounce international corporations backed by foreign money and to make other evangelical revelations. Called on the carpet by the head conglomerate figure, Arthur Jensen (Ned Beatty, nominated for the best-supporting acting Oscar), Beale, thinking that he has encountered the Great Spirit, soon becomes a prophet of affirmation for the international Corporate Way, so denouncing individual initiative that his ratings slip disastrously. Unable to fire Beale because their positions are also controlled by Jensen, Diana and her boss, Hackett (Robert Duvall), decide to use the radicals' Ecumenical Liberation Army to assassinate Beale in midrant during his program. The film ends with an offscreen announcer commenting,

"This was the story of Howard Beale, the first man killed because he had lousy ratings."

As *Dog Day Afternoon* benefits from what Lumet learned about minimizing exposition in directing *The Sea Gull*, so do *Network* and ensuing comedies such as *Just Tell Me What You Want* and *Garbo Talks* benefit from the director's work to improve his comic touch in *Murder on the Orient Express* (1974). In an interview Lumet commented on his delight in learning more about a new style:

One of the main reasons I did *Orient Express*, aside from liking to get back to melodrama now and then, was that I knew that stylistically it had to be gay in spirit, even though it was about a murder. . . . it's not a comedy, but you are smiling through that movie even at your most tense. There's a sense of gaiety, among the actors too. And you've never seen anybody work so hard to get gaiety, this grim little Jew knocking himself out. . . . I couldn't have done the job I did on *Network* without *Orient Express*. . . . One of the reasons *Orient* worked so well was that I had one foot firmly planted in an area I know well, melodrama, a murder mystery, so I could step out tentatively with the other foot, without getting too damaged.[29]

While *Daniel* represents subtler political art than the humorous social criticism of Lumet and Chayefsky in *Network*, the latter film effectively uses caricature and exaggerated situations to make its important sociocultural point. *Network* is Lumet's sole film that presents him in the role of sociological pamphleteer. Despite Chayefsky's frequent sermons in scenes involving the love triangle of Holden, his wife (Beatrice Straight), and Dunaway, Charles Michener in his *Newsweek* review praised Lumet's "steely assurance" in the direction, which recalled to the reviewer Preston Sturges's great social comedies of the 1940s.[30] The film earned Lumet his third Academy Award nomination for best director and garnered ten Oscar nominations, including Straight's for best supporting actress. Dunaway, who can be a flat, passive performer despite her intelligence and beauty, gives an outstanding performance. Stephen Farber notes, "Sidney Lumet is a wizard at drawing things out of actors that no other director has tapped. Dunaway has never before given a performance of such dizzying energy: her work here is a revelation. . . . The scheming, commanding Diana [resembles] the black widow heroines of forties movies—the striking, aggressive, ambitious bitches played by Barbara Stanwyck and Bette Davis."[31]

Lumet's decision to abandon his usual "very definite camera pattern" and controlled color progressions to "chaos" to depict the irrationality of Dunaway and Duvall's world strengthened both the comedic and serious aspects of *Network*. Lumet remarked, "Here it was scrambling, and in a couple of instances I tried to make camera jokes, like before Holden and Dunaway go to bed . . . the proverbial 180-degree romantic dolly around the table, the wood-burning fireplace in the background. The basic visual attack was to corrupt the camera as we went, since everything in the picture got corrupted . . . so we began on a fairly realistic level and by the end of the movie it looked like an ad commercial." [32] Thus within minutes, Lumet shows images of the stately columns of the four television network buildings, the home videos of black radical leader Great Ahmed Khan (Arthur Burghardt), filming his own bank robbery, and the pristine white office of Diana the huntress. As Beale has his vision in blue-purple light, Diana munches a sandwich almost without visual transition. The now-mystic Beale wanders the streets in the rain mumbling about bearing witness, and network flunkeys follow him with camera and sound equipment. Shortly afterward in the Great Ahmed Khan's hideout, the leader incessantly eats his favorite food, Kentucky Fried Chicken. Then the Marxist screams to network executives, "Don't fuck with my distribution costs!" after interrupting their bargaining process with a pistol shot. When Jensen summons Beale, Lumet shoots the two at opposite ends of a long conference table, with Jensen framed between two rows of dim green lights, the corporation magnate's white hands flashing in the scant light of the darkened room. As the pathology climaxes with Beale's assassination and the anchor lies in his own blood, a television camera dollies in to show the event several times on different screens, alongside a commercial lushly celebrating an airline. The film's credits begin over competing news chatter, and still on the lower left screen, Beale's body reminds us of Lumet's persistent concern with the forces awaiting our increasing social passivity and abandonment of reason.

Prince of the City: Film as Literature

Andrew Sarris, who early in Lumet's career was not convinced of the director's superior merits, demonstrates his capacity for critical re-evaluation and fairness by his assessment of Lumet's crime master-piece, *Prince of the City* (1981):

[It] is the most profoundly disturbing film I've seen this year in terms of both its moral ambiguity and its aesthetic complexity. . . . Unlike most other contemporary entertainments, it is not a fairy tale about 'them' versus 'us.' Far from satisfying our yearnings for our lost innocence, it scourges us with our most persistent uncertainties and guilts. Indeed, *Prince of the City* seems much of the time less like a movie than a surgical incision into the corpus of our society. In the process, the distinctions between right and wrong, good and evil, honor and dishonor have been swept into the gutters of New York street life. . . . I have absolutely no reservations about *Prince of the City*. It is certainly a prodigious enough achievement to deserve unqualified praise.[33]

In *Prince of the City*, Lumet creates an original literary film from nonfictional material, one that while using cinematic space intelligently reveals its excellence centrally in literary terms. In the story of Daniel Ciello, a New York City narcotics detective who decides to become an informer for the crime commission, based on Robert Daley's journalistic biography of Robert Leuci, Lumet, for the first time in his career officially sharing screenwriting credit with head scenarist Jay Presson Allen, achieves a high level of sophisticated characterization, tragic irony, and complex moral theme. Ciello's reasons for his decision to inform, even to inform on his closest partners and friends whom he swore not to implicate, remain implicit throughout, worked out through action in a well-structured plot that allows no easy answers or rationales. An amalgam of Ciello's desire for atonement for his own inevitable misdeeds within the corrupt arena of his work as an elite narcotics agent, his fear of rumored investigations that may include him, his sincere Serpico-like admiration for the police profession, and his anger at fatcats in the criminal justice system who often remain unpunished for serious crimes, Ciello's motives are as complicated as the social and legal machinery he thinks he can govern but that ultimately swamps him and nearly destroys his life. Lumet probes Ciello's increasing isolation as he discovers the inevitability—early predicted by his loyal wife—that the social process he has set in motion must end with his betrayal of his closest friends, his ambivalence over his relationships with lifelong family friends who are members of the mob, and his rage at the cool, rational—and ultimately humane and understanding—attorneys whose privilege and comfort he assails: "I'm the only thing between you and the jungle!"

The film explores the horrendous pressures placed by society upon its defenders in the continual trench warfare against major crime—particularly the drug trade eating away the democratic and moral fabric of the nation. *Prince of the City* posits the dilemma of whether it is a higher value for the cop to protect his coworkers (upon whom his life frequently depends) or to inform higher-ups about the constant and ubiquitous police corruption, as in Serpico's world, among narcotics enforcers, in an effort to encourage the growth of abstract justice in the crucial drug war. In his perennial concern with personal responsibility, Lumet also examines the arguable rightness of Ciello's actions as balanced against their terrible consequences for himself, his loved ones, and his friends, in a film termed "An American Tragedy" by critic David Ansen, "which is not only about crime and punishment, but the whole fabric of society—class, race, our notions of family and law and morality." [34]

The "princes" of the city constituted a special force, the Special Investigating Unit (SIU) of elite undercover narcotics agents who, after breaking the French Connection drug ring in the early 1960s, were permitted to operate without supervision in return for waging war against multimillion-dollar drug operations. As described in Robert Daley's book, the SIU detectives' corruption stemmed from their daily work among and dependence upon drug addicts and dealers. [35] Because they continually moved in a seamy world, the agents' crimes included supplying junkies with heroin in return for information about dealers, employing illegal wiretaps, and skimming thousands of dollars from drug busts. Robert Leuci (Daniel Ciello in the film) and his colleagues felt that they dealt more effectively than the rest of the criminal justice system with the drug menace, never taking bribes to free dealers and maintaining great loyalty to their partners in their ever-perilous work. Of the seventy special detectives in the SIU, fifty-two would be indicted for crimes, and two would commit suicide and one would become insane because of the testimony of their colleagues.

For Lumet these events presented "a genuine tragedy in which everyone involved, with the best intentions, creates a disaster." [36] During an interview, the director said of his nearly three-hour film that

It's an enormous picture—130 locations, 280 scenes, 126 speaking parts. . . . Leuci . . . is not your conventional hero. He's as complex a man as I've ever met in my life, and he's in as complex a situation as I've ever known about. The picture is also about cops and how pressured they are, what they have to live with day in, day out, and how they try to keep some sort of equilibrium, whether it's staying honest or not becoming cynical. The difficulty of separating villains from heroes intrigued me. . . . Whether Leuci was a rat or a hero was one of the things I had to work through for myself while making the movie. [Growing up] poor . . . on the political left, I was brought up on this idea about an informer being a rat. I went into the movie feeling great ambivalence but concluded that Leuci was a hero. Political informing is [unforgivable]. Criminal informing—that's a different cup of tea. In *Prince of the City,* we're dealing with dope, something that's destroying large segments of our population. [37]

Shot on location in New York, as three-fourths of Lumet's films have been, *Prince of the City* features some unusual but successful choices among its many actors. Lumet interviewed some five thousand people, including nonprofessionals: the role of a sleazy bail bondsman, DeBennedeto, is played by Ron Karabatsos, in real life a New Jersey detective. Telling management that he would cast no stars—originally, Brian De Palma had been set to direct the production, with John Travolta considered in the starring role—Lumet told the *Village Voice,* "The point was that this would be an honest piece of work, and I didn't want to hear any nonsense from management that they can't identify with the Treat Williams character because he's not a conventional hero. I told them, 'We're going to rub his nose in shit because he's been living in shit and behaved shittily.' "[38] The director chose the relatively unknown Williams to portray Ciello, observing that "Treat has great power, but also an innate sweetness and naïveté," useful qualities in depicting the story's gray moral antinomies.[39]

Playing Ciello's wise wife, Lindsay Crouse appeared in her first Lumet film, to be followed by fine performances in *The Verdict* and in *Daniel*. To a female critic's charge that Crouse was not "Hollywood cinematic," Lumet defended Crouse: " 'Cinematic' is what reveals human behavior. And Lindsay does that better than almost any other actress working."[40] Coscenarist Jay Presson Allen, who wrote the screenplay for Hitchcock's *Marnie*, also wrote Lumet's earlier comedy-drama *Just Tell Me What You Want* and would work with him on the melodrama *Deathtrap*. Visually the film was notable for Lumet's discovery of "a young Boris [Kaufman]," cinematographer Andrzej Bartkowiak, who would serve as Lumet's director of photography during the 1980s and early 1990s for such films as *The Verdict, Daniel, Power, Garbo Talks, Family Business,* and *Q & A*. Lumet encountered the Lodz film school graduate through Bartkowiak's work in the PBS dramatization of John Cheever's story "The Five-Forty-Eight," and he praises highly the young Pole's ability to achieve black-and-white effects in color photography, saying that "he's going to be one of the great cameramen in the world."

Lumet advances the film's literary ironies and ambiguities through a cinematic style evocative of its troubling themes. A metallic-sounding file card device introduces the separate plot strands, as identification pictures of the many characters flash on the screen to aid us in comprehending their diversity, backed by a peculiar high whining sound, reminiscent of a similar noise in *Fail Safe*, suggesting the more subtle societal mechanism enveloping all the participants. At one point, as

Ciello painfully removes the tape holding an undercover recording device to his chest, Lumet shows a window behind him, partly open, and five shadows cross behind him in visual containment. Early in the film, Ciello and his wife stand in line for the film "Ship of Fools," as he tells her gently of his childhood idealism concerning police work. Before the suicides of both of Ciello's apprehended friends, Lumet's camera steadily and very slowly pulls up and in upon their harrowed faces, revealing again Lumet's career-long preoccupation with the importance of the individual and with moral choice. When Ciello and his wife are kept under guard by the investigators in the mountains, during a walk in the woods they are forced by a false alarm to hurl themselves to the ground. A guard's legs straddling them, they are surrounded by thickets of brush suggesting the spiritual chaos and confusion that Ciello's decision has brought upon everyone he cares for.

During Ciello's grilling by yet another in the parade of attorneys, Lumet shows the gleaming face of an insistently smiling stenographer reflected in the surface of a wood table, itself reflecting the false smiles of many present at his degradation, several of the investigators perhaps more concerned with their own career-building than with the human elements of the morass they uncover. When Ciello visits the house of one of his partners to inform him of the suicide of one of their closest colleagues, Lumet shoots the silent scene, punctuated only by the scream of the partner at the news, in the carefully enclosed small space of a backyard. In the penultimate sequence as the lawyers and investigators at last judge with reasoned compassion Ciello's plaint, "I know the law . . . the law doesn't know the streets," sparing him from indictment and allowing him to continue on the force, Lumet shoots Ciello's judges seated in the sun's dying light, bathed in somber golden-brown rays that do not reach all present in the room.[41]

But visually most remarkable is the sequence just before Ciello's decision to try to rise above his past. Faced with his troubled younger brother's recognition of his misdeeds, Ciello physically drives the youth into a corner of his room, but Lumet positions Ciello also confined visually in the corner, cracked paint visible behind the brothers. Just before Ciello visits the first investigator, however, Lumet reveals the detective in all the moral squalor in which he must work, as Ciello goes out on a rainy night to help a junkie informant. Pursuing a dealer at 3 A.M. Ciello viciously assaults him with his fists, bloodying his mouth, even accidentally knocking to the ground during the chase the junkie he tries to aid. As all three run, all are oppressed by shadows of the seamy walls in the moral darkness they share. Showing compassion toward the dealer who pleads with the detective to allow him to keep a little of the dope for his own need, Ciello, after supplying his informant with drugs, guides the dealer to his abysmal home, where bulbs hang from the ceiling over his rack of a bed and the walls have a greenish tinge. There he must endure the man's screams as he and a woman fight over their need for the drugs.

In a memorable reaction shot of Ciello—the same meditative shot used in the closing freeze-frame of the film—the detective stands for several seconds poised against a barely visible wall, to his left a filthy window with rain coursing its length. Somewhat statically in the manner of Carl Dreyer, whom Lumet greatly admired, this nuanced film unfashionably suggests that, especially in such a nether world, moral considerations matter, that they have significance. Unlike much of contemporary nihilistic, easy relativism, *Prince of the City* affirms the value of reason and moral action, though it does not propose pat versions of either actions or motives, as Danny Ciello comes to accept responsibility for his life. Part of the reason for his survival is that he always retains the power over himself at least to attempt to choose and to accept, if not fully to understand, the multiple and diverse effects of these attempts, acknowledging but not completely submitting to the fact of moral compromise. As film writer and attorney Myron Meisel writes, the film's "seriousness restores some sanity to our considerations of crime, of moral standards and of just what meaningful action is possible for us in an increasingly treacherous and intractable world." [42]

Chapter Seven

A Major American Director

In twenty significant films Sidney Lumet has consistently addressed such culturally important themes as the possibility and the nature of meaningful action in the contemporary world through a variety of visual techniques and styles appropriate to his subject matter in each film. In a career that has included "more films . . . than any of his contemporaries . . . over the same period of time," he has frequently created excellent cinematic equivalents of notable literary works, directing at least four films that can stand with the important achievements of any American film director.[1] Nevertheless, Lumet has not yet received the critical acceptance or standing of a major artist in the film medium. While usually treated with critical respect as a vital, versatile, and competent director who possesses a "dogged, professional persistence," as a "talented and conscientious technician with a passion for the theater and an ability to handle actors," as a director who has "kept up the pressure of a prolific and varied output" and whose "career has been spectacularly uneven," or as a director whose "every move should be closely watched in the future" and whose "nearly proverbial 'unevenness' is the direct consequence of his versatility and pragmatism, of a concern with material output rather than personal input," Lumet has engendered a critical estimate that falls considerably short of its deserved position.[2] Frequently, as the foregoing critical analyses show, critical commentary on Lumet tends toward the general and the subjective, as if observers are uncertain of where to place him and of criteria by which to assess his work. This blatant discrepancy between the director's achievement and its reception has its source in the frequently impressionistic writings, influential far beyond their merit, of Andrew Sarris and Pauline Kael during the 1960s. In an attempt to rectify the imbalance, these two critics' views must be carefully examined.

In *The American Cinema*, Sarris places Lumet in his seventh category, "Strained Seriousness" (between "Lightly Likable" and "Oddities, One-Shots, and Newcomers"), along with such directors as Jack Clayton (*Room at the Top, The Innocents*), Jules Dassin (*The Naked City, He Who Must Die*), John Frankenheimer (*Birdman of Alcatraz, The Man-*

churian Candidate), Robert Rossen (*Body and Soul, The Hustler*), Robert Wise (*The Set-Up, The Day the Earth Stood Still*), and Stanley Kubrick (*Paths of Glory, 2001: A Space Odyssey*). Sarris charges Lumet and the other directors in this rubric with unevenness and "pretentiousness" (which presumably includes lack of a "personal vision of the world," the central standard for Sarris's "Pantheon Directors," a category that includes Chaplin, Griffith, Welles, Ford, Keaton, and Hitchcock). Lumet is "efficiently vehicular but pleasantly impersonal," or not a subscriber to the French auteur theory, possesses "innate good taste" that alone "saves him from utter mediocrity," and "lacks the necessary temperament of a tyrant on the set." Sarris condemns the "masochism" of *The Pawnbroker* and the "sadism" of *The Hill* as results of a "humorless temperament" and ends by dismissing the "middle-brow aspirations of his projects."[3]

Two years before the appearance of Sarris's volume, Pauline Kael was invited to attend the production of *The Group* from casting to editing. In her long essay for the *New Yorker,* Kael praises *The Group* for its "vitality" and for its treatment of "the specific experiences of women in our time," while affirming Lumet's close involvement in the casting and detailed planning, including "the camera position for each shot, the lens to be used, and just about everything the technicians need to know." She applauds *Long Day's Journey into Night,* and in the same paragraph says, "Lumet had been getting work directing movies for several years because he was cheap, fast and reliable." She implies that television experience makes a director a "mechanic," who afterward has "little . . . left of his own to express." Because "Lumet was television-trained . . . [h]e was no dangerous artist; he was out to do a job." Making no distinction between American television of the 1950s and of the decade during which she is writing—indeed, mentioning no Lumet television work specifically—Kael expresses her fears, just after the appearance of *The Pawnbroker* and *The Hill,* that movies may be turned into television shows: "It is possible that in the next few years television will wreck movies." In the same sentence she says, "And yet he still is, in his methods of work, basically a TV director." Kael writes—just after Lumet's successive direction of *Long Day's Journey into Night, Fail Safe,* and *The Pawnbroker*—that he is not concerned with "discovering the possibilities in the material and shaping it." She implies that because the mass audiences of the mid-1960s want merely "the immediacy of foreground action and as many climaxes as possible," Lumet's television background will aim him toward "the really big audience" and give film audiences the worst level of mid-1960s television programming.[4]

Kael continues, saying that because of Lumet's television training, he directs films "one-dimensionally." The "camera will rarely move within a shot; 'movement' will be accomplished by the actors moving within the frame and by the rapid juxtaposition of shots." Effects will be obtained by "turning loose the actors, and by emphasizing . . . emphatic climaxes, shocks, excessive and thus surprising bits of action." She continues, "He cannot use crowds or details to convey the illusion of life. His backgrounds are always just an empty space; he doesn't even know how to make the principals stand out of a crowd. If he moves the camera, it's just a form of conspicuous expenditure—to prove he can do it. He has only TV foreground action. . . . it basically represents a loss of *the whole illusionary delight of movies*" (italics mine). Kael also criticizes Lumet's fast, live television-like pace in making the film, saying that he had "slammed through" making *The Pawnbroker* and *The Hill* within a six-month period. She condemns Lumet's liking for speed in shooting as producing rushed, careless work including insufficient directorial interpretive assistance for the actors and adds that Lumet was considering his next film while still making *The Group*. Because of these alleged deficiencies, Kael goes on to accuse Lumet of work that is "slovenly," of emotion tending to "excess," of "coarse effects," and of "a basic emotional vulgarity in his work." Impressionistic even in her praise of the director, she calls him "a very uncommon man with a common touch" and then uses his remarkable and acknowledged energy to label him as not reflective, questioning his precision and "ear for dialogue." [5]

Kael makes few specific indictments of *The Group*: she complains that Lumet does not do enough retakes, that she would prefer "long fluid scenes" in certain places in the film, and that the editing is faulty and is done to cover up mistakes in the shooting. [6] She claims that Lumet had not read the novel before he read the screenplay ("it's doubtful if he'd ever read any Mary McCarthy"), that Lumet deemphasizes the political satire of the novel in preference to psychological themes. Kael does not explore Lumet's statement to her that Lakey and Polly were "the only ones of the Group who completed themselves. The others are all wrecked by trying to be something else, something they're not." Kael protests that the beginning is too fast for viewers easily to gain their bearings, that Lumet makes mistakes on details, such as Helena once substituting *class* for *group,* and that two of Libby's sets reflect a 1940s ambience rather than the "*art moderne* décor of the thirties, which was such an important part of the novel." This, similar mistakes involving Kay's coiffures in certain scenes, and Lumet's "emphasis on immediate results," Kael says, show "the almost total lack of nuance, subtlety, and even rhythmical and structural development in his work." But astonishingly in the same essay, Kael also writes that "the movie is a considerably more realistic and sophisticated account of modern male-female relationships and what goes wrong in them than we've had on the screen." She says that Lumet has a kind of "pragmatic genius" giving his films "some charge or energy which may in some crazy way be more important than perfection anyway" and that "in watching Lumet work, I was torn between detesting his fundamental tastelessness and opportunism and recognizing the fact that at some level it all *works*. It obviously, too obviously, wants to be moving, but damn it, it is."[7]

If the diction and overheated statement of these frequently overgeneralized comments, together with some contradictions between them, reveal some confusions in Kael's thinking and perhaps some personal animus against Lumet, her motives for writing in such a manner remain obscure. During interviews with me, Lumet was polite concerning Kael's frequently impressionistic views, saying that "with certain kinds of movies you need the reviews in order for them to succeed." Starting in 1968 he simply stopped reading all reviews of his films except for those in his morning *New York Times*. "It was the only solution," he said, "because what happens is—and anybody who says [such reviews] don't hurt is lying, of course they hurt—you start to censor yourself, you start thinking, 'what'll Pauline think of it,' which is madness, and so the only other solution was to not read them. . . . Pauline is so eager to force her *own* ideas onto whatever she's watching that I think very often Pauline could do her review off the titles because from there on she's just interested in how it meshes with her feelings. She's *not* open to the movie." In another interview, Lumet commented that he thought he was unpopular with Kael and Sarris because "I won't be put into a mold of their expectations. I have seen more good talent ruined by trying to live up to an idea of itself." Lumet added that he thought the rift between him and Kael occurred when they spoke about the function of the critic: "There were two other people present, and she said to them, 'My job is to show him'—pointing at me— 'which direction to go in.' I looked at her and said, 'You've got to be kidding.' She said, 'No, I'm not.' I said, 'In other words, you want the creative experience without the creative risk.' And that was it. She's never written a good word about me since."[8]

Although Kael accuses Lumet of carelessness with certain details in *The Group* and in aspects of its filming, she is herself uncertain in her grasp of some areas of the film's action. The early action is, in fact, marked by some fluid camera movements that emphasize the young women's unexamined actions that betoken the unhappiness ahead for most of them (see chapter 3). Stephen Farber, in his discriminating article on Lumet's films of the later 1960s, notes that Lumet's frequent thematic interest in the relationship of a character's past to his or her present life finds good stylistic equivalence in the "gentle, lyrical montage of the girls at college," which lends to their youthful idealism a quality of evanescence and predicts Lumet's adaptational emphasis upon "life's continuing betrayal of youthful optimism."[9] Kael over-simplifies nuances in both novel and film when she says that "deter-mined Kay . . . goes mad; good sweet Polly gets a dear understanding husband to depend on." Her statement that both Polly and Gus "use" analysis in their failed relationship fails to recognize that only Gus succumbs to this preoccupation. Kael accuses Lumet's approach of sexism: "By treating the girls as poor, weak creatures, as insignificant 'little women,'" the director "betrayed" women. She scores the film's treatment of the "quiet girls who don't come on strong com[ing] off best as human beings," charging Lumet himself with having a sexist view: "For Lumet, a woman shouldn't have any problems a real man can't take care of. If she does, she's sick."[10] Kael's observations of the film's sexual politics are misguided: several of the men in the film have as little self-understanding or maturity as the unhappiest of the wo-men, and Lakey (who is hardly dependent upon men, or women for that matter), Polly, and Helena are hardly "insignificant" figures or mainly dependent ones.

True, even these frequently strong women characters are not strongly interested in politics, for Lumet typically chooses to represent political themes and issues in personal, psychological ways. In an era during which "politics," especially among many film and academic critics, has come to mean only activity of a frequently unconsidered pop-Marxist or deconstructionist persuasion, so fashionable in recent years, Lumet has suffered critically for treating currently unfashionable liberal themes and subjects in his films. Only once did Lumet venture into the documentary form, with the 1969 film *King: A Filmed Record . . . Montgomery to Memphis* (codirected with Joseph Mankiewicz), which garnered an Academy Award nomination for best documentary. Lumet's usual sociopolitical stance is that noted by Andrew Sarris and Tom Allen during a revival of *12 Angry Men:* Lumet "captured in pristine form the emotional voltage and transcendental face of the New York–trained actor . . . a great acting exercise for conflicting person-alities in a tight space . . . one exquisite frame after another. . . . [It's] not just a cast. That's an honor roll of the key male character actors who have most sensitively incarnated the liberal social conscience that New York prides itself on bringing to the American tube and screen."[11]

In a recent interview, Lumet commented on his view of radical politics, saying that Gus, the violence-prone radical in his 1988 film, *Running on Empty*, is "really running on empty. . . . he's isolated."[12] Lumet added of the sixties' new leftists:

[They] succeeded at something very romantic. And then when it all didn't go their way, they ran out of gas. Certainly politically they did. First came exhaustion and then a refusal to engage. . . . I had tremendous admiration for . . . the stopping of a major war without overthrowing our own government in a revolution . . . [but the movement] also revolted against its own father, which was the old Left. And laughed at it, dismissed it. . . . Didn't even bother really to learn about it. . . . The agrarian and labor movements at the end of the 19th century were wonderfully moving, touching things, and of great importance. And by cutting themselves off from the Left, they made themselves a one-action generation. The war, but after that, nothing—these people grew up, a lot of them voted for Reagan. . . . I felt that the societal elements [of the 1960s] were rather naive and laughable. I'm just not thrilled by a rock 'n roll drug culture. It doesn't seem to be enormously contributive to a way of living. . . . it has nothing to do with what one does about economics . . . about very important forces in our lives.[13]

Offscreen, Lumet is a civil libertarian rather than an ideologue in politics, one of fifty charter members of the Performing Arts Committee for Civil Liberties, formed by Woody Allen in 1982 to oppose threats to free expression. (With Allen, Lumet has vigorously opposed the "colorization" of old black-and-white films.) In the 1930s, Lumet "recalls attending a single Communist party meeting, and was asked to leave after he pointed out that Soviet society was not classless because the artists lived better than the masses."[14] Not only in *Daniel* and in *Prince of the City* has the director made films with sociopolitical implications, but also, for example, in *Q & A, Power, Dog Day Afternoon*, and *The Verdict*, as well as in *Running on Empty*, Lumet has explored characters who risk much to challenge dominant, powerful systems. The rather broad treatment in *Network, The Anderson Tapes*, and *The Verdict*, in fact, seems to result from an attempt to reach a politically unsophisticated audience with melodrama and sometimes caricature so the "common viewer" can experience a change in attitude regarding matters such as the abuse of legal systems, technology and mass communications. Despite Kael's dissatisfactions, Lumet's art, if not overtly ideological, is political when, as in these films, it addresses the national phenomena of political reaction, social passivity and malaise, as well as the lack of personal responsibility noted by the director in many of our social institutions.

Another criticism raised by Kael, that Lumet "pulls it all out of his *own* background" in reaching thematic interpretations in his films, that he is "a Method director: he looked for the meaning and motivation of everything in himself and his own experience," seems to counter a charge frequently leveled against the director that he is insufficiently "personal," insufficiently an auteurist. This has been Sarris's central objection to Lumet's career, until his eventual recognition of the high artistic quality of *Prince of the City;* there he favored Lumet over the more "auteurist" director originally assigned to that film. "I cannot imagine [Brian] De Palma's displaying Lumet's patience and scrupulousness in exploring the thorny issues of *Prince.* . . . I would have expected instead more fireworks, more facile cynicism, and possibly, even some facetiousness." [15] Lumet himself prefers his versatility and range rather than confinement within one immediately recognizable style. "I'm accused of not having a signature—I don't want to have a signature. That's taking yourself seriously, putting yourself on the library shelf. I don't know how good I am yet—or how bad. But I'm not afraid to try anything." [16] While the auteur theory is valuable for its emphasis upon the director's controlling creative vision, the theory has unrealistically subordinated attention to the essentially collaborative nature of film art. In an interview, Lumet observed, "I've never been a fashionable director. The whole *auteur* nonsense is repugnant to me. I won't take the billing 'a Sidney Lumet Film.' . . . When I go out shooting, I'm dependent on the weather, the sun, and 120 people around me knowing their work. And I don't want to settle into a particular style, because to me the style is determined by the material itself. I think this has sort of left me in a vacuum from a critical point of view." [17]

Lumet considers the term *auteur* "pretentious"; Shewey notes that "to Lumet, the term is only a justification of directorial self-indulgence" and praises the director's creative control over *The Verdict* as similar to that of a director like Truffaut. Shewey cites Lumet's and cinematographer Andrzej Bartkowiak's conscious use of Caravaggio-prompted lighting and color in the film to complement and reflect its dark themes of self-entrapment in the past, something, in Shewey's view, "that distinguishes an artistic director from an indifferent one." Lumet feels that any careful, creative director "has been doing that for years anyway. So all the auteur theory did was make what had been natural self-conscious. . . . [It] had a bad effect critically, because it's

trained critics to look for the wrong things."[18] Lumet expanded upon
his dissatisfaction with the auteur theory:

[Sarris] would like to . . . see forty pictures of which four are mine, and without
knowing who directed them be able to say, 'Those four were Lumet's pictures.'
Well . . . you'd never say [*Prince of the City* and *Murder on the Orient Express*]
came from the same man! . . . I have a million reasons for doing different
movies. I once did a movie [*The Appointment*] because I was having trouble
making the transition from black and white to color and had a chance to work
with a cameraman [Antonioni's Carlo Di Palma] who I knew could get me past
my block. I did *Murder on the Orient Express* because I love melodrama. . . . I
wanted to have fun. It turned out to be some of the hardest work I've ever done,
because the piece was highly stylized, but *Network* would never have been as
good as it was if I hadn't done *Murder on the Orient Express*. . . . I consider my
career . . . an ongoing process. . . . I know I'm good, but I don't know how
good. And I'm not going to find out unless I keep pushing against the borders. . . . They can't be Andrew Sarris' borders, they can't be Pauline Kael's
borders. They can't belong to anyone but me.[19]

Of course, one quasi-"auteurist" aspect of Lumet's directorial career is his continuing literary vision, his love for significant written
language, for which he has received criticism especially from Sarris.
Lumet has said, "The writing is better in the theater. I love language.
. . . if words are going to be used, I want the best in words. Playwrights tend to write better language, more revelatory language, more
profound language, than most screen writers."[20] Through a variety of
approaches, Lumet projects a personal vision that makes use of exist-
ing art, which he transmutes and shapes into independent works of
cinematic art through his considerable body of adapted work, echoing
Bazin's view that literature and language are important to the art of
film. That art in Lumet's view is collaborative, and he has distinguished
it by his association with fine cinematographers, actors, and artists in
other fields. Lumet's collaborative sense is shown by his saying of
Oswald Morris, the cinematographer on his black musical film, *The
Wiz*—and also his cinematographer for *The Hill, Equus*, and *Just Tell Me
What You Want*—that, while there were other cameramen of equal
technical ability, "He's the only one that I know of that I could talk to in
terms of the story, the fantasy, the style, the internal meaning—and
who would make it his way of thinking from then on."[21]

Following his effective collaboration with cinematographer Freddie
Young in color design on *The Deadly Affair*, Lumet worked with production designer Tony Walton on *The Sea Gull* (Walton also served with the

director on *The Wiz, Equus,* and *Murder on the Orient Express*) to achieve
subdued color textures: "In *The Sea Gull,* there was a combination of
filtering and choices made in the actual art direction. That's one of the
basic things I've learnt about color—it begins with the art director and
that's who you have to do your heaviest work with. Why leave it all to
the camera? Let the camera augment it." Commenting on the close
relation of color to the theme in *The Sea Gull,* Lumet continued, "In *Sea
Gull,* it's . . . beauty that's important. It was not a desaturation, but
rather a muting—to get autumnal, nostalgic, gentle. To get a seagull's
color against gray sky and water." [22] From early in his career, Lumet has
firmly believed in the collaborative process. His 1960 interview with
Peter Bogdanovich discloses a close working relationship with Tennessee Williams and Meade Roberts in forming the final screenplay for *The
Fugitive Kind* that demonstrates that Lumet, who has claimed screenwriting credit for only two of his films, *Prince of the City* and *Q & A,*
frequently contributes to the finished verbal work of art. He described
his method to Bogdanovich:

The method for myself is one simply of letting [the writers] do their work, then
going *back* into work in terms of whatever specifics are needed, whether it's
structural or dialogue. On *Fugitive Kind,* for instance, there was a good deal of
re-writing between the original draft and what wound up on the screen. . . .
    [Bogdanovich]: Did you have a say in that?
    [Lumet]: Oh, yeah. And the working procedure was that Tennessee and
Meade brought in the first draft, then all of us together talk, talk . . . back,
another draft, talk, talk . . . back, another draft—I think it was the fourth draft
we used. [23]

In the Bogdanovich interview, Lumet, as he has often done,
praised his frequent collaborator in the early films, cinematographer
Boris Kaufman. Kaufman, Jean Vigo's cameraman in the 1930s for *Zero
for Conduct* and *L'Atalante* and a master of visual lyricism, is lauded not
only for his great technical virtuosity but also for his strong "sense of
dramatic interpretation" and his ability to suit camera style to thematic
purpose. [24] While Lumet emphasized to me, "*I* make the frame, I pick
the lens, I make my own set-ups," he said of Kaufman, "Boris was in
perfect keeping with the kinds of movies I was doing. In terms of the
kind of dramatic intensity nobody could have been better. . . . Boris
was never really able to make the transition into color, and I was having
my own problems adjusting to color, so finally the relationship ended.
But he was a genuine kindred spirit from the creative point of view; to
sit and discuss script with Boris was a joy, what he absorbed, what he
understood of what was wanted and what was not." [25]

As Lumet has encouraged his cinematographers to share in cinematic creativity, so he also has enjoyed a similar relationship with other artists. Film editor Ralph Rosenblum writes in his professional autobiography that for *The Pawnbroker* Lumet first wanted to use for the musical score the work of the cerebral pianist and composer of the distinguised Modern Jazz Quartet, John Lewis, but Lumet accepted Rosenblum's advice of the more accessible, also distinguished jazz arranger Quincy Jones, formerly composer for the Count Basie orchestra. Rosenblum praises the director highly in several respects: "Clearly, if a picture needed astute editorial consideration, Sidney was the director to handle it. But despite his mastery of editorial technique, Lumet was respectful of the editor's point of view and contribution; he never rejected something of value simply because he did not originate it. Under Lumet I rarely had an opportunity to work out long stretches of film on my own, and I would have found working with him in recent years unsatisfying for that reason; but we operated as a team, and I always felt well used."[26]

Probably Lumet's most well-known collaborative element is his relationship with actors, his outstanding ability in drawing from them superior performances. The director's psychological sensitivity, so present in the films, significantly contributes to his ability to work with actors in both a liberating and a disciplined manner. He once commented, "Good work in movies involves personal exposure, personal risks, showing how you feel about something. The actor is infinitely more exposed than anyone else, and he's exposed at the very moment of creativity. Actors are the infantry, the ones in the line of fire."[27] Actor Christopher Reeve, a major player in Lumet's melodrama *Deathtrap*, gives a revealing description of Lumet's varied abilities in this collaborative relationship:

He knows how to speak a variety of languages, whereas an insecure or tyrannical director often fails to communicate with anybody who doesn't understand him immediately. He knows how to talk technical language—if you want to work that way—he knows how to talk Method, he knows how to improvise, and he does it all equally well. Michael Caine had his part nailed from day one, so Sidney left him alone; they just cracked jokes and had a good time. Irene Worth brought a lot of ideas; Sidney's job was to refine and edit the wealth of material she brought him. My way is improvisation as a process of finding out what I *don't* want in order to get what I *do* want. Then during shooting Sidney would often come up at the last minute and give me a new idea I'd never thought of—not a major change, but something fresh to put on my plate. That, combined with the work we'd done in rehearsal, made for spontaneous work."[28]

Unlike such directors as Hitchcock and Bergman, Lumet chooses not to control his actors rigorously but to discuss with them ideas and character as they relate to the entire film, using an extensive preplanning and rehearsal period to make each central actor familiar with the range and depth of the film.[29] His professional flexibility and his respect for the artistic importance of the film effort, which he considers equal to that of the literary effort, has prompted actors of Ralph Richardson's caliber to turn down far greater fees for a chance to work with Lumet.[30] In an interview with Kenneth Chanko, Lumet spoke reflectively about the importance to him of this collaborative aspect of filmmaking:

Good acting is really self-revelation, and that's a very painful, complicated and frightening process. And it takes time to get people free enough to do that. That self-revelation is done much better, and better nurtured, off the set, away from strangers and in a private atmosphere, where you can try things and not feel foolish. . . . So it's a much more concentrated time than you ever get on the set, and therefore you can use the time much better—both for me and the actor. I think I spend more time in pre-production rehearsals with the cast than most directors. . . . you can get away with more in the theater; you can fake it easier than you can in film. But that cliché about how you have to reduce the performance, make it smaller on film, isn't true. You just have to work more honestly. . . . I like being described as the actor's director because it comes primarily from the fact that they open up with me more than they do with most directors.[31]

He discussed the matter further in an interview with me:

The trust becomes enormous. Also they know, on the human level, that I won't violate them. One of the things that I establish very early is that I'm never going to lie, I'm never going to be going for one thing while they think I'm going for another; if we can't get it out of mutual craft, I'd rather let it go, I'd rather not get it. . . . I've had actors, I remember once, very early on, I tried that subterfuge, and the actor loved it! She was just totally surprised by what happened, thought it was great, and I'd made the most intense violation of her, on a human level, and from then on I never even wanted to see her again because if her self-respect was that little it was nobody I wanted to be around. What I did was the old trick, saying keep going no matter what I do, say the line, and we rolled and I whacked her right across the face, I hit her hard and tears came, and she was just happy that the moment worked out. If it takes that to get it then it's not worth getting. So I think that combination of they know that no violation will take place and they know that I'm aware of what they're offering up . . . that *respect* I've got for their feelings is what allows them to open themselves up for me.

If Lumet is justly esteemed by actors and film professionals for his patience and meditative pace in the preproduction stages of filming, he is undeniably fast-paced, as Kael points out, in the actual shooting stage. In *The Group* Lumet's energy and passion for filmmaking may occasionally result in insufficiently considered details concerning the social texture of a period, but a detailed, probing examination of Lumet's most important films reveals no such carelessness. Even interesting, but for this director minor, films such as *Murder on the Orient Express* and *The Wiz* are notable for their accuracy in period detail. Just as artistically and commercially successful writers such as Joyce Carol Oates are criticized for their prolific output, so Lumet has been pilloried for having directed thirty-six feature films in thirty-three years. Given that twenty of these films, at least, constitute major work, Lumet's abundant output would seem to require no apology. He has said that he loves to work, strives continually to experiment and to try to develop new talents and subjects and styles. And certainly, given the difficulty of sustaining even as successful a career as Lumet's in a market so devoted to the sensationalistic and the trivial, it is necessary for him continually to produce commercially viable films, the success of which may allow him to gain financing for artistically more serious works. To gain the opportunity to make *Daniel*, one of his greatest works, Lumet promised the studio that he would make another film of their choice; and after the commercial success of *Serpico*, he told an interviewer, "I'm not one to be cool about a hit. . . . I know the marketplace, and I know you need hits to survive in it."[32] And of course Lumet's reputation throughout his career for coming in under budget and under schedule has given him added commercial muscle with cost-conscious producers.

Yet his commercial pragmatism and keen survival sense did not lead him to make a film in Hollywood until *The Morning After* (1986), starring Jane Fonda, whom Lumet praises as a "brilliant comedienne." Even in perfecting the glossy style of *The Morning After, Murder on the Orient Express, Deathtrap,* and the later sections of *Network,* Lumet managed to combine commercial appeal with thematically congruent atmosphere and technique. If Lumet's directorial weaknesses centrally comprise his several minor films in the melodrama genre as well as his frequent lack of facility with comedy—although *Family Business* (1989) reveals a comic lightness reminiscent of parts of *Dog Day Afternoon* and *Network,* admirably fused with a psychologically mature treatment of fathering within an ostensible "caper film" format—then his interview statements bear chilling witness to the increasing commercial pressures on creative directors in recent years. The producers of *The*

Anderson Tapes forced Lumet to change the ending so that the Sean Connery burglar character would be punished; "They were afraid they wouldn't get a good TV sale." *Power* was released in August instead of in March as had been originally planned, at Lumet's suggestion. "Chevy Chase starts falling down stairs with a monkey on his back and we're into the popcorn season come Memorial Day. If we were lucky enough to start hitting some sort of commercial success in March or April, we'd be out of bucks and finished before summer."[33] Concerned about the reception of *Prince of the City*, Lumet told David Ansen how difficult it is to make "my kind of movies": "There's a reveling in mindlessness. Now the summer fluff movies are wintertime movies. You've got January and February for your flop serious movies."[34]

Despite his prolific pace and output, Lumet even in his minor films usually aims above solely commercial appeal, his frequent base in melodrama, while serving his other art well, reaching in these films a larger audience with important social ideas and themes. For example, *The Anderson Tapes* and *The Verdict* emphasize ideas rather than violence or sensationalism, and in major films that concern crime, Lumet seldom uses shock effects. The respected film editor Dede Allen lauds Lumet's speed and enthusiasm: "We get infected by his enthusiasm . . . excitement. . . . it's contagious," and Lumet himself explains his fast pace as the best mode for sustaining realism in mood and atmosphere. It also helps "the actors stay hot. The thing that exhausts them . . . is waiting. . . . Because of my theater and TV background, I'm trained to make the dramatic selection in advance. So I rehearse, and then commit to one attack." And, in keeping with his drive to keep progressing and learning, Lumet comments, "My job's to keep directing. If I'm not directing, I'm not a director. I'm just a man with opinions."[35]

"There is a loveliness exists, / Preserves us, not for specialists," writes Snodgrass in "April Inventory."[36] It is Lumet's dedication to improve himself, to learn new styles and to expand his already considerable range of cinematic subjects that, in addition to his impressive number of excellent films, stamps him as a major American film director. His many characters who undertake substantial risks reflect the director's own intent to "keep pushing against the borders" of his abilities and his art; Lumet's musings about possible film projects concerning Malcolm X, war, compulsive careerism, and television evangelism suggest continued expansion. He is well known for making most of his films in New York, usually avoiding Hollywood in order to gain independence that will allow greater experiment in subject, theme, and appropriate styles. Of his reasons for making his satiric

New York comedy, *Just Tell Me What You Want*, he said that it is "a pure comedy with no dramatic extensions. It is about something—I hope it's about hypocrisy—but its form is comedic, its spirit is totally gay, the lines are witty, it requires wit in the performances, in the direction. . . . I think in the future the dramatic work's going to be helped because of this." Lumet asserts, "I don't believe in waiting for the masterpiece. Masterful subject matter only comes up rarely. The point is, there's something to advance your technique in every movie you do."[37]

Lumet's visual techniques reveal frequent interest in images of spatial fragmentation and enclosure to represent the spiritual trunca-tions of the modern era. But they also embrace a more open-ended, lyrical cinematic style to suggest the world's purposive possibilities. Cinematographer Owen Roizman, Lumet's director of photography on *Network*, says that Lumet's theory of camera movement is to establish "very important moves . . . when they're dramatically called for."[38] *The Pawnbroker*, renowned for its harsh, angular style, also contains carefully conceived depth compositions that disclose Mendel's charac-ter and Nazerman's attempt to establish human contact on Marilyn's balcony, and camera positions and movements that reveal, for exam-ple, Mabel's progress through the street life, Ortiz's jostling path toward Tangee and destruction, and Nazerman's children's commun-ion with the natural world. Whiteness in Rodriguez's apartment im-portantly supports theme in the same film. In *The Morning After*, as the confused Jane Fonda character wanders the Los Angeles streets, searching for the explanation of a murder as well as for the meaning of her disappointing life, Lumet visually juxtaposes her to a horizontally color-divided white and brown wall similar to the white images that background Anouk Aimée in *The Appointment*. Spacious shots or cam-era movements disclose Myrtle and Chicken's tentative safety at the end of the Tennessee Williams-based *Last of the Mobile Hot-Shots*, the lake's world in the pensive pans at the beginning of *The Sea Gull*, the young lovers' walk by the sea in *Running on Empty*, the searchers' mythic journey in the tiny red auto and Morroe's walk among the dead in *Bye, Bye Braverman*, and the "eerie, dreamlike" early views of Carla that "match Federico's sense of dislocation" and the ironically romantic helicopter perspective of the lovers on the island in *The Appointment*.[39] Spacious shots or camera movements also reveal the Ben Shahn-like background of Paul Newman's initial talk with Lindsay Crouse in *The Verdict*, the flow of flashy glitter at Henry Fonda's party as well as the lyrical snow scenes in *Stage Struck*, and the gathering at the first wake in *Family Business*, the elder and his grandson visible amid the drunken singing of "Danny Boy," while, significantly, reached last by the slowly moving camera, apart in his unknowing of himself, is the seated Dustin Hoffman.

Lumet interviewer William Wolf comments on reasons for Lumet's lack of wider critical acceptance: "Critics have in recent years tended to worship style over content, bestowing kudos on newcomers who make a splash with self-conscious visual pizzazz, often lavished on escapist entertainment or violent chic. There is also the general resistance in our country to films that concentrate on—as so many of Lumet's do—social themes and the complexities of relationships."[40] Such personal and social complexities are an inextricable part of Sidney Lumet's literary vision, a vision that has encompassed Shaw and Camus in the theater, O'Neill and Reginald Rose in television direction, and in his long film career such literary figures as O'Neill, Chekhov, Miller, Williams, McCarthy, Doctorow, and Edward Lewis Wallant. Lumet's essentially Modernist literary and cinematic vision is unfashionable in a contemporary period in which film more and more is regarded as merely a means of escape from increasingly unpleasant, even barbaric, social realities into infantile fantasy, as merely an emotionally seductive medium, designed to titillate the ultimate feel-good consumer with, in Kael's unfortunately reductive phrase, "the whole illusionary delight of movies."

Film, like all art, of course *is* pleasure, an important component of which stems from mature consideration and reflection upon the most serious and profound human events and dilemmas. Lumet has addressed our minimalist, casually relativistic culture with films that— from *12 Angry Men* to *Q & A*—in theme and style attempt to restore the importance of reason as well as of personal and institutional responsibility. Among some twenty major films, he has made at the very least ten that in depth and scope of thematic conception and in artistic congruence of idea and imaginative form are of outstanding quality: *12 Angry Men*, *Long Day's Journey into Night*, *Fail Safe*, *The Pawnbroker*, *A View from the Bridge*, *Daniel*, *The Group*, *The Sea Gull*, *Dog Day Afternoon*, and *Prince of the City*. While working below the artistic level of Kurosawa or Bergman, who usually create the written bases for their films, Lumet is crucially important to an increasingly decadent culture as a major director who frequently transmutes literature, or infuses literary seriousness, into cinematic art. For even in such lesser films as the 1984 *Garbo Talks*—Ron Silver, in a brilliant serio-comic visual choreography, must arduously forge his way through the flea market toward his beloved mother's elusive fantasy, unable here to proceed in an easy straight line but forced finally to venture risks, to circumnavigate many layers of humanity, to face life's continual surprise and opportunity rather than settling into his accustomed security—Lumet continually creates urgent, necessary metaphors of what is for him an underlying personal purpose in the creation of film, to challenge himself as well as his society, to extend that self, and "to see what's *there!*"

Notes

Introduction

1. David Margolick, "Again, Sidney Lumet Ponders Justice," *New York Times*, Dec. 31, 1989, sec. H, p. 9.

2. Kevin Lally, "Versatility Gives Lumet Staying Power," *Film Journal* 89 (Jan. 1986): 8.

3. Bernard F. Dick, *Anatomy of Film* (New York: St. Martin's Press, 1978), 131.

4. Stephen Farber, "Lumet in '69," *Sight and Sound* 38 (Autumn 1969): 193-95. Yacowar judges *Last of the Mobile Hot-Shots* "a provocative minor work by a major American director," in *Tennessee Williams and Film* (New York: Ungar, 1977), 136.

1. A Cinema of Conscience

1. John Lombardi, "Lumet: The City Is His Sound Stage," *New York Times Magazine*, June 6, 1982, pp. 26, 29.

2. *Current Biography*, Sept. 1967, p. 26.

3. Don Shewey, "Sidney Lumet: The Reluctant Auteur," *American Film* 8 (Dec. 1982): 34.

4. William Wolf, "Director with a Conscience," *New York*, Aug. 10, 1981, p. 55.

5. Joseph Heller, *Catch-22* (New York: Dell, 1976), 450.

6. Jill Kearney, "What's Wrong with Today's Films?" *American Film* 11 (May 1986): 53-56. See scenarist Steve Tesich's comment that contemporary films feed the national "drift away from the strength and beauty of the human experience" (55); producer Edgar J. Scherick's view that film increasingly concerns "violence, lack of respect for human life, the antidemocratic theses" (56); and Lumet's observation that the predominant characteristics of today's films include "sentimentality instead of emotion, tactile sensation and shock instead of thrill" (54). For Lumet's earlier analysis that "the industry itself actually stops good pictures from being made," see Fred Baker, ed., *Movie People: At Work in the Business of Film* (New York: Douglas, 1972), 35-40.

7. A.H. Weiler, "A Funeral Grows in Brooklyn," *New York Times*, April 23, 1967, sec. 2, p. 20.

8. Guy Flatley, "Lumet—The Kid Actor Who Became a Director," *New York Times*, Jan. 20, 1974, sec. D, p. 11.

9. See Robert Alter, *The Pleasures of Reading in an Ideological Age* (New York: Simon and Schuster, 1989).

10. Fred Baker, ed., *Movie People: At Work in the Business of Film* (New York: Douglas, 1972), 47.

11. David Margolick, "Again, Sidney Lumet Ponders Justice," *New York Times*, Dec. 31, 1989, sec. H, p. 9.

12. Peter Travers, *Rolling Stone*, May 17, 1990, p. 27.

13. Gary Giddens, *Village Voice*, May 1, 1990, p. 74; David Ansen, *Newsweek*, May 7, 1990, p. 65.

14. Vincent Canby, *New York Times*, April 27, 1990, sec. C, p. 20.

15. Lombardi, "Lumet," 81; Gavin Smith, "Sidney Lumet: Lion on the Left," *Film Comment* 24 (Aug. 1988): 37. Lumet's careful preproduction planning and script sessions resemble those of Kurosawa. Donald Richie, *The Films of Akira Kurosawa* (Berkeley: Univ. of California Press, 1965), 185, 191-92.

16. Kevin Lally, "Versatility Gives Lumet Staying Power," *Film Journal* 89 (Jan. 1986): 8; Smith, "Lion on the Left," 38.

17. *Variety*, Jan. 29, 1986, p. 14.

18. Jack Kroll, "The Selling of the Candidates," *Newsweek*, Feb. 10, 1986, p. 79.

19. Rick Lyman, *Omaha World-Herald*, Feb. 16, 1986, p. 11.

20. Shewey, "Reluctant Auteur," 35; Kenneth M. Chanko, "Sidney Lumet: An Interview," *Films in Review* 35 (Oct. 1984): 452.

21. Tom Burke, "Suddenly, I Knew How to Film the Play," *New York Times*, July 24, 1977, sec. D, p. 20; Stephen E. Bowles, *Sidney Lumet: A Guide to References and Resources* (Boston: G.K. Hall, 1979), 4 (For additional biographical information on Lumet's early career, see pp. 4-11); Smith, "Lion on the Left," 38.

22. Flatley, "Kid Actor," 11.

23. Ibid.

24. Shewey, "Reluctant Auteur," 33-34.

25. Arthur Bell, "Not the Rosenbergs' Story," *Village Voice*, Sept. 6, 1983, p. 42.

26. Patricia Bosworth, "Grouptalk—Groupthink," *New York Herald Tribune*, Aug. 22, 1965, p. 12.

27. Smith, "Lion on the Left," 38; Flatley, "Kid Actor," 11.

28. Lombardi, "Lumet," 36.

29. Elaine Dundy, "Why Actors Do Better for Sidney Lumet," *New York*, Nov. 22, 1976, p. 82.

30. *New York Times*, May 26, 1948, p. 29.

31. Bowles, *Sidney Lumet*, 7.

32. Smith, "Lion on the Left," 34.

33. Chanko, "Sidney Lumet," 452.

34. Bowles, *Sidney Lumet*, 11.

35. Chanko, "Sidney Lumet," 452.

36. Gerald Mast, *A Short History of the Movies*, 4th ed. (New York: Macmillan, 1986), 314.

37. Gene Moskowitz, "The Tight Close-Up," *Sight and Sound* 29 (Winter 1959-60): 127.

38. *Cue Magazine*, July 19, 1952, p. 6.

39. Ibid.

40. Ibid.

41. Lumet's *Iceman*, of which Jack Gould wrote, "To television has come a moment of enrichment and excitement unequalled in the medium's thirteen years" (*New York Times*, Nov. 16, 1960, p. 83), will be discussed with *Long Day's Journey into Night* in chapter 4.

2. The Loner and the Struggle for Moral Capability

1. Molly Haskell, "An Unstable Fable," *New York*, Nov. 7, 1977, p. 91.

2. Andrew Sarris, "Reining in the Prance," *Village Voice*, Oct. 31, 1977, p. 45. Sarris adds: "an unbelievably elegant temptress in an antiwoman fantasy. What did she ever see in Firth's clod of a stableboy to make her humiliate herself and her whole sex at the smelly shrine of the Great God Equus?"

3. Stanley Kauffmann, "Ill Wind," *The New Republic*, Nov. 5, 1977, pp. 24-25.

4. In an interview, Lumet revealed at least his partial approval of Shaffer's thesis: "We wanted to get the Dionysian side on a more realistic level, so that it could be presented squarely in both its horror and its magnificence." *Films and Filming* 24 (May 1978): 14.

5. Gordon Gow, *Films and Filming* 24 (Oct. 1977): 28.

6. Adler's individual psychology is useful here in revealing that over-compensatory efforts can lead to acts of hysteria as well as acts of genius. Alan's deep feelings of inadequacy in social areas remind us of Adler's view that "dependency is the root of all feelings of inferiority." H.H. Mosak, ed., *Alfred Adler: His Influence on Psychology Today* (Park Ridge, N.J.: Noyes, 1973), 1.

7. *New York Times*, July 24, 1977, sec. D, p. 20.

8. James M. Welsh, "Dream Doctors as Healers in Drama and Film: A Paradigm, an Antecedent, and an Imitation," *Literature and Medicine* 6 (1987): 125.

9. *Films and Filming* 24 (May 1978): 15.

10. Lumet said in an interview, "Kitt West does incredible masks. He did the animal heads for the Royal Ballet's *Tales of Beatrix Potter*. He made me six heads; the eyes, mouths, tongues moved, all controlled by one person, the hand in the neck. In the eye sockets and in certain areas of the horse's skin were pockets where we could insert blood capsules."

11. Lionel Trilling, *The Liberal Imagination* (Garden City, N.Y.: Anchor, 1953), 64.

12. John Kirk, introduction to *The Incongruous Spy: Two Novels of Suspense by John Le Carré—Call for the Dead/A Murder of Quality* (New York: Walker, 1963), iii, iv. All quotations from *Call for the Dead* will be taken from this edition and cited in the text.

13. Kirk, introduction to *The Incongruous Spy*, v.

14. Dehn was also the screenwriter for Martin Ritt's 1965 film of Le Carré's *The Spy Who Came In from the Cold*. Lumet has said that Le Carré's theme "is always concerned with betrayal—at every level, not just in plot but in emotion" (*New York Times*, May 15, 1966, sec. 2, p. 11).

15. Several reviewers impressed with the film especially lauded Lumet for his direction of the actors. Mike Sarne, in *Films and Filming* 13 (April 1967): 6-7, wrote in, "technique, photography, cutting, acting, and literacy, the film must be regarded as one of the very best in the genre." See also Arthur Knight in *Saturday Review* 50 (Jan. 28, 1967): 49, and the *New Yorker*, Feb. 4, 1967, p. 98. Harriet Andersson's role was her first English-speaking one after her acclaim in Ingmar Bergman's films.

16. David Warner, who portrays Konstantin in Lumet's *The Sea Gull*, appears as Edward, with Michael Bryant as Gaveston and Charles Kay as Lightborn. Lumet's film marked the company's first appearance in a special portion of a film. *New York Times*, Feb. 11, 1966, p. 36.

17. Young, who won Oscars for cinematography for *Lawrence of Arabia* and *Doctor Zhivago*, wrote about his technique of preexposing Eastman color negative to obtain a subdued color in order to enhance the threatening mood of the film in "A Method of Pre-Exposing Color Negative for Subtle Effect," *American Cinematographer* 47 (Aug. 1966): 537. Lumet said of the muted color process, "This way we can knock out glamor. The phony edge is taken off and everything is real." *New York Times*, May 15, 1966, sec. 2, p. 11. Lumet was among the first American directors to employ color with darker hues to attempt to communicate life's more serious aspects, as is evident in Boris Kaufman's cinematography for *Bye, Bye Braverman* and *The Group*.

18. Tennessee Williams, *Orpheus Descending with Battle of Angels* (New York: New Directions, 1958), 114, 115. All quotations will be taken from this edition and cited in the text.

19. Writing of this film and of *A View from the Bridge*, Graham Petrie notes, "In both cases, Lumet has done his best to tone down the weaknesses of the original, and, at the very least, each film seems to me to be an improvement on the original play." Graham Petrie, "The Films of Sidney Lumet: Adaptation as Art," *Film Quarterly* 21 (Winter 1967-68), 10.

20. Signi L. Falk, *Tennessee Williams*, 2d ed. (Boston: Twayne, 1978), 104-5.

21. In *Tennessee Williams and Film* (New York: Ungar, 1977), Maurice Yacowar stresses the "physical realism" of the film compared with that of the play, citing such mythic resonances as Val as bringer of "music, love, and vitality to a deadened Eurydice." Yacowar thinks that generally "the film is the best version of the basic material" (60-66). Gene D. Phillips agrees that the film is the artistically superior version in *The Films of Tennessee Williams* (Philadelphia: Art Alliance Press, 1980), 206. This study, which concentrates on Williams's drama, provides information about the troubled background production of the film (210-13), as does Peter Bogdanovich, "An Interview with Sidney Lumet," *Film Quarterly* 14 (Winter 1960): 18-19. Positive reviews include two by Bosley Crowther, in the *New York Times*, April 15, 1960, p. 13, and April 24, 1960, sec. 2, p. 1. Negative and impressionistic commentaries include Hollis

Alpert, *Saturday Review,* April 23, 1960, p. 28, and Parker Tyler, *Films and Filming* 8 (Summer 1960): 47-49. Tyler's review treats the film only as Williams's play, sees Val only as a fugitive "from the mental clinic" (48), and is typical of the unfortunately impressionistic commentary often encountered in Lumet criticism.

22. Lumet achieved this unusual effect by placing lamps "on low just beyond the crest of a hill; [we] laid them right on the deck." For a fine discussion of lighting and of techniques of camera fixture prior to shooting, including cinematographer Boris Kaufman's observations on lighting in this and other key scenes, see Frederick Foster, "Filming *The Fugitive Kind*," *American Cinematographer* 41 (June 1960): 354-55, 379-80, 382.

23. Yacowar observes that "further poetic dimension is supplied by some exceptional photography" (*Tennessee Williams and Film*, 63).

24. Yacowar comments that Val is also stayed by Lady, who obsessively desires revenge upon her husband for destroying her father's arbor and seeks to reopen it to spite Jabe while he still lives (ibid., 65).

25. I of course disagree with Phillips's moralistic interpretation of the lovers' deaths, which emphasizes a "purification-by-fire theme of the play" (*Films of Tennessee Williams*, 210).

26. Gerald Weales observes that Alfieri is "a cross between the Greek chorus and Mary Worth." Weales, *American Drama since World War Two* (New York: Harcourt, Brace, 1962), 12.

27. Arthur Miller, *Collected Plays* (New York: Viking, 1957), 439. All quotations of *A View from the Bridge* will be taken from this edition and cited in the text.

28. Negative and impressionistic, misconceived reviews include Norm Fruchter, *Sight and Sound* 31 (Spring 1962): 95-96; Jonas Mekas, *Village Voice*, Feb. 22, 1962, p. 11; and Pauline Kael, *Film Quarterly* 15 (Summer 1962): 27-29. Favorable commentaries include Bosley Crowther, *New York Times*, Jan. 23, 1962, p. 36.

29. Lumet, who treats a homosexual theme in *Dog Day Afternoon*, does not seem to me to do so in *Bridge*, despite this interpretation of Eddie's kissing Rodolpho in Pauline Kael, *Film Quarterly* 15 (Summer 1962): 29. Kael ignores the total context in this scene and also forgets Bea's recognition, in the end of both play (437) and film, of Eddie's true need: "You want somethin' else, Eddie, and you can never have her!"

30. Another perspective on effective use of the long shot in *Bridge* is discussed in Roy Huss and Norman Silverstein, *The Film Experience* (New York: Delta, 1968), 117-18.

31. Andrew Kopkind, "Broken Hearts and Minds," *The Movies*, Oct. 1983, p. 71; Stephen Farber, "*Daniel*," *Film Quarterly* 39 (Spring 1984): 32.

32. Pauline Kael, *New Yorker*, Sept. 5, 1983, pp. 110, 111. See also Richard Corliss, *Time*, Aug. 29, 1983, p. 61, and Edward Guthmann, "In Doctorow's Den," *San Francisco Bay Guardian*, Sept. 21, 1983, pp. 23-25. An intelligent discussion of the historical issues is provided by Peter Kihss, "The Movie 'Daniel': How Close Is It to History?" *New York Times*, Aug. 31, 1983, p. 20.

33. Andrew Sarris, "The Rosenbergs, the Isaacsons, and Thou," *Village Voice*, Sept. 6, 1983, pp. 45, 51. Kopkind correctly identifies cinematographer Andrzej Bartkowiak's sepia hues in these sequences ("Broken Hearts and Minds," 70).

34. Sarris, "Rosenbergs, the Isaacsons, and Thou," 45; Guthmann, "Doctorow's Den," 25. Farber suggests a possible political motive behind the "curiously smug and scolding tone" of most of the film's reviews. "A film that recalls the dangers of that hysteria [the anti-Communist attitudes of the 1950s] is definitely going against the grain. Although they might try to deny it, mainstream movie critics have almost always reflected rather than defied the prevailing political mood in the country, and this film clearly makes them uncomfortable . . . We have come full circle; the Cold War madness of the fifties is resurgent in the eighties, and that is one reason why this film is such a courageous and pertinent plea for sanity" (*"Daniel,"* 32).

35. E.L. Doctorow, *The Book of Daniel* (New York: Bantam, 1979), 227-30. All quotations will be taken from this edition and cited in the text.

36. Arthur Bell, "Not the Rosenbergs' Story," *Village Voice*, Sept. 6, 1983, p. 41.

37. Judy Stone, "Director Defends Movie Version of 'Daniel,'" *San Francisco Chronicle*, Oct. 4, 1983, p. 42.

38. Sarris, "The Rosenbergs, the Isaacsons, and Thou," 45.

39. P. Michael Campbell, "Lumet and Hutton, in defense of 'Daniel'," *Daily Californian*, Sept. 30, 1983, pp. 10-11.

40. Edward Guthmann, "Timothy Hutton Talks Back," *San Francisco Bay Guardian*, Sept. 28, 1983, pp. 32-33.

41. Campbell, 11.

42. Kopkind, "Broken Hearts and Minds," 70.

43. Ibid., 71.

44. Ibid., 70.

45. Ibid.

46. See ibid., 71, and Farber, *"Daniel,"* 35.

47. Bell, "Not the Rosenbergs' Story," 42.

48. Guthmann, "Hutton Talks Back," 33.

49. Deborah Mason, *"Daniel*: Love and Protest," *Vogue*, Aug. 1983, p. 379. Andrew Sarris says of what he believes to be Lumet's final implication that the Rosenbergs are redeemed by the 1960s peace movement: "The children of Spock have turned out as shallow in their political commitments as in their awareness of history" ("Rosenbergs, the Isaacsons, and Thou," 51).

50. Kopkind, "Broken Hearts and Minds," 71.

3. Woman and the Progress of Self-Understanding

1. Lumet remarks that in the film the young women's "vulnerability shows." Raymond Durgnat praises the film as "one of the most sympathetic" American films in his experience and, while praising the atypical casting highly, says that Lumet's women emerge with "delicate humor and tender-

ness" (*Films and Filming* 13 [Sept. 1966]: 14-15). A favorable *Time* review, March 11, 1966, p. 99, disagrees with Pauline Kael's well-known attack on the film and the director by noting that Joanna Pettet, in the leading role of Kay, "etches a jittery, wounding image of pride slowly strangled." *Saturday Review,* March 26, 1966, p. 46, praises Lumet for eliciting great performances from mainly inexperienced actresses. Bowles notes that, to that point in Lumet's career, the film had his longest shooting schedule and his biggest budget, over 2.5 million dollars. At that time it was the most expensive film ever made in New York.

2. Pauline Kael's negative essay, "The Making of *The Group,*" in *Kiss Kiss Bang Bang* (New York: Atlantic Monthly Press, 1968), 65-100, disagrees with Lumet's psychoanalytic interpretation of the novel. For a full response to Kael's sometimes critically inaccurate and contradictory comments, see chapter 7. Other negative, impressionistic responses to the film include Judith Crist, *New York Herald Tribune,* March 20, 1966, p. 33, and J.H. Fenwick, *Sight and Sound* 35 (Autumn 1966): 200. The most thoughtful of the positive reviews is by Durgnat. See also Elliott Sirkin, *Film Comment* 8 (Sept. 1972): 66-68; background material is provided in Patricia Bosworth, "Grouptalk—Groupthink," *New York Herald Tribune,* Aug. 22, 1965, pp. 12-18.

3. Mary McCarthy, *The Group* (New York: Harcourt, Brace, 1963), 7-8. All further quotations from the novel will be taken from this edition and cited in the text. (Particularly tedious is the description of the Baked Alaska and its reception by various group members on p. 24.)

4. In the fourth edition of *A Short History of the Movies* (New York: Macmillan, 1986), 443, Gerald Mast adds a paragraph on Lumet, indicating the director's "conviction that reason will eventually prevail in human affairs."

5. *The Group* was the first color picture for Kaufman as Lumet's director of photography.

6. Lumet leaves no visual doubt that Kay's fall is accidental: Pettet carefully balances herself on the ledge, momentarily teeters, then rights herself firmly before leaning out to attempt to see with binoculars the plane she has heard. Then she loses her balance and topples off.

7. Willard Beecher and Marguerite Beecher, "Memorial to Dr. Alfred Adler," in H.H. Mosak, ed., *Alfred Adler: His Influence on Psychology Today* (Park Ridge, N.J.: Noyes, 1973), 1.

8. Charles A. Fenton, ed., *The Best Short Stories of World War II: An American Anthology* (New York: Viking, 1957), 67-87. All quotations of "Layover in El Paso" will be taken from this edition and cited in the text.

9. Quoted in Fenton, ed., *Best Short Stories,* 65.

10. Negative commentary, which praises Boris Kaufman's realistic New York City photography and impressionistically criticizes the film for belonging to the romance genre while neglecting Lumet's contributions to this genre, includes John McCarter, *New Yorker,* Sept. 19, 1959, p. 89; Bosley Crowther, *New York Times,* Sept. 12, 1959, p. 12; and Richard Roud, *Sight and Sound* 29 (Winter 1959-60): 40.

11. Lumet commented, "The first forty-five minutes of that movie are excellent," adding that he did not have the final editing rights on *That Kind of*

Woman and did not authorize the sentimental music accompanying the film's conclusion.

12. Larry McMurtry, *Leaving Cheyenne* (New York: Harper and Row, 1963), epigraph. All quotations will be taken from this edition and cited in the text.

13. Larry McMurtry, "Approaching Cheyenne . . . Leaving Lumet. Oh, Pshaw!" *New York*, April 29, 1974, pp. 64-66. McMurtry is particularly concerned about the revelation of Ms. Danner's stretch marks and that two major characters are shown in shoes, not boots. McMurtry accuses Lumet of wordiness but betrays his prejudices by grouping Lumet with Eric Rohmer while disparaging both. Both directors employ ideas in their films, a fact that seems to induce discomfort in the regional novelist. See also an intelligent and amusing review, more critical of the novel than of Lumet's film: Penelope Gilliatt, *New Yorker*, April 22, 1974, pp. 138-40.

14. McMurtry, "Approaching Cheyenne," 64-66.

4. Lumet at Zenith

1. James Joyce, *Ulysses* (New York: Modern Library, 1961), 213.

2. A.H. Weiler, *New York Times*, April 27, 1957, sec. 2, p. 1.

3. The then seventy-three-year-old Sweeney had first acted on Broadway in *The Klansmen*, which gave rise to *Birth of a Nation*. Lumet had first acted with him as a child actor and chose him for this part because of his "special inner energy."

4. Boris Kaufman, "Filming *12 Angry Men* on a Single Set," *American Cinematographer* 37 (Dec. 1956): 724-25.

5. See Andrew Sarris's impressionistic account of Lumet's career in *The American Cinema: Directors and Directions, 1929-1968* (New York: Dutton, 1968), 198; Kaufman, "Filming *Twelve Angry Men*," 725.

6. Don Ross, "A Dozen Happy Actors Become 'Twelve Angry Men,'" *New York Times*, July 15, 1956, sec. 4, p. 3.

7. See Sarris, 198, and Pauline Kael, "The Making of *The Group*," in *Kiss Kiss Bang Bang* (New York: Atlantic Monthly Press, 1968), 65-100, and my discussion in chapter 7.

8. Interview with the author. See also Dale Luciano, "*Long Day's Journey into Night*: An Interview with Sidney Lumet," *Film Quarterly* 25 (Fall 1971): 20-29.

9. In his television version, roughly half the length of Lumet's film, Rose had to cut much dialogue that gave dimension to character. Rose, *Twelve Angry Men*, in *Six Television Plays* (New York: Simon and Schuster, 1956), 157. Rose comments, "As a motion picture . . . I think that *Twelve Angry Men* has grown in stature. . . . much of the extra time has been spent in exploring the characters and their motivations for behaving as they do toward the defendant and each other." In "Author's Commentary," Rose says that *Twelve Angry Men* is one of his most difficult plays to read, since the visual element enables the audience to delineate the characters; Rose labeled them only by number and included only

thumbnail descriptions of their characteristics. Quotations from Rose's play are cited in the text.

10. In William I. Kaufman, ed., *Great Television Plays* (New York: Dell, 1969).

11. *Time,* April 29, 1957, p. 96.

12. John Harrington, ed., *Film and/as Literature* (Englewood Cliffs, N.J.: Prentice-Hall, 1977), 3.

13. Graham Petrie, "The Films of Sidney Lumet: Adaptation as Art," *Film Quarterly* 21 (Winter 1967-68): 13; Robin Bean, "The Insider: Sidney Lumet Talks about His Work in Films," *Films and Filming* 11 (June 1965): 12.

14. Sidney Lumet, "On a Film 'Journey,'" *New York Times,* Oct. 7, 1962, sec. 2, p. 7.

15. Dale Luciano, *"Long Day's Journey Into Night*: An Interview with Sidney Lumet," *Film Quarterly* 25 (Fall 1971): 25-26.

16. Bean, "Insider," 13. Lumet added some observations on his and Stock-well's interpretation of Edmund that attest to his sensitivity in adapting O'Neill: "It was in fact the most difficult [part] to play. O'Neill always wrote himself badly. In *Iceman* the part of [Parritt] had the same problem that Edmund has in this. It is full of self-pity. . . . O'Neill had such self-hatred that he almost didn't dare to write himself in any sort of active way because . . . he felt that any time he did anything it . . . hurt or injured someone. . . . I felt thematically that we would lose a great deal [if we portrayed Edmund as passive] because in the stage production in New York [the 1957 Quintero production] the play was about the father and the brother. I felt that [O'Neill's play] was about the mother and Edmund. As a result we really had to activate [Edmund]. . . . We got a sort of level of pain going; in other words got the passivity coming out of what I said I felt about O'Neill, which is active, restraining oneself; not acting because if you do you'll kill something . . . which is a very different thing from passive" (13).

17. Lee R. Bobker, *Elements of Film,* 3d ed. (New York: Harcourt, Brace, 1979), 153. Film editor Ralph Rosenblum praised Lumet as "the only director I've worked with who could tell me cut-for-cut what he wanted in a scene. . . . An example arose during the editing of *Long Day's Journey.* I had always cut dialogue scenes by carefully choosing whether to focus on the speaker or the listener. Lumet came up with an alternative approach, 'mathematical cutting,' in which we cut back and forth from one actor to the other in evenly matched but progressively shorter snippets of film, totally ignoring who was talking and who was listening, and markedly increasing the tension." Ralph Rosenblum and Robert Karen, *When the Shooting Stops . . . the Cutting Begins: A Film Editor's Story* (New York: Penguin, 1980), 152.

18. Luciano, "Interview with Sidney Lumet," 20. O'Neill scholars discussing Mary's tragic importance include Travis Bogard (*Contour in Time,* rev. ed., 1988), Normand Berlin (*Eugene O'Neill,* 1982), and Virginia Floyd, *The Plays of Eugene O'Neill,* 1985).

19. John Gardner, *On Moral Fiction* (New York: Basic Books, 1978), 6.

20. Robin Bean notes that Lumet resented the impressionism of several of the reviews of the film. (*Time,* Oct. 12, 1962, p. 102, labeled the film "merely a

photographed play," and even the usually discerning Arthur Knight wrote impressionistically in *Saturday Review,* Oct. 6, 1962, p. 30.) Lumet said that such commentary reflected a "lack of understanding of cinema technique. . . . All their eyes were capable of seeing was scenery; they didn't know cinema technique from a hole in the wall. There was more sheer physical technique in that movie, in its editing and its camera work, than anything you are liable to see for twenty years. In the University of Southern California they use it to illustrate a certain level of camera work" (Bean, "Insider," 10-11). Graham Petrie notes in support of the director that "Superb [as the performances] are, however, they would have counted for little if Lumet had not found the exact cinematic equivalent for the dramatic world created by O'Neill" "Films of Sidney Lumet," (11). See also Luciano, "Interview with Sidney Lumet," 24-25.

21. Writing in *Theatre Arts,* Byron Bentley praises Lumet's use of confined space, saying that the adaptation's success depended on the "extent to which it heightens the illusion of inescapable reality" (Oct. 1962, p. 16). Petrie adds that Lumet's "characters are trapped, forced into physical proximity to each other" ("Films of Sidney Lumet," 11).

22. Eugene O'Neill, *Long Day's Journey into Night* (New Haven, Conn.: Yale Univ. Press, 1956), 12. All quotations will be taken from this edition and cited in the text.

23. Lumet observed that he also used the bright light at the opening to avoid "tragic omens." Luciano, "Interview with Sidney Lumet," 21.

24. Sidney Lumet, "On a Film 'Journey,'" *New York Times,* Oct. 7, 1962, sec. 2, p. 7; Alfred Adler, *The Individual Psychology of Alfred Adler,* ed. H.L. Ansbacher and R.R. Ansbacher (New York: Basic Books, 1956), 267. Mary's obsessive need for approval can be observed elsewhere in the play, for example, on pp. 86, 93-95, and 105.

25. Petrie comments, "Even the few moments of virtuoso camerawork are used, not to escape the spatial restrictions of the setting, but to emphasize them. The 360-degree pan which watches Mary Tyrone pace around the living room like a caged beast . . . emphasizes both the physical and mental traps in which she finds herself" ("Films of Sidney Lumet," 12).

26. John Orlandello, *O'Neill on Film* (Rutherford, N.J.: Fairleigh Dickinson Univ. Press, 1982), 145.

27. Lumet, "On a Film 'Journey,'" 7.

28. Speaking to Luciano about his and Kaufman's creative collaboration, the director observed, "Boris' triumph, from a lighting point of view in *Long Day's Journey,* lies in the fact that if you take the same close-up of Ralph Richardson from Act One, and a close-up of [him] from Act Four, the exact same size, and put those two faces next to each other on the screen, they will look like a different man. It'll almost be hard to think the same actor is in both shots. That is Boris' triumph, and it's a tremendous one, through the use of light." Luciano, "Interview with Sidney Lumet," 23.

29. Bernard F. Dick writes that mobile camera movement can draw the viewer into a character's mind: "The [ending] crane shot . . . is one of the great feats of film making. . . . If regression could be visualized, it would consist of

gradual diminution." Dick, *Anatomy of Film* (New York: St. Martin's Press, 1978), 21.

30. Petrie comments that Lumet's cinematic treatment of Mary's great final speech makes it even more effective: "Just as the camera has previously *created* the emotional relationship between the characters, now it sums them up for us: we are shown Mary's loneliness and isolation from her family; the isolation of each of them from the others; the family's complete withdrawal from the outside world; and finally the fragile unity which still keeps them together to torment and comfort each other. The effect is quiet, compassionate, and almost unbearably moving" ("Films of Sidney Lumet," 12-13).

31. *Newsweek*, Oct. 15, 1962, p. 109.

32. Kenneth Tynan, *Observer* (London), April 25, 1965, 24, was a rare early review that preferred Lumet's "fiercely intelligent film" as making "the logic of catastrophe seem much more intimate and irrefutable." See also Bosley Crowther, *New York Times*, Sept. 16, 1964, p. 36. Negative and impressionistic reviews include Penelope Houston, *Sight and Sound* 34 (Spring 1965): 97, and Stanley Kauffmann, *The New Republic*, Sept. 12, 1964, pp. 26-27. Graham Petrie notes that *Fail Safe* was made before *Dr. Strangelove*, and he regards Lumet's film as "much more honest, and much less simple-minded" ("Films of Sidney Lumet," 13).

33. Eugene Burdick and Harvey Wheeler, *Fail-Safe* (New York: McGraw-Hill, 1962), 88. All further quotations from the novel will be taken from this edition and cited in the text.

34. Lumet considers excessive the exposition concerning Groteschele: "There have always been the Kissingers and Herman Kahns with us, and that's what the Matthau character was supposed to be. It would have been perfectly clear just to leave his arguments within the war room."

35. Discussing early cinematic influences upon his films, Lumet said, "Just as an aspiration, because I couldn't ever think of getting where he got—Carl Dreyer."

36. Lumet discussed this shot in remarks concerning the unintentionally amusing bureaucratic coda attached to the closing credits: "It is the stated position of the Department of Defense and the US Air Force that a rigidly enforced system of safeguards and controls insure that occurrences such as those depicted in this story cannot happen." Lumet said, "Columbia put it on. . . . it happened after we'd been refused not only government cooperation but every bit of stock footage. That take-off of the bombers I did with one stock shot of a plane taking off that was available to anybody." Lumet and film editor Ralph Rosenblum "kept blowing it up, took one plane and made it look like six. It's the same shot, done six different ways, on an optical machine." See also Rosenblum and Karen, *When the Shooting Stops*, 3-4. Elizabeth Trotta adds, "Moreover, major firms like IBM and General Dynamics have refused to let [Lumet] even see machines involved in defense work. Consequently, the War Room furnishings are the product of a fertile imagination coupled with pho- tographs from Popular Science Magazine." Trotta, "Director Lumet at Work: A Hectic Day in New York," *Newsday*, May 7, 1963, sec. C, p. 3.

37. Lumet's director of photography on *Fail Safe*, Gerald Hirschfeld, writes informatively about technical aspects of lighting and using lenses in cramped space in "Low Key for *Fail Safe*," *American Cinematographer* 44 (Aug. 1963): 462-63, 482-84. Bowles confirms that "Lumet enjoys the challenge of filming in spatially restricted environments." Stephen E. Bowles, *Sidney Lumet: A Guide to References and Resources* (Boston: G.K. Hall, 1979), 57.

38. Robin Bean discusses Lumet's uses of melodrama, conjoined with the director's "great strength . . . his intense interest in people," in his review of *Fail Safe*, which he calls a "devastating . . . brilliantly made" film. *Films and Filming* 11 (June 1965): 245.

39. Edward Lewis Wallant, *The Pawnbroker* (New York: Harvest/Harcourt, Brace, 1978), 3-4. All further quotations from the novel will be taken from this edition and cited in the text.

40. Gabriel Miller views this scene, repeated and completed at the end of the film, as a reflection of Nazerman's sense of helplessness at his inability to save his family, "which is the major cause of his profound guilt." Miller, *Screening the Novel: Rediscovered American Fiction in Film* (New York: Ungar, 1980), 182. Alan Casty refers to this scene in his discussion of Lumet's realism in "*The Pawnbroker* and the New Direction in Film Realism," *Film Heritage* 1 (Spring 1966): 3-14.

41. Gordon Gow praises Lumet's shock cuts as "superb cinema, essential cinema," expressing Nazerman's wish to shut out the world and his consistent inability to do so. *Film and Filming* 13 (Dec. 1966): 6. In an interview Lumet said he felt that the shock cuts were a technique appropriate to thematic need. "I began with the basis that for Sol the past is not past, it is much more present than what is going on at the moment around him." Lumet, "Keep Them on the Hook," *Films and Filming* 11 (Oct. 1964), 18. Most of the cuts to Nazerman's past are more harshly lighted than the present events in Nazerman's life. See also Rosenblum and Karen, *When the Shooting Stops*, 139-66.

42. Lumet significantly de-emphasizes Morton's importance, omitting the sentimentally improbable telephone call made by Sol to Morton in the novel following Ortiz's death. This omission concentrates Nazerman's latent affection for Morton onto Ortiz and also concentrates Wallant's issues and characters. "I felt, actually, we helped the novel. I think we were totally within Wallant's intent. I think what hurts Wallant—a potentially great writer—in all the novels is the intent to create too great a texture, to create too much about subsidiary characters."

43. While praising highly Steiger's magnificent performance, Lumet said, "It's just that as an actor he is *in*capable of feeling *nothing*." Lumet added that perhaps James Mason, whose performance in the director's *Child's Play* "is one of the great screen performances, and it's absolutely ignored," might have been even more suited for his conception of the part than Steiger, so that the character could have been "even more detached. . . . Mason could have literally gone so dead inside that when the eruption came it would have been terrifying. . . . I think I should have gone for an even colder performance from Rod."

44. Joseph Lyons complains that Lumet's omission of Wallant's paragraph (169) concerning Ruth's rape in the camp bordello and the husband and wife's shared look during which "finally she was able to award him the tears of forgiveness" is unjustifiable, since it establishes that Nazerman is, compared with his wife, "weak and shallow." Lyons misses the intrinsic sentimentality in Wallant's scene: it is hardly likely that Ruth feels Sol is to blame for her sexual abuse at the hands of Nazis who oppress them both. Lyons, "*The Pawnbroker*: Flashback in the Novel and the Film," *Western Humanities Review* 20 (1966): 24.

45. Lumet intended the loud, abrasive jazz score at this point to dispel sentimentality, not to allow the audience "the conventional catharsis. . . . The kind of insane joy that starts with the music at the end with its wildness, is joy in the sense that Sol's alive again" ("Keep Them on the Hook," 17). Petrie disagrees, finding the jazz discordant and intrusive, while otherwise praising the ending and Lumet's controlled camera style ("Films of Sidney Lumet," 14-16).

5. Comic Misconnections and the Universality of Loss

1. Cleanth Brooks and Robert B. Heilman, *Understanding Drama* (New York: Holt, Rinehart and Winston, 1948), 456.

2. The unpublished Budberg translation is available in typescript at the Library of Congress Motion Picture Division. Lumet saw the Budberg-translation production of *The Three Sisters* in London and commissioned this translation.

3. Constance Garnett, trans., *The Sea Gull* (New York: Modern Library, 1929), 7. Stark Young's fine 1939 translation also strives, with frequent success, for a lighter touch; but his rendering of Sorin's speeches too often settles for such obvious evidences of emotional dislocation as "and so on" and "and all the rest of it" as fillers at the ends of sentences. Stark Young, trans., *The Sea Gull* (New York: Scribners, 1939), 5, 7, 11.

4. In an interview with the author Lumet said that *The Sea Gull* is a favorite among his films.

5. Lumet said that "on *The Sea Gull*, my only reservation is that I wasn't tougher on Simone in terms of her English because she is bilingual. Simone can get to a point where you can just feel the French accent, and that would have been marvelous." Lumet asked Signoret to work with him on her English pronunciation for two and a half months before filming, but because of other commitments she could not do so. John Simon regrets Signoret's accent in *New Leader*, Feb. 17, 1969, p. 28. Detailed, positive reviews include Louise Sweeney, *Christian Science Monitor*, Dec. 27, 1968, p. 4, and Roger Greenspun, *New York Free Press*, Jan. 9, 1969, p. 7. For an alternately intelligent and impressionistic review see Andrew Sarris, *Village Voice*, Jan. 9, 1969, pp. 47-48.

6. Young, trans., *Sea Gull*, 23.

7. John Gassner, ed., *A Treasury of the Theatre: Ibsen to Ionesco*, 3d ed. (New York: Simon and Schuster, 1963), 206.

8. Wallace Markfield, *To an Early Grave* (New York: Simon and Schuster,

1964), 255. All further quotations will be taken from this edition and cited in the text. Few early reviewers understood Lumet's attempt to universalize the novel's themes, such as the negative, impressionistic commentaries in *Time*, March 15, 1968, p. 90, and *Saturday Review*, March 2, 1968, p. 40, which said that Lumet failed to generalize beyond a satire of the *Partisan Review* group. More perceptive, though mixed, reviews were written by Andrew Sarris, in *Village Voice*, March 21, 1968, p. 47, who praised the film as poised "on the edge of enchantment whenever the frailties and sensibilities of the four nonheroes intermingle," and by Paul D. Zimmerman, in *Newsweek*, March 11, 1968, p. 92, who praised Lumet's avoidance of sentimentality and his "scrupulously honest translation" of the novel.

9. Stanley Edgar Hyman, *Standards: A Chronicle of Books for Our Time* (New York: Horizon, 1966), 214.

10. Ibid., 216.

11. Frank Campenni, "Wallace Markfield," *20th-Century American Jewish Fiction Writers*, ed. Daniel Walden (Detroit: Gale, 1984), 176.

12. Lumet's discipline over the material is also notable because much of it was so personally familiar to him. "My God, these four, post-Depression Jewish intellectuals are everyone I grew up with. Me, in fact. . . . In a strange way, this is the most personal picture I've ever made. . . . It's the irreverent but wholly universal humor of the bookish, Jewish intellectual. But there is also much more—the depth, affection, sometimes tragic aspect of the middle-aged intellectual who refuses to grow up." A.H. Weiler, "A Funeral Grows in Brooklyn," *New York Times*, April 23, 1967, sec. 2, pp. 15, 20.

13. Hyman, *Standards*, 218.

14. Interview with the author.

15. *Braverman* was the second Lumet film shot in color by the cinematographer most associated with the director in the earlier films, Boris Kaufman. Zimmerman, sometimes critical of *Braverman* in his *Newsweek* review, praises "Lumet's beautifully sunny location shots that transform Brooklyn into a wonderland of church kiosks, tattered temples and infinite files of red brick houses" (March 11, 1968, p. 92).

16. Hyman notes that "Markfield has clearly taken *Ulysses* as his model, but . . . has aimed more modestly at writing just Mr. Bloom's day in Brooklyn" (*Standards*, 218).

6. Major Films from Nonliterary Sources

1. Stephen E. Bowles, *Sidney Lumet: A Guide to References and Resources* (Boston: G.K. Hall, 1979), 20.

2. Among favorable reviewers, Arthur Knight wrote, "Neither technically nor emotionally has Lumet worked so brilliantly before." *Saturday Review*, Oct. 2, 1965, p. 30.

3. T.S. Eliot, *The Complete Poems and Plays 1909-1950* (New York: Harcourt, Brace, 1958), 83.

4. William Avery, *Films in Review* 24 (Aug.-Sept., 1973): 440; Stephen Farber, *New York Times*, June 3, 1973, sec. 2, p. 11.

5. Richard Schickel, *Time*, June 4, 1973, p. 97.

6. Sidney Lumet, "Sidney Lumet: *The Offence*: An Interview with Susan Merrill," *Films in Review* 24 (Nov. 1973): 527.

7. Ibid., 528.

8. Frank Serpico, "A Letter Home," *Village Voice*, Feb. 3, 1975, p. 8.

9. Win Sharples, Jr., "The Filming of *Serpico*," *Filmmakers Newsletter* 7 (Feb. 1974): 30.

10. Andrew Sarris and Tom Allen, "Revivals in Focus," *Village Voice*, Jan. 5, 1982, p. 52.

11. Jay Cocks complained that the film insufficiently delineated Serpico's motives for his honesty, though Lumet clearly implies these in the film's scenes of the policeman's family life. Cocks, *Time*, Dec. 31, 1973, p. 51. Among the majority positive reactions, see Sharples, "Filming of *Serpico*," and Kathleen Carroll, *New York Daily News*, Dec. 16, 1973, p. 7.

12. Carroll, *New York Daily News*, Dec. 16, 1973, p. 7.

13. Sharples, "Filming of *Serpico*," 31.

14. Ibid., 33.

15. Carroll, *New York Daily News*, Dec. 16, 1973, p. 7.

16. Bernard F. Dick interprets Serpico as mythic Christ figure, "god-man doomed to suffer for his love of humanity . . . a cop who found his apostolate on the streets." Dick, *Anatomy of Film* (New York: St. Martin's Press, 1978), 92-93.

17. Serpico, "Letter Home," 15.

18. See Vincent Canby, "Lumet's Quintessential New York Film," *New York Times*, Sept. 28, 1975, p. 13, and James Monaco, "*Dog Day Afternoon*," *Sight and Sound* 45 (Winter 1975-76): 57-58.

19. Jack Kroll, *Newsweek*, Sept. 29, 1975, p. 84.

20. Mort Sheinman, "Sidney Lumet: Letting It Happen," *Women's Wear Daily*, Oct. 2, 1975, p. 12.

21. Monaco notes, "There is a real sense here of the subtle, non-verbal modes of communication between people" ("*Dog Day Afternoon*," 57).

22. Paul Bailey, *London Times Literary Supplement*, Oct. 3, 1980, p. 1098.

23. Kroll, *Newsweek*, Sept. 29, 1975, p. 84.

24. Ibid.

25. Vincent Canby, "A Surreal Attack on American Life," *New York Times*, Nov. 28, 1976, sec. D, p. 17.

26. Allan Wolper, *The Soho Weekly News*, Nov. 11, 1976, p. 7.

27. Richard Schickel, *Time*, Nov. 29, 1976, p. 79.

28. Ibid.

29. *Orient Express*, *Dog Day Afternoon*, and *Network* were consecutive commercial successes for Lumet. While not as visually variegated as some of his films, *Orient Express* allowed Lumet to direct a gallery of superlative actors (Sean Connery, John Gielgud, Vanessa Redgrave, and others and garnered an

Academy Award for Ingrid Bergman as best supporting actress and a best-actor nomination for Albert Finney as Hercule Poirot.

30. Charles Michener, *Newsweek,* Nov. 22, 1976, p. 107.

31. Stephen Farber, "See It Now: It Won't Be on ABC," *New West,* Nov. 8, 1976, p. 94.

32. See cinematographer Owen Roizman's long article, "*Network* and How It Was Photographed," *American Cinematographer* 58 (April 1977): 384ff., for details of Lumet's plan for the film. Roizman received an Academy Award nomination for his cinematography for *Network.*

33. Andrew Sarris, *Village Voice,* Aug. 25, 1981, p. 41.

34. David Ansen, "An American Tragedy," *Newsweek,* Aug. 24, 1981, p. 68.

35. Robert Daley, *Prince of the City* (Boston: Houghton Mifflin, 1978). Nicholas Pileggi, writing in *New York,* Aug. 31, 1981, pp. 28-30, questions Daley's version of the SIU affair, alleging more widespread and serious SIU corruption.

36. Pileggi, *New York,* Aug. 31, 1981, p. 30.

37. William Wolf, "Director with a Conscience," *New York,* Aug. 10, 1981, pp. 54-55.

38. Arthur Bell, *Village Voice,* Aug. 11, 1981, p. 38. Lumet also commented to Bell, "Orion . . . was unhappy with the [De Palma] screenplay, but had [Robert] de Niro given a definite 'yes' they'd have filmed the phone book."

39. Orion/Warners Production Notes to *Prince of the City.*

40. Deborah Mason, "*Daniel:* Love and Protest," *Vogue,* Aug. 1983, pp. 321, 379.

41. John Lombardi expands upon the visual stylization in *Prince:* "There's a definite progression in the way it's shot that's pure Lumet. In the beginning, things are back-lit; people don't stand out so much. They literally come into focus as the movie goes on. In the end, the background is somewhat out of focus. Technically, everything in the film reverses, which parallels what's happening to the characters—most end up doing exactly the opposite of what they wanted to do." Lombardi, "Lumet: The City Is His Sound Stage," *New York Times Magazine,* June 6, 1982, pp. 78-79. Lumet adds, "*Prince,* though it's generally perceived to be highly realistic, isn't. It's very stylized. The closest lens to what the eye sees is approximately 35 mm, 40 mm; those two lenses were never used in the picture" (Lombardi, 81).

42. Myron Meisel, "A Cop Alone," *AirCal Magazine,* Oct. 1981, p. 11.

7. A Major American Director

1. Jean-Pierre Coursodon, "Sidney Lumet," in *American Directors, Vol. 2* (New York: McGraw-Hill, 1983), 209.

2. Peter Cowie, *50 Major Film-Makers* (London: Tantivy, 1975), 164; Georges Sadoul, *Dictionary of Film Makers,* trans. and updated by Peter Morris (Berkeley: Univ. of California Press, 1972), 159; Richard Combs, "Sidney Lumet," in *Cinema, A Critical Dictionary: The Major Film-Makers,* Vol. 2, ed.

Richard Roud (London: Secker and Warburg, 1980), 651-52; Coursodon, "Sidney Lumet," 215, 209.

3. Andrew Sarris, *The American Cinema: Directors and Directions, 1929-1968* (New York: Dutton, 1968), 197-98, 39.

4. Pauline Kael, "The Making of *The Group*," reprinted in *Kiss Kiss Bang Bang* (New York: Atlantic Monthly Press, 1968), 65-100.

5. Ibid., 82-84, 75.

6. Distinguished film editor Ralph Rosenblum, who edited several of Lumet's films, including *The Pawnbroker* and *The Group*, in addition to Woody Allen's *Annie Hall* and *Sleeper*, in explaining the tediousness of cutting and the boredom it can induce in observers of his work, writes that Kael stayed with him a total of twenty minutes to comment on the film's editing. Ralph Rosenblum and Robert Karen, *When the Shooting Stops . . . the Cutting Begins: A Film Editor's Story* (New York: Penguin, 1980), 184.

7. Kael, *Kiss Kiss Bang Bang*, 69, 80, 84-97.

8. Don Shewey, "Sidney Lumet: The Reluctant Auteur," *American Film* 8 (Dec. 1982): 36.

9. Stephen Farber, "Lumet in '69," *Sight and Sound* 38 (Autumn 1969): 191.

10. Kael, *Kiss Kiss Bang Bang*, 77, 96-98, 80-81.

11. Andrew Sarris and Tom Allen, "Revivals in Focus," *Village Voice*, Oct. 9, 1984, p. 64-65.

12. Gavin Smith, "Sidney Lumet: Lion on the Left," *Film Comment* 24 (Aug. 1988): 35. Smith sees Lumet as "one of the only surviving political filmmakers in American cinema" and regards *The Fugitive Kind*, foreshadowing southern turmoil in the 1960s, with *Fail Safe* and *The Pawnbroker* as "sophisticated ideological critiques of postwar American society" (32).

13. Ibid., 36.

14. Shewey, "Reluctant Auteur," 35; Smith, "Lion on the Left," 32. During his interview with Lumet, William Wolf stated that Lumet's career was threatened during the early 1950s by Harvey Matusow concerning the director's alleged attendance at Communist meetings and that the occasion contributed to his conception of the Leuci character in *Prince of the City*: "Lumet hopes—and believes—that he would have behaved honorably had the matter escalated and had he been pressured, as others were, to name names. But he is convinced that one can never know with certainty how one will react under duress until actually in the situation. . . . (Also present was Hearst columnist Victor Riesel.)." Wolf, "Director with a Conscience," *New York*, Aug. 10, 1981, p. 55.

15. Kael, *Kiss Kiss Bang Bang*, 89, 88; Andrew Sarris, *Village Voice*, Aug. 25, 1981, p. 41.

16. David Ansen, "New York's Finest," *Newsweek*, Aug. 24, 1981, p. 68. Elsewhere the director observed, "Fred Astaire said it better than anybody. . . . 'I take my work very seriously, but I don't take myself seriously.'" Kevin Lally, "Versatility Gives Lumet Staying Power," *Film Journal* 89 (Jan. 1986): 26. Lumet wittily spoofs the "personal signature" in the opening sequence of *Family Business*; as the moving camera vertically surveys the elder McMullen's

(Connery's) urban turf, visible on the extreme right edge of the frame is a tall, slender sign that reads, "Network Entertainment Company."

17. Wolf, "Director with a Conscience," 54.

18. Shewey, "Reluctant Auteur," 33.

19. Ibid., 36.

20. Kenneth M. Chanko, "Sidney Lumet: An Interview," *Films in Review* 35 (Oct. 1984): 455.

21. Dan Yakir, "Wiz Kid," *Film Comment* 14 (Nov.-Dec. 1978): 53.

22. Ibid., 53.

23. Peter Bogdanovich, "An Interview with Sidney Lumet," *Film Quarterly* 14 (Winter 1960): 20.

24. Ibid.

25. Kaufman underscores the fruitfulness of their creative collaboration in Frederick Foster, "Filming *The Fugitive Kind*," *American Cinematographer* 41 (June 1960): 354-55.

26. Rosenblum and Karen, *When the Shooting Stops*, 152.

27. Guy Flatley, "Lumet—The Kid Actor Who Became a Director," *New York Times*, Jan. 20, 1974, sec. D, p. 11.

28. Shewey, "Reluctant Auteur," 33.

29. See Lumet's interview with Dale Luciano for his detailed description of this gestation process during the filming of *Long Day's Journey into Night*. Luciano, "*Long Day's Journey into Night*: An Interview with Sidney Lumet," *Film Quarterly* 25 (Fall 1971): 21-22.

30. Robin Bean, "The Insider: Sidney Lumet Talks about His Work in Films," *Films and Filming* 11 (June 1966): 13.

31. Chanko, "Sidney Lumet," 451.

32. Flatley, "Kid Actor," 11.

33. Arthur Bell, *Village Voice*, Aug. 11, 1981, p. 38. For corroborative statements from other contemporary creative talents in film, see John Stanley, "Keeping the Faith in Movie Making," *San Francisco Chronicle Datebook*, June 25, 1989, pp. 38-40, and Nick Pasquariello, "Odd Man Out: A Conversation with Maverick Filmmaker Carroll Ballard," *East Bay Express*, June 30, 1989, pp. 1, 11-15.

34. Ansen, "New York's Finest," 68.

35. Elaine Dundy, "Why Actors Do Better for Sidney Lumet," *New York*, Nov. 22, 1976, p. 82; Shewey, "Reluctant Auteur," 33; Kathleen Carroll, *New York Daily News*, Dec. 16, 1973, p. 7.

36. W.D. Snodgrass, "April Inventory," in *Norton Anthology of Modern Poetry*, ed. Richard Ellmann and Robert O'Clair (New York: Norton, 1973), 1087.

37. Shewey, "Reluctant Auteur," 31-32.

38. Owen Roizman, "*Network* and How It Was Photographed," *American Cinematographer* 58 (April 1977): 402.

39. Farber, "Lumet in '69," 194. Farber writes that the color in the film, "enhanced by Piero Gherardi's brilliant, asymmetrical set designs, is among the finest non-naturalistic uses of colour since Antonioni's own experiments" (195).

40. Wolf, "Director with a Conscience," 54.

Bibliography

This bibliography contains only references to major interviews with and secondary sources about Sidney Lumet. For additional items, see Bowles's reference volume and the notes to this book.

Appelbaum, Ralph. "Colour and Concepts." *Films and Filming* 24 (May 1978): 13-16.

Bean, Robin. "The Insider: Sidney Lumet Talks about His Work in Films." *Films and Filming* 11 (June 1966): 9-13.

Bogdanovich, Peter. "An Interview with Sidney Lumet." *Film Quarterly* 14 (Winter 1960): 18-23.

Bosworth, Patricia. "Grouptalk—Groupthink." *New York Herald Tribune*, Aug. 22, 1965, pp. 12-18.

Bowles, Stephen E. *Sidney Lumet: A Guide to References and Resources.* Boston: G.K. Hall, 1979.

Burke, Tom. "Suddenly, I Knew How to Film the Play." *New York Times*, July 24, 1977, sec. D, pp. 9, 20.

Casty, Alan. "*The Pawnbroker* and the New Direction in Film Realism." *Film Heritage* 1 (Spring 1966): 3-14.

Chanko, Kenneth M. "Sidney Lumet: An Interview." *Films in Review* 35 (Oct. 1984): 451-56.

Combs, Richard. "Sidney Lumet." In *Cinema, A Critical Dictionary: The Major Film-Makers, Vol. 2*, ed. Richard Roud, 650-52. London: Secker and Warburg, 1980.

Coursodon, Jean-Pierre. *American Directors, Vol. 2*. New York: McGraw-Hill, 1983.

Cowie, Peter. *50 Major Film-Makers*. London: Tantivy, 1975.

Cunningham, Frank R. "The Insistence of Memory: The Opening Sequences of Lumet's *Pawnbroker*." *Literature/Film Quarterly* 17, no. 1 (1989): 39-43.

_____. "Sidney Lumet's Humanism: The Return to the Father in *12 Angry Men*." *Literature/Film Quarterly* 14, no. 2 (1986): 112-21.

Dick, Bernard F. *Anatomy of Film*. New York: St. Martin's Press, 1978.

Dundy, Elaine. "Why Actors Do Better for Sidney Lumet." *New York*, Nov. 22, 1976, p. 82.

Farber, Stephen. "*Daniel*." *Film Quarterly* 39 (Spring 1984): 32-37.

_____. "Lumet in '69." *Sight and Sound* 38 (Autumn 1969): 190-95.

Flatley, Guy. "Lumet—The Kid Actor Who Became a Director." *New York Times*, Jan. 20, 1974, sec. D, pp. 11, 13.

Foster, Frederick. "Filming *The Fugitive Kind.*" *American Cinematographer* 41 (June 1960): 354-55, 379-80, 382.

Friedman, Lester D. *Hollywood's Image of the Jew.* New York: Ungar, 1982.

Gow, Gordon. "What's Real? What's True?" *Films and Filming* 21 (May 1975): 10-16.

Hirschfeld, Gerald. "Low Key for *Fail Safe.*" *American Cinematographer* 44 (Aug. 1963): 462-63, 482-84.

Insdorf, Annette. *Indelible Shadows: Film and the Holocaust.* New York: Random House, 1983.

Kael, Pauline. "The Making of *The Group.*" In *Kiss Kiss Bang Bang,* 65-100. New York: Atlantic Monthly Press, 1968.

Kaufman, Boris. "Filming *12 Angry Men* on a Single Set." *American Cinematographer* 37 (Dec. 1956): 724-25.

Kearney, Jill. "What's Wrong with Today's Films?" *American Film* 11 (May 1986): 53-56.

Kopkind, Andrew. "Broken Hearts and Minds." *The Movies,* Oct. 1983, pp. 70-71.

Lally, Kevin. "Versatility Gives Lumet Staying Power." *Film Journal* 89 (Jan. 1986): 8, 26.

Lombardi, John. "Lumet: The City Is His Sound Stage." *New York Times Magazine,* June 6, 1982, pp. 26ff.

Luciano, Dale. "*Long Day's Journey into Night*: An Interview with Sidney Lumet." *Film Quarterly* 25 (Fall 1971): 20-29.

Lumet, Sidney. "Keep Them on the Hook." *Films and Filming* 11 (Oct. 1964): 17-20.

———. "Le Point de Vue du Metteur en Scène." *Cahiers du Cinéma,* no. 94 (April 1959): 32-34.

———. "Notes on TV." *Cue,* July 19, 1952, p. 6.

———. "On a Film 'Journey.'" *New York Times,* Oct. 7, 1962, sec. 2, p. 7.

———. "Sidney Lumet." *Cahiers du Cinéma,* nos. 150-51 (Dec. 1963-Jan. 1964): 56-57.

———. "Sidney Lumet: *The Offence*: An Interview with Susan Merrill." *Films in Review* 24 (Nov. 1973): 523-28, 556.

———. "Sidney Lumet on the Director," in *Movie People: At Work in the Business of Film,* ed. Fred Baker. New York: Douglas, 1972, pp. 35-50.

Miller, Gabriel. *Screening the Novel: Rediscovered American Fiction in Film.* New York: Ungar, 1980.

Moskowitz, Gene. "The Tight Close-Up." *Sight and Sound* 29 (Winter 1959-60): 126-30.

Orlandello, John. *O'Neill on Film.* Rutherford, N.J.: Fairleigh Dickinson Univ. Press, 1982.

Petrie, Graham. "The Films of Sidney Lumet: Adaptation as Art." *Film Quarterly* 21 (Winter 1967-68): 9-18.

Phillips, Gene D. *The Films of Tennessee Williams.* Philadelphia: Art Alliance Press, 1980.

Roizman, Owen. "*Network* and How It Was Photographed." *American Cin-ematographer* 58 (April 1977): 384ff.

Rosenblum, Ralph, and Robert Karen. *When the Shooting Stops . . . the Cutting Begins: A Film Editor's Story.* New York: Penguin, 1980.

Sadoul, Georges. *Dictionary of Film Makers,* trans. and updated by Peter Morris. Berkeley: Univ. of California Press, 1972.

Sarris, Andrew. *The American Cinema: Directors and Directions, 1929-1968.* New York: Dutton, 1968.

Sharples, Win, Jr. "The Filming of *Serpico.*" *Filmmakers Newsletter* 7 (Feb. 1974): 30-34.

Shewey, Don. "Sidney Lumet: The Reluctant Auteur." *American Film* 8 (Dec. 1982): 31-36.

Smith, Gavin. "Sidney Lumet: Lion on the Left." *Film Comment* 24 (Aug. 1988): 32-38.

Steele, Robert. "Another Trip to the Pawnshop." *Film Heritage* 1 (Spring 1966): 15-22.

Weiler, A.H. "A Funeral Grows in Brooklyn." *New York Times,* April 23, 1967, sec. 2, pp. 15, 20.

Welsh, James M. "Dream Doctors as Healers in Drama and Film: A Paradigm, an Antecedent, and an Imitation." *Literature and Medicine* 6 (1987): 117-27.

Wolf, William. "Director with a Conscience." *New York,* Aug. 10, 1981, pp. 54-55.

Yacowar, Maurice. *Tennessee Williams and Film.* New York: Ungar, 1977.

Yakir, Dan. "Wiz Kid." *Film Comment* 14 (Nov.-Dec. 1978): 49-54.

Young, Freddie. "A Method of Pre-Exposing Color Negative For Subtle Effect." *American Cinematographer* 47 (Aug. 1966): 537.

Index